CONTENTS

A PEOPLE'S HISTORY OF DÚN LAOGHAIRE-RATHDOWN

A PEOPLE'S HISTORY OF DÚN LAOGHAIRE-RATHDOWN

DEIRDRE NUTTALL

EASTWOOD BOOKS

First published 2024 by Eastwood Books
Dublin, Ireland

www.eastwoodbooks.com

First edition

Eastwood Books
The Wordwell Group
Unit 9, 78 Furze Road
Sandyford
Dublin, Ireland

The Wordwell Group is a member of Publishing Ireland,
the Irish Publishers' Association.

ISBN: 978-1-916742-55-0 (paperback)
ISBN: 978-1-916742-62-8 (ebook)

The publishers and author would like to acknowledge the kind support of
Dún Laoghaire-Rathdown County Council in the publication of this work.

Typesetting and design by the Wordwell Group
Cover design by Fiachra McCarthy
Printed in Ireland by Sprint Books

Cover photograph: Lily Howe with her children at the sea in the 1940s. Kind
permission of Jimmy Howe.

The Publishers gratefully acknowledge the kind support of the following bodies:

 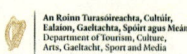 

Supported by the Department of Tourism, Culture, Arts,
Gaeltacht, Sports and Media under the Decade of Centenaries 2012-2023 initiative.

ACKNOWLEDGEMENTS

Thanks above all to the many interviewees who shared their own and their families' memories as part of the People's History of dlr programme (2021–2023). These have now been added to the National Folklore Collection at University College Dublin, and they form the basis of this book. The generosity, openness and kindness with which interviews were given was utterly remarkable and is very much appreciated. The full interviews can be accessed in the National Folklore Collection. Pseudonyms have been used in this book for all who generously contributed as interviewees.

Very many thanks to the team at the National Folklore Collection, and in particular to Dr Críostóir Mac Cárthaigh, whose professionalism, kindness and support enabled our collecting project and the writing of this book every step of the way.

Many thanks also to Patricia Corish, the Local Studies Librarian at the Lexicon Library, for her help in sourcing materials, and to all the staff for accommodating meetings and interviews.

And thanks to Ronan Colgan at Wordwell Books, and to copyeditor Neil Burkey, for all their work in getting *A People's History of Dún Laoghaire-Rathdown* ready for the public.

Deirdre Black, Heritage Officer, Dún Laoghaire-Rathdown County Council
Deirdre Nuttall, Researcher and Author

DÚN LAOGHAIRE
-RATHDOWN

The boundaries we impose on the map may sometimes trace natural features like rivers and mountain ranges, but they are also fundamentally administrative decisions that demarcate certain territories for practical purposes. By drawing the map, we create the place.

County Dublin has existed as an administrative district since Norman times. During the nineteenth century, as suburbs and satellite communities grew, various local townships and, later, urban district councils were founded, including Blackrock, Killiney, Dalkey and Kingstown (now Dún Laoghaire; we will refer to the town – which has variously been known as Dunleary, Kingstown and Dún Laoghaire – by the era-appropriate name in its various contexts). In 1898, a bill reorganising local government was passed, transferring authority, including township and sanitary authorities, to county councils.[1] The Borough of Dún Laoghaire was founded in 1930. The county area of Dún Laoghaire-Rathdown – the study area for this book – was formalised in 1994, following a Local Government Act in 1991, which arranged to divide County Dublin, for administrative purposes, into the three counties of Fingal, South Dublin and Dún Laoghaire-Rathdown.[2] Through these various changes, the citizens of Dún Laoghaire-Rathdown, to paraphrase James Joyce's Leopold Bloom, have always simply been the people, living in the same place. We will therefore use the modern county designation

'Dún Laoghaire-Rathdown' in discussing anywhere in this geographical area, from both before and after the administrative division.

At a glance, the most striking thing about Dún Laoghaire-Rathdown is its extraordinary diversity: geographic, socioeconomic, professional, denominational and occupational diversity have marked this area for centuries, and to a remarkable degree. The county encompasses a coastal area stretching from the southern part of Dublin city, a series of former villages and towns – some on sites inhabited since antiquity – sprawling modern suburbs, relatively sparsely populated uplands and areas where agriculture is still actively practised. Nomadism, while less common than before, remains an active way of life. The area has historically been the home to a notably diverse population regarding socioeconomic status and political and ethno-religious allegiance. In a small geographical space, we find examples of practically every type of occupation and identity present on the island of Ireland, south and north. We also find that many of the social and cultural trends that have marked modern Ireland happened here first: the suburbanisation of urban areas and mass disengagement from formal religion, to name just two examples. In short, if we understand the intricacies of Dún Laoghaire-Rathdown, we also understand Ireland.

Yet despite this remarkable variety of experience, the voices of ordinary people have been much less recorded and heard than those of the gentry and the wealthy business families, so many of whom have notable histories here. No conspiracy theory is necessary to understand this exclusion, which is a common pattern in historical matter everywhere. Inevitably, people with bigger public profiles are more written about in the print media. Wealthy people are more likely to have lived in architecturally important homes that eventually are designated as protected structures and become the subject of historical tours, that become permanent records in the landscape of their former inhabitants, beautiful focal points in estates transformed into parkland. Historic graveyards often contain lavish funerary art honouring the memory

Lily Clare in Dún Laoghaire in the 1920s. Kind permission of Jimmy Howe.

of the dead whose families could afford gravestones – or whose heroic deaths prompted the state or other benefactors to foot the bill – while others' earthly remains have returned to nature marked only by a simple, unmarked stone, or by nothing at all. Throughout history, the wealthy and well-connected leave a much more detailed paper trail, and far more tangible material heritage. Conversely, the equally rich lives of those with modest incomes can be almost invisible in both the landscape and the written record. It can be almost as if they never existed.

The histories of the wealthy and well-connected are, of course, extremely important – but so are the histories of the poor and the not-so-wealthy, of the many whose rich, complex lives can seem to have vanished without a trace, or to survive only in the minds of those who knew them: an archive of memories that is, by definition, time-limited. Data such as census returns and the records of institutions such as schools and work-houses can give us insights into the lives of ordinary people, but only in a two-dimensional way. For example, many worked in domestic service and show up in the various censuses in the homes where they worked, but what do we know about their daily lives? Thousands of children grew up in institutions or in fosterage in the county. Were most of them treated well? Or not?

When it comes to understanding the lives of the less well-connected, there are many unanswered questions. This imbalance in the historical

Little boys in Glencullen, c.1950s/early 1960s. Kind permission of National Folklore Collection.

record is not really anybody's fault. But it is a pity. Fortunately, by talking to people about what they remember, and about the stories handed down in their families and communities, we can claw back a lot of vital information that fills in many of the gaps and sheds light on many of the grey areas of history.

By their very nature, oral histories are different to documented histories. They rely on memories, which can be flawed or incomplete. People can be vague, for example, about exactly when something happened. Was it 1926? Or perhaps 1932? Before or after Auntie Margaret moved to Liverpool? But oral histories do provide something that even the most thoughtful historian working exclusively with printed sources never really can: real punch-in-the-gut insights into what it *felt* like living through a particular period, above all from the viewpoint of those who typically leave little by way of a paper trail. Best of all, when we can match oral histories and ethnologies with historical certainties, we can gain incredible insight into what it was like living through a particular period of time as a particular type of person.

But before we visit the many stories of Dún Laoghaire-Rathdown, let's start with a glance at the natural and cultural backdrop, the physical and social context, against which the many stories in this book played out.

The area's archaeological profile is well-studied. In 1845,[3] researchers examined elk skulls and skeletons following reports from local farmers who had dug deep into the ground during a drought: apparently, about 100 skulls were found near Kilternan between 1847 and 1876. Pádraic, growing up nearby, heard they were the remains of animals 'trapped during Noah's floods'. Pádraic was a little boy in 1934 when, as part of a government scheme to provide work to the unemployed, some of the locals were hired by the Office of Public Works to help excavate them.[4] The supervisors – Knud Jessen, Professor of Botany at the University of Copenhagen, and geologist Anthony Farrington – let him help, leaving Pádraic with childhood memories that he would never forget.[5]

With respect to human habitation, this region was originally inhabited during the Mesolithic (from *c.*6000 to 4000 BCE) and then underwent rapid change during the Neolithic (from *c.*3000 BCE), when agriculture was introduced, and people settled long-term. These early farmers left behind tools and other items, and the portal tombs found in locations including Ballybrack, Brenanstown and Kilternan. Bronze Age tools and weapons have been found on Dalkey Island and in Cabinteely, Glencullen, Newtown, Killiney Hill and Rathfarnham. Tombs from that era are found in Kilmashogue, Foxrock and Shankill. Late Bronze Age and Iron Age sites, dating from *c.*1200 BCE to the early Christian era, have been found in Cabinteely, Newtown, Carrickmines and Kilgobbin,[6] with further evidence of habitation dating to the Viking period – when there was an active slave trade, apparently operating from a prison camp on Dalkey Island[7] – and beyond.[8] The name Dún Laoghaire, meaning 'Laoghaire's fort', is believed to refer to King Laoghaire, who lived primarily in Tara in the fifth century, and is thought to have had a fort – or to have given his name to a fort – in an area near the seafront.[9] Important sacred sites date from the early Christian and medieval period, notably Tully Church, with its two ancient crosses and tombstones featuring carvings that apparently combine Christian and pagan motifs,[10] and Old Rathmichael Church, where one can see the base of a round tower (known locally as a 'skull hole')* and a collection of engraved Hiberno-Norse slabs, known as the Rathdown Slabs and unique to this area.[11] The church of Clonkeen was founded in the late seventh century.[12] By the middle ages, ecclesiastical settlements occupied swathes of land in the southwest, serviced by agricultural hinterland, and memorialised in placenames including Monkstown, Deansgrange, Kill o' the Grange, Tobernea Terrace and Taney Parish.

---

* In old graveyards, where burial rights associated with particular families were asserted for generations, space could run out, resulting in 'the piling up of skulls, bones and coffins' (Whelan, 2018, 93); presumably the origin of the term 'skull hole', as the base of the round tower would be a convenient location for such remains. At the time of writing the base of the tower was used for composting flowers and grass cuttings.

Anglo-Normans settled from the early medieval period. By 1326, for example, more than half the residents of the Clonkeen area were Anglo-Normans.[13] Numerous tower houses built and inhabited by the Anglo-Normans can still be seen, notably the well-preserved Puck's Castle in Rathmichael and Kilgobbin Castle in Kilgobbin.[14] Post-Reformation, lands held by religious orders, and by Catholic landowners, were taken and given to loyalists to the English crown. After the Cromwellian conquest in the seventeenth century, many big Catholic landowners were forcibly replaced by Protestants integral to the colonial ruling class. From the late seventeenth century, these families inhabited stately homes with large estates, like Marlay Park.[15] During this period, much of the older infrastructure associated with the Catholic Church was badly damaged or fell into disrepair. During the Penal Laws, Catholic worship was carried out discreetly, in homes, outdoor spaces or mass houses. Brian, whose family's history in the Glencullen area dates to the 1600s, and whose father was born in 1875, could point to ruins in the family farm that are believed locally to have been a mass house during the penal era. When he was growing up in the 1930s and 1940s, stories were still told about it, and about how someone was always on lookout during Mass, in case of a raid.* Writing in 1899 of Monkstown in 1766, Francis Elrington Ball discussed a series of large homes and their residents, and made just one reference to their presumably numerous employees – the 'native servant' of a Robert Elrington who had arrived from Jamaica, bringing

---

* Stories about the days of the Penal Laws were still being related in 1979–80, when the Urban Folklore Project took place. The following story, referring to the Dublin uplands, hints at ongoing anger in the context of a story about the supernatural: 'near St Columba's [a Protestant boarding school]... there is a story that during the penal days there was a carriage travelling along, taking some people to midnight mass on Christmas Eve. During the penal days there was no church; they were bringing them to an altar; a wayside altar somewhere. The British soldiers heard about this and they waylaid the coach and cut off the driver's head with a sword and the horses continued and brought the people to where the mass was being celebrated, and the legend is that on Christmas Eve every seven years it can be seen.' National Folklore Collection, Urban Folklore Project (henceforth NFC UFP), vol. 1979, pp.98–9.

said unnamed servant (who may actually have been a slave; black slaves were more common in Ireland than is often assumed[*]) with him.[16]

Until the eighteenth century, Dunleary was settled only by small clusters of fishing families. From the mid-eighteenth century, it was an increasingly important port and channel of communication with Britain, and the first pier (which silted up quickly) was built. By the early 1800s, the Martello towers (built amid Britain's anxiety that war with Napoleon might be imminent, and that Ireland might provide him with a convenient back door)[17] and new roads had been constructed, and port traffic had increased dramatically.[18]

Legislation for the construction of the harbour was passed in 1815 (a welcome development amid memories of the terrible events of 1807, when two ships were wrecked on the rocky west shore, and nearly 400 died). It was the vision of Richard Toutcher who, following this tragedy, campaigned to have a sanctuary harbour built. This led to an Act of Parliament in 1815, establishing the Dunleary Harbour Commissioners. In 1817, the foundation stone was laid. By the 1820s, about a thousand labourers, often with their wives and children, were present.

While many of the workers were local, skilled stonemasons but others also came from further afield, including Scotland. Some families still trace their descent from these, like Kate's family: 'the father and four sons came initially [to work on the construction of the harbour] and they married Irish women and stayed'. Building the harbour was arduous, dangerous work, and living conditions were poor, and as the numbers in the area rose, so did the cost of living, while services and amenities like pubs sprang up. Funicular rails, along which horses pulled carts, were constructed to bring stone from Dalkey Quarry. The route remains an important local feature; the tracks are long gone, but it is still known as 'The Metals' (today a popular walking and cycling route). In 1821, following a royal visit from George IV, Dunleary became known as Kingstown, and was on course to becoming one of the most important ports in

---

[*] See Hart, 2002, 19–32 for a discussion of black people in Ireland in the 1700s; an estimated 1,000 individuals in the 1790s.

Britain and Ireland. The mailboat ran regularly between Kingstown and Britain from 1826,[19] transforming the area into one of Ireland's foremost gateways to the world. In 1834, Kingstown was the first Dublin suburb to become a township.[20]

Dalkey, a Viking and then a medieval trading settlement, had become a small fishing village in the early nineteenth century, when permission was granted to Richard Toutcher to quarry granite there. By 1823, Dalkey Commons was home to about a thousand people living in insanitary, squalid conditions, many labouring in the quarry. By the mid-nineteenth century, developers had acquired rights over the former Commons, and while Dalkey would retain an important working- and middle-class population, large, fashionable homes with impressive views began construction. This trend remained controversial throughout the second half of the nineteenth century – *Freeman's Journal* strongly criticised the privatisation of public rights-of-way and the demise of the use of the Commons for general leisure purposes.[21]

Kingstown Harbour was considered completed by 1842,[22] and the development of the entire area had been set in motion. By the 1860s, the pier was a major transport hub, receiving vast quantities of coal; four new, modern Mail Packet ships were regularly crossing the Irish Sea, and a coastal building boom, all along the southern shores of Dublin Bay, was underway. Many of the well-known buildings of the area were constructed then, including the Royal Marine Hotel.[23] Ever since, the harbour has been not just a place of comings and goings and an important site of employment but a stage on which many pivotal scenes of Ireland's story – the tragedies and the triumphs – have been enacted.

Given the early roll-out of public transport here, its transformative effect on the county, particularly the coastal areas, cannot be underestimated. A train line running along the coast from Dublin to Kingstown opened in 1834 and was still, as the twentieth century approached, one of the 'best paying lines', for its length, in the world, with huge passenger numbers. Especially in the summer, city-dwellers could enjoy a day at the seaside and the fashionable promenade of the East Pier, from which they could view Dublin Bay and contemplate its alleged superiority over the Bay of Naples, then in vogue among the fashionable set.[24]

The introduction of reliable public transport also had a dramatic impact on the inland parts of Dún Laoghaire-Rathdown. Whereas previously they were dominated by wealthy landowners with demesnes, those working in agriculture as landlords, tenant farmers or labourers, and those working in service, public transport enabled a wider range of people to live here while working in Dublin.[25] The construction of the railways, and provision of reliable, affordable public transport, was one of the most significant influences on settlement patterns from this period,* with the construction of suburbs and the growth of extant communities tending to occur along railway corridors.[26] In 1854, the Dublin, Wicklow and Wexford Railway Company opened a line from Harcourt Street to Bray, with each train capable of carrying 300.[27] At the time, the suburb of Ranelagh marked the end of the city to the south, and beyond that lay farmland punctuated by villages and stately homes. The railway made the entire inland area to the south of the city and north of the Wicklow border attractive to those seeking clean air and an easy commute.

Between 1851 and 1861, the population of Kingstown increased by 43 per cent to about 21,000, as new, elegant terraces filled the seafront and developments crept down the coast and inland.[28] In the late nineteenth century, 'G.R.D.' noted approvingly that the second-class carriages on the Dublin and Kingstown Railway (with its 'atmospheric continuation' to Dalkey, referring to the system used to propel the train,[29] whereby trains were propelled by air rather than by steam engines[30]) were more comfortable than English equivalents, and that the train stopped at 'some of the best bathing houses'.

---

* It also had an interesting impact on the local ecosystem. Booterstown Marsh – now a nature reserve with an array of birds and plants – was effectively created by the construction of the railway. What had once been cultivated land became a marsh, marking the transition from fresh to saltwater, and a natural oasis in an increasingly urban environment.

Throughout the second half of the nineteenth century, the population of Dublin had increased rapidly, with the influx of poor people, mostly Catholics, from rural areas. Many of them were illiterate, lived in poor housing and worked in unskilled jobs.[31] The Protestant middle and upper classes, who inhabited the new suburbs in numbers very disproportionate to their numbers in Ireland overall,[32] along with rapidly growing numbers of highly educated middle-class Catholics, increasingly chose a comfortable life on the periphery. In 1860, *The Irish Builder* boasted, 'Our suburbs are extending, green fields are metamorphosed into populous districts… "bustle" is the word… and the welcome sounds of the hammer and trowel are met at each step.' By 1871, 5 per cent of Dublin's entire workforce – about 6,500 men and 3,000 women – was working in building, with many of the less-skilled labourers leaving squalid tenements every morning to help construct the growing suburbs to the south. Property developers worried that labourers' poor living conditions might compromise their work, as they were often ill and hungry, and tempted to seek better working conditions overseas.[33]

The growing suburbs needed a new source of water, and from 1879 water to the coastal area was provided by the Vartry Reservoir in Wicklow. This reliable source of clean water – a breakthrough in urban sanitation[34] – facilitated yet further development.[35] Adequate sanitation and drainage were significant challenges. The proximity of the homes of the very poor to those of the well-to-do meant that wealthier people were more exercised about the squalor in which the poor lived than elsewhere, because communicable diseases relating to poor living conditions might impact on them too. The village of Glasthule, for example, was home to many desperately poor families, unable to maintain reasonable standards of hygiene and without sanitation. Consequently, in 1866, a cholera outbreak linked to a sewer opening onto a stream used for drinking or washing claimed 127 lives.[36] In 1880, there was a 'lengthened controversy' with the Board of the Rathdown Union and the Local Government Board regarding conditions in the small village of Newtown-Park, which lacked both a water supply and adequate drainage. In 1890, addressing the Dublin Sanitary Association, Frederic Pim – the association's president – referenced the diseases caused by poor sanitation, and the 'years of embarrassment and privation' that could result when a sick breadwinner could not work for an extended period.[37] The following year, he pointed out that the well-to-do were not immune to the ravages of diseases associated with the poor: 'Every autumn,' he said, 'we have an outbreak of typhoid among our well-to-do classes, by which prominent citizens are struck down, some never to rise again.' The larger population also meant more sewage, much of which was discharged into Dublin Bay in Kingstown and Blackrock, where it failed to discriminate between the social classes. In 1892, Pim remarked that public bathing was under threat, as the flat strands 'are being clothed with a foul and noisome deposit'.[38]

Nonetheless, with much higher levels of squalor and disease in the inner city, the southern suburbs were increasingly touted as a place for the middle classes and affluent. Estate agents maintained, for example, that living in Kingstown could cure the sick, including those suffering from 'depressed nervous temperament', boasted of recent improvements to the 'sanitary arrangements' and compared it favourably to similar settlements in Britain.[39] Numerous epidemics, including the devastating cholera epidemic of 1832 and a serious outbreak of smallpox in 1865, were well within living memory, and the suburbs were promoted as healthier places to be,[40] which indeed they were. For the ten years from 1865 to 1874, the death rate in the city was 30.9 per thousand, and in the suburbs 22.7 per thousand,[41] for reasons relating to sanitation, air quality and residents' socioeconomic status.

By 1898, Dublin city was surrounded by ten separate councils administering new suburbs dominated by comfortable Victorian homes, raising their own taxes, and electing their own administrators, among them the township of Kingstown.[42] The suburban areas of Dún Laoghaire-Rathdown were ever-more popular. The Dublin Southern Districts Tramway had launched tramlines from the city centre to Blackrock and from Kingstown to Dalkey in 1870. Initially horse-drawn along tram-tracks, the trams were electrified from 1896.*

Blackrock was home to numerous well-to-do families, who in turn supported working-class families in domestic service, service and agricultural positions, as well as a range of retail businesses. It became a township in 1863.[43] In 1889, a publication sponsored by a local estate agents, Talbot Coall and Son, promoted Blackrock as beautiful and cheerful, just fifteen minutes on public transport from the city centre, but a much nicer place to live, with clear air when Dublin was immersed in polluted fog. In the mid-nineteenth century, Foxrock was still a predominately rural, inland parish. It too was soon being promoted as 'the healthiest part of Dublin' to middle- and upper-class families. Churches (Church of Ireland and Catholic) and sporting facilities, including the Foxrock Golf Club (opened in 1893) and the Foxrock Independents GAA Club (founded in 1900), were established as Foxrock grew. From the early twentieth century, modest homes for the working classes were constructed in Foxrock. For example, Brighton Cottages had running water and outdoor sanitation and were considered high-quality homes for working families, even if they were concealed from view by trees and hedging, so the wealthy did not have to see them. Working-class families in Foxrock had some access to local sporting and other facilities: they could have picnics on the golf course, and some kept ferrets to hunt rabbits there.[44]

By 1911, many of the southern suburbs were well-established. The flight of more affluent people from the inner city had resulted in over 60 per cent of the residents of the inner city being working-class.[45] The suburbs of Dún Laoghaire-Rathdown were physically dominated by villas and grand homes, and were popular among the aspirant middle classes, while they also had significant working-class populations. The southern suburbs continued to grow amid the turmoil of the first two

---

* They would run until 1949, when they were discontinued. The last was effectively dismantled by a 'howling and shrieking' mob of souvenir hunters who took off all the lights and brought them home. McAsey, 1967, 91.

decades of the twentieth century and in early independence. Between 1926 and 1936, for example, the population of parts of Blackrock grew by between 25 and 40 per cent, and by a further 21.8 per cent between 1936 and 1946.[46]

In parallel with the rapid development of the area throughout the nineteenth and early twentieth centuries, there was an ambitious programme of church-building, especially in areas with large, affluent Catholic populations. In the years immediately after the famine of the 1840s, beautiful Catholic churches were erected, including the Church of St Patrick in Monkstown, completed in 1866.[47] The parallel growth of suburbs and of Catholic church buildings and infrastructure would continue throughout much of the twentieth century,[48] serving also as *de facto* monuments to the relative decline in influence of families from the Protestant elite and middle classes, who nonetheless remained in the area in considerable numbers. Placenames reflect the ongoing cultural and political shifts, with older homes and streets often bearing names that sound quite British, reflecting the power of the Anglo-Irish families who lived there, alongside newer homes and streets – and renamed grand houses – that reflected the interest in Gaelic culture and heritage fostered in early independence. They were an important marker of the interests of the rapidly emerging elite of well-educated, comfortably off Catholic families with important positions in government, in the public sector and in the professions. Attending both groups, the area was also home to an army of domestic servants, gardeners and labourers with their own ambitions, plans and hopes. Many were migrants from rural Ireland, often seeking to leave behind the old ways at home. Audrey's mother left Mayo for Shankill to evade her father's plans for an arranged marriage that she did not want, and Joe, also from Shankill, reported a succession of female relatives from his mother's remote place of origin in Mayo coming to study nursing at Loughlinstown Hospital and improve their prospects.

In the early twentieth century, both established and emerging forms of transportation combined to make the suburbs increasingly accessible from the city. Lexicon Library Collection.

The Ticket Booking Office at Sandycove, 1965. Photo by Kevin Murray, Archive of the Irish Railway Record Society, courtesy Ciarán Cooney.

Public transport improved steadily. The Great Southern Railways, operating rail, bus and lorry services, came into existence in 1925, when all the railway companies lying wholly within the Free State were amalgamated. The Transport Acts of 1932 and 1933 gave the Great Southern Railways the right to compulsorily acquire its road competition. Córas Iompair Éireann (CIÉ) was founded on 1 January 1945 under the Transport Act of 1944, uniting the Great Southern Railways and the Dublin United Tramway.[49] Before, private bus services also ferried people around. Many of the workers on these services were absorbed into CIÉ. Those who had run private companies lost money, but CIÉ's new employees had 'jobs for life', and improved public transport made it progressively easier for suburbanites to travel into Dublin to work and contributed to yet further suburban growth.*

In 1948, as Ireland recovered from the Emergency, Dún Laoghaire Borough Council celebrated a Civic Week, with a brochure lauding the area's suitability for 'the invalid, the semi-invalid and the not-so-young', listing its many attractions, and asserting that only the 'fussiest of housewives' would ever need to go elsewhere. It also claimed that local girls were so attractive that 'Englishmen, Scotsmen and Welshmen' travelled to the area to select brides.[50] Upwardly mobile families continued to move from the inner city and from rural areas to suburbs like Mount Merrion, with homes like those built by property developer John Kenny – the 'Kenny-built' houses.[51] Property developer M.P. Kennedy was also active locally, building Trimleston Estate in Mount Merrion, among other developments, comprising relatively modest, but comfortable houses in an attractive location for the middle classes, with similar houses constructed in the Maretimo Gardens development in Blackrock by developer Thomas Archer.[52] With comfortable homes and access to schools and parkland, these settlers created growing communities in which aspirational parents could work to ensure continued upward

---

* Public transport was also locally noted as a means by which young people from a wider area could meet, fall in love and get married; for example, the tramway from Stillorgan to Blackrock was regarded as a vector by which matches were made. Rochford, 2006, 5.

social mobility. Oisín grew up in Mount Merrion then, and he noted the preponderance of civil servants, with the size of the houses roughly in line with the seniority of the civil servants who lived in them: 'within a half a mile of our house, we had… Secretary of the Department of Industry and Commerce, Secretary of the Department of Lands, a senior civil servant in Áras an Uachtaráin, a man from the Department of Justice'. Many families in these areas had roots in rural Ireland and their homes became the foci of chain migration from rural areas into Dublin and good jobs in the civil service, the professions and emerging industries. Sally, for example, grew up in a 'Kenny-built' house in Mount Merrion in the 1940s and 1950s, the child of civil servants (her mother having been forced to retire on marriage). She remembered, 'there was always somebody in the house'. Sally's mother was from a modest rural background and, having come up in the world, she now accommodated relatives who wanted much the same: 'My aunts came up… they did their civil service exams, or did their nursing exams.'

Council estates were also being constructed in large numbers, in areas including Dún Laoghaire, Monkstown, Sallynoggin and Glasthule, providing decent-quality homes for families leaving crowded, often unsanitary accommodation in the inner city or in built-up satellite communities, and for lower-income families migrating from rural areas. Throughout the 1950s and 1960s, agriculture witnessed growing numbers of young people leaving the land as farming became more mechanised, educational levels rose and expectations for young country people shifted. Rising car ownership* also made it easier for people working in the city centre to commute from dormitory suburbs.[53] By 1961, the population of Dublin had increased to 595,288 (from 472,935

---

* While cars made the roads more dangerous and less inviting for children and pedestrians, road accidents occurred before cars were common too. An elderly woman, Elizabeth Rushby, speaking in 1980 about the early twentieth century, remembered a dreadful accident in Dún Laoghaire that occurred in her childhood, when a horse pulling a car kicked a small boy so hard that his brains came out, 'right down on the road like a big gut out of a fish'. NFC UFP, vol. 1994, 357.

in 1936) and that of Dún Laoghaire to 68,101 (from 39,785 in 1936).[54] Levels of property ownership continued to grow dramatically. In 1946, 52.2 per cent of households owned their own home; by 1971, 70.8 per cent did, placing Ireland among the countries with the highest levels of home ownership in the world.[55] By 1979, over a third of the Irish population lived in the Dublin area.[56] From 1984, the Dublin Area Rapid Transit, or DART, linked the southern suburbs with increased efficiency to the centre.

By now, the suburbs generally, and perhaps the southern suburbs particularly, had become so successful in establishing themselves as pleasant places to live, well connected to places of work and sites of leisure, that they posed an existential threat to retail and other businesses in the city centre, which increasingly featured swathes of dereliction as business owners eyed sites and customer bases in the suburbs and abandoned inner-city areas that were often inconvenient for drivers.[57] While Ireland was in recession for much of the 1980s, the misery was far from equally spread. Rural areas saw ongoing depopulation and the inner city remained largely poor and even squalid, while comfortable new housing developments in Dún Laoghaire-Rathdown, like The Park in Cabinteely, provided homes for aspirational, successful young families. David, who lived in The Park with his wife and their young family, remembered the 1980s as a time of hard work and success: 'I didn't even *know* there was a recession. We were busy. We were doing things. We were getting on with our lives.' In 1987, Brian Kennedy stated that 80 per cent of the inhabitants of South County Dublin had parents from provincial towns and rural areas. The unprecedented increases in formal education from the mid-twentieth century, especially after the introduction of free secondary education in 1967, meant that there were plenty of highly educated, skilled young professionals poised to take senior positions in the civil service and in diverse professions, while also urging their children towards academic prowess. The same year, 35 per cent of children in the Foxrock/Carrickmines area progressed to university.[58] Growing levels of female employment meant that more families were now dual-income.

The Cowzer family from Blackrock, day tripping in Glencullen, c.1963. Rising prosperity and the growing affordability of cars made day tripping increasingly accessible to ordinary families. Those who lived in Dún Laoghaire-Rathdown didn't have to venture far to enjoy the mountains and the sea. Courtesy Linda Cowzer.

Works on the DART in the early 1980s. Good public transport links between Dún Laoghaire-Rathdown and Dublin have been a major driver of settlement and development in the area for centuries. Archive of the Irish Railway Record Society, courtesy Ciarán Cooney.

* * *

Given its proximity to Dublin city, and its high average levels of education and income, Dún Laoghaire-Rathdown can hardly be described as
marginalised. But even the best statistical and historical data provide only
a partial picture of what it is like living somewhere, and what it feels like
to belong to a particular place at a particular time. The important historical events and people that Ireland has chosen to commemorate and
celebrate, while ignoring many others, continue to facilitate a partial,
and even partly imagined, understanding of the past and its influence on
the present.[59] While historians have often turned their attention to this
area and its vicissitudes throughout history, it has rarely been the subject
of serious ethnological investigation. The National Folklore Collection,
held at University College Dublin, which has vast holdings from all over
the country, has very little from here. In the academic year 1937–8, the
Irish Folklore Commission embarked on an ambitious programme to
use the schoolchildren of Ireland as folklore collectors.[60] In the booklet
sent to all the participating schools, they invited children 'to participate
in the task of rescuing from oblivion the traditions which, in spite of
the vicissitudes of the historic Irish nation, have, century in, century
out, been preserved with loving care by their ancestors'. Schools from
the cities of Dublin, Cork, Limerick and Waterford could opt out, as
the Commission was primarily interested in rural tradition.[61] Of all the
schools in the area now known as Dún Laoghaire-Rathdown, only some
are included* and the information they offer is relatively sparse, perhaps
partly because the handbook provided by the Commission was written
with rural people in mind, and many of the numerous sample questions were not very relevant to urban or suburban communities. In 1979,
the Urban Folklore Project, also carried out by the National Folklore

---

* The Mercy Convent in Blackrock, the Loreto Convent and the Harold's Boy's School in
  Dalkey, Taney School and Dundrum National Schools C and B, the Christian Brothers
  in Dún Laoghaire, St Brigid's in Foxrock, St Joseph's Boys and the Convent School in
  Glasthule, Killiney, Rathfarnham Boys', Sandyford Boys' and Stillorgan National School.

Collection, collected material from Dublin city and surroundings, with some collected in Dún Laoghaire-Rathdown, above all in its more rural areas, but the material still pales in comparison to holdings from elsewhere in Ireland, particularly the west.[62]

However, a vast wealth of material resides in the memories of the people of this extraordinary county, and we will use it here to look at what living through the ebbs and flows of history has been like for them. To explore the vast diversity of Dún Laoghaire-Rathdown, we have spoken to its people from all sorts of backgrounds, so as to piece together their collective experiential jigsaw.[63] There have always been huge economic disparities here, but how did the locals, along the economic spectrum, interact with and feel about one another? What was it like growing up here during the massive social and economic shifts of the twentieth century? Historical data provides some clues, but it remains largely silent on the subjective experience of the individuals involved.

Lily Clare and a friend with a fireman in Dún Laoghaire, 1930s. Kind permission of Jimmy Howe.

Carrickmines, 1967. O'Dea Photographic
Collection. National Library of Ireland.

Fortunately, this project, carried out in collaboration between Dún Laoghaire-Rathdown County Council and the UNESCO-recognised National Folklore Collection at University College Dublin, has been able to tap the personal and family memories of the 268 people – mostly in their sixties, seventies, eighties and nineties – who contributed to the People's History of Dún Laoghaire-Rathdown oral history programme between 2021 and 2023. Pseudonyms have been used in this book for all who generously contributed as interviewees. While many families have stories about recent ancestors in the nineteenth and early twentieth centuries, where a date is not specified here, the material reflects the age profile of the majority of interviewees, and refers to events in the mid-twentieth century, a key moment in Ireland's pivot from tradition to modernity, when so many of the social and cultural innovations taking place were observed here first. And, because of the area's exceptional diversity, in the process we gain insight into the journey of the whole island of Ireland through the recent past towards the present, and can address at least some of the imbalance inherent in most historical research.* The People's History of Dún Laoghaire-Rathdown has created a rich archive for future researchers – about three million words of audio recordings and of transcribed text that is now part of the National Folklore Collection, a public archive – and the primary research material for this book.

---

* The project was co-funded by the Heritage Council of Ireland as part of the implementation of the dlr County Heritage Plan 2021–2025, the Department of Tourism, Culture, Arts, Gaeltacht, Sport and Media as part of the Decade of Centenaries Initiative 2013–2023, the dlrcc Heritage Office and was generously supported by the staff of the National Folklore Collection at UCD.

WHO'S WHO

In matters of identity, as in landscape, occupation and socioeconomic difference, Dún Laoghaire-Rathdown is strikingly varied. For centuries, residents have dwelt in a complex web of personal and professional relationships, with lives intersecting in many different ways, both with one another and with the geography and history of their home. Historically, we find identities tending to coalesce around families' socioeconomic, ethno-religious and political backgrounds, as well as location and profession, as well as strong local identities associated with geographical place – with the latter often as strong as or stronger than the former.

Mary Richardson and Joan Richardson, c.1954. Rural children in agricultural parts of the area often travelled into Dublin City to attend school. Kind permission of Mary White.

Throughout the nineteenth and most of the twentieth century, people from different socioeconomic backgrounds had significantly different experiences, with people from the same social class but different ethno-religious or political backgrounds having much more in common, in most ways, than those from the same ethno-religious background but different social classes. Isobel grew up in Monkstown in the 1930s and 1940s. At about twelve years old, she was already taller than many of the lower-income adults she saw. This she attributes to being well-fed, whereas many of the older local residents had suffered from childhood malnutrition, leaving them with 'rickets and bandy legs'. The difference between her appearance, as a middle-class child, and that of the poorer children in the area was also striking. She saw many whose heads were shaved because they had ringworm, who were poorly dressed and shod: 'ill-fitting clothes, too small or too big and very, very ragged… lots… had no shoes whatsoever'. The poorest adults at the time often had no coats; women wore shawls and men improvised on rainy days with hessian sacks draped across shoulders. Edward grew up in Dún Laoghaire and Glasthule in the 1930s and 1940s. His parents had long roots in the local working-class community. Edward was keenly aware of social distinctions and of how difficult life could be for the working classes. Life, he said, was 'pressing you down'. Young working-class people clearly received the message: they should not get 'above their station'.

Wealthy people tended to socialise and work with other wealthy people. George, for example, grew up in a very wealthy Dalkey family. The difference between his home and those of local working-class families was startling. As a small child in the 1950s, he quickly learned that there were certain children who could never be his friends. 'We met them in the park,' he remembered, 'there was a kind of a social division'. On the few occasions when George invited local children from much poorer families home to play, he was told not to do it again. Francis, from Sallynoggin, recalled a vast gulf, mid-twentieth century, between the wealthy and the working classes: 'We were no more aware of [them]… than the cat would be of people living in houses.' Francis's father worked part-time as a gardener, and sometimes Francis helped at the weekends: 'But the life that they lived was totally alien to me,' he said. 'It never occurred to me that they were exactly the same as the rest of us.' Andrew remembered a local woman in the Rochestown area from whom his family purchased eggs in the 1950s: 'She had a little cottage there, which had no electricity, no running water, a mud floor... She was a lovely lady. But she had practically nothing.' Growing up in Sallynoggin in the 1960s, in a working-class family that was doing well, Rob was aware of dreadful poverty: 'kids who didn't have any clean clothes and nits... head lice... and the fingernails and all... they used to get sandwiches in the schools... It might be just margarine one day, cheese the next, jam the next... and that might have been the only decent food that those kids got.' People who were children in wealthy families in the 1940s, 1950s and 1960s often recall their elders quite routinely referring to the working classes with terms such as 'guttersnipes'.

Vera's husband was educated at a boarding school in England, which was quite common among upper-class Catholic families in the first half of the twentieth century. On returning to Ireland, this cohort was exempt from the ban on Catholics attending Trinity, as they had never studied Irish. They progressed to further education alongside the Anglo-Irish and other mostly comfortably off Irish Protestant students, with whom they had much more in common than with their poorer coreligionists. While there was a working-class Protestant community in Dún Laoghaire-Rathdown, the Protestant working classes were, generally, concentrated in inner-city areas, where they might be the subject of charitable works on the part of wealthy Protestants from the southern suburbs, who were important funders of organisations like the Association for the Relief of Distressed Protestants (ARDP), founded in 1836.[1]

In Catholic churches, until the mid-twentieth century, worshippers were often divided into poorer and better-off by the requirement of donating six pence to enter by a particular door, attend Mass alongside wealthy parishioners and receive Holy Communion first.[2] In Booterstown Parish Church, for example, red ropes separated the side aisles from the centre, the latter reserved for those who could afford six pence. These barriers were removed in 1945.[3] Hugh Leonard, from Dalkey, remembered that, 'There were red ropes half-way down the aisles so that the twopennies could not sneak into the sixpennies at the front. The quality and the Holy Marys sat near the altar, the cornerboys and wasters stood at the back… and the ordinary people sat between them.'[4] Debbie's family attended Foxrock Church when she was growing up in the 1940s. The first ten rows were reserved for the well-to-do. The less wealthy tried to sit as near those special rows as possible, to gape at the stylish, fashionable clothes of the rich. Then, she said, people generally accepted their place in life. With the benefit of hindsight, her view has changed: 'the rich really lived off the poor. I would have thought of it as the other way round until I got older and realised… they were living off the workers rather than the workers living off [them].' Ailish moved to Cabinteely to work in domestic service in 1948 and settled locally with her husband, a butcher, in the 1950s. Then, wealthy locals entered through one church door and the less wealthy through another. The McGrath family, who lived in Cabinteely House, a stately home, were in the front. 'Well, we were used to it, I suppose,' Ailish concluded.

Liz, who grew up in Blackrock in the 1950s, remembered the local priest's preference for the rich. He made a point, she said, of walking through wealthy areas and shaking hands with everyone he met there, but would not shake hands at all with poorer parishioners. William, from Shankill, recounted how his father worked as a sacristan in the local church. Despite his lengthy service, few of the priests saw him as their social equal, and they tended to make this clear. Some were also tough with parishioners who struggled to pay church dues. One threatened those struggling to pay with having their name 'called out' from the pulpit in Mass.

Wealthy and lower-income Protestants, conversely, tended to worship in different churches, and to interact largely in employer/employee or recipient of social assistance/grandee relationships. Poorer Protestants frequently benefited from the philanthropic efforts of wealthy Protestants, and often worked for them too. Wealthy Protestant families in the nine-teenth and early twentieth centuries often endeavoured to hire Protestant servants, but as the population – particularly the working-class popu-lation – was overwhelmingly Catholic, inevitably they were rarely able to have an all-Protestant domestic staff.[5] Depending on the family, and the closeness of their relationship with their staff, they might adapt their behaviour in recognition of the 'mixed' household. Speaking in 1980, Eileen Hughes remembered her Church of Ireland family all eating fish on Friday because the housemaid, Katie, and their neighbours, were Catholic, were not allowed to eat meat and preferred not to smell cook-ing meat on those days.[6]

Personal hygiene is a recurring theme in any discussion of social class. Throughout the nineteenth and the first half of the twentieth century, and in some cases into the 1960s, 1970s and even 1980s, the poorest local residents did not have bathroom facilities indoors and/or had to share limited facilities between many. It was impossible for mothers of large families to wash children more than once a week. It was even more dif-ficult for Traveller families, who generally lived on roadsides and might depend for access to water on local settled families who did not always cooperate, or who even restricted their access. Rosie said that one of the main reasons why better-off people in Dalkey paid more to attend Mass was because they were anxious not to sit beside the poorest con-gregants, who often smelled bad because they lived in homes in which it was impossible to keep clothing clean and dry, especially in winter. Many of the poorest people also had fleas, she said, and others worried about catching them. Rob remembered classmates in school in Ballybrack in the 1950s, 'who smelt to high heaven, who quite clearly weren't washed as they should be'. Medical reformers throughout the first half of the twentieth century often noted that poor hygiene, often practically una-voidable, was a contributing factor to higher rates of disease among the working classes. Most, of course, did their best to be as clean as possible, even when facilities were limited. The phrase used to instruct children on how to wash effectively with only a basin and a washcloth was: 'You washed down as far as possible, and then you washed up as far as possible, then you took the basin upstairs and you washed possible.'

* * *

Even in wealthy families in which girls were well-educated, they were often expected to be subordinate to their brothers until well into the twentieth century. Families from all social classes often opted to provide boys with more, and more rigorous, education, as girls' higher education was seen as wasteful. Girls generally got married and were thereafter expected to dedicate themselves to home and family, an occupation not considered to benefit from higher education. Nonetheless, educational standards rose steadily for both sexes throughout the twentieth century, with the difference between female and male educational attainment steadily eroding. As educational differences continued to decline, girls increasingly experienced their subordinate position in the household as galling. In the 1950s and early 1960s, Priscilla and her sister, from a comfortably off, highly educated Dalkey family, were expected to make their brothers' beds and cook their meals during the school holidays. Tomatoes – considered scarce – were set aside for their father and brothers. And even though girls like Priscilla did get a good education, boys typically got an even better one. 'The focus was on the boys,' she remembered, 'and the boys getting a job, and the money was for the boys… the boys could sit at the table and the girls would come and bring them their food.' Among less well-off families, parents might decide to let the boys remain in school and do their Intermediate or even Leaving Certificate, but not to waste school fees on the girls, who would probably only have a few years to use their training before marriage. With the introduction of free secondary education in 1967, amid dramatic social change, girls' educational levels rose rapidly, as discussed in 'Getting Ahead'.

Another important distinction was between urbanites and rural-dwellers and, in the rural context, between comfortably off and small farmers, and between landowners and labourers. Farmers with more land and bigger incomes tended to be well-networked with suburban and urban areas, while those with small parcels of land tended to have much more local identities and less access to major retailers to sell their produce. Whereas farm labourers and the rural working classes might have had more in common in some ways with the urban poor, rural districts often also had strong local identities, facilitated by the fact that smaller farmers often worked on a seasonal basis for farmers with more land, and by the cooperative work that was a feature of farm life generally before mechanisation. There were significant social and class differences between farming people. Bigger farmers often sent their children into Dublin, or to a suburb like Dún Laoghaire or Dalkey, to attend secondary school. Smaller farmers rarely could support a family to a reasonable standard on just a few acres, and the smallest farmers often lived with significant levels of poverty, well into the 1970s and 1980s.

Generally, the relationship between bigger and smaller landowners was cordial, but sometimes the disparity between social standing could lead to tensions. In one uplands community, a local landowning family was treated with considerable deference until the 1960s or 1970s, with people even bowing to them. By the mid-1970s, Brendan had had enough. At Mass with his children, he occupied the seat usually taken by this particular family. 'Down they come with the big stick, walking down the aisle of the church,' Brendan remembered. 'And he stood. He didn't say anything, he just pointed out, "Out. Get out." We just told him, "No. Feck off!"' By now, educational disparities between the richest members of the community and others had narrowed considerably, while employment opportunities had widened. Even people's homes were getting less dissimilar. Fewer people felt a need to display deference to families that had traditionally been local employers.

* * *

Ethno-religious differences have historically marked every aspect of life here, from industry and commerce to recreation. Since the seventeenth century, Dún Laoghaire-Rathdown has notably been a place where the Church of Ireland, with its favoured position under British rule as the state religion, has had a very substantial presence – more than in any other part of the territory that would become independent Ireland. Other Protestant denominations, including Methodists, Presbyterians, Unitarians, Plymouth Brethren and so forth, were also represented in greater numbers than in most of the country. Throughout much of modern history, the relationship between ethno-religious status and socio-economic trends in Dún Laoghaire-Rathdown mirrored that of Ireland (excluding Northern Ireland) as a whole, with members of the Church of Ireland, and to a lesser extent other Protestant denominations, heavily over-represented among the professions, as landowners and in 'the upper levels of financial and commercial life'.[7] Church of Ireland members were not, however, universally well-to-do; in the mid-nineteenth century, parishioners in Kilternan were described as 'very poor', attending church barefoot, even in bad weather,[8] while, as we discuss in 'A Roof Over Their Heads', the workhouse in Loughlinstown offered refuge to substantial numbers of destitute Protestants.

By the middle decades of the nineteenth century, notwithstanding the challenges facing ordinary people, the Catholic Church was ever-ascendant, there was a rapidly growing, educated Catholic middle class, and the Church was constructing impressive buildings and consolidating its authority over huge swathes of society, notably education, healthcare and the care of the vulnerable. Religious vocations were high, with many bright young men and women, often from relatively modest backgrounds, who wished to pursue a religious life while also accessing a better standard of education than was accessible to their families before. Whereas members of the Church of Ireland had previously enjoyed considerable group privilege (the entire agricultural Irish population had to contribute to the financial support of the Church of Ireland, for example), that had waned greatly as the twentieth century approached, especially following the disestablishment of the Church of Ireland in 1871.[9] By 1889, when a local estate agents, Talbot Coall and Son, was advertising Kingstown as a desirable location for the middle and affluent classes, it listed the thriving Catholic parishes as one of its attractions.[10] By 1907, just fifteen years pre-independence, a record of the parishes of the area pointed out how Kingstown may have been developed by the English and 'all the resources of modern civilisation', but that 'the spiritual sentinels on the watch-tower, the Archbishops of Dublin, tended its growth, and nurtured it into an energetic and zealous Catholic community'.[11]

Contemporaneously with the dramatic growth in power and influence of the Catholic Church, smaller Protestant denominations also grew. In Ireland generally, for example, Methodists increased rapidly in numbers at the time, with thriving congregations particularly in areas with large Anglican populations; Methodists tended to convert from the Church of Ireland.[12] Small denominations, like the Kellyites, who had a presence in Blackrock, also form part of the picture. The Kellyites followed the teaching of Thomas Kelly, originally a Church of Ireland cleric, who broke with the Church of Ireland in 1803 and had his own small following until his death in 1855, after which the congregation dissipated.[13]

By the mid-twentieth century, Dún Laoghaire Borough remained significantly more religiously diverse than elsewhere in Dublin. In 1946, for example, the overall Protestant population of the city was 8.7 per cent (down from 10.8 per cent in 1936) and trending downwards; in Dún Laoghaire Borough, it was 18.5 per cent.[14] By now, the educated Catholic upper and middle classes, who tended to have better Irish language skills and to be well-connected with important political and Church figures, were increasingly dominant. The substantial Protestant community, including many who were well-educated, well-to-do and well-connected, continued to wield considerable influence, but was declining in relative power. Many Protestant parents were also now anxious for their children to be competent in Irish, so as not to be excluded from good public-sector jobs.

Significant levels of separation were maintained along denominational lines in all sectors of life throughout most of this period,
generally amiably. Nicola grew up in a Methodist family in Dalkey.
Because of their faith, her family was notably stricter than the other
people living in the Bullock Harbour area. As a child in the 1930s
and early 1940s, she often wished she was Catholic, so that she could
go to the pictures and football matches too. But, she said, there was
never any sectarian 'carry-on'. In early twentieth-century Blackrock,
however, larger shops were run by Protestants, employed mostly
Protestants and mostly dealt with the Ulster Bank, whereas smaller
shops employed Catholics and mostly dealt with the National Bank.
Protestants and Catholics were often served by different chemists,
while religious worship, education and social welfare were, until the
second part of the twentieth century, mostly provided by religious
and other philanthropic organisations. Kate recalled that the understanding in Dún Laoghaire was that many of the Protestant-owned
businesses endeavoured to promote other Protestants to management
positions, so the prospects of their Catholic employees were limited,
right into the 1960s. Rosaleen, who worked for Boland's Biscuits – a
Protestant-owned company – in the 1960s, remembered that all the
management positions 'seemed to be' filled by Protestants. Protestant-
owned businesses also tended to provide apprenticeship positions to
young Protestants, who often came from small rural towns and either
'lived in' in dormitory-style accommodation or were housed locally
as lodgers. Fintan, who worked for Murdoch's, a prominent Dún
Laoghaire business in the mid-twentieth century, remembered, 'a lot of
young chaps who were Church of Ireland, from the country, who came
to work'. Ita and Nora's paternal great-grandfather was English, so the
family surname gave the impression that the family were Protestants,
although they were Catholics. When their grandfather established a
furniture-removal business in Dún Laoghaire, he quickly built up a
client base among local Protestants, who assumed that he was one of

'them'. So as not to disabuse them of this convenient belief, he went to a very early Mass on Sunday mornings, to avoid being seen.

While some families were happy to socialise outside of their own ethno-religious group, leisure activities – including children's, women's and men's social organisations, dances and sports – were largely separated along denominational lines until well into the twentieth century.[15] Gabriel, from a Catholic background, remembered that, 'all the soccer, rugby, tennis... you didn't mix with Protestant, or any other religion, you stuck with your own crowd'. But for some, social class superseded denominational difference. Janet's father, a working-class Catholic, grew up with a Protestant best friend, and they remained close all their lives. He considered himself 'a Catholic *and* a Protestant', happily attending both types of service, playing hockey (sometimes regarded as a 'Protestant' game) rather than hurling, and participating in local musical groups dominated by Protestants. He also volunteered, together with his friend, in doing odd jobs around a local Protestant church, for which they were rewarded with boxes of food. Eventually, the parish priest learned that he was attending Protestant services, and he was 'put out' or excommunicated (Janet is not sure when this happened, but some time before the Second Vatican Council).

* * *

In 1849, ten warships accompanied a young Queen Victoria into Dublin Bay.[16] Her Jubilee was celebrated with gusto by many in 1887. According to local marine historian Vincent Delaney, although they were invited by the crew of HBS *Belleisle* – a guard ship in Kingstown Harbour – to celebrate aboard, the Water Wag sailors (the characteristic Water Wag yachts are discussed in the 'Fun and Games' chapter) opted to celebrate on Dalkey Island, where they consumed copious quantities of alcohol, fired a Howitzer gun, and drunkenly sang 'God Save the Queen'. A generation or two later, Victoria's last royal visit commenced in Kingstown, where she and her retinue landed on 4 April

1900. Amid nationalist rumblings, her visit asserted British authority over its neighbouring island. For locals, it was also a super day out. The waterfront had been lavishly decorated, the harbour staff were formally dressed in frock-coats, and the streets were lined with excited crowds as the aged queen and her entourage left the royal yacht and boarded their vehicles before being whisked into the city centre for further pomp and ceremony. Everyone had dressed in their smartest clothes, the children whose parents could afford it had extra pocket money, local bands performed and businesses sold commemorative souvenirs. It must have been extremely irritating for everyone when Victoria's cavalcade rapidly bypassed the centre of Kingstown.[17] In 1980, Ann Burns still remembered Victoria as 'a little old lady' and 'very small'. Ann stood 'at the top of Seafield Avenue in Monkstown with… the children of the house and the other maid [Ann worked in domestic service]… all the flags and bunting and the whole place, of course, all red, white and blue'.[18] Brian, who grew up in Glencullen and whose father was twenty-six then, recalled his father's stories of how a huge, celebratory fire was lit at Three Rock Mountain. Jennifer's grandmother – a member of the Gaelic League who considered herself a nationalist – was also a great monarchist who was one of the many who lined the streets of Kingstown, hoping to see the elderly queen: 'she stood there for two hours, waiting for them to go past, and she was thrilled with herself, because she actually saw them!' Gladys and Noreen's mother was a little girl at the local Dominican convent at the time, and when Gladys and Noreen were small, she often talked about how the children were walked down to the seafront to watch the queen go by. The day out was fun but Victoria was an anticlimax: a 'little old woman in a carriage', sadly lacking a glittering crown.

Many nationalists had objected to Victoria's visit, regarding it as a provocation, or asserting that the British stance in South Africa and behaviour during the Boer War was abominable.* W.B. Yeats, then

---

* Irish nationalists supported the Boers, who were in fact treated appallingly by the British forces; they were largely uninterested in the native South Africans, who had been treated badly all along, and were oppressed for many years to come.

Children dressed as soldiers in a kitchen garden, c.1910. Their costumes suggest they may be playing a game inspired by the recent Boer War. Kind permission of Rosaleen Miller and Jennifer Nuttall.

prominent in the Celtic Revival, stormed: 'Whoever stands by the road-way cheering for Queen Victoria cheers for that Empire, dishonours Ireland and condones a crime... her crime in South Africa.'[19] For those who were anxious about the nationalist movement, of which Yeats represented the cultural wing, Victoria's visit was an opportunity to make a public statement of loyalty. For locals attached to the idea of monarchy, who felt this visit represented something important about them and about Ireland generally, it must have seemed that British authority in Ireland would never end.

Just ten years after Victoria's visit, her successor, Edward, died. Ann Burns, quoted previously, was now working in another house, apparently with very different attitudes towards the British monarchy. She describes her employers as 'great friends of all in the university [UCD]'. The night Edward died, they celebrated merrily: 'Bastards went high that night at dinner,' Ann remembered, 'half-drunk enough from knocking decanters of whiskey and everything.'[20] But sectors of Dún Laoghaire-Rathdown maintained a strong sense of Britishness and attachment to Britain long after independence and long after such sentiments had waned, even among most former unionists elsewhere in independent Ireland. The reasons why are quite complex. One is more obvious than others: the substantial Protestant, particularly Church of Ireland, population in the area, which had historic and other links to Britain, and among whom many had business interests relying on British partners. Generally, in early independence, there was a tendency to view Irish Protestants as of a culture oppositional to Irish tradition. Writing in 1938 of Dundrum, national school teacher Andrew T. Walsh, of Dundrum Boys' School, described the area as 'a stronghold of Protestantism until recently, with a dominating Protestant outlook, and pro-British bias'. He highlighted impressive Protestant church buildings and their symbolic role and stated that that, 'Most of the inhabitants [of Dundrum], until a comparatively recent date, were servitors of the ruling Protestant order.' Glumly, he concluded that 'The cumulative effect of this continuous influence… produced in time conditions, social and psychological… fatal to the preservation of tradition.'[21] Andrew's family, from the Rochestown area, were the sort of people to whom Andrew T. Walsh referred. Even in the 1950s and early 1960s, the family retained a sense of Britishness. This, however, was shifting when Andrew was coming of age: 'I felt I wanted to be Irish… But… I flew a British flag… from the top of a big tree we had in the place.'

Other reasons for a lingering sense of Britishness are more nuanced. Among the poorer elements of the population in early independence were many who had fought in the First World War, and even in the Boer War, who now benefitted from support in the form of subsidised housing, among other benefits (discussed in more detail in the 'Getting Ahead' chapter). Jim described, as late as the mid-twentieth century, a lingering sense of Britishness among elements of the York Street community in downtown Dún Laoghaire, a largely working-class area home to families linked to the sea in diverse ways. 'I mean,' he said, 'it was nothing unusual to see pictures of the queen hanging on the wall in houses down there.' Moreover, the area's geographical location – from which Britain was literally visible on a clear day, from which so many migrated seasonally to Britain seeking work, or emigrated to Britain on a more permanent basis, and from which sailors and fishermen frequently left to explore the Irish Sea and meet and work with British counterparts – played a role. Seafaring folk often felt a greater sense of community with their counterparts all around the Irish Sea than with Irish people who lived inland. Dublin Bay and the Irish Sea beyond it was, for them, not a barrier between Ireland and Britain, but a bridge.

Displays of a 'British' identity could coalesce around commemorations and other collective events that were, to some extent, a counterpoint to the lavish public displays of faith common until the final decades of the twentieth century. Following the First World War, the purchase and display of the poppies sold to fundraise for army veterans was an important identity marker. At the Armistice ceremony in Dublin in 1924, crowds of about 50,000 poppy-wearers, waving British flags, gathered to cheer on the approximately 25,000 veterans marching through the streets. The poppy would become a contentious symbol in the 1920s and 1930s, seen by many as representing British imperialism, and by others as representing pride in the noble sacrifice of the Irish soldiers.[22] The marking of calendar occasions associated with British history, like the Girls' and Boys' Brigades'[23] activities around Remembrance Day, persisted in some areas well into independence. Hannah, growing up in the 1950s and early 1960s, was a member of the Girls' Brigade, and recalled they had a service on Remembrance Sunday: 'And we always wore the poppies and they played the "Last Post" on the bugle.' As many locals had family members who had fought with the British forces in one or other of the world wars, for them, Remembrance Day felt quite personal.

Lingering feelings of Britishness, or of a sense of loyalty to Britain, tended to decline rather rapidly among those of Protestant or Anglo-Irish descent as independent Ireland matured. Ambrose remembered his father, who had grown up in a rather Anglo-Irish environment, adopting a strongly republican viewpoint by the 1960s: 'he became sort of a radical Sinn Féiner... quite staunchly anti-Brit'. But the idea of certain people as 'British' persisted among their friends and neighbours, sometimes long after these individuals had relinquished such notions. Roberta's father visited his neighbours – 'we were surrounded by Protestants' – when Nelson's Pillar on Dublin's O'Connell Street was destroyed by the IRA on 8 March 1966: 'he went in and apologised to them… as if they weren't even Irish!'

* * *

With its substantial Anglo-Irish population and growing, educated anglophone (and sometimes anglophile) population, Dún Laoghaire-Rathdown is not the most obvious place to look for evidence of the renaissance of Irish. Yet the Irish language and Gaelic culture were influential here even pre-independence. From the late nineteenth century, interest in Irish (then severely threatened in Gaeltacht areas, largely because of poverty and emigration), and in Gaelic games, folklore and other aspects of Irish traditional culture, grew rapidly.[24] Learning Irish, using Celtic motifs in art and design – for example, the Oratory of the Sacred Heart in Dún Laoghaire, richly decorated by artist Sister Concepta Lynch, Dun Emer Industries in Dundrum, where Evelyn Gleeson, Elizabeth and Susan Yeats ran an arts and crafts cooperative movement for women, where Celtic motifs and stories were frequently evoked, Cuala Press in Churchtown, which was run by Elizabeth Yeats from 1908, and numerous examples of funerary art in Deansgrange Cemetery – and reading traditional Irish stories were ways in which people from varied backgrounds could express a sense of Irishness. Geologist Maxwell Henry Close, descended from a wealthy Anglo-Irish family, lived in Blackrock. Maxwell developed a love of Irish while working in the west. He would become a stalwart of the Society for the Preservation of the Irish Language from 1876, and of the Gaelic Union from 1880 and, when he died in 1903, he left money to assist with the publication of an Irish dictionary. A Maxwell descendant remembered him saying that their family 'ought not to be [in Ireland] at all' because they owned property that had once been confiscated from the native

Irish, suggesting that his interest in the language may have been at least partly an expiation of ancestral sins.[25]

Liam's grandfather was a senior civil servant whose career began pre-independence. Under the 'British Raj,' Liam said, his grandfather was urged to change his surname to the English version. Post-independence, he had the 'great pleasure' of going to his former boss, an Englishman, to say that his services were no longer required. In early independence, the new government boldly decided to restore the Irish language as a mother tongue. Teachers were now expected to be able to speak Irish, and new boarding schools were established to prepare teachers who would be competent in the language. Many incentives were established to encourage the use of Irish.[26] Irish language schools, discussed in the chapter 'Getting Ahead', were an important aspect of the local educational landscape from the mid-twentieth century. Rachel's mother was a young Montessori-trained primary school teacher in early independence. From a Quaker background, she had an English mother and had grown up in Dalkey with little to no knowledge of the Irish language or Gaelic culture. The more she learned about both, the more fascinated she became – and she also knew that her work prospects as a teacher were limited without adequate Irish. One of her close friends was a teacher at Coláiste Moibhí, a Church of Ireland secondary school in Shankill in which young people were trained through Irish to teach in Protestant national schools. Through this friendship, and through a series of visits to a Gaeltacht area, she learned Irish. In the process, her political views tended to become increasingly nationalist.

Young people from Gaeltacht areas migrated to Dún Laoghaire-Rathdown to serve apprenticeships, assume domestic positions and work as nannies for middle-class couples. Some families of means sought young women from Irish-speaking areas to care for their children and speak Irish with them, as the language was an increasingly valuable form of social capital. Rob's mother, an Irish-speaking Kerrywoman, arrived in c.1930 to work as a nanny for such a family. She would settle in Ballybrack after her marriage. Her own family grew up English-speaking, but familiar with certain Irish words that she used routinely: 'My mother would talk about,' Rob remembered, 'going and "do your *uisce* [water]", which was "go and urinate"… I thought this was hilarious, when the teacher talked about *uisce*.' Other young people from Gaeltacht areas were drawn by work opportunities in the civil service and other professional positions.

Families with a good command of Irish and/or interest in cultural nationalism moved into the area in greater numbers in the 1930s and 1940s, benefiting from growing educational standards, and excellent opportunities for educated Irish-speakers in well-paid public-sector positions. Conversely, some people without Irish now found it difficult to obtain work in the national school system or in certain forms of public-sector employment. Richard's father, a teacher, ultimately moved to Wales in *c.*1950 for this reason. Organisations dedicated to teaching Irish and promoting Gaelic culture also provided opportunities to socialise and pursue education. Eden's mother attended a branch of the Gaelic League in Shankill in the 1920s and/or 1930s. 'Éamon de Valera and Bean de Valera,' she said, 'started a Gaelic League in Shankill. And my mother went to it… she loved the Irish language.' Some have suggested that, among Irish-speakers, a new form of snobbery emerged with the passage of time, a sort of 'More-Gaelic-Than-Thou' approach to the language. By the late 1950s and early 1960s, Niamh felt that some Irish speakers were inclined to look down on those who were less conversant with the language, a stereotype that tended to linger and that was often less than helpful in terms of encouraging a positive view of the language. Commented Tadhg: '*Nuair a chloiseann daoine b'fhéidir nach bhfuil Gaeilge acu an téarma "Gaelgóir", cruthaíonn siad íomhá istigh ina gcloigeann gur duine saghas* fanatic *iad.*' ['When people who may not speak Irish hear the term "Gaelgóir" (Irish-speaker), they create an image in their head that they are some kind of fanatic.'] Nonetheless, education through Irish became increasingly available with the establishment of Irish language schools like Coláiste Íosagáin, which opened in 1971, which we discuss in more detail in 'Getting

Ahead'. Families associated with the school were often also active in other areas of Gaelic life, including GAA sports and traditional music, and some of them had family roots in Gaeltacht areas, and were anxious to maintain their linguistic and cultural connection to their places of origin.

* * *

Alongside the major ethno-religious groups living in this area were smaller communities, including Travellers, Italians and others, who had made their home here for diverse reasons.

Travellers are, of course, a subset of the Irish generally, but throughout history they were viewed, and treated, as quite separate by most settled people. Various extended families, often travelling between areas in Wexford, Wicklow and South Dublin, or the midlands and South Dublin, have long and complex histories here, referenced at numerous points throughout this book, while larger numbers of Travellers – like many others from rural Ireland – migrated seeking opportunity in the

Travellers at a roadside campfire, June 1963. The 1960s was a period of mass migration of people from rural areas to Dublin, in search of work and opportunity. A large number of Traveller families took part in this movement of people. Many Traveller families also had long historical connections with Dún Laoghaire-Rathdown, migrating in and out of the area during different seasons of the year for generations. Photo by Richard Tilbrook. Tilbrook Photographic Collection, National Library of Ireland.

1960s, 1970s and beyond. Aidan's family was one of many that moved to Dublin from their traditional areas. He was about eight in the early 1960s, when his family travelled up from Galway; he remembered how sad he was ('roaring crying') to leave his pet dog, Tiny, behind. Tiny ran behind the car taking them to the train station until he could no longer keep up.

The Italian-Irish were a small group, forerunners of the massive inward migration that occurred much later, whose influence on modern Ireland has been considerably greater than their numbers might suggest. After Catholic Emancipation in 1829, the Church entered a period of church and cathedral building in Ireland (over 2,000 Catholic churches were constructed between 1790 and 1847).[27] This required craftsmen in the areas of mosaics, stonemasonry and *terrazzo* flooring, skills found in abundance among Italian artisans, but uncommon among Irish. Other Italians came to work in the area of music. Between 1841 and 1881, Italians

Members of the Borza family outside their family business in Dún Laoghaire in the 1960s. Courtesy of Camillo Borza.

represented between 2 and 4 per cent of the foreign-born population.[28] The 1901 census shows that many Italians in Dublin were skilled artisans, engaged in making frames, laying floors, painting, gilding and so on, while others were selling ice cream and confectionary.[29] By 1912, there was a stable resident population, with about 300 in Dublin. Many of the Italian surnames that are now familiar were already evident, including Borza, Fusco, Macari and Cafolla.[30] The number of Italians in Dublin grew gradually until 1946, with a boost from Northern Irish Italian-Irish avoiding British internment during the war years.[31] The Italian-Irish population increased sharply in the post-war years up to the 1970s[32] due to a process of chain migration that saw Italians coming to work for their relatives and, ultimately, establishing their own businesses.

Massimo, whose family ran a well-known café in Dún Laoghaire, is descended from a cohort that originates in a specific area in Italy, with very large numbers from just one small community, the little town of Casalattico south of Rome. Casalattico and its surrounding communities, including Montattico, in an area that was quite undeveloped before the Second World War, were devastated by the hostilities. Many immigrants from this area came with little or nothing except a willingness to work extremely hard. As with many Irish people at the time, some had little formal education. After just one or two generations, many of the Italian-Irish were thriving, and the dishes they introduced – such as fish and chips, initially sold by Italian-Irish in the late nineteenth century – had been adopted as staple foods. Generally, the Italian-Irish became an accepted facet of society, facilitated by the fact that they shared Ireland's majority faith (Massimo described the typical Italian-Irish premises as '*riddled* with Padre Pio, and Virgin Mary, and Jesus on the wall, and the Last Supper'). Eva, who grew up in Stillorgan, remembered the arrival, in the 1950s or early 1960s, of an Italian family who opened a 'chipper'. The parents, who still spoke very little English, managed to communicate their hope that Eva and their daughter could walk to school together. It was the beginning of a childhood friendship in which Eva taught her new friend English, and had her first taste of spaghetti.

Despite the ease with which Italians assimilated, into the 1960s and 1970s some Italian-Irish families observed a preference for their children to marry within the community. But a marked tendency for upward social mobility meant that, by the 1970s and 1980s, growing numbers of Italian-Irish were attending university or undergoing other forms of higher education or training, amid which this preference for endogamy waned rapidly.

The relatively few immigrants from places considered 'exotic' attracted a lot of attention before the modern era of multiculturalism, like the students from former British colonies in the West Indies, who came to Dublin to study subjects like medicine, law and engineering. Often far more educated than most residents of the communities where they stayed, they could attract both fascination and derision. Isobel's parents were Quakers from Monkstown deeply involved in progressive activism. Through Quaker circles, they became friendly with three Nigerian students attending Trinity College in the 1940s. They invited the young men to visit them, and allowed their three teenaged daughters to accompany them on trips into Dublin. 'Now *that*,' Isobel said, 'was unheard of.' She recalled walking with one of them – a law student – on O'Connell Street while people shouted 'Prostitute!' at her, assuming that no 'respectable' girl would go out with a black man. 'I was both proud and embarrassed,' she remembered.

* * *

Tensions around social class and identity were most evident among the young. Racquelle remembered some tension, mid-twentieth century, between the middle classes and groups of children considered 'rough': 'We always had to beware of the boys, the "Deansgrangers"... I suppose we were very middle-class.' James remembered minor conflict between the Presentation School in Glasthule, considered slightly 'posher', and the Harold School: 'We'd throw stones at each other... it wasn't vicious, but... there was a divide... like a class divide.' Anthony also remembered that he and his friends harboured resentment towards the Presentation students: 'We'd run around, chase them, punch them, because these were the posh-ies.' Margaret, from a comfortably off family, remembered Glasthule being known as 'Indian territory' (a reference to the popular 'cowboy and Indian' films) and that children from wealthier families were instructed never to go there. Conor remembered: 'when I was walking down [from school] I would meet all the guys from Eblana [a Christian Brothers school in Dún Laoghaire that primarily educated the urban working classes], who didn't like the posh kids, so I'd have to fight my way down the York Road'. Barry, also from Dún Laoghaire, said: 'if any of the guys [from the York Road area] saw you in a school uniform they'd come down and they'd threaten you'. Hannah's family ran a clothing manufacturing business in Stillorgan employing a small workforce. On her way home from school, she sometimes encountered name-calling that was superficially sectarian ('proddy dog') but that she believed was really about socioeconomic difference and resentments, as the parents of the other children may have been her family's employees.

People who could not afford fruits and vegetables, and who had poor housing without gardens, often lived near enormous homes with acres of land with orchards, kitchen gardens and an abundance of homegrown food. It was galling to see all the apples and fruit on their trees – sometimes lying on the ground, going to waste. In 1774, robbing an orchard was a crime serious enough to make the papers. The *Saunders Newsletter* reported that 'persons unknown' had scaled a wall in Milltown and absconded with apples, unripe peaches and cabbages.[33] Orchard-robbing remained, into recent decades, a popular way to strike a blow for social justice and get some fruit at the same time. 'You know,' commented Marianne, whose family lived in Glasthule, 'if they'd steal apples or fruit… they'd nearly feel they could take it… if you're hungry, you will do anything.' Many remembered orchard-robbing fondly as a victimless crime and an entertainment. But fruit-growers did not always share this benign view. In 1941, girls who had stolen gooseberries and currants from a Dundrum farm were issued with a hefty fine.[34] Arthur grew up in a large house in the Sallynoggin area. His father was a doctor, and the socioeconomic difference between their family and those in local council estates was stark. Arthur remembered 'the big wall… which separated us from them, and the orchard… we had as much fun catching boys stealing apples as they were having fun stealing them'. One day, Arthur's father encountered a boy 'with his jumper full of apples' and said to the dog 'get him'. The dog injured the boy's knee and he had to be brought to the surgery for stitches. 'Now,' Arthur reflected, 'today my father would have been sued… then it was understood that the boy was… in the wrong.' As late as the early 1980s, children who robbed orchards sometimes still had to contend with robust responses. Eoin and his friends robbed an orchard in Blackrock, and the owner used a shotgun loaded with salt to teach them a lesson. 'It hurt like hell!' Eoin remembered.

The over-representation of Protestants among the elite groups could be resented, although there was little overt conflict.* Tension can be seen, again primarily among children, in discussions of the afterlife and perceptions of morality. Aiden Traynor recalled being told in the 1940s and 1950s that all non-Catholics would go to hell, and finding this difficult to reconcile with his 'very nice Protestant acquaintances'.[35] Jacinta was a young child in the 1940s, and one of her playmates was a Protestant boy. When Jacinta was given a holy medal, she wanted to show it to her friend, but another child warned her not to: 'He's a Protestant. The devil will get you.' Ita and Nora remembered an absence of tension between the varied religious denominations in Dún Laoghaire, but also recalled watching local Methodists file into church, and pondering: 'Lord, they're all going to go to hell!' Ambrose grew up near Sallynoggin in the 1950s in a relatively modest apartment in a formerly grand, now subdivided, 'big house' – a visual reminder of Ireland's history of inequality. He

---

* Some legendary narratives contributed from this area to the National Folklore Collection in 1937–8 hint at an undercurrent of religious tension, interlaced with resentment about socioeconomic difference, including dramatic legends that focus on showcasing the 'reality' of transubstantiation, the evils of blasphemy, the ignorance of Protestants and the perils of dying without absolution. Villains and the misguided often suffer suitably gruesome and dramatic fates. See, for example, material collected by E. Johnston, a student at St Joseph's School for Boys in Glasthule. National Folklore Collection, Schools Collection (henceforth NFC SC), vol. 796, 111–12.

remembered conflict with other local boys with a sectarian edge: 'and a bunch of fellas… surrounded me and sort-of… half-kicking, "Proddy dog, proddy dog"… "Martin Luther was the most evil man who ever lived!"' Kate, who grew up in Dún Laoghaire, remembered: 'we used to sneak into… Protestant churches, and have a little look… and then we'd feel we had to confess it, like a big sin!' Henry, from Shankill, was beaten by the school principal when he and some friends were caught looking around the local Protestant church. Jennifer remembered that, as a little girl in the 1950s, she 'wanted to play with the little girl in the house opposite, and Granny said, "No, her mother is a black Protestant!"' In Monkstown in the 1950s, Nuala's best childhood friend was a Quaker girl, and one Sunday Nuala attended Sunday school with her. When the nuns in her school discovered, 'there was uproar'. Also growing up in Dún Laoghaire in the 1950s, Janet had neighbours who cleaned a local Protestant school. They were often given leftovers from the dining hall to bring home. They shared them with the neighbours, but some said they would not eat 'Protestant' food. As late as the 1960s, in the Kilmashogue area, Tim recalled considerable feelings of difference: 'And we… looked at [a local Protestant family] as if they were two-headed monsters.' An old story about how if you walk backwards around a Protestant church a certain number of times you'll see the devil is sometimes related still, if never seriously, in the context of conversations about how much things have changed with the years. Eoin remembered doing it once as a dare as a little boy in the 1970s, by which time the Second Vatican Council, the ecumenical movement and a general trend towards liberalisation, had eroded much of the tension and feelings of difference that had lingered in early independence.

Many Protestant children, especially those from more evangelical backgrounds, were receiving similar messages about their Catholic peers until the second half of the twentieth century or so, although adults from Protestant backgrounds appear more reluctant to discuss them now. Among families that would have been pro-British in the early twentieth century, resentment could coalesce around anger towards the Free State and its rules, especially those seen to disadvantage Protestants. The father of a friend of Donnacha, was a 'very bigoted man' who sent his son to school in England, apparently 'in case he'd be contaminated by learning Irish'.

'Mixed' marriage was regarded with horror by many Protestants and Catholics alike throughout much of the twentieth century and was a particularly active issue here. There are many stories of potential matches that faltered because of parental opposition, and of difficulties following such marriages. Ann Burns, who was interviewed in 1980, married her husband George, a Protestant, in the early twentieth century, and George converted to Catholicism. Ann's in-laws never forgave her.[36] Ann and George had had to fight hard for their relationship: before their marriage, when they were courting, Ann went to church to say her confession, and was asked by the priest if her boyfriend had any intention of marrying her and what religion he was. When she said that he was a Protestant, the priest 'let out a roar at me... he eat [*sic*] me, he devoured me... he never gave me absolution'.[37] Sam Blackmore, a Protestant who married a Catholic woman, remembered in 1980 how his wife, a domestic servant, had had to 'get letters' from each parish where she had worked before the marriage (presumably attesting to her good character), and that the couple could not marry in her local parish of Monkstown, and so had to settle for a side room in Foxrock Church.[38] Gladys and Noreen's grandmother was a nurse in Dalkey in the 1870s when she married a local Catholic gardener. Her Church of Ireland family disowned her. Although she had formally converted, and raised her children as Catholics, she attended Protestant churches all her life, which distressed her daughter – Gladys and Noreen's mother – who longed for her mother to be a real Catholic. Harry and Derek's grandfather was a sailmaker who came to Kingstown in 1898, where he met and married an Irishwoman. He was a Plymouth Brethren and she was Catholic; their children were raised Catholics, and when their father died in the 1950s, they had to ask permission from their parish priest to attend his funeral. Gareth's mother was a Catholic and his father a Protestant; they married in the

1920s and settled in Barnacullia. There was never any serious trouble, but a lingering feeling of being 'left on the outside with Protestants'. 'And do you know what I was terrified of at school?' Andrew remembered, of his young days in the 1950s and early 1960s. 'That I would meet a Catholic girl, would fall in love with her, and want to marry her, and know that my parents would not accept that.' Francis recalled a conversation with his mother about a suitor of hers. 'Why didn't you marry him, Mammy?' her children asked. 'Oh well,' their mother said, 'he was a Protestant, and my mother wouldn't have let me.' A thirteen-year-old girl in the 1950s, Liz and her family were invited to a Protestant relative's wedding. After some debate, they decided to visit the parish priest in Blackrock to receive a dispensation. The priest gave permission, but instructed them to remain at the back of the church and not to sing hymns. Kathleen worked in a bank in Dalkey. When a Protestant colleague was getting married in Blackrock in 1967 – shortly after the Second Vatican Council – she opted not to attend, but she did check later with a priest as to what would have happened if she had sought permission to go. 'Had you asked for permission,' he told her, 'you would have been refused.' Protestants anxious about 'mixed' marriage often danced in Protestant-only (or at least notionally Protestant-only) venues, including parish socials and dances at Protestant tennis clubs. Some were stricter than others in enforcing the in-community nature of the events. The stricter requested a letter from the would-be dancer's rector to confirm that he or she was Protestant.[39] By the 1970s, however, most of these anxieties and restrictions had vanished or were no longer taken as seriously as before, and from then onwards, for most families, 'mixed' marriages were no longer considered a serious problem.

Overall, overt, serious tension between the different religious denominations and social classes was rare. The intricate social and commercial links between the residents of Dún Laoghaire-Rathdown, and the nature of the built environment, in which people from very different backgrounds, and with very different incomes, lived in close proximity, seems to have helped to foster local identities that, usually, superseded differences.

Until the advent of large supermarkets and discount shops and the near ubiquity of the family car, for example, rich and poor often went to the same local shops. 'We would see both sides,' said Adam, whose family had a well-known Dún Laoghaire grocery. 'The very wealthy families who expected service and big orders, and fancy stuff… then the very poor… [who would] have a quiet word with [Dad] in the back… saying they couldn't afford to pay.' Kimberly, speaking of her family's experience in the two or three generations before her own 1970s childhood, explained the lack of tension locally as relating to different social classes inhabiting different, adjacent areas: 'everybody kind of just stayed within their own unit'. If anything, she said, families on lower incomes were happy to live near the wealthy, making it easier to find work in domestic service and labouring positions. Nellie, a Traveller who grew up in tents and caravans, largely in the Monkstown area, in the 1980s and 1990s, commented on how the close proximity of people from all sorts of backgrounds meant they could see one another as individuals. She also remembered a strong sense of community: 'we lived on one side of our road… we had houses that were anywhere up to a million and then on the other side we had… social housing and [my family] lived in a field'. Despite these yawning differences (and harrowing stories of anti-Traveller discrimination that we discuss elsewhere), Nellie's childhood memories are of an area with a strong local identity encompassing considerable social difference.

The coastal area also benefitted from good public transport used by people of all social classes, bringing residents from very diverse backgrounds together, and perhaps contributing to local identities that seemed more important than socioeconomic difference. The tram, for example, without private or first-class carriages, united those who rarely or never interacted socially, at least for the duration of their journey. In 1907, A. Peter noted that 'the tramcar has done more, perhaps, to break down social distinctions… than is realised. If one sits opposite the washerwoman… for a quarter of an hour, a different impression is created in one's mind of this estimable personage [than]… if she were simply waiting in the hall.'[40] The same applied to the DART train system, which opened in 1984.

* * *

Public commemorations in an area with such great historical and social diversity can be complex. Whereas pre-independence monuments tended to glorify various aspects of British colonialism, popular affection for figures like Queen Victoria became divisive in independence, as did any public monuments associated with her reign. Remembering with pride the sacrifices of the soldiers of the First World War became tricky too. New monuments commemorating fallen patriot heroes, and sacred spaces associated with nationalism, like the Republican Plot in Deansgrange Cemetery, started to appear, bedecked with gravestones in the Celtic Revival style, with many in the form of Irish High Crosses decorated with complex interlace, serving both as monuments to the dead and as assertions of cultural identity.[41] They all remain in testimony to the complex history and shifting trends of this fascinating region.

A ROOF OVER THEIR HEADS

While monuments of all sorts stand in official commemoration of the long gone, so do many of their homes. Dún Laoghaire-Rathdown has a rich architectural heritage: vernacular architecture including stone-cutters' and labourers' cottages, farmhouses, assorted urban dwellings, Victorian villas and terraces, grand Big Houses, twentieth-century housing estates, and subsidised and council housing dating from pre-independence to contemporary times. Travellers add their covered wagons, tents and other forms of mobile and portable habitation. All have stories to tell about the inhabitants, the challenges they faced, and their hopes and aspirations for their own and their children's lives.

* * *

For generations, the poor of Dún Laoghaire-Rathdown lived in challenging circumstances. In the nineteenth century, some inhabited urban slums in Kingstown, Blackrock, Booterstown, Dundrum and Glasthule, and others lived in poor conditions in rural and suburban areas; shanty-houses constructed on Commons, for example, or estate land made available for general grazing.[1] Many endured squalor in laneways and alleys closely adjacent to middle- and upper-class homes.[2] Kingstown had 'courts' that were simple homes with earth floors, often located down laneways, originally intended as temporary housing for workers constructing the harbour and the railway. In the 1840s, the authorities were concerned about the hovels with poor ventilation, little light and no sanitation, when large families inhabited one-room dwellings, and landlords were not required to provide adequate housing.[3] The courts housed about a third of the people of Kingstown by the 1860s.[4] They depended on communal wells for water, which were frequently contaminated by sewage, leading to disease.

In Dalkey, there was an area known as The Common (local landowners had a right of commonage, proportionate to the amount of land they had; the tendency for land to be enclosed and privatised dated to the early medieval period, but in some areas commons persisted).[5] In about 1834, squatters moved in and, by staying for long enough, acquired the right to remain.[6]

By the late nineteenth century, there was growing interest in providing adequate housing for the working classes.[7] Then, in Glasthule, some housing was of poorer quality than local accommodations for pigs and cattle,[8] and the Tivoli Buildings below Sandycove were notorious for dreadful conditions and associated social problems.[9] In response, between 1897 and 1899, the Dublin Artisans' Dwellings Company built the Eden Road Housing Scheme, with attractive, comfortable homes for working families. In 1900, there were still about 300 tenement dwellings in Kingstown.[10] By 1904–5, the Urban District Council had constructed well-built, modest houses for the poor, but they were considered too small and expensive for most working families.[11]

Post-independence, the Free State embarked on building social housing, but demand consistently outstripped supply. In 1925, the Dublin Civic Survey Report, prepared by the Civics Institute of Ireland, sought to provide the information necessary to develop an overall plan for Dublin, still partly in ruins following 1916 and the War of Independence. The report highlighted that many lived in appalling conditions linked to high infant mortality and poor health generally. While this was common in the inner city, there were also dreadful slums in many suburbs. The 1926 census reveals, for example, that 16 per cent of the Blackrock population lived in one-room homes.[12] Certain jobs came with housing as part of the package, or subsidised housing, but its quality was extremely variable. Jacinta, who grew up in a coastguard's cottage in Dún Laoghaire in the 1930s and 1940s, remembered her childhood home as notably damp, the walls stained and the floor-tiles 'humpy', with toilets and running water outside. Indoor sanitation was installed in 1962, resulting in a rent increase.

In the suburbs there was room to expand and create homes for working people, with state support and intervention.[13] The Housing Act was passed in 1931 to increase government aid to those needing better housing. In 1932, under a Fianna Fáil government, the clearance of Dublin slums began, leading to the creation of huge new housing estates for working families.[14] Living in a new council home in the 1930s had immediate positive repercussions for families, particularly for the health and safety of pregnant and recently delivered women and their babies.[15] Council housing was generally offered to those considered in greatest need. In 1934, sixteen council houses in Ballinteer were made available to 'deserving tuberculosis patients', among others – it was thought that the good air in the area would assist with their recovery. A few years later, the authorities received 245 applications for ninety-six good-quality council homes that became available in 1940.[16] But already-established residents local to new council housing estates could be hostile to them. Terence, who grew up in Sandyford in the 1930s, remembered one known as 'Madrid' in reference to the ongoing Spanish Civil War and the estate's reputed roughness, and another as 'Abyssinia' in reference to the second Italo-Abyssinian war, also then ongoing.

Social housing projects continued to be an important instigator of development and change in areas like Monkstown Farm, Sallynoggin and smaller, more rural developments. But despite government efforts to improve housing stock, council housing remained insufficient, and the quality of many working-class homes inadequate through the first half of the twentieth century, even in otherwise affluent areas. For example, by the mid-twentieth century, a former hotel in Foxrock had been converted into poorly maintained flats, with thirteen families sharing one

John Charles McQuaid blessing the foundation stone of the new church of Our Lady of Victories at Sallynoggin as the new suburb became increasingly established, 1953. Independent Newspapers, National Library of Ireland.

outdoor tap and insufficient sanitation, requiring families to 'slop out'. The Buildings in Glasthule remained notorious. Richard remembered that they accommodated 'a particularly unfortunate bunch of people', and that wealthier people 'weren't encouraged to mix with them'. 'It wasn't so much the quality of the *people*,' he explained, 'as the impetigo and fleas.' One woman who grew up there with her grandmother remembered a wonderful sense of community: 'every door was open; you wouldn't be short of anything… Nobody was better off than anyone else'. But she also remembered dreadful poverty, and her grandmother helping at a local soup kitchen providing food for those in difficulty.

Among those living in poor housing, young mothers particularly longed for better homes for their families. Catherine remembered going for walks with her mother and her mother's friends around social

A builder helping to construct vast new suburbs to accommodate a growing population, Blackrock, 1961. O'Dea Photograph Collection. National Library of Ireland.

housing estates under development, like St Begnet's Villas in Dalkey, constructed in the 1940s. The women brought holy medals and secreted them in the chimneys of unfinished homes, hoping to be given a council house.* Edward and two of his siblings spent their early years living with their parents in a one-bedroom home in Dún Laoghaire, sharing a single outdoors toilet with several other households, and the kitchen with the owner of the subdivided house and another household. In 1946, through Edward's father's work with the lifeboat, they were finally able to move to better housing in Dalkey and then Glasthule, and the family's standard of living 'shot up'.

Help to obtain better housing was sought in many ways. Ailish, a young wife and mother in the early 1950s, desperately wanted her own home, as she and her husband were renting unsuitable accommodation quite far from his work in Cabinteely. Her sister, a nun, sent her the text of a special prayer to St Joseph. 'Here's the secret, Ailish,' she said, 'if you want to get a house.' Six weeks later, they had a place to live. 'Joseph was

---

* A wonderful example of the principle of sympathetic magic being used in a relatively modern, literate context. The concept was coined by James Frazer in *The Golden Bough* in 1889 and examples of sympathetic magic in practice can be found all over the world in both archaeological and diverse cultural contexts.

Builders at work in Blackrock,
1961. Photo by James P. O'Dea,
O'Dea Photograph Collection,
National Library of Ireland.

my best friend ever since!' Ailish laughed. Some other families apparently could invoke old loyalties relating to the troubled years of the 1920s to get a council house, even years later. Jim's aunt related to him a story of how the family could petition W.T. Cosgrave – a senior Fine Gael politician – for access to a good house by referencing Jim's grandfather, in the IRA during the War of Independence. When religious orders were involved in the construction of social housing, a family's standing with the Church could impact on whether they would be considered for a new home. Philo's family moved into a new house on Temple Hill in the 1940s, on a small estate built on land donated by the Vincentian Sisters, who retained some influence over who was offered accommodation.

The initial phase of building in Sallynoggin, between 1948 and 1951, was the fulfilment of a vision for a new town. The scheme involved 550 homes in four distinct types, including houses with up to five bedrooms for larger families. The trees planted were positioned within future residents' gardens in the hope that a sense of ownership would encourage locals to care for them.[17] Many young families were eager to move to one of the new council houses. Jennifer's family lived in inadequate housing in Dún Laoghaire. While Jennifer was six, in October 1951, they were offered a house in Sallynoggin. The area was considered quite rough then and was locally known as 'Korea' – a reference to the then-raging Korean War. Nonetheless, Jennifer's parents were thrilled to have a comfortable, three-bedroom home, with indoor plumbing, access to green spaces and security of tenure. Catherine's family was living in Northumberland Avenue in Dún Laoghaire in 1951 when she was twelve years old, the year she contracted tubercular meningitis and was confined in Cork Street Fever Hospital in the city centre for eight months. The *Evening Herald* published updates about the condition of patients in the hospital – 'critical', 'some improvement', 'satisfactory' – and every night her classmates checked to see how she was. Catherine's parents were told that she would not be discharged until they had moved to less crowded accommodation. They moved to a new house in Sallynoggin, although her mother regarded it as 'the back of beyonds'. The people of Dún Laoghaire teased Sallynoggin residents, Catherine recalled, implying that they lived in the Wild West: 'Did you see any Indians on the way in? Did you miss any bullets?' Theresa remembered Maureen Potter, a comedienne, causing hilarity in a theatre audience in the 1950s just by saying 'Sallynoggin' in reference to the council housing estates here, which were very much looked down on by many other residents of south Dublin.

The era from the 1950s to the 1980s was a significant period for house-building, a time of rapid urbanisation and the expansion of both public housing and private developments. Contributing social trends included the increasing embrace of free-market conditions, a dramatic shift from the predominance of agriculture to urban industrial and professional occupations, and the beginning of the shift towards a more secular world view that would accelerate towards the latter part of the twentieth century. In 1955, Taoiseach John A. Costello told the Dublin Master Builders that the best way to make each Irish person into a good citizen 'is to give everyone a stake in the country... to give him his own home'. At the time, 75 per cent of all capital spent on housing was invested in public housing projects.[18] Thousands lived in good-quality housing with access to ample green spaces for the first time. Clodagh remembered moving into a new home in Ballybrack in the 1960s, as a young mother of three: 'I couldn't believe the amount of doors… Wow!'

The Small Homes Acquisition Act made it easier for working families to buy homes. The initial legislation was passed in 1899, empowering local authorities to advance money to buyers to purchase family homes, with a system in place for repayment. The legislation was updated and extended in 1957. Through this system, for example, a newly married James could buy a new-build house in Birch Grove on the outskirts of Dún Laoghaire, a pleasant estate in which his family could grow up not far from James's childhood home downtown.

Occasionally, innovative solutions were found for those with incomes too high to qualify for social housing, but too low to easily access most forms of private housing. Notably, the Ballybrack Cooperative Housing Society was composed of families who worked with architect Noel Downey in the late 1960s and early 1970s to create a development. The society was, in turn, an 'offshoot of the South County Dublin Housing Cooperative' founded in 1969 when Dún Laoghaire Corporation provided sites to thirty members on a 150-year leasehold, and committed to provide them with roads and services.[19]

Meanwhile, people with grand houses, and people who had simply enjoyed country life, resented seeing their panoramic views and the hedgerows where they had once picked blackberries disappear as the suburbs continued to spread.

* * *

The first 'Big Houses' in Dún Laoghaire-Rathdown were tower houses and fortified homes built from the early thirteenth century by the Anglo-Norman elite. Substantial estates were also owned by monasteries and other religious authorities. Post-Reformation, religious estates were seized and granted to loyalists of the British crown, and during the

Cromwellian period, lands were taken from wealthy Catholics, who were replaced by a Protestant elite.[20] The manor houses and grand homes of this elite would be important employers for many years – and powerful symbols of power, oppression, inequality and more.

Many of the Big Houses in the area have had chequered histories tracking the ebbs and flows of their owners' fortunes. In the first half of the twentieth century, many grand homes were subdivided into apartments and smaller dwellings, which were rented to individuals and families, often from formerly well-off families in reduced circumstances. Ambrose, who grew up in one such apartment, remembered the house, with its 'faded grandeur', as divided into ten separate dwellings in rather poor condition. Other Big Houses were bought by religious orders, who lived in them and ran schools, orphanages and so on (as discussed later). Others, of course, remained the homes of the wealthiest residents and both significant employers locally and emblems of remarkable socio-economic inequality.

* * *

In newly independent Ireland, providing for veterans of the First World War was an obligation for the British, who had to rely on the Free State's cooperation. This was a challenging situation. Many of the British authorities still struggled to understand that Ireland was now autonomous, while the Irish authorities had to balance the former soldiers' needs with antagonism and competing demands from other elements, while also dealing with the Civil War, which began in June 1922, less than a year after the end of the War of Independence in July 1921.

Pre-independence, the Land Act of 1919 legislated for the provision of land and housing to veterans of the war.[21] In 1922, the Irish Sailors' and Soldiers' Land Trust was established for this purpose. It began operation on 1 January 1924 as a non-political body involving cooperation between Britain, Northern Ireland and the Free State.[22] In 1923, the government passed the relevant legislation, the Land Trust Powers Act, despite considerable opposition from those who felt that 'enemies of the republican state' should not be rewarded. By 1926, the trust had completed 1,000 homes for ex-servicemen, amid demand for more.[23] Ex-servicemen's homes were generally located in areas near towns and cities, where it was easier to find work,[24] and homes were constructed in various areas, including Sallynoggin and Dundrum.[25] The ex-servicemen's homes helped to raise the standards of working-class housing generally, as they were typically well-designed, attractive buildings with good-size gardens and high-quality building materials.[26] In recognition of her father's service, Regina's family inhabited an ex-serviceman's home in Rosary Gardens in Dún Laoghaire, a housing estate built specifically for the purpose. Kate's family lived there too, and she attributes much of her grandmother's positive attitude and good quality of life to the fact that she and her close friends lived in such well-built, comfortable homes.

* * *

For generations, it was extremely difficult for most single women, particularly working-class women, to obtain homes of their own. They typically earned far less than men with similar jobs. Kate's aunt never married – her fiancé had died tragically – and although she worked very hard, she never had enough money to rent a little place of her own. Like most women in her position, she relied on the kindness of relatives, and moved from one family home to another. In the mid-twentieth century, in her fifties, she was eventually offered a small council home, the first place that she could call her own.

It could also be extremely difficult for widows to provide adequate housing for themselves and their children. Even women who had worked in skilled jobs before marriage often had to do badly paid casual 'women's work' to augment meagre widow's pensions. Jimmy's mother was widowed in the 1950s, when she was in her early thirties, and supported her family by working as a cleaner. As there was no man's salary, the council relocated the family from a three- to a two-bedroom home in Sallynoggin, as the rent was lower and easier to meet with a woman's earning capacity. Despite working hard for little money and raising five children alone, Jimmy's mother was very houseproud and they had a 'good room… for the priest when he came'. The children quickly learned to be very protective of their mother, who worked so hard to keep a roof over their heads. Jimmy lined his shoes with cardboard to make them last a little longer once holes started to appear in the soles.

In 1976, Roberta was a single woman in her thirties with a successful career. Having not taken a huge interest in the issue of women's rights before, she suddenly became very aware of women's rights activism when she wanted to buy her first home. It was much more difficult for a single professional woman to buy her own home than for a single man with a similar salary. Roberta had to sign an affidavit giving her occupation as 'spinster', although she had been working for many years. Simultaneously, she realised that her own mother had no rights to the home she lived in, that her husband could have sold the house without her permission had he wanted to. 'Oh,' she remembered, 'I was *really* angry about that!'

* * *

Pre-independence, the most destitute were provided with housing and food in workhouses, where they endured a strict regime according to principles established by the Poor Law Act of 1834,[27] which presented seeking help as the last possible option, dissuading all but those in direst need. A Poor Law Commission was sent to Ireland to establish workhouses in line with the Poor Law in England.[28] The Rathdown Union was formed in 1839, and by 1840 a workhouse on Loughlinstown Commons was planned. On 12 October 1841, the Rathdown Union Workhouse, including an infirmary, opened in Loughlinstown (despite local opposition from those who feared it would devalue property). Among the first inmates were people aged from four months to eighty years, sixteen Catholics and seven Protestants, many disabled and/or unwell. Throughout the 1840s, the workhouse catered largely for destitute women, children and the sick of both sexes, including those with health disorders relating to the famine (a graveyard dating to famine times is located behind the building).[29] Children could be admitted alongside their parents, or with just their mothers in the case of the 'illegitimate'.[30] Larger numbers of women than men resorted to the workhouse, among them elderly former domestic servants, no longer strong enough to work, and unmarried mothers.[31] In 1861, there were about three times as many able-bodied women as men in Irish workhouses.[32] Those deemed 'idiots' (with intellectual disability or various types of mental illness) were isolated in a special ward. Anyone who broke the workhouse rules could be punished by having their food ration reduced, being put into isolation or being expelled.[33] Those capable of work were given jobs: men most often worked in farming and maintenance, and occasionally in road repair, while women did the domestic labour, including washing, ironing and sewing. Conditions were harsh, and many inmates perished in periodic outbreaks of disease.[34]

Considerable stigma was associated with having to enter a workhouse. While receiving alms from private bodies in times of need was considered acceptable, the workhouse was universally seen as an absolute last resort and a source of shame. Those in receipt of private alms were generally considered the 'deserving poor', while those who ended up in workhouses were thus, by extension, 'undeserving', because of the widespread view, informed by religious norms, that 'the virtuous poor would endure almost any privation rather than enter the workhouse'.[35] Even within this generally harsh environment, a hierarchy prevailed. 'Immoral' people – typically prostituted women and unmarried mothers – were separated from the rest of the population.[36] Women who had two or more children outside marriage were often also deemed to have an intellectual disability. Unmarried mothers were excluded from the 'better' jobs available within the workhouse. Writing in 1913, H. Nelson Hardy described a workhouse doctor selecting female assistants from among the women and rejecting unmarried mothers automatically.[37] Attempts were made to improve the futures of workhouse children. They were given basic training in agriculture, girls were taught needlework and other skills necessary for domestic positions, and some of the boys were taught basic shoemaking or tailoring skills and placed with tradesmen to learn their craft.[38]

By the 1890s, the relative numbers of workhouse inmates with mental health problems, known as 'lunatics', had soared, particularly in urban areas.[39] From 1899 (when about 1 per cent of the Irish population lived in workhouses),[40] the religious order of the Poor Servants of the Mother of God – founded by Frances Margaret Taylor, who had worked with Florence Nightingale in the Crimean War – ran the workhouse and, shortly thereafter, the infirmary also. In 1980, Ann Burns remembered of the late nineteenth and early twentieth century that 'Things were very, very bad in those days, there was nothing for a poor woman when the husband died or if she'd no one but herself… there was nothing but Rathdown Union [Workhouse]'.[41] Loughlinstown Workhouse was disbanded in 1920, although its infirmary would continue to operate.[42] The Poor Servants' association with the institution (operating as St Columcille's Hospital from 1952) ended in 1991.[43] The stigma attached to the workhouse lingered for years after its closure. Jennifer was a little girl in the 1950s, out for a family day trip in her father's car, when they passed the old workhouse. 'My granny was in the back seat of the car,' Jennifer remembered, 'and she grabbed me and she said, "Don't *ever* let them send me there!"' Her granny's father had been sent to the workhouse many years earlier after stealing from his employer. One of his daughters was driven to suicide by the shame. This awful story had never left Jennifer's granny, and the sight of the building just brought it all back.

* * *

Throughout the nineteenth and much of the twentieth century, Ireland was heavily influenced by conservative nationalist views of what Irish society should be like.[44] Girls and women were presented with the unattainable goal of being both virgins and mothers. Women whose behaviour or circumstances placed them outside the parameters of acceptable behaviour, particularly when these involved unregulated female sexuality and fertility, were often seen as significant threats to the integrity of the home and, by extension, to Irish society generally. A Magdalene asylum and laundry, St Patrick's Refuge, was opened in Kingstown in 1879, serving 'destitutes and penitents'.[45] It was run by the Sisters of Mercy until 1963. ('They used to take in girls off the streets,' remembered Regina.) The rate of births outside marriage increased in early independence, leading to great concern in government and among religious and other moral authority figures.[46] Consequently, unmarried mothers, particularly from poor backgrounds, were generally approached from a 'crime and punishment' viewpoint, intended to punish them for their transgression and to offer moral rehabilitation, ideally in the form of an institution run by the Church.[47] In 1927, the Commission on the Relief of the Sick and Destitute Poor argued that unmarried mothers who had 'fallen more than once' were 'incorrigible' and that the authorities should be allowed to prevent those in workhouses from leaving the institutions after their children were born.[48]

Terence, born in 1929 to a single mother, was a rare example of a child born outside wedlock in the early decades of the twentieth century who was entirely accepted by his family. Following Terence's birth, his mother – a nurse – went to England to find work, and he was raised by his grandmother, who already took in foster children and was a kind and generous woman. In that era – in England as in Ireland – nurses were expected to be of 'high moral character', and the prevailing wisdom was that this did not include women who had given birth outside marriage.

Rob reported that his aunt became pregnant outside marriage in the late 1940s. Her baby was placed in Neptune House in Blackrock, run as St Patrick's Infants' Hospital since 1930. She visited him frequently and then one day he was gone. She and her brother 'paid a few bob extra so the child would have better conditions'. So that she wouldn't look like 'a fallen woman', they visited together, giving the appearance of a couple visiting a child. One day, Rob said, 'they went in and the child wasn't there'. The nuns said that the child had gone to Scotland. Rob's aunt lived with the grief of this loss all her life. It later transpired that her child had, in fact, been adopted by an American couple. Rob's father supported his sister, losing a longed-for opportunity to become a Cistercian monk in the process. He never forgot how she was treated, and years later, when he and his wife were raising a large family, their home was a safe place for pregnant girls to stay. Rob grew up with a succession of frightened pregnant girls, mostly from rural locations, coming and going from his childhood home.

While women of all social classes whose sexual behaviour was considered inappropriate were seen as challenges to the integrity of the home, the outcome for women from poor backgrounds was generally far worse than for women from middle-class or affluent families, in which 'arrangements' could be made. Poor women were much more likely to end up in a Magdalene asylum or the workhouse. If they were more fortunate, they

Flyer seeking funds and support for a children's home in Blackrock. Lexicon Library Collection.

ST. JOSEPH'S ORPHANAGE

BUILDING FUND COMMITTEE

present

BON PRODUCTIONS

IN

Annual Grand Variety Concert

WITH GUEST ARTISTES

DUN LAOGHAIRE TOWN HALL

Mon. 19th., Tues. 20th. & Wed. 21st. May, 1958

This programme is presented with the Compliments of the Organsing Committee and the Advertisers

Flyer seeking funds for St Joseph's Orphanage in Dún Laoghaire. Lexicon Library Postcard Collection.

might be provided for by a charity that arranged for unmarried mothers who had given up their babies to be employed as domestic staff. Martin recalled family members who had acquired maids through this means: 'it was seen as charity,' he said, 'but... they got cheap labour'. Unmarried girls and women from well-to-do backgrounds who became pregnant could have their babies in discreet nursing homes – often in England – and give them up for adoptions that might be facilitated by well-placed senior clergymen, before returning to polite society. For example, one woman who gave birth following an affair outside her marriage stayed in the family home, while the baby was adopted from a local children's home by an American family.

Isobel grew up in a Quaker family in Monkstown with parents who were very socially progressive. When a young Catholic girl became pregnant by her Protestant boyfriend in about 1942, she found a refuge with them. The girl's mother attempted to have her committed to an 'asylum', six local priests remonstrated with Isobel's parents, and their name was read from the altar. This story, unlike so many, has a happy ending. The couple married in the Unitarian Church in Dublin and settled down. After that, Isobel's parents developed a reputation for helping pregnant girls and they had a 'constant stream of unmarried mothers' – sometimes girls whose boyfriends were from different religious backgrounds, seen as a barrier to marriage – who were told that they would help. Inevitably, Isobel's family attracted a lot of attention locally. For Isobel, an adolescent girl then, it could be tough. She was mortified, but also proud of her parents' actions.

As the 1960s progressed, young women and girls continued to dread the prospect of pregnancy. Sarah-Jane remembered how the words 'the mailboat' evoked thoughts of terror in association with the idea of getting pregnant as an unmarried young girl. 'You'd hear stories,' she said. Her father would say, 'You better not get pregnant because, I swear to God, you'll be *on the mailboat* out tomorrow!' By the mid-1970s, attitudes towards unmarried mothers had started to soften. Increasingly, they were seen as deserving of 'a second chance' and less as a threat to the stability of the home. Organisations like Ally, established in 1971 by Dominican priest Father Fergal O'Connor, provided alternatives to mother and baby homes. Ally placed unmarried mothers with families who accommodated them during their pregnancies in exchange for help with housework and childcare. Sally, who was then a young mother and busy medical doctor, accommodated several. She remembered bringing them to hospital when they went into labour: 'And this is the sad thing,' Sally said, 'they would come home without the baby.' Most gave their children up for adoption: 'Mostly they had nothing, and no prospects. And adoption gave the children a better chance.' Other young women took the mailboat and gave birth in England. The children were adopted overseas and the girls who returned would pretend there had never been a baby at all. As Ireland moved into the 1980s and 1990s, the stigma attached to unmarried motherhood receded further and it started to become easier for single women to raise their own children.

* * *

As elsewhere in Ireland, excepting the workhouses, institutional care for orphans and other vulnerable children was almost invariably provided by religious organisations, or at least organisations run with a distinct religious ethos, generally either Catholic or Church of Ireland. Written in 1891, the promotional literature of Talbot Coall and Son estate agents stresses the proximity to the coastal suburbs of the glories of the Dublin/ Wicklow Mountains, proposing several itineraries, and outlining some of the natural and historical sites of interest that could easily be seen on a short journey from home; among the possible sites to see was the Glencree Reformatory for 'youthful criminals under Roman Catholic direction', where visitors were 'warmly received' and invited to view the inmates.[49]

Many of the residents of orphanages and children's homes had at least one living parent. Children could be taken into care if one parent had died, if a parent had tuberculosis – rife until the 1950s – or if there was mental illness in the family, for example, and of course children also entered institutions from mother and baby homes, if they were not adopted. Often, the state funded the running of these organisations, but did not have a role in governance.[50] Clodagh remembered children attending St Joseph's orphanage in Dún Laoghaire when their mother died in childbirth and their father – who had to work – could not care for them. Kate remembered children from one family in her national school whose mother had died. Their father was doing his best, but he had to work. Periodically, 'the authorities' came to take the children away. Other local children hid their friends and ultimately things got better and this family stayed together.

St Joseph's Orphanage was founded in Kingstown by the Daughters of the Heart of Mary* in 1860, initially caring for up to eight orphans and teaching them how to be industrious and orderly.[51] Jennifer, who attended National School at St Joseph's Orphanage together with 'house children', said that some had mothers in hospital with tuberculosis, that others were occasionally visited by their mothers, and that one small family was from Wales, placed in the orphanage by their widowed father, who worked on the mailboat and could visit them on his time off. Carmel, who joined the Daughters of the Heart of Mary as a girl of eighteen in 1948, said that the children generally came to the orphanage when a parent or other relative, or perhaps a parish priest, made contact – as opposed to through official channels like the courts – and that many were there because one or both parents had died of tuberculosis. There were also a few children of dual heritage whose fathers were Africans – often students – who had been in Ireland briefly. These children were referred to St Joseph's from mother and baby homes, as most potential adoptive parents were only interested in white babies. Whereas most of the children had experienced some family life and many had at least

---

* An order founded in France in 1790 during the French Revolution, when the sisters had to eschew habits to go undetected. Mary Anne O'Farrell joined the French order in 1850 and founded its first orphanage in Ireland, on Sussex Street in Dublin, in 1856. Scudds, 2001, 18.

one living parent, these children had spent their early years in institutional settings and were often, Carmel remembered, 'very disturbed'. St Joseph's also maintained close links with the Legion of Mary's Regina Coeli Hostel in the city centre, which provided accommodation and training for, among others, single mothers, including domestic servants 'taken advantage of' by their employers, and formerly prostituted women. Whereas these women were often under considerable pressure to give up their babies for adoption, many, Carmel said, were determined to keep them. St Joseph's could care for their children while they were finding their feet. Carmel remembered the weekends when these mothers and other relatives of the St Joseph's children visited. At one stage in the 1950s, a bus strike lasted several weeks, and the mothers walked all the way from the Regina Coeli Hostel to Dún Laoghaire to see their children. Families of children at St Joseph's generally made a small contribution for the children's upkeep – what they could afford, often very little – and the sisters also raised funds by providing laundry services and by running a care home for elderly women. There was no state funding until the mid-1960s.

St Joseph's Orphanage was an outlier regarding the care the children were given, with much more attention provided to their welfare, and considerable effort taken to provide them with an environment as warm and nurturing as possible. The orphanage encouraged local families to take the children into their homes to play and to visit. As a young woman in the 1960s, Marianne visited St Joseph's to see if she could take a child occasionally for the weekend. They said, 'Well, we have a little one here.' An important provider of institutional care, St Joseph's would operate until 1985.

St Philomena's Orphanage was opened in Stillorgan in 1933, and subsequently split when the administrators, the Daughters of St Vincent de Paul, opened an institution for little boys in Blackrock.[52] St Patrick's in Blackrock was founded in 1910 to care for 'unwanted babies' born to Catholic mothers considered capable of 'redemption'. It was run by a board known as St Patrick's Guild, which produced annual reports and applied for funding using material stating that 'The work is national, it is Irish, it is Catholic'. The organisation arranged for the children to be adopted, provided a place to stay for the pregnant women, and sometimes found them work. From 1929, the orphanage was located at Neptune House in Blackrock, and was generally known as 'Temple Hill' in reference to its location. It employed a matron as well as women doctors, nurses, housekeepers and nurses-in-training and described itself as providing refuge to 'expectant mothers of the better class, genuine first offenders, of previous good character'. Many of the mothers were domestic servants, often pregnant by their employers. In 1943, control of the orphanage was handed over to the Sisters of Charity, after which arranging foreign adoptions became a pressing concern. By the 1960s (by which point domestic adoptions had been legalised), Temple Hill housed almost 100 babies.[53] Karen remembered passing the institution as a child in the 1930s and asking her mother about it. 'Oh,' her mother said. '[The women employees] are learning to be nannies.' Philo grew up in a nearby housing estate, and from age ten or twelve, in the 1940s, she was allowed in to play with the babies. For her, the whole place was 'beautiful', with about twelve well-cared-for babies in each room, and staff who were 'delighted' to see her because she entertained the infants waiting to be adopted overseas.

The Bird's Nest in Dún Laoghaire was founded by Mrs Smyley in 1859 to care for orphans in an atmosphere of Protestant evangelism. Early applicants were expected to be at least seven, free from disease and able to provide their parents' marriage certificates.[54] Girls were trained for domestic service and boys graduated to other 'homes' around Dublin.[55] Richard grew up locally and worked in education as an adult. He had been vaguely familiar with the Protestant children's homes as a child, as various acquaintances were involved in fundraising for them. As a young adult in the 1950s, he was helping at an event in the Bird's Nest and found it 'perfectly dreadful… the rooms were plastered with texts like "Prepare to meet thy doom"'. Eugene was brought there in the 1960s aged three, having spent his earliest years in the Children's Fold in Monkstown, a

Protestant home for very small children. Among Eugene's earliest memories are the velvet gloves worn by the woman who handled his intake and the Smarties Easter egg he was given, presumably to make the transition a little easier. The Bird's Nest at the time was home to thirty or forty children raised in an evangelical Church of Ireland ethos. It was a dark place, he said, but, 'I can't say it was sad. You know no better.' The children became more aware of their 'difference' going through primary school. They were more likely to have academic difficulties, as there was nobody to care about or help them with their homework. They wore distinctive uniforms. They ate separately. As Eugene neared the end of his primary education, some of the parents with children in the school objected to the large numbers of students from the orphanage, after which the older Bird's Nest residents were educated separately, in special prefabs. By then, they were all keenly aware they were never invited to anyone's birthday party. They barely knew when their own birthdays were, as they were never celebrated. Outside school, the children only left the Bird's Nest in large, supervised groups. 'Are youse from the orphanage?' other children might ask them, curiously. Because the Bird's Nest was a Protestant institution, many of the locals were aware of it, but rarely interacted directly with the children or staff. One shop gave them a box of sweets to share on their Sunday walks. At Christmas, the children attended an event at the Town Hall at which they sang hymns and were given second-hand toys. The strong Anglican representation in local government, Eugene feels, gave them this small place at the table. Without ceremony, Eugene left the Bird's Nest for a residential home for older children when he finished primary school: 'We'd a large cornflakes box each with our toothbrush... and a pyjamas... and my few books... And we arrived [at the new home]... I remember a man saying to me, "Youse are filthy, you'll have to have baths. And have you got lice?"' Eugene was pragmatic about his childhood experiences. 'But,' he commented, 'I think that my experience as a child politicised me.' In the 1950s, 1960s and 1970s, the Bird's Nest was also home to children whose parents were young African students of medicine and local women. Eugene also recalled child refugees from the Biafran War (from 6 July 1967 to 15 January 1970 a civil war was fought between Nigeria and the Republic of Biafra, a secessionist state that declared independence from Nigeria in 1967). One little girl, Alice, arrived in her traditional dress. It was taken from her and Eugene saw one of the cleaning ladies using it as a duster a few days later. Little Alice spoke no English and must have been, Eugene recalled, utterly confused. In the latter stages of its operation, the Bird's Nest was involved in clinical trials for vaccines carried out on babies and children in orphanages in the 1960s and 1970s, including trials for a 3-in-1 vaccine for diphtheria, tetanus and pertussis, and separate polio immunisation for a 4-in-1 vaccine for the illnesses. It closed in 1977. Until its closure, the Bird's Nest was a commonly invoked threat to local children, who were told they would 'end up there' if they misbehaved. 'We were afraid to walk past,' recalled Francis, 'in case someone came out and grabbed us.' Catherine remembered one family walk when she and her sister kept fighting: 'And my father opened the gate on the Bird's Nest... and put us into it. And he said, "Now!" And my mother said, "You get a fiver each for Catholic children". You want to hear us screaming!'

The Cottage Home in Kingstown was founded in 1880. By 1889, located in a 'large and commodious house', it cared for the children of poor Protestants who were orphaned, motherless or in need of care because their mother was mentally ill, or because their father had died and their mothers had to work.[56] It also provided day care for the children of working mothers (often widows), who were expected to pay a modest fee.[57] Child refugees of the First World War were temporarily housed here too.[58] Ita's grandmother's home in the 1950s backed on to the Cottage Home, and she often played in the garden. She remembered that 'all you ever heard, all evening long, was children crying'. As Ita's family was Catholic, they never met the Protestant children who inhabited the home. The Cottage Home did, however, figure in the social and philanthropic lives of local Protestants, involved in fundraising and other forms of support, some of whom volunteered there.

While industrial schools were a feature of life in most European countries in the nineteenth and early twentieth century, Ireland was an outlier regarding the numbers of children raised in such institutions. Following the Industrial and Reformatory Schools Acts of 1854 and 1858, they could receive government funding. By the early twentieth century, most industrial schools were administered by Catholic religious orders.[59] In many Catholic institutions, members of religious orders involved in running orphanages and other such institutions were often seen as occupying less prestigious positions compared to colleagues elsewhere.[60] In 1924, the newly formed Department of Education noted that there were more children – in absolute terms – in industrial schools in the Irish Free State than in the UK; many were the children of single mothers but children could also be detained for reasons including school truancy. Three years later, the government expanded the list of reasons for detaining children in them.[61] Many were a prominent feature of the social and architectural landscape for decades. Kevin, growing up in Blackrock in the 1940s and 1950s, remembered the horror with which industrial schools were viewed. Everybody seemed to know some family, down on their luck, whose children had ended up in one: 'because they robbed… or wouldn't go to school… we didn't know what was happening in them, but… it wasn't the place to go to'.

St Anne's Industrial School for girls in Booterstown was founded in 1870 by the Sisters of Mercy, and 113 were detained there in 1879.[62] It was still operating as a children's home in the 1960s and 1970s, when Vera was a young mother living adjacent to the building: 'there was a sort of balcony to a fire escape and the kids played up there, so they were looking directly down into our garden'. The school still ran a laundry to which many locals sent their clothes and linen to be washed.

Carriglea Park in Kill o' the Grange was purchased by the Christian Brothers in 1893 and operated as an industrial school from 1896 until 1954. Years later, the Report of the Commission to Inquire into Child Abuse[63] stated that it was 'dilapidated and run-down' and that the boys at the institution were often badly dressed and unshod, even though there were sufficient funds to provide them with adequate clothing and footwear.

Karen, a little girl in the 1930s, remembered her mother threatening her 'many times' with Carriglea when she misbehaved: 'That's where all the bad boys go. I'm sending you there!' and Lina, a small child in the 1940s, remembered seeing them: 'out on a Sunday, all marching along with the Christian Brothers in all their gear… and that was a threat to boys as well, "I'll send you to Carriglea!"' Harvey, who grew up in Sallynoggin in the 1940s and 1950s, often saw the children from Carriglea on their Sunday walks: 'They'd have herringbone tweed suits on, all in short trousers and hobnail boots, and Brothers walking either side with them. They were all like soldiers… there wouldn't be a word out of them.' Harvey's father teased: 'That's where youse are going if youse get out of line.' Years later, Harvey befriended an older man who had grown up in Carriglea, 'the saddest person … His mother put him in there. She didn't want him.'

Young people typically left institutions in their teens, often ill-equipped for the outside world. Many travelled to Britain to seek work in manual labour and domestic service. Graham remembered meeting a young man of about sixteen, fresh from an industrial school, on his way to Coventry in the 1950s to work on the building sites. Used to institutional life, he was young, vulnerable and alone in the adult world.

As the twentieth century advanced into its second half, the numbers of children confined to institutions dropped, because of lower mortality rates resulting in fewer orphans, the growing reluctance of the courts to commit children to such places, and declining poverty. From the 1960s, there was growing concern for the welfare of children and young people in care, and the churches and other interested parties inspected the institutions, often reporting that the residents were poorly clothed and cared for.[64] Nonetheless, a surprising number continued to reside in institutional care: in the year 1968–9, across Ireland 162 children were sent to industrial schools for reasons including a lack of proper guardianship and school non-attendance.

* * *

Formally arranged 'fostering out' has a long history in Dún Laoghaire-Rathdown, while informal fosterage arrangements within extended families were also common. Formal fostering dates to a system of 'boarding out' established by the Poor Law Commission in 1862, initially to provide foster care to children up to the age of five. Typically, working-class women, the wives of small farmers, labourers, fishermen and certain types of tradesmen, acted as foster mothers.[65] From 1869, penniless children alone in the workhouse system were sent to live with foster families, as a workhouse was unsafe for children, particularly unaccompanied. This scheme was known as the 'children at nurse' system,[66] and foster children were known as 'nurse children' until the second part of the twentieth century – they are remembered as such to this day. When children were sent to live with foster families, who received a small stipend in return, they always stayed with coreligionists, as clerics of both the majority Catholic faith and the minority Protestant faiths had very strong feelings on this matter.[67] Gareth, from a Church of Ireland family, remembered his family as one of the few in Barnacullia when he was growing up in the 1930s and 1940s not to have nurse children. Gareth's family was otherwise the same as everyone else, the absence of nurse children from their home – because the supplying institution was Catholic-run – being one of the few visible differences.

In theory, fosterage gave children without families a better start in life, as they were moving from crowded institutions to family homes, and often from areas with terrible air contamination to locations with clean air. In practice, the outcome for these children was extremely variable, as very little oversight was given to where they went, and the common view that they were damaged goods influenced their treatment. In March 1924, at an inquest into the death of an infant nurse child, the coroner described the situation as 'scandalous', saying that he had seen the bodies of fifteen deceased nurse children already that year.[68] Many nurse children had very difficult childhoods. Some parents would not allow their children to play with them and felt that when a nurse child misbehaved, they were simply revealing their flawed nature. While some families treated foster children kindly, others exploited them for cheap labour.

Terence's grandmother – who also raised him – cared for about thirty foster children over the years. Terence's foster siblings came from an institution run by the Holy Faith, on Eccles Street in Dublin. They typically spent their early years with Terence's family, after which they were placed in industrial schools. However, as they formed a close bond with Terence's grandparents, many returned when they were sixteen, leaving the industrial school and staying in the Sandyford area for a while before emigrating.

Matthew, who grew up in Glencullen in the 1930s and 1940s, remembered that some nurse children there were used as labour on host families' farms, even from very young ages: they 'got it rough'. Two young boys he knew had to mind cows on the road during the day and drive them back home in the evening, and another small boy had to carry heavy buckets of pig-swill back to the farm, and spent hours on the hillside cutting ferns for use as bedding for the pigs. Joseph, who grew up in Glencullen in the 1940s and 1950s, remembered many nurse children. They were usually about six when they arrived from the children's homes where they had spent their early years. To his knowledge, most of the foster families treated the nurse children kindly, but their lives were still difficult. Many of the teachers at the National School were violent generally, but they tended to be more restrained with children who had parents. The foster children, he said, were subjected to much more violence, because the teachers knew that their guardians were less likely to complain. Brendan remembered several of the nurse children in his class in the 1950s regularly being punished for being late to school because they were attending to the agricultural duties the host families demanded of them. Their experience of education was so difficult, he said, that they learned very little, and the teacher made them hide in the cloakroom when the priest or a school inspector visited.

* * *

Traditional building methods shifted over the course of the twentieth century. Joseph remembered mid-twentieth-century farmers in Glencullen, an upland area, gathering ferns as animal bedding, as the available straw was all used for thatching houses. Thatched homes were common in parts of the uplands until the 1950s, when thatch was increasingly replaced by tiles; Aileen, also from Glencullen, remembered her childhood home being tiled in the early 1950s.

Outside primary urban centres, the provision of piped water to rural housing was gradual. In Glencullen, for example, locals relied on pumps provided by the council until 1963, when piped water was introduced with the help of local labour. This also made it possible to install indoor sanitation. Some homes in Cabinteely, still relatively rural, also had no piped water until the 1960s, with householders relying on pumps on the street. Tim grew up in a farming family in Kilmashogue in the 1960s, when locals still used wells for their drinking water. As a small child, he recalled being sent to get water with a 'little can'. The day a child was deemed big enough to manage a bucket was 'a very special day'. 'I remember having the can,' he said, 'and then one time, one of my uncles saying, "Tim… do you think you can carry a bucket of water up the field?" I felt really proud.'

Indoor sanitation was introduced gradually throughout the area from the nineteenth century, initially to the grander homes of the wealthier, down through to the more humble homes of the urban working classes, and eventually to smaller homes in the uplands and more rural areas. In some rural areas, indoor sanitation was gradually introduced from a period starting roughly in the 1940s and 1950s, with some homes remaining without until the 1970s and 1980s. Charlie, who grew up in a rural uplands community in the 1940s and 1950s, remembered of his childhood that they used 'buckets in the bedrooms', slopped out into holes in the garden where the family grew fruit trees: 'the garden was very fertile altogether!' In 1950s Kilmacud, many homes remained without sanitation. Nicky's family home had a chemical toilet, which grew to be a source of embarrassment as sanitation increasingly became the norm in urban areas. During Nicky's courtship of his future wife, the family was under strict instructions not to use the toilet before her visit.

Coal was the most common form of fuel, contributing to poor air quality inside houses and in the urban environment generally. Stories abound of how hard it was for poor families to keep their homes warm. Jacinta remembered how, in the 1940s and 1950s, coal was collected from the Coal Quay in Dún Laoghaire by drivers with horses and carts. When a driver passed friends, 'he'd give a little shake', causing a small amount of coal to tumble onto the road: 'we used to collect the coal in a little box for the fire'. Firewood was also an important fuel, with poorer families in rural and suburban areas often dedicating significant time to gathering wood, until at least the second half of the twentieth century. Philo recalled her mother's absolute mortification when she – along with many others – received a summons in the 1940s for gathering firewood from the ground in Mount Merrion Woods, not having realised that this was illegal. Henry, growing up in Shankill in the 1940s, when it was still a rural village, said that all the children in the National School were expected to gather wood for the family hearth on their way home from class, and that families also gathered dried horse dung to burn in open fireplaces used for cooking as well as heating. Breda, growing up in Cabinteely in the 1950s and 1960s, remembered how, after storms, local women used prams to gather wood that had fallen from trees on local estate and convent land. Most owners of substantial properties did not object to the women gathering firewood on their land, but one large landowner refused access, leading to considerable local resentment. Joseph, a child in Glencullen in the 1940s and 1950s, remembered turf as the primary fuel for heating homes in the uplands. Particular local households had turbary (turf-cutting) rights that belonged with the house, and 'went with the house' if it changed hands. Families on lower incomes gathered turf from a bog owned by Mr Fitz-Simon, a local landlord: 'no one paid for turf up there. You went up and just cut it.' The estate gamekeeper allocated 'banks' for cutting, and expected to be given a 'few bob' in exchange for a good section, ideally conveniently near the road. In the latter decades of the twentieth century, various items of legislation restricted the burning of smoky coal, and homes were increasingly likely to be centrally heated.

The electrification of Dublin was gradual. The Dublin Electric Light Company was established in 1880. A year later, seventeen new electric lamps were erected in the city centre. Gradually, electricity spread to major cities and towns.[69] The process of suburban and then rural electrification was extremely gradual. By 1903, the Kingstown area could have had electricity, but the Urban District Council opted to continue with gas lighting rather than develop a generating station locally. By 1935, however, all public street lighting was converted to electricity.[70] Many residents, even of developed urban areas, remember a time before electricity in their home, while the more rural areas were electrified even later. Joseph, growing up in the Glencullen area in the 1940s and 1950s, remembered the dim oil lap that illuminated his childhood home: 'There was a little Sacred Heart lamp. It was a ritual. That was filled about four o'clock on a winter's evening, and that was the oil lamp for the table. It was set in the middle of the table... that was the only bit of light you had.' Stephen, from the uplands of Kilmashogue, remembered the area being electrified when he was a child in the 1950s. Some of the local men got temporary work using their horses to drag the electricity poles up the steep road. 'I can remember when we got the power in,' he said, 'the electrician lifting up one of the lads to switch on the light.' At first, many opted out because of concerns about the expense; the first electricity wire served just two houses. Some homes in the uplands and some other areas electrified only in the 1960s and 1970s. Gene, growing up in Kilternan in the 1960s, remembered seeing a neighbour's home lit for the first time.

* * *

Typified by boxy semi-detached homes, the architecture of the new suburbs that increasingly filled Dún Laoghaire-Rathdown from the mid-twentieth century has sometimes been dismissed as 'dreary' or 'monotonous'.[71] But for many of the inhabitants, these new suburbs offered an exciting, novel way of life and even liberation. Suburbanites were often leaving something they experienced as old and tired for an environment where dreams could, and sometimes did, come true. The suburbs could be wonderful for young families who wanted to forge their own path, away from their hometowns and, perhaps, from stifling parental or community expectations, or from difficult memories of conflicts like the Civil War, to start off somewhere brand new.

Many of the new homes in Mount Merrion were built such that they incorporated ideas about lifestyle, aspiration and social class in their very bricks and mortar. Oisín remembered 'the layout of the houses had, off the kitchen, a maid's room'. Phillip's family moved from Rialto in the city centre to Mount Merrion in the 1930s. They had bought their home – one of the ('very modern… beautiful') 'Kenny-built' houses mentioned before – when their young daughter was ill with tuberculosis. The air quality was very poor in the city centre, and they hoped that she would improve in Mount Merrion, where the housing was much less dense and the air quality much higher. Their daughter died, aged thirteen, just before they moved in. At that time, the Kenny-built houses made homes for couples with ambitions for themselves and their children, who wanted to live in a clean, safe area but did not always have huge amounts of disposable income. Phillip remembered of his childhood in the 1930s and 1940s that 'it was a rather nice estate to be in… you thought some people looked as if they had a bundle, but there wasn't that amount of money. Money was very scarce… we were very lucky to come up to Mount Merrion.' Roberta's family moved to Foxrock from Dún Laoghaire in the 1950s when her mother was convalescing with tuberculosis. 'Now,' said Roberta, 'the only reason we lived in Foxrock was that when Mammy got sick… the medical advice was "get her up out of the mist".'

The development of new suburbs continued briskly throughout the second half of the twentieth century as houses were built on previously agricultural land, including estate lands and the former home farms of institutions like convents and hospitals. Most of the new estates were built with young families in mind. Throughout the 1960s, 1970s and 1980s, many were almost entirely populated by young couples with growing families. It was wonderful for stay-at-home mothers in particular to be surrounded by others of the same age, with similar interests and needs. It was easy, in those comfortable suburbs, to make friends, share childcare and reap the benefits of higher educational standards and more opportunities. Yvette and her husband Roy moved into a new-build housing estate in Dundrum in 1967. They had chosen it partly because, as a young Protestant couple, they did not want to settle in a 'Protestant' area, as the older generation of Protestants had tended to do. They wanted to live in a broad-minded, diverse community. They found like-minded neighbours in their housing estate: 'it was very forward-looking... They didn't feel that they had to obey social norms.' As they were all young parents together, it was easy for adults and children alike to make friends.

In 1966, Lisa and her new husband won a house in a 'newlywed draw'* held at the Mansion House in Dublin, and shortly afterwards they moved into a new home in Milltown. As their family grew, they bought in a new suburb in Ballinteer. An area that had been green fields was now filled with terraced and semi-detached three-bedroom homes inhabited by young couples who had migrated from rural areas or from the inner city. Lisa, who had grown up in a working-class neighbourhood near the inner city, remembered feeling anxious about moving to Ballinteer, worrying that everyone else might be a bit snobbish. 'Oh my God,' she recalled thinking, 'I think this is just a bit above me.' But instead she found her suburb a warm, companiable place to live, with neighbours

---

* 'Newlywed draws' were held periodically by the corporation for the allocation of new council homes. The draws were often held at the Mansion House and were feel-good events attended by excited young couples starting out in life.

Construction of Pine Valley in the mid-1970s. Kind permission of Linde Lunney.

Pine Valley on completion. Kind permission of Linde Lunney.

who – like her – enjoyed the diversity of occupations and backgrounds among the community and looked to the future, not the past.

But residents of more established areas often regarded the new suburbs with a jaundiced eye. New private developments could change a residential area dramatically. Theresa, who moved to Killiney as a child in the 1940s, recalled considerable irritation as housing estates blossomed all over the locality: 'Of course we resented it... land being built on, which was open fields, and we're seeing these green fields... eaten up by housing.' In the early 1970s, poet Eavan Boland and her husband settled in Dundrum at a time when it was, she wrote, already moving into the foothills of the Dublin Mountains. She was, she said, at the time, 'oblivious' of the suburb's Anglo-Norman past as she settled into life in a village that was becoming a suburb.[72]

The N11, starting as the Stillorgan Dual Carriageway, was built to improve access to and from the suburbs. The first piece of dual carriageway ever built in Ireland was constructed in the 1950s between the junction of Stillorgan Road and Newtownpark Avenue and Foxrock Church, with further stretches built in the early to mid-1970s, and gradually connected over the subsequent years. By the mid-twentieth century, roads servicing the area were far too small for the volume of traffic, and increasingly dangerous. Noleen grew up on the side of the Old Bray Road. She remembered locals' anxiety as new developments were built and the existing road became too small: 'a total nightmare. Every single weekend, going to bed and you'd be literally lying there waiting for something to happen. There was always accidents.' Darragh, a child in the 1970s, remembered huge worry about the roads: 'For decades people were going, "God, please bring the N11 bypass, please make it happen."' Tragically, a young girl was killed on the new Cabinteely Bypass shortly after it opened in 1985.* Overall, however, road safety

---

* 'Girl Killed by Car', *Irish Times*, 30 March 1985. Strikingly, in the mid-1980s, even such a tragic accident as this only received scant media attention compared to today, a sign of the much improved road safety that makes such accidents today more newsworthy because they are rarer.

increased significantly with the change and, as the N11 bypassed the new suburbs increasingly consuming satellite villages, it facilitated yet more development of new housing estates with good access to Dublin. For some residents who had grown up in those villages, the N11 removed the last vestiges of the places they remembered. For Eva, from Stillorgan, 'the heart, the soul went out of Stillorgan'. But the N11 was, Larry remembered, one of the main reasons why he and his wife, returning émigrés, decided to settle in Cabinteely in the early 1980s and raise their young family there: 'That was the swing factor… all I had to do [to get into the city centre] was point the car one way.' Larry and his family, and countless others, settled and raised their families in the comfortable suburbs that extended all along this new major artery.

Suburban housing estates are contested territories, often invoked by writers, artists and filmmakers as symbols of either all that is good or all that is bad about modern living. They are safe havens for ambitious families, away from the chaos and dangers of the inner city, but also seen as distant from centres of 'culture', the intellect, excitement. They are places towards and from which people flee. Lloyd's parents settled in a new-build housing estate in Blackrock in the 1960s, attracted by all the area had to offer: 'a nice, clean, cosy suburb… that idea that they had worked hard to get there, together… they'd arrived! … able to give their family things that they'd never had themselves, and very proud of it'. Darragh's socially upwardly mobile family grew up in a Blackrock suburb offering access to good schools, the seaside and many local amenities, but as a young adult he increasingly saw the suburbs as a problem – as a cause of, more than an answer to, urban decay: 'the inner city was dying… the suburban outer belt was getting ever stronger… it seemed so anodyne and irrelevant… I was going home at night to sleep and eat… thinking, yeah, this isn't where I want to ultimately end up.' This idea was in turn challenged by many others, including Eavan Boland, who deemed the suburban life worthy of poetic interrogation.[73] The debate continues to rage.

* * *

Many Traveller families had long-established links with Dún Laoghaire-Rathdown, particularly the rural areas where many had done seasonal work for farmers. In the academic year 1937–8 Máiréad Ní Ghríobháin, a schoolgirl in St Brigid's in Foxrock, stated, 'They are always very kind towards each other and try to help each other in their time of need.'[74] Lil Ní Shíoradáin, also of St Brigid's, described a Traveller family, associated with Enniscorthy and periodically camping on the Ballyogan Road, as 'very clean people' whose wagons were beautifully kept with 'very white sheets' and pillow cases with a lace trim they also sold, along with homemade paper flowers. A named family member – Miley Cash – is described as a 'nice, jolly old man', who played dance music for 'all the boys and girls'. Síghle Ní Shíoradáin discussed the Connor family, who also stayed periodically on the Ballyogan Road, as living in a 'nice big caravan' in the summer, engaging in tin-smithing, carpentry and making paper flowers, and as the owners of more horses than they needed to pull all their wagons and carts.[75]

Residents who remember the 1940s and early 1950s often have positive stories about their relationship with Travellers at the time. Harvey, for example, grew up in a newly built Sallynoggin in the 1940s and 1950s, and remembered Travellers who camped locally: 'They were nice… they'd be cooking on the fire and they'd chat to you… They used to always come to our house… and Mam used to give them their water.' Molly's mother, who farmed in a rather isolated area of Kilternan, enjoyed opportunities to chat when Travellers were staying locally: 'She was very friendly with them. She was always very interested… she would spend a lot of time with them and round the campfire with them.' Jennifer moved to Sallynoggin when she was six, and spent most of her childhood there. Although the area was increasingly urban, Sallynoggin remained a popular halting site, and the relationship between Travellers and settled people was, according to Jennifer, generally positive: 'My father used to say, "Never refuse water to the Travellers!" And they'd sharpen lawnmowers for us… they'd mend buckets and pots and things like that.' Jennifer played with the Traveller children who camped opposite her house until the Corporation decided to build houses there too, and the Travellers had to move on.

But through the 1930s, 1940s and 1950s, the Travellers were becoming increasingly marginalised. The Acquisition of Derelict Sites Act of 1940 impacted on them, as they often used unoccupied or otherwise derelict sites in urban areas for encampments. The Local Government (Sanitary Services) Act of 1948, originally intended to control holiday camping, could also be read as applying to Travellers' camps.[76] In 1949, the then Minister for Justice was asked to remove 'itinerants' from camps around Dublin.[77] Better-off Traveller families still lived in covered wagons, often with additional tented accommodation, and offered useful services to settled communities. Very poor Travellers lived in extremely challenging conditions. Iseult, a little girl of ten or eleven in the late 1950s, often walked past a Traveller camp on her way to school in the Ballycorus area. One day, she met a young couple in their tent, which looked to Iseult 'like a bowl turned upside-down'. 'And they were sitting on the ground,' Iseult remembered, 'it was freezing cold. There was rain… She had the baby in her arms, and she wasn't much older than I was.'

By the early 1960s, more Travellers lived in urban and suburban areas, when the use of public spaces was increasingly prone to legislation.[78] This was partly because Travellers' traditional skills were much less in demand with the explosion onto the market of plastic goods replacing the metal items they had worked with before, while as farming was increasingly mechanised, less casual, seasonal work was available. Like many others, Travellers migrated towards urban areas in search of opportunity. At the same time, Dublin and its suburbs were growing quickly, with housing increasingly occupying the formerly rural hinterlands where Travellers had traditionally spent some of the year. New housing estates, both council and private developments, were often built on or beside areas that had been traditional halting sites, perhaps for many generations, and the Traveller way of life was increasingly seen by settled people as unacceptable. A relationship that, however unequal, had been experienced by most as broadly positive, was rapidly souring. Elaine moved into a housing estate in Stillorgan in the early 1970s. Half the houses had been built. On the other side of what had recently been a field there was a small encampment of Travellers in wagons and tents, along with their animals and hens. Elaine described her relationship with the Travellers as good. Elaine's children and the Traveller children all attended the local school and they walked down together in the mornings. But, Elaine said, 'we [estate residents] all knew they were gone, or going', and they had to leave when the second stage of the housing estate was constructed.

The Commission on Itinerancy, established in 1961, was the first attempt to focus on Travellers as a specific group with unique needs,[79] but it also focused on Travellers and their nomadism ('the feeling inside of longing to be on the move'[80]) as a problem to be fixed. Throughout the 1960s and 1970s, the relationship between settled people and Travellers in Dún Laoghaire-Rathdown deteriorated dramatically. Frequently, the new residents of recently completed housing estates formed community groups that petitioned the authorities to break up and remove Traveller campsites. While settled people often disapproved of Traveller nomadism, generally they also did not wish to have settled Travellers living near them. Travellers could be targeted for eviction from temporary sites, while not offered housing elsewhere, and often also excluded from various forms of welfare then available to the poor, if they did not have a fixed address, as many did not.[81] Lawrence, a Traveller, spent some of his childhood in the 1960s in a camp near the Martello tower on the Rock Road in Blackrock. It was quite an exciting place for children to live, because when the circus also set up camp nearby they could hear the tigers and elephants. His family was never able to stay for long – just a month or so, until the authorities moved them on. The process of being evicted was frightening for the children, as typically the Gardaí would come very early, at six or so, and start the eviction process with what sounded like very aggressive shouting. Victor Bewley – a Quaker philanthropist whose work with the Itinerant Settlement Committees is discussed in 'Fighting and Fighting Back' – described two young Traveller families living in tents, in very poor conditions, in Milltown. One visited a local convent seeking help with their baby, and the child died in the mother's arms on the way there. A month later, the other young couple's baby died of pneumonia.[82] Despite efforts from some quarters to support Travellers, by the 1970s they were increasingly viewed as an entirely separate and inferior caste,[83] and as a problem to solve rather than another group of local residents.

The first officially recognised halting site for Travellers was founded at Labre Park in Ballyfermot,[84] but it housed only a fraction of the Travellers in the Dublin area, many of whom had long-standing relationships with Dún Laoghaire-Rathdown. At this time, Travellers had few officially recognised halting sites, traditional halting areas were being built over and the ongoing construction of the N11 had displaced many families, while measures to evict Travellers were ongoing. Noleen remembered Travellers camping opposite her home just after the N11 bypass of the area was completed. The council evicted the families and planted trees on the side of the road to prevent further camps. Gareth's cousin, originally from the Barnacullia area, lived on the Clonkeen Road. He was known for having a 'cure' for warts. He was visited by people from all over Dublin seeking a remedy, including various Travellers. He had always got along well with Travelling people, but as the area became increasingly developed, and Travellers started camping nearby with greater frequency, for longer periods, he lost patience. He could leverage his reputation for healing to persuade a family to cease camping on his land, by intimating that, just as he had the power to cure warts, he also had the power to inflict them.

Some Traveller families simply moved onto public or private land, including the grounds of Foxrock Catholic Church, Salthill DART station and Sandyford Industrial Estate, and refused to leave until they were given somewhere to stay. Locals reacted in diverse ways, with some organising anti-Traveller groups[85] that sometimes took part in vigilantism, while others engaged actively with Travellers towards finding resolution, and even became involved in activism, as we will explore in more detail in 'Fighting and Fighting Back'. Poverty remained a significant issue. Conor remembered visiting Travellers' sites during the hard winter of 1981: 'I remember the astonishing poverty… going up to see a caravan alone on a snow-covered derelict site and knocking on it, and… everybody was just keeping warm, head to toe.'

For a new generation of Travellers, literate and increasingly politically aware, their understanding of nomadism as central to their identity developed a political edge. Many settled people, well-meaning and otherwise, simply could not understand why anyone would want to be nomadic, but many Travellers saw nomadism as central to their identity. Mick, whose parents had moved into a house when he was little, returned to the road when he got married, spending a year or so near the N11 and then in Sandyford, which was much less developed in the 1980s than it is now, as well as a series of camps in the summer. On the road, he felt able to connect to his tradition in a way that had eluded him growing up in a house in a community that had never really accepted him: 'you'd tell the old stories and you kept tradition going… You'd do the old tradition about lighting the fire and… the old black kettle… putting everything in that pot… these were things that will long stay in our memory.' In the 1980s and 1990s, Nellie, born in a tent in Dublin city centre in 1983, grew up in tents and on halting sites, largely along the coast: under a railway bridge in Dún Laoghaire, behind the train station in Seapoint and in other locations. Although she experienced individual kindnesses from various locals, things were still very hard for most Travellers.

In 1998, the Housing (Traveller Accommodation) Act was passed, requiring housing authorities to work with Travellers to meet their housing needs, including the provision of halting and transient sites.[86] Travellers were then regularly required to move under threat of legal action (the 1948 Sanitary Services Act was frequently invoked),[87] while the provision of halting sites and other arrangements for Traveller accommodation remained inadequate, with much of the money set aside for Traveller accommodation spent on forced evictions.[88] The painted, covered wagons associated with the Traveller community were becoming rare. Hand-made wagons represented an enormous investment of funds and work and were much harder to replace than mass-produced caravans. Lawrence, a Traveller child in the 1960s, remembered accompanying his father to timberyards to buy the materials needed: 'there's a number of different timbers on a barrel-top wagon… He used to measure everything… with pieces of string… he'd be carving out the wood… and then getting the paint and painting it… that kind of design on the side… a circle of different kinds of plants.' By the time Lawrence was a grown man, few families were using wooden wagons. Nellie identified forced evictions as one of the reasons behind the rapid decline in tradition: 'the trespass laws… stopped a lot of Travellers from learning that trade of building wagons'. Caravans and other items on sites were often impounded or badly damaged during evictions. As wooden wagons were increasingly replaced with modern prefabricated caravans and mobile homes, a significant form of folk art was seriously threatened, and opportunities to preserve wooden wagons were often overlooked.

* * *

Various good-luck charms and other objects and amulets were associated with homes of all sorts. The use of a holy water font near the front door is well-known in Catholic homes from all over the country, of course, and other traditional practices were also popular. Horseshoes, for example, could be secreted in the roof of a house during building, for example – Roy recalled finding one built into the scullery of a family-owned property. Douglas recalled finding an old coin, dated 1826, inside the garden wall of the family home – perhaps, as he suggested, a 'time capsule' placed there by the builders – or maybe a good-luck charm intended to bring prosperity to the household.

While the use of holy water and other objects and substances supposed to keep the residents of a home safe, or to protect the house itself, has waned with the years, these traditions are relatively persistent. Alongside the decline in observance of formal religion, and an increase in inward migration, a greater diversity of amulets and other tokens intended to keep the house safe or attract good luck was seen from the latter decades of the twentieth century, although perhaps these were not always taken as seriously as they once were. However, the instinct to protect the home – for most the place where they are supposed to feel safest and most loved, and for many the biggest financial investment they will ever make – remained as strong as ever.

MOUTHS TO FEED

We all work to provide for ourselves and our families. To put meals on the table, food in the mouths of our dependants. The geographical and socioeconomic complexities of Dún Laoghaire-Rathdown have contributed to what is probably the greatest occupational diversity in Ireland. The range of activities that falls under the category of 'work' includes a wide array of paid and unpaid activities, all of which have contributed to the economy of this area throughout history.

* * *

People have been working in agriculture here since prehistory. Subsequently, issues of land ownership and production have been influenced on every level by the shifts and changes in history. By the 1780s, when British power in Ireland had been thoroughly consolidated, landlords owned more than 95 per cent of productive land.[1] The poorest farmers worked small tenant farms and utilised any common land they could. In 1834, the *Dublin Penny Journal* described how Dalkey cattle farmers accessed the eighteen acres of good pasture on Dalkey Island: 'They fasten one end of a rope around the beast's horns, and then tie the other to the stern of a boat… they drag the animal into the sea and force it to swim after the boat.'[2] With land reform in the late nineteenth century, and into early independence, the landlord system waned. Tenant farmers became smallholders, dramatically impacting on their relationship with the land. The growth of Dublin and its suburbs in the nineteenth century also had a major role in shaping local agriculture. Landowners in the uplands and other rural and semi-rural areas kept cattle for dairy and domestic consumption, sheep and goats,* which often grazed areas considered commonage, and pigs.[3] As means of transporting produce from more distant areas to the city improved, local agriculture increasingly focused on providing urbanites with perishable foodstuffs, particularly dairy, vegetables and poultry and eggs, with farmers ever-more creative in finding arable land as it was increasingly consumed by housing.

Dairy produce has been one of the major calorie sources for Irish people since antiquity, with dairy herds present since the Neolithic.[4] In modern history, before refrigeration and the centralisation of dairies, the local population was served by many dairies.[5] Roy's family had dairies in Glasthule from approximately the late 1700s to the early 1980s. During much of that period, there was a dairy every 200 yards or so along the coast.[†] The stories of some families in the dairy industry suggest that arranged – or at least convenient – marriages helped to keep the business among themselves. Dairies were significant employers of women and men, working as herders, milkers and in delivery. In the early twentieth century, for example, as the primary breadwinner for a family of siblings living in Glasthule in challenging circumstances, Jennifer's grandmother – who also had a full-time job – did an early-morning milk round.

---

* Goat raising, an important source of income for farmers from at least the eighteenth century (see Ball, 1895, 210) (memorialised in the name of the suburb of Goatstown), declined from the 1950s, roughly in parallel with the decline in tuberculosis, possibly because of distressing associations with goats' milk, considered an ideal food for the sick.

† Local variations in some elements of material culture associated with dairying are reported, like the one-legged milking stools used in one Glasthule dairy; the children were presented with their own stools, with a degree of ceremony, when they were big enough to help with milking. As the stool had just one leg, the milker used their own two legs to provide stability, and could leap backwards swiftly if the cow started to kick.

Above left: Josephine O'Brien (1888–1959), pictured with a working dog (to help with herding cows) and milk churns. Kind permission of the O'Brien family.

Above right: Peter O'Brien (1890–1965), owner of O'Brien's Dairy in Glasthule. The handcart was used to bring feed to the cows and the horses that pulled the milk carts. Kind permission of the O'Brien family.

Many dairy owners in more built-up areas did not have substantial grazing lands of their own, so they rented fields from convents and other landowners, and supplemented the cows' diet with other foods, including spent hops from the Guinness brewery in the city centre.[6] Roy remembered, in the 1960s, the hops arriving from Guinness's and being stored in a grain pit: 'the steam would still be rising and the smell would come into the house'. Cattle had ample grazing land in rural areas, but dairy farming was always very hard work. Molly's mother farmed full-time in Kilternan from the late 1920s. She cared for herds on the home farm and her aunt's land: 'she would get on her bicycle and go down...

to her aunt's farm and milk the cows there. And then come back here and then do the same again in the evening.'

Standards of hygiene and quality control in dairies were variable into the late nineteenth century and beyond. In 1892, addressing the Dublin Sanitary Association, Frederic Pim remarked on the many children dying from diarrhoea, which he attributed to 'unwholesome' milk.[7] Liam MacAonghusa of Blackrock remembered the milk delivered to his home in the mid-twentieth century as 'usually still warm with cow hair frequently floating on top'.[8] Less-scrupulous dairies sometimes watered milk, and the water could contain contaminants that were a risk to children's health, particularly poor children, who often died from gastrointestinal disorders.[9] Dairies tended to collaborate – if one was short of milk, they could buy in supplies – so in cases of disease spreading, or of watered milk, it could be difficult to pin down who was responsible. Tuberculosis could also be spread by infected herds. In 1928, 2.66 per cent of random samples of Dublin milk contained the tuberculosis bacillus, and of cows slaughtered in Dublin in 1926, 24 per cent showed evidence of the disease.[10] Contracting tuberculosis was also an occupational risk for dairy workers. Roberta's family had a dairy farm in the Dún Laoghaire area in the early twentieth century; a series of brothers died from tuberculosis.

The proximity of the countryside to growing urban and suburban areas meant that animals raised for meat, including cattle, sheep and pigs, were herded into urban locations and slaughtered there until into the second half of the twentieth century, their gruesome deaths a source of fascination to local children.[11] In Dún Laoghaire in the 1930s, little boys asked butchers for cows' udders, which could be stuffed, sewn up, and used as improvised footballs until they disintegrated, and which were otherwise discarded. For Liz, growing up in the 1950s, the butchers in Blackrock were endlessly fascinating: 'on Wednesday evening, you'd see the... blood being washed down the streets... That was my *favourite* thing, to watch the animals hanging up.' Brian, whose family had a sizeable farm in Glencullen and also rented land in north Dublin, recalled bringing cattle into Dublin to sell, and herding sheep, in the

1940s, all the way from Glencullen to the north inner city for transport to Northern Ireland.

Country families often kept pigs, of course, and many families in suburban and urban settings kept a pig for personal use until the mid-twentieth century. There were also piggeries locally until the mid-twentieth century and beyond. Roy's family, in Glasthule, kept pigs for the extended family in the 1950s and 1960s. Denny, growing up in Dún Laoghaire in the 1950s, often helped the family to collect slops (left-over foods) from townspeople for their quite substantial piggery: 'We had a pull truck... with the... buckets on it. So the neighbours would just come out... or we'd go and pick up the bucket and come out and empty it into our main bucket and bring it back... for boiling up.' Nicky's family lived in a council house in Kilmacud in the mid-twentieth century under a special arrangement whereby his father worked six months a year for the Corporation, and used the half-acre supplied with the house to provide for the family for the other six. On that half-acre, they kept 200 hens and up to ten pigs in a council-provided pigsty. From twelve or so, Nicky helped by collecting slops from neighbours. The council also supplied pigs to families in council housing in the Glencullen area. Davy remembered families selling their pigs to raise money for occasions like Christmas, or a child's Confirmation or Holy Communion. 'It was,' he said, 'the only way... of keeping a few pound together... if an issue come up – you needed money quick. The pig had to go.' It could be hard to say goodbye to an animal that, often, had been like a pet. Remembered Charlie, who grew up in an uplands area in the 1940s and 1950s: 'We'd had a sow for a number of years, and she came to the time when she was no longer any use, and she had to go... my mother cried her eyes out all day and all night.' Sinéad, growing up in Blackrock in the 1970s and 1980s, remembered a piggery still operating locally, although urban and suburban animal husbandry were then in precipitous decline.

It was common until well into the mid-twentieth century and beyond for anyone with even a very small piece of land to engage in small-scale agricultural activity, in areas peripheral to urban and suburban developments. Much of this work was done by women whose husbands were employed elsewhere, and sometimes by elderly, otherwise retired men and women. When families had very small farms, it often made sense for men to have 'off-farm' jobs, which might be full- or part-time jobs for the county council, or in construction or other heavy work, while their wives did most of the farm work. Charlie remembered of his uplands stone-cutting community that: 'The women did everything [on the farm]… there was vegetables, potatoes and fruit and all those things… [they also had] hens… and pigs.' Richard remembered a very poor family in Dún Laoghaire with no land of their own, permitted by a local school in the 1930s and 1940s to graze their goat on school property: 'he came down every afternoon to milk the goat, and we were told as schoolboys, "You're not to tease the goat… That's his way of getting his milk."' Harry and Derek's family moved from downtown Dún Laoghaire to a brand-new council house in Sallynoggin in the 1950s. For them, it was like moving to the deep countryside. But there were perks: a nearby poultry and pig farm discarded male chicks, boiling them with the slops for the pigs. Enterprisingly, by the 1960s, when he was big enough to have a part-time job and help out with the slops, Harry saved male chicks, raising them in small batches under the stairs. When they were grown, the family occasionally had one for Sunday dinner. ('Where's Timmy?' the younger children would ask. 'Timmy's missing!')

* * *

The Irish Land Commission was originally established under the Land Act in 1881 to facilitate the transfer of land from landlords to tenants and to establish fair rents. This process, a fundamental aspect of rural policy, continued post-independence.[12] By 1923, over 80 per cent of tenant farmers had become landowners. More substantial farms were typically family-run businesses on which men and women both worked, with men – typically the property owners – doing the heavier physical work, and women caring for poultry, milking and making butter, and often doing administration, such as bookkeeping. Some farms were owned and worked by women, typically widows or unmarried women who had inherited land. In 1933, the government of the Free State passed the Land Act, extending the Land Commission's powers; it was no longer necessary for landowners to consent to their lands being acquired for redistribution, even if other suitable land was available locally. At this time, the government felt pressured to reward veterans of the War of Independence, who tended to be given 'special consideration' in land redistribution.[13] As well as compulsorily acquiring land from large landowners and giving smallholders incentives to acquire land, the commission could acquire land from smaller farmers whom it felt were not using it efficiently. The Land Commission ceased acquiring land in 1983, and ceased operations completely in 1999.

Before farming became heavily mechanised, larger farms and better-off farmers were significant employers of full-time and seasonal workers. Men were more likely to be employed full-time, and women and men alike did seasonal work, such as picking crops or stones. Matthew joined his father's Sandyford-based ploughing business aged fourteen, in 1945. They had a horse-drawn plough and worked on farms across south Dublin, including in Dalkey. Gradually, they acquired land and cattle and started a small dairy business supplying the Tel-el-Kebir dairy in Monkstown, eventually buying a reasonably sizeable farm in Glencullen, where Matthew would spend much of his working life. William's grandmother worked as a farm labourer in the Shankill area in the early twentieth century: hard, physical work like digging potatoes and turnips. In her later years, she reminisced about women doing this sort of work until late in their pregnancies. Women employees for mid-to-large-sized farms could also combine farm labour with housework. Elinor, for example, remembered an employee of the family. Bridget, originally from Kilkenny, was already elderly when Elinor was a child in the late 1940s and 1950s. She milked cows, made butter and cared for poultry, as well as carrying out domestic duties. Schoolchildren in more rural areas, as soon as they were old enough, also worked, seasonally picking potatoes and fruit, both on their own families' farms and as casual labour for larger farmers.

A threshing machine with Eddie Fox Sr in the late 1960s, at a time when threshing machines were steadily being replaced with newer technologies, and the suburbs were increasingly encroaching on farmland in the area. Kind permission of Eddie Fox.

A threshing mill in the early 1960s, demonstrating the need for rural cooperation, and possibly also hired help, at busy times in the agricultural year. Kind permission of Eddie Fox.

Institutions including hospitals, convents and monasteries, and industrial and boarding schools, were also employers of farm managers and labourers, who might be younger sons of farming families who did not inherit, until the mid-twentieth century, as many provided their own vegetables, and even dairy and meat. Breda's parents both worked for Loughlinstown Hospital in the 1920s and 1930s, her father as a farm worker, primarily growing vegetables for the patients, and her mother in the hospital laundry. Farm managers were typically quite poorly paid, but generally had free accommodation and a generous supply of farm-grown food, while often their wives – like Patricia's mother – also worked for the institution in areas such as cleaning, cooking and laundry. Catherine's father worked for the Mercy Convent in Blackrock and held a dim view of his employers: 'He always said the only mercy was [written] on the gate.' Debbie's father had a similar job on a farm in Ballyogan that provided produce, including dairy, to Blackrock College. Polly's father worked on the home farm of St Augustine's, a St John of God's establishment, from the early 1930s. The pay was quite modest ('not overpaid'), but the family lived in the gate lodge and they could also use the produce for themselves: 'buckets of apples and loads of tomatoes, cabbages, potatoes'. While the family had a good relationship with the Brothers, it was also quite distant, and in particular the Brothers did not interact much with Polly's mother: 'if any of the Brothers came from the Big House and walked down towards the lodge… they had to bow their heads and avert their gaze. They couldn't look at a woman.'

Agricultural workers in the Peach House, Convent of the Sacred Heart, Mount Anville. Lexicon Library Postcard Collection.

Farming at the Convent of the Sacred Heart, Mount Anville. Lexicon Library Postcard Collection.

While all farmers tended to work cooperatively during busy times of the year – harvest, hay-making and so forth – wealthier farmers could pay seasonal labourers. Poorer farmers depended heavily on local coopera-tion, which was informally arranged, and enforced through social norms. Joseph, from Glencullen, remembered collaborative work – referred to with the Irish word *meitheal* ('a *meitheal* of men') throughout the agri-cultural calendar. It included activities like turf-cutting and collecting and saving the hay: 'neighbours would… give you a hand and bring the turf home… You'd help them as well… Same as collecting the hay. One neighbour would help another neighbour.'

In parts of the uplands, such as the Glencullen area, long-established farms could use common land on the hills in the spring and summer for planting crops, while in the winter everyone with hill rights could release their animals to graze and consume whatever had been left behind of the plants. These rights were particularly important for farmers with small-holdings, who often had little land of their own. Similarly, in the Mullins Hill area of Killiney, smaller farmers depended heavily on the commonage to graze their animals. Siobhán commented on how herds of dairy goats, grazed on common land, were important to the local economy when tuberculosis was rife, and goats' milk considered better for those with the disease.

Agriculture, dairying and the keeping of livestock generally in urban areas could lead to relationships of mutual benefit. As mentioned previously, piggery owners generally collected food waste ('slops') from households, and dairies and horse owners provided gardens with manure – Isobel, who grew up in Monkstown, remembered an enterprising man collecting horse manure with a wheelbarrow and shovel, and selling it to householders with gardens.

Better-off farming families often tended to marry within their communities (and faith groups) until well into the twentieth century, partly because they tended to meet mostly other farmers, but also – especially for families with substantial properties – to consolidate farms and keep land within extended families or particular communities. Marriages 'with a degree of convenience' were common. For example, a woman who owned land and needed a man to help with heavy physical work might be seen as a good match for a hardworking landless man, perhaps a younger son of a farming family; an older man seeking a younger wife might be seen as a good catch for a young woman from a poorer family seeking upward social mobility; or a comfortably off farming family might marry into a mill-owning or grocery retail family, with useful business dividends for all concerned.

Whereas most women married to farmers also participated in running the farm, married women were not typically landowners. A few women owned and worked substantial farms, but most women in farming worked alongside their husbands or the property owners, or worked on a smaller scale while also caring for their families. Rural

A woman with her sheep in Kilternan, c.1930. Farming, including animal husbandry, was an important part of the rural economy into the 1970s, although in steady decline from the mid-twentieth century onward in response to the growing suburbs and to other factors, including the industrialisation of farming, and to emerging technologies such as refrigerated vehicles. Kind permission of Mary White.

women often kept at least a few hens, and maybe a pig or turkeys, even on very small smallholdings. For rural women, this sort of enterprise had long been a way to supplement the family income, and to earn a little money for themselves. With the help of organisations like the Irish Countrywomen's Association (ICA), from early independence growing numbers of rural women became more skilled in marketing their produce and selling it directly to customers, to outlets like the ICA's Country Shop in Stephen's Green, or at cooperatives such as the Country Market in Kilternan. Polly's mother lived in the lodge of St Augustine's in Newtown Park, owned by the St John of God order, where her husband was the farm manager from the 1930s. She was an active ICA member and very industrious, raising hens for sale and curing sheepskins for rugs. By the mid-twentieth century, growing numbers of rural women were running relatively substantial income-generating enterprises, generally from their homes, often after having to leave paid work on getting married. Emily lived in Kilternan and had been fired from her clerical job on getting married in 1962. She and a local friend decided to open a poultry farm. As poultry rearing was traditionally seen as women's work, there was an infrastructure in place to support them. The state hired women experts to provide professional instruction, exempting them from the marriage bar. Olive and her friend contacted a 'poultry instructress' who showed them how to kill and process the birds. They built up a flock, selling birds for the table to private customers and at the local country market.

* * *

The origins of the industrial era can be traced to the large number of water- and windmills dating to the early modern period. Areas with mills included Dundrum, Milltown, Kilternan, Stillorgan, Carrickmines[14] and Rathfarnham.[15] Milling remained an important industry for centuries. By the 1800s, mills were increasingly linked with industrial activity and were important employers, to the point that settlements often developed around them.[16]

Lead mining, smelting and associated operations were active from the early 1800s. Lead mining and smelting occurred at several locations, with some mines dating to the mid-eighteenth century. Lead was excavated from a mine in Killiney, and lead and, later, tin in Dalkey.[17] While these initiatives were relatively short-lived, lead mining also began in 1806 in Ballycorus, where the chimney constructed in 1858 remains a prominent feature of the built landscape.[18]

Stone quarrying has been an important sector for centuries. Dalkey Quarry, which provided materials for the construction of Kingstown Harbour, was abandoned in c.1890.[19] Quarrying was also important in the foothills of the Dublin/Wicklow Mountains, such as in Glencullen, where it was an important source of employment, and played a signifi-cant role in establishing local identities and hierarchies of power, and in Ticknock, where much of the stone used in the construction of Georgian Dublin was quarried.[20] Men employed in quarries were typically extremely protective of their profession. More highly skilled positions passed from father to son in the hierarchical uplands communities. Stonemasons did the most refined finishing of the stone. Stonecutters

Granite cutter, Glencullen, 1962. Courtesy of National Folklore Collection.

shaped the rocks removed from the quarries. The quarrymen did the rougher, heavier work, and could rarely dream of becoming stonecutters or stonemasons, with no older male relatives to get them into the profession. Skilled stonemasons and stonecutters were so protective of their work that sometimes they strove to ensure that it would pass to the next generation through strategic marriages. Charlie, descended from a line of stonecutters thought to date to the late 1700s, commented that 'It was a closed trade. You couldn't get into the trade unless your father was a stonecutter.' Many families preferred daughters to marry into another stone-cutting family, and thus produce the next generation. Charlie's grandmother married a gardener instead; her disappointed family refused to hold her wedding breakfast at home.

Throughout the nineteenth and twentieth centuries, quarry workers belonged to various unions, including the Operative Stonecutters'

Society of Stepaside, which was founded in 1860, registered in 1898 and required members – who came from across the Dublin/Wicklow Mountains – to have served an apprenticeship. The society protected stonecutters' interests, including reinforcing the distinction between them and the less-skilled quarrymen.[21] Joseph, from Glencullen, was a stonecutter who followed in his father's footsteps in the mid-twentieth century. He started his seven-year apprenticeship at fifteen, qualifying for 'full money' at twenty-two. From 1970, the Stonecutters' Union of Ireland amalgamated with the stonecutters' section of the Ancient Guild of Brick and Stonelayers and Allied Trades Branch of the Builder Workers' Trade Union, granting them access to building sites.[22] Working with stone is hard, physical, dangerous work. Silicosis was a professional hazard, and despite considerable trade union activism, many stone workers never got old enough to receive a pension.

Other skilled trades and craft professions were often 'closed' professions too. The right to join a union, and therefore to practise, was passed from father to son. There were both practical and emotional reasons behind the drive to protect the skilled professions. Restricting the numbers of skilled workers helped to keep salaries higher, and also protected their social status. 'It was a status symbol to say you were a tradesman or a craftsman,' Julian explained. 'You could say it with pride… you were a step above the common man.' It was often almost impossible to get accepted onto an apprenticeship as an outsider. These norms could be enforced through a combination of tradition, aggression (actual or threatened) and ostracisation. Gradually throughout the twentieth century, training for skilled professions shifted from an apprenticeship system into schools and post-secondary centres of learning, and professions that had once been 'closed' opened to anyone with the appropriate training.

With the boom in property development of the mid-to-late nineteenth century came a range of related industries. From 1771, brickworks were banned from a two-mile radius of Dublin.[23] Bricks were in great demand, but because of the health risks associated with brickworks, in 1861 an injunction was granted against a Mr Alexander Edie, disallowing him from erecting a brick kiln in Blackrock. Developers had to import British brick or pay for its transport from outlying areas, but residents continued to object, as building remained a very significant sector into the late nineteenth and throughout the twentieth century. Gráinne's father purchased an out-of-use pottery on Pottery Road in 1935, and started manufacturing drainpipes and flue liners. The business operated until 1965, when ceramics in building were rapidly being replaced with plastics.

Many large estates were purchased by religious orders in the nineteenth century, and their lands became extremely valuable as pressure for new housing mounted. Ambitious builders often courted influential members of religious orders. Sarah-Jane's father regularly delivered whiskey to senior Catholic clerics in the 1950s and 1960s, and frequently provided local nuns with lifts. 'My father got a *rake* of work out of the priests and the nuns,' said Sarah-Jane, 'and I can tell you truthfully my father did [them favours] to get business!' He also joined the Opus Dei and attended Mass daily. While this, of course, may have been partly because of piety, according to Sarah-Jane, 'if you joined things like that, you got an awful lot of work out of [religious orders]… that's how he built up his business, really'.

Maureen's father followed his own father into the blacksmithing business, with a forge in Kill o' the Grange, shoeing horses, mules and donkeys. In particular, he served the large number of distribution businesses working from the area, delivering products like bread and dairy produce to homes and premises all over Dublin. When Maureen was a child in the 1940s, this was still a thriving business, but it waned quickly when petrol rationing ended after the Second World War, and as carts and buggies were steadily replaced by cars and vans.

Industrial laundries, like IMCO on the Rock Road, were significant employers, particularly of women like Kimberly's mother, who worked there in the mid-twentieth century, managing large, heavy machinery to wash heavily soiled sheets and towels from local hospitals. Laundries also supported an array of service professionals, such as boiler engineers and

Women at work in Manor Hill Laundry, Dundrum. Lexicon Library Postcard Collection.

Workers in Bradmola, 1948. Bradmola was just one example of the growing industrialisation in the area. It was a significant local employer, particularly of young women, who often went straight to work in the Bradmola factory on leaving school at the age of fourteen or so. Working at Bradmola was generally seen as a more attractive option than going into domestic service, which had historically been the greatest source of work for working-class girls. As factories became more widespread, it became more difficult for wealthier families to find women and girls for domestic service positions. *Dún Laoghaire Borough Civic Week Souvenir Handbook 1948.*

plumbers. In many ways, these were precursors to the diverse types of industry that would become steadily more common.

Sinéad's father worked at the Irish Glass Bottle factory in Ringsend in the 1970s and 1980s, but the factory had been a significant employer in south Dublin since its foundation in 1855,[24] attracting workers from a wide catchment area and the subject of considerable national pride. In 1932, it boasted of being the 'most modern type' of glass bottle factory in the world, as it was now producing clear glass, while heretofore it had produced only green.[25] In 1967, it announced further expansion amid a shift in consumer behaviour towards increased acceptance of 'one trip' (not recycled) jars and bottles.[26]

During the first half of the twentieth century, electrification, steam power and other new and emerging technologies were replacing mills and other old industries, reducing reliance on water-driven mills and negating the importance of physical strength in many factory jobs, contributing to a significant rise in the numbers of women in manufacturing, in parallel with a decline in women entering domestic service.[27] While enterprises such as Dun Emer Industries and Cuala Press, mentioned in 'Who's Who', trained small numbers of women in creative professions, a growing number of working-class women employed outside the home worked in industry. Whereas her mother and her mother's sisters had worked in domestic service, for example, in the early 1960s Philo and most of her friends found work at the Bradmola factory in Blackrock, which made hosiery. The work was excruciatingly dull, but the young women on the factory floor made the time pass by singing, and made more money than earlier generations could have as servants. The Pye Factory in Dundrum,* which made radios from 1935, and later televisions, was a significant local employer, particularly of girls and women, performing tasks including

---

* The British company of which the Dundrum branch was a subsidiary that originally entered the radio business in 1922, when it started making laboratory equipment to teach students about wireless transmission, rapidly spreading into making radios for the mass market. It probably established a branch in Ireland because of de Valera's protectionist policies, which would have imposed heavy taxes on radios imported from Britain. https://www.pye-story.org/history/early-days. Retrieved 5 May 2023.

soldering and assembly. Throughout the 1950s, Pye continuously adver-
tised in national and local newspapers for 'Girls, 17–20 years' to apply for
assembly positions at their premises in Dundrum, offering trade union
wages, a profit-sharing scheme and an on-site canteen.[28]

* * *

Fishing in Dublin Bay dates to the earliest years of human habitation;[29]
fish traps from the Mesolithic have been uncovered in the Liffey
estuary.[30] Fishing was still a significant employer in Dún Laoghaire-
Rathdown in the nineteenth and much of the twentieth centuries.
Kimberly's grandmother ran a fishmonger's in Dún Laoghaire, selling
fish caught by the men of the family, and other fishermen. Her daughters
spent their afternoons mending fishing nets. Séamus's grandfather fished
with a long line from Coliemore Harbour in Dalkey from the early to
the mid-twentieth century. Using a relatively small boat, he trailed a

John 'Gunger' Hammond, a fisherman at Coliemore Harbour, Dalkey. Colman
Doyle Collection, National Library of Ireland.

line with up to 600 hooks, baited with lugworm or ragworm gathered from locations such as Sandymount Strand. From the early twentieth century, lobster was increasingly prized by upmarket restaurants and wealthy householders as a luxury food item, and the lobster fishery became important. In response, fishermen become skilled in making their own pots: 'the traditional pot,' Séamus remembered, 'was an actual drum... less than a two-foot diameter circle, and about three foot long... you knitted a mouth into [the net] where the lobster would hopefully go in and sit down.' Constructing the pots was skilled work: 'You had timbers... one-inch laths, and you bent them in a smoke tube, you put smoke down into the tubes... to bend them into a ring.' Mark's father made his own pots too, in Mark's young days in the 1970s, using slats from old Guinness barrels, referred to as 'sallies',* two-by-one timbers for the battens that he retrieved from skips outside building sites, and ropes for the openings or 'gobs' at either end of the pot, sewn with a large needle. Mark's father became so skilled at ropework that he started making other things too: decorative ropes for pulling bells, ornate rope handles for the coffins of seafaring men. By the late 1970s, the wooden sallies were generally replaced by pieces of black plastic hose, but were still referred to with the same term.

A code of conduct informally agreed by lobster and crab fishermen determined where pots could be laid – for example, it was unacceptable to lay pots such that the ropes might interfere with someone else's ability to raise theirs. Lobsters were sold to fishmongers, to city-centre markets, and directly to restaurants and wealthy householders, with small, deformed or otherwise subpar specimens consumed at home by the fishing families themselves. Lobster fishing could be quite lucrative, but like all fishing, it had its dangers. A sudden shift in the direction of the wind while shifting pots could tip someone overboard.

---

* The term 'sallies', which remains in many Irish placenames, refers originally to willow (trees from the *Salix* genus) sticks used in basket-making across much of Europe, an ancient and still-practised craft, and by extension to any small sticks used in similar craft contexts.

Even before Dún Laoghaire Harbour was constructed, mariners' safety and the presence of lighthouses along the coast were pressing matters. From 1763, pilotage became essential for ships entering or leaving Dublin Port, and a formal training system was instigated. Many also worked unofficially as pilots, or 'hobblers'. They rowed out to incoming ships and guided them to port, where they arranged for them to be berthed and discharged by relatives or friends in complementary roles. In Dún Laoghaire and Dalkey, hobblers and their boats – from the mid-nineteenth century typically clinker-built skiffs[31] – persisted until well into the twentieth century.[32] Among hobblers, there was intense rivalry between extended families and communities competing for access to the same ships. Sometimes this manifested as hard feelings and even violence. Two well-known hobbling families clarified to their respective children that intermarriage was unacceptable – a restriction that lasted longer than hobbling itself, into the second half of the twentieth century.

Hobbling was extremely dangerous. Séamus's grandfather often told his family of the dangers he faced. He illustrated these accounts with the (presumably apocryphal) detail of how a finger was saved after being accidentally severed early one morning after he and his fellow hobblers had spent the night sleeping in their boat. Sailors in the ship had tossed down a grappling hook, which had severed his finger, but later that day, he said, it was successfully sewn back on by a local doctor. James's family also worked in the hobbling business. Several relatives died in and around the harbour in the 1920s – one run over by a 'steamer', which completely destroyed his body, and another by falling from his boat, hitting his head and presumably drowning, the body recovered by divers from the seafloor near the bandstand on Dún Laoghaire pier the following day. In 1928, three hobblers died when a steamer cut their wooden boat in half in the middle of the night, and on 5 December 1934, Dún Laoghaire dockers Richard and Henry Shortall, and John and Gareth Hughes, rowed out to a schooner in their skiff *Jealous of Me* (according to Al, grandson of the boat's owner, the name was a reference to the intense competition between groups of hobblers). They unloaded in Ringsend and Gareth stayed onshore to wait for their money and to bring it home, while the other three rowed back to Dún Laoghaire. The three rowers were seen passing the Poolbeg Lighthouse, but they never came home. Their boat was washed up in Irishtown the following day. Following this tragic incident, hobbling – already in decline – became much rarer. From 1936, it was outlawed.[33] In 2002, the Dún Laoghaire Harbour Board commissioned artist Fiona Mulholland to create a monument in memory of hobblers who died exercising their trade.

The modern system of maintaining lighthouses springs from 1786, when the Corporation for Preserving and Improving the Port of Dublin was established to maintain local lighthouses, and 1810, when the British Parliament transferred the control of all Irish lighthouses to this corporation.[34] As Dunleary pier was constructed, temporary wooden lighthouses were used on either end of the growing West and East Piers; the present lighthouses, together with keepers' homes, were established in 1847 (on the East Pier) and 1852 (on the West Pier).[35] In 1867, a time of rapid development in lighthouse technology, the Commissioners of Irish Lights was formed as a distinct body (previously it was part of the Dublin Ballast Board).[36] Post-independence, Irish Lights remained an all-island organisation and a very significant employer in the coastal areas, with men working on board lightships, on mobile ships circumnavigating the coast and in diverse support jobs. Maurice's grandfather, for example, was a diver in the early twentieth century, with 'heavily weighted boots and... rubber suits with a huge brass helmet that had to be screwed on'. James worked with Irish Lights in boat building and maintenance from the early 1950s, travelling up and down the coast.

Irish Lights was considered a good employer, but conditions on the lightships were tough. The men had to spend quite long periods at sea in circumstances that could be dangerous – 'the constant rolling and pitching, the ever-present risk of breaking adrift without propulsive power; the hazard of collision in bad weather'.[37] The Kish lightship was run down four times, including one occasion, in 1902, when it was sunk by the Dún Laoghaire mailboat.[38] (That said, the lightship was sufficiently enticing in the summer that Peter's father, a child in the late 1940s, would spend a week or so on it with his dad, an employee of Irish Lights – 'and that was his holiday.') By the mid-twentieth century, conditions were increasingly comfortable,[39] although employees still contended with significant periods away from home, and inclement weather still caused problems. Right up until 1965, the Commissioners of Irish Lights frequently received applications for grant aid for the purchase of false teeth to replace sets lost overboard in harsh weather. Many of the men in Caroline's family worked on the lightships. Sometimes they were away for months, missing family occasions and dealing with boredom and the very limited diet on board. At home, their wives listened to the Irish Lights broadcast to learn when their men were due back. Emer's father worked on the *Isolde*, servicing lighthouses all around the Irish coast, and occasionally as far away as Scotland. He was often away for weeks. Emer's mother, at home, listened to the Irish Lights broadcast every day in hope of hearing news.

While working on the lightships and their service ships could be stressful and demanding, it also involved many long, rather dull evenings. Many of the men who worked on them kept themselves endearingly busy with a range of creative projects. 'The men used to knit,' recalled Kate, 'and they'd make rugs… and my grandfather told me there were Fair Isle jumpers they would knit… and ships in bottles.' Emer's father used coloured sweet wrappers to make beautiful collages of exotic birds, and transformed glass bottles into lamps. James recalled sailors making ships in bottles, rugs and home-made clothes brushes, using horsehair, contrasting white hair with black to write their initials in the bristles.

In 1963, work began on the Kish Lighthouse, which would be a breakthrough for lighthouse technology. The chief engineer on the project, Desmond Martin, had served with the British Army in the Second World War and was familiar with the technology behind the Mulberry

Near the seafront in Kingstown, c. 1990 Sailing and maritime life in general has a long history as a major employment sector in the region. Photo by John J. Clarke, donated by Brian P. Clarke, Clarke Photographic Collection, National Library of Ireland.

Harbours,* floating harbours brought from England to France and sunk to create safe places for the Allies to land. Public interest was such that a 'viewing stand' was constructed so that visitors to Dún Laoghaire could observe the work underway.[40] The lighthouse was towed to the Kish sandbanks on 29 June 1965.[41] In August, the *Belfast Telegraph* reported that, if it fared well in bad weather, it was probable that lightships elsewhere on the island of Ireland would be replaced with similar structures.[42]

'Deep-sea' sailing, so-called to differentiate it from sailing the Irish Sea or around the coast, was an attractive profession for adventurous young men. Kevin's father went to sea as a young man, had many adventures

---

* The prefabricated elements of the harbours were made over the course of seven months in the latter part of the war, involving the efforts of more than 240 contracting companies, which collaborated to fabricate over 120,000 tons of steel and a million tons of concrete which would go into the revolutionary floating infrastructure. Somehow, the work was kept secret and, with the element of surprise, was instrumental in ending the war with a victory for the Allies. Beckett, 2004, 171–2.

and stopped sailing when he settled down in his thirties. As a child in the 1950s, Kevin was fascinated by his father's stories of life on the high seas ('What are you going to be when you're grown up?' 'Going to be a sailor like my dad!') and wondered why he had stopped for the relatively unadventurous work provided by Dublin Port and Dock: 'He's sitting there… cup of tea, and he's rolling a cigarette, and I looked at him and thought, "He steered a ship through the Panama Canal. He steered a ship through the Suez. He was in storms with waves crashing across the deck… And he gave it all up!" When Kevin asked his father why, 'without even looking at me or stopping rolling his cigarette, he just said, "My wife and family were more important"'. After his father died young, Kevin followed in his footsteps: first training in Gravesend in Kent, then pursuing a career as a deep-sea sailor and having many adventures, and retiring from seafaring when he became a husband and father.

Occupations that are risky, in the sense of being dangerous for those engaged in them, or in terms of making a living, tend universally to be associated with beliefs and traditions predicated around reducing risk and optimising luck. The marine sector was risky in every aspect: sailing, hobbling and fishing were all high-risk activities with many casualties and injuries, and hobblers and fishermen also depended to a great extent on luck to get a job or find fish, and therefore being able to make a living. In this highly charged context, there is a rich corpus of tradition and belief relating to the sea.[43] Séamus's grandfather, who was a fishermen and rented out 'pleasure boats', never learned to swim, but was sure that he was perfectly safe, as he had been born with a 'skull cap' – a caul, known for protecting those at sea from drowning. Interviewed in 1980, Ann Burns also related the well-known belief that a baby's caul could keep a sailor safe. When a child in Dún Laoghaire was born with a caul, she said, it was carefully preserved and 'given to young men now that would go out on sea' as 'they would never be drowned'.[44] Al's father was a sailor and fisherman, descended from men who knew the sea intimately. When Al was a child in the 1960s and 1970s, his father earned his living primarily by fishing, and observed many traditions relating to the trade:

it was unlucky, for example, to mention rats or pigs before going fishing for the day. One morning, Al inadvertently did both. They had no luck that day, returning to shore in the evening with almost no fish.

The mailboat was a significant employer locally, with jobs for hands on board, porters and clerical and administrative workers. The City of Dublin Steam Packet Company was founded in 1833, running the mail between Holyhead and Kingstown. In 1860, five mailboats – state-of-the-art vessels the *Ulster*, *Munster*, *Leinster*, *Connaught* and *Ireland* – were constructed by Laird of Liverpool.[45] Anthony's great-grandfather was employed as a stoker on the mailboat at around that time, shovelling coal into the furnace as the vessel traversed the Irish Sea. In the mid-twentieth century, Barbara's father worked as a porter for the mailboat (operating as British Rail then). He was offered office work but preferred to continue as a porter, as the tips were generous and often effectively doubled his salary (he received an enormous tip from Laurel and Hardy during their famous stay at the local Royal Marine Hotel in 1953).

The sea was a source of livelihood and a bridge between Dún Laoghaire-Rathdown and the rest of the world, but it was dangerous, too. Wives at home, remembered Mark, prayed fervently for the safety of the seamen and everyone had a healthy respect for the dangers: 'The sea is the boss. It doesn't matter what you know. When it wants you it'll take you.' Yet people were not entirely fatalistic. In the early 1800s, the Dublin Port Authority became one of the first in the world to create a formal lifeboat service. It acquired three boats, one of which was kept at Bullock Harbour in Dalkey.[46] In 1830, a Northumberland lifeboat was brought to Dunleary[47] for use as a lifeboat. The Lifeboat House in Dunleary was constructed in 1860.[48] The lifeboat service continued to work in extremely dangerous conditions; in 1895 a Finnish ship, the *Palme*, experienced difficulties and the lifeboat took to sea – while all on board the *Palme* survived, all fifteen of the lifeboat men died from drowning or exposure.[49] In 1980, Ann Burns, then ninety-two, remembered her encounter with one of them, dressed in his oilskins and sou'wester, rushing down Tivoli Terrace towards the sea. Ann's mother had dropped her groceries from her apron, and the young man paused to help her pick them up. Later, Ann and her mother heard that he and the rest of the crew had drowned.[50] Janet's family was badly impacted by the tragedy, losing several family members from different generations. The trauma, she said, lingered for years, long after all those who had personally known and loved the dead were themselves deceased. Some of the extended family emigrated to America and England after the disaster and were never seen again, while Janet's own father – whose recent ancestors were among those lost – spoke of the disaster often, and brought the children to see the memorial stone and pray for those who were lost, many years before. Kimberly's great-grandfather married one of the widows of the disaster, who had had to surrender all six of her children to institutional care. She had a further three children with her second husband; the first family stayed in care. One of the children of the second family – Kimberly's grandfather – would work on the lifeboat too, which must have been a huge worry to his mother, who had already lost so much. Kimberly's father himself went to sea in 1946, aged just fourteen, with the memories of all the family had lost a full two generations before still very present.

In 1947, a lifeboat with a diesel engine, operating since 1938, was used to rescue the crew members of the *Bolivar* when it ran aground and broke in two. Edward's father was on the lifeboat, determined to save the lives of the Norwegian crew despite treacherous conditions and the fact that one of the lifeboat's two propellers was broken. 'The ship was stuck on the bank,' recounted Edward, 'so she wasn't moving. But as the waves were coming in, it was lifting the lifeboat. So [Dad] manoeuvred the lifeboat alongside the ship. And as the lifeboat lifted up, the passengers were passed down one at a time.' The rescue was a resounding success.

Bríd remembered the children of Dún Laoghaire taking a huge interest in the lifeboat when she was growing up in the 1950s and 1960s: 'Every time the flare would go up… you'd see kids coming from everywhere… God forgive us… in the hope of seeing somebody being hauled out of the harbour.' The lifeboat reminded the children that the sea was

Kingstown Harbour, c.1900. Lexicon Library Postcard Collection.

A double-ended Dublin Bay Water Wag outside what is now the National Yacht Club in Dún Laoghaire, c.1860–1924. Photo by Joshua H. Hargrave, Joshua H. Hargrave Collection, National Library of Ireland.

dangerous, but also that there was someone looking out for all those in danger on the water.

Many men were employed in the harbour and dock of Dún Laoghaire for heavy physical work: taking luggage and other items off the mail-boat, loading and unloading commercial vessels and so on. This was a common source of employment for men who had spent some time at sea and now wanted to work closer to home. The heaviest work in this category may have been unloading coal in the coal pier. Edward's father did this in the first half of the twentieth century, and Edward himself did a short stint later on. It was backbreaking. The coal was dropped down to the men in lots of about a tonne, and they had to move it with shovels.

Ship building, boat building and sail making were all important employment sectors throughout the nineteenth and early twentieth centuries. Small-scale fishermen and sailors typically had clinker-built craft purchased from local boat makers. Wealthy yacht owners hired professionals to construct yachts and make sails. Nicola's grandfather migrated to Dalkey from Cork in the late 1800s, drawn by opportunities in boat building: he made boats and yachts, including many of the Water Wags popular for leisure purposes among the middle classes from the 1880s (discussed in more detail in 'Fun and Games'), and he repaired many of the significant boats in the area, including lifeboats. Harry and Derek's recent ancestors were sail makers, originally from the Isle of Wight, who moved to Dunleary in 1898 to make sails for yachts, then soaring in popularity. Initially working for a local firm called Perry's, they would open their own business. 'I remember my father having sails in our back garden on the clothes line,' Harry said. When Harry was a child in the 1960s, the family had diversified into also making tents for Irish circuses like Fossett's (Harry and his friends got free tickets).

James was a fully trained boat builder, having served his apprenticeship at a ship-building yard in Dún Laoghaire in the 1940s. After a long period working for Irish Lights as a shipwright, repairing vessels, he established his own small yard. His primary business was the construction of clinker-built yachts – including the local Water Wags – for local yacht club members. It was skilled, interesting work, but getting customers to pay on time was a constant challenge.

Yacht clubs provided employment to local working-class men and women, the former generally as boatmen and hired hands, and the latter as cooks, cleaners and servers. Local marine historian Vincent Delaney described the duties of the boatmen and paid hands as rowing people from the clubhouse out to their boat, anchored in the harbour, making sure that boats weren't leaking and performing general maintenance. Some paid hands lived on the boats and ensured they were properly rigged when the owners wanted to use them. In the winter months, they painted and repaired boats, and otherwise prepared them for the next sailing season. Women in service positions in the club – cleaners, cooks and so on – endured poor working conditions and were expected to pay from their own modest wages for anything that broke as they worked.[51]

The Strand, Killiney (shown here c.1880–1900) and Seapoint have long been popular destinations for days out at the seaside, and by extension a business opportunity for local families. Photo by Robert French. The Lawrence Photograph Collection, National Library of Ireland.

Day trippers in Dalkey. Local families rented boats and took people on boat trips around Dalkey Island and environs. Lexicon Library Postcard Collection.

The marine leisure sector became progressively more important as an employer through the late nineteenth century, as the middle classes expanded and, in parallel, access to the yacht clubs as short holidays – or at least occasional days out – became available to more working-class families. As tourism grew from the 1940s onwards, growing numbers of enterprising fishermen and hobblers, along with other seafarers, found seasonal employment in renting 'pleasure boats' to tourists or day trippers, or taking tourists on fishing or sightseeing tours of Dublin Bay from locations including Dún Laoghaire and Dalkey harbours. Until the 1950s, most of these boats were rowboats, with the addition of outboard engines from the 1950s onwards. Séamus's grandfather ran a successful small business from Coliemore Harbour in Dalkey, with seven or eight boats stored, upside-down, in the garden behind their cottage throughout the winter months.

The Baths in Dún Laoghaire, Blackrock and to a lesser extent Seapoint (the latter had no indoor facilities) were significant employers. Honorah's father, a former council water inspector, ran the Baths from about 1920. The job came with accommodation that was quite large, but initially not very well-organised for a growing family. Of course, they had abundant supplies of hot water for washing dishes, clothing and children, unlike many local families then. The Baths hired certain essential staff, including a boiler engineer whose work was so important that he was regarded, Honorah said, with reverence. Many employees were on seasonal contracts, hired for the spring and summer, and had to find other employment during the winter. Kate's aunt worked at the Dún Laoghaire Baths, serving the customers who came 'for steam baths, seaweed baths and just fresh water baths', as opposed to the swimming baths, which were for fun. Seaweed baths tended to be frequented by better-off

Dún Laoghaire Baths in the 1920s. Lexicon Library Postcard Collection.

Jim Hanney in Station Box, Dún Laoghaire, 1967. O'Dea Photographic Collection, National Library of Ireland.

customers, as they were much more expensive than the regular baths. Kate's aunt washed and dried towels and cleaned the baths after use, and collected heavy buckets of seaweed for the seaweed baths, which was heavy work. Other staff included men who pulled live seaweed off the rocks in Dublin Bay for use in the seaweed baths.

* * *

Desmond's great-great-grandmother Catherine, from Shankill, managed her own hackney firm in the nineteenth century, employing her two sons to run horse-drawn vehicles serving a wide area, inland as far as Rathfarnham and south to Bray and beyond. Catherine was said locally to have been among the first in Ireland to install rubber wheels on her vehicles;* stories were still told of Catherine and her business generations later. A tendency to work in transport filtered down through the family, with Desmond's grandfather operating a truck in the 1930s and 1940s. Transport was an important source of employment generally, with many men employed by the mailboats – on and offshore – and on the rail and tram networks. While numbers declined in the 1960s and 1970s,

---

* Vulcanised rubber was first produced on an industrial scale from 1844, using a technique developed in the 1830s by Charles Goodyear.

when car ownership started to become the norm, transport remained an important employment sector.

* * *

From the seventeenth century, Big Houses and their estates were important local employers of both sexes. The houses needed an army of servants, mostly women, while the estates required farm workers, gardeners, managers and even millers.[52] By the nineteenth century, over 24 per cent of the Dublin workforce was engaged in domestic service.[53] In 1881, 48 per cent of all women employed in the formal economy were in domestic service. Some were trained at an institution like the House of Mercy on Lower Baggot Street in Dublin, which taught Catholic girls of 'good character' how to work as laundresses and domestic servants, or the Domestic Training Institute for Protestant Girls on Charlemont Street, providing similar training to Protestants.[54] In Stillorgan Park in 1911, the Power family – a wealthy Catholic clan – had a chauffeur, cook, parlourmaid, housemaid and ladies' maid. The chauffeur was Protestant; the rest of the staff were Catholic.[55]

The Big Houses, and the smaller but still grand homes of minor gentry, business families, successful professionals and the middle classes, as well as religious orders, remained important employers following independence.[56] Even families on relatively modest incomes, and in smallish homes, often hired live-in staff, possibly just one girl in her teens, from a rural area or a working-class home, prepared to work long hours for very little pay. Well-paid civil servants, for example, were generally expected to have at least one live-in 'girl'.[57] Many families also employed casual workers for laundry, heavy cleaning and other demanding domestic tasks. In 1926, almost two-thirds of girls between thirteen and fifteen and no longer in education, but not engaged in agricultural work, were in domestic service. Domestic service involved migration – of primarily young girls and women, often starting as little more than children – from rural to urban areas, and from working-class homes to middle-class

Mary Geoghegan, a native Irish speaker from Galway who worked in domestic service in the Dalkey area in the late 1940s. Kind permission of Marie, Michael and Thomas Clancy, Mary Geoghegan's children.

or affluent homes. Anthony's mother, aged fourteen, left a seven-acre Roscommon farm in 1928 to work in service in Dún Laoghaire. She was employed by a kind, generous family who provided good working conditions and reasonably good pay. She would work for them all her life, continuing on a daily basis after her marriage. In this movement of the countless girls and women like Anthony's mother, there was a significant influx of traditions, customs, belief and linguistic influences from rural to suburban areas, which have all contributed to the complexities of local culture and identity.

Live-in domestic staff occupied an ambivalent position – simultaneously household members and lower-status individuals, often with extremely limited workers' rights. Even casual staff, who typically provided cleaning or laundry services, were often privy to many of the family's secrets while excluded from their circles. Some were treated badly; others were dearly loved; none were particularly well-paid. Maids were often known simply as 'the girl' and viewed as largely interchangeable. Social roles were usually strictly enforced. Ann Burns, a servant in Dún Laoghaire in the early twentieth century, pre-independence, remembered another maid being told not to wear her new hat in public, as the daughter of the house had just bought the same one.[58] George grew up in a wealthy family in Dalkey in the 1950s. He remembered the social division between families who hired servants and those who provided services. 'Well, you know,' his mother said, 'they come from a *different part* of the town.' As well as hiring women for casual work, the family had live-in servants: 'Bridie and Nora… from Connemara… Joanna… we called her "Nurse" but she was really the nanny.' Andrew grew up in a well-to-do family in the Rochestown area. In his childhood in the 1940s and 1950s, his parents had a live-in maid, Bridie. Bridie's room, known as 'the outside room', was near the kitchen. 'It held a washing machine,' Andrew remembered, 'and it had the electric meters… it must have been absolutely miserable… cold as sin.' Liam grew up in Blackrock in the 1940s and early 1950s, the child of a senior civil servant with a brand-new house in a pleasant, middle-class development. Then, 'nearly every family had a live-in maid… a girl… from some country farm'. For years, Liam's family had Mary, who was intimately involved with raising the family, and much-loved. Mary had Sundays and Wednesday afternoons off, and the children were instructed not to go into the kitchen then, as she might be entertaining guests. Mary met a man, married and settled in Dublin. Ailish came to Dublin in 1948, aged eighteen, to work as a cook for the British attaché and his wife near Cabinteely. She liked her employers, but it was very hard work, as they did a lot of entertaining: 'Oh, we had an awful lot of parties,' she remembered. 'Nothing in the house. No fridges.

A housekeeper with a child of the house. Women who worked in domestic service and who did not marry often remained with the same family for many years. Bridget would remain with her employers until her death. Kind permission of Mary White.

No hot water... and all the parties they had to have.' She also had very little time off, just half a day on a Sunday. Philo's mother grew up in a farming family in Malahide. They were poor and all the girls went into service aged fourteen. Philo's mother worked in a house in Blackrock, where the hours were long and the money poor – and she also met and fell for a local Blackrock man. Throughout her married life, she continued to work part-time in domestic service.

The ambivalent situation of domestic staff was particularly marked among those caring for children, whose lives were intimately entwined with those of their employers. Andrew's mother, growing up in an affluent household in the early twentieth century, was raised by a nanny, whom she loved dearly: 'she loved Nanny more than her mother'. Cyril's father, born into a well-to-do family in 1923, had a governess with whom he remained close until her death in the early 1970s. She was, Cyril believes, among the many women of her generation who remained unmarried because so many men had died in the First World War. She dedicated her life, instead, to raising the children of others.

In many families, especially those with rural origins, domestic staff could be relatives or family connections – perhaps relatives from more modest backgrounds, looking for a start in Dublin. Sally, who grew up in Mount Merrion, remembered the young girls who worked in her childhood home in the 1940s and 1950s. They came, she said, from very poor backgrounds in Sally's mother's home area, and were excited to have a bedroom of their own for the first time: 'I always remember the furniture in this small room was very much a truckle bed, and Mammy had made a little bedside table out of an orange box… and she put gingham around it. And these girls thought they were in heaven! You know, because they came from places where they had no… water, one of fourteen or fifteen… not enough to eat, disease …'

While some legislation introduced in the early twentieth century improved the lot of domestic staff,[59] they still had few legal rights. They could, for example, be summarily dismissed if they suffered ill health that compromised their work, and employers were not obliged to provide financial assistance with healthcare. Ann Burns, working in domestic service in the early twentieth century, injured herself at work and had to spend six months in hospital with a 'running tumour'. She lost her job: 'they couldn't expect the mistress to wait for me that length'.[60] Domestic servants often worked long hours, and for those who lived with their employers, there could be ambiguity about when they were on duty and when not. Jim's mother, working in Dún Laoghaire in the 1930s, was supposed to be off on Wednesday afternoons, and liked going to the cinema with her boyfriend, but her employer always found her a task just before she was due to go out, so she never saw the beginning of the film. 'What struck me,' Jim reflected, 'was her lack of outrage at this. She just accepted this as normal… because she was working-class.'

Social distance characterised most relationships between employers and domestic staff, evident even in how servants were named within the household. Sometimes employers used interchangeable first names that didn't belong to them, like a succession of servants known as 'Kitty' or 'Biddy' regardless of their real names, or with nicknames that might not always have been used affectionately. Douglas's grandmother was a bank manager's wife, for whom having a maid was a 'social necessity'. She would only hire women whose name was 'Kathleen', presumably as this made it easier to remember what they were called (or perhaps she just referred to all maids as 'Kathleen'). There were, of course, exceptions. Isobel, growing up in Monkstown in the 1930s and 1940s, has fond memories of the family's maid, Maggie. Isobel's parents, Quakers, felt strongly about the essential equality of all people. 'Whereas all my friends, if I went to their house… the maid had her food in the kitchen,' remembered Isobel. 'Maggie always sat at a table with us, and she was always family, and we regarded her as family and loved her as family.' In the 1950s, Anthony's mother worked part-time as a cleaner for two elderly sisters, who also employed his father as a part-time gardener. The sisters – 'very nice people' – invited Anthony's family to garden parties at their home, together with their other friends.

Young girls were vulnerable to sexual predation on the part of employers or senior members of staff, were likely to be blamed if they complained and had no meaningful legal recourse in the event of pregnancy. Pregnant servant girls were often 'put out' as soon as their condition became apparent, after which they might be forced into prostitution and/or an institution, as many would not hire unmarried mothers.[61] A 'good reference' was essential, and girls and women fired because of pregnancy were unlikely to get one. Again, there were exceptions. Ann Burns, recorded in 1980, remembered that in her own young years in the early twentieth century, she became pregnant while unmarried and in a relationship with the man whom she would eventually marry. The pregnancy was miscarried and her employers were kind to her despite the situation.[62] Graham's grandmother worked as a maid for a wealthy family in Sallynoggin in the early twentieth century. She had three children fathered by one of her employers. She considered herself relatively fortunate, as the family supported her, she kept her children – although their father never officially recognised them – and she would marry another man. Jennifer's great-aunt was a young girl of about sixteen, working in service in the early twentieth century, when she gave birth to a child assumed to have been fathered by her employer. The family took her back as a servant, and she would work with them all her life until she literally died on the job, serving lunch. Cecilia's mother, born in 1900, was working in domestic service in a Big House when, one day, 'she was kneeling cleaning out the fire grate and [her employer's nephew] was home... he made a pass at my mother, and she hit him with the poker'. Cecilia's mother expected to be fired, but in a display of female solidarity across the social classes, her employer told her that she 'did the right thing' and that 'he deserved it'.

A vast but unquantifiable number of working-class women, often middle-aged or older, often excluded from the formal economy because they were married, performed informal cleaning services, frequently for multiple clients, for long hours and for small wages, sometimes supplemented by gifts like food and clothing. This work, while sometimes providing a substantial proportion of the income of working-class families – sometimes the main income where women were widowed or husbands were absent – was typically paid in cash and rarely recorded officially, and is therefore almost invisible in much historical documentation, although it is frequently referenced in literature, drama and other creative works.[63] In some fishing families, during the summer children accompanied their fathers on their fishing boats, leaving their mothers free to work as cleaners. Casual domestic servants might receive gifts from employers to augment their pay, often second-hand clothing and other items for the house and family. The best were sold, with the rest distributed among extended families. For servants who felt appreciated by their employers, gifts of clothing and toys for the family cemented these warm feelings, but for those who did not, the clothing was a reminder of their dependence on someone who might not treat them well. A cleaning lady might attend Mass wearing her employer's old dress, her children in the cast-off clothing of the young misses and masters of the house, frequently while also separated from the wealthier members of the congregation by the red cords that divided the church into sections for rich and poor.

Liz's grandmother, who lived in Blackrock, was widowed young. With a family to raise, she went out to work in the late 1920s and early 1930s as a housekeeper for a wealthy family in Dalkey. Thankfully, her employees treated her well, supplementing her income with food and other useful items. Every Christmas, she was allowed to use their ingredients to make her own family's Christmas cake. Séamus's mother lost her husband to tuberculosis, and had to return to casual, poorly paid domestic work in Dalkey in the mid-twentieth century. Christine's grandmother, who lived in Dalkey, was abandoned by her husband, and had to support her family by cleaning a local bank. Eddie's mother, from Blackrock, was widowed at twenty-seven when her husband died of tuberculosis. With three small children, she had to do poorly paid casual domestic work, mostly for middle-class families in the quite new suburb of Mount Merrion, where young, educated couples were settling then, mid-twentieth century. Jimmy's father died of tuberculosis in 1954, aged thirty-two, leaving his widow and their five small children, one a newborn, shortly after they had moved to a new house in Sallynoggin. Well-meaning relatives suggested that the new widow surrender at least some of the children to an orphanage, but she refused, undertaking a series of gruelling casual cleaning jobs instead. Kevin's father died suddenly, aged forty-seven, in the mid-1950s, when Kevin was in his early teens. Kevin's mother had to go into domestic service, and do extremely long hours, as her widow's allowance from Dublin Port and Docks was a pittance. 'Our home,' Kevin remembered, 'went from being an emotional and physically warm home to an emotional and physically cold house, because my mother had to go out to work… all over Foxrock, doing housework for people.' Thankfully, her employers were kind women: 'the personal support that she got… saw her through the rough, emotional side'. Ingrid's mother, and subsequently Ingrid herself – who grew up in Glasthule – worked in domestic service for a wealthy local family that she remembered with huge fondness. They provided funds to her mother to help with Holy Communions and Confirmations and they helped when Ingrid's sister was seriously ill. Ingrid's mother took great pride in her work and her professionalism, and

Ingrid loved watching and learning from her from the moment she hung up her coat and donned the special rubber shoes she wore for work. Ingrid herself started working at about thirteen, carrying out tasks like cleaning the skirting boards. It was hard work, but she liked it. Perhaps because she had confidence in her own work and abilities, and such a good relationship with her employers, Ingrid's mother felt able to stand up for the rights of young girls moving from the country into live-in domestic positions. One young girl was given a bedroom so wet that her clothes were permanently damp. Ingrid's mother firmly told the employer that these were not fit conditions and things improved.

Clearly, women in domestic service were not just doing essential household work, but were also important vectors of cultural, gastronomic, linguistic and other influences from areas outside Dún Laoghaire-Rathdown. They were also vectors of new foodways and different ways of living acquired from their experience of working in affluent homes into the working-class communities they typically married into. Cooks or parlourmaids, for example, learned how to prepare and present foods – lobster bisque, perhaps, or beef Wellington – they might not have grown up with. These skills were retained after marriage, and could be both a source of pride and a means to obtain casual or part-time work to supplement the family income. Marianne's grandmother had worked as a parlourmaid. Afterwards, she remained 'very particular about table settings' and proud of the refined habits that she had learned at work. 'She'd lovely touches,' Marianne remembered, 'which you wouldn't have got coming from a farming family... Now we didn't have much silver... but what *was* there was shined to within an inch of its life... she said, "This is what we always did in the Big House."'

When the workhouse system was in place, many retired domestic servants ended their days there when they got too old for heavy physical work, particularly unmarried women, who might have worked for the same family all their lives.[64] With small incomes, little time off and considerable social pressure to display 'high moral standards', they often had few opportunities to meet men. They typically earned too little to save for retirement, and depended on employers' good will and ability to provide for them in old age, or on extended family who might take them in. Even after the state introduced modest pension incomes for all, former domestic servants often struggled. Marianne's grandmother was friends with the cook alongside whom she had worked; when the cook retired in the mid-twentieth century, she had a home with Marianne's granny. But many had nowhere to go. Sometimes employers requested favours from the council or other providers of subsidised housing. This housing, if it were made available, was often of a very poor standard.

Barbara's aunt, originally from Cork, came to Dublin to work in domestic service for a very wealthy family. She spent almost her entire adult life doing everything for them. She got up early to empty grates, set fires, clean the house and do all the cooking. She made the beds and filled hot water bottles, placing them in the family's beds before they turned in for the night. She had half a day off per week and visited her sister – married locally – for tea on Sunday evenings. Once a year, she visited a sister in Cork. When she was too old for this heavy work, her employers – whom she loved dearly – started phoning her relatives: 'We think she should go into a home because we can't look after her.' After she died in St Vincent's Hospital ('conveniently for [her employers]'), the doctors handed Ellen the small bag of clothes that she had brought to hospital. Barbara went to the house where her aunt had worked to empty her little bedroom, but there was nothing there. Her aunt had never earned enough to save any money or buy anything for herself beyond the bare necessities. 'But [her employers] were nice, gentle people,' Barbara reflected, 'and upper-class, and I suppose that's the way people treated their maids in those days. But she was happy. She knew no other life.' Many of the girls from her home area in Cork had worked in domestic service for local farming families, and apparently many were sent home in disgrace, pregnant by their employers. In contrast to them, Barbara said, her aunt's situation seemed relatively good.

Bridget worked for most of her adult life for Elinor's family doing housework and farm work – milking the cows, making butter and so on. Despite sharing decades of her life, and a close and even loving relationship, with her employers, Bridget's life was also quite separate. Her bedroom adjoined the kitchen. She ate separately. On Sundays, she went to Mass by herself. Bridget worked until the day she died. 'She was like a member of the family,' Elinor remembered, 'and she was part of the furniture… very much part of the house, and the only time I remember her going out was when she went to church on a Sunday, on her big bicycle.' When she died in 1956, Bridget was waked in the small bedroom off the kitchen that had been her home for decades.

Harry's aunt worked 'for yonks' as a maid for a family in Dalkey, and was apparently well-treated by them. But when the family – and his aunt – got old, she had to leave. Maids earned so little that she had never been able to save for retirement. She moved into the Glasthule Buildings, notoriously substandard in the 1960s, and lived her final years in what Harry described as 'squalor'. She used a candle for light, as she dreaded the electricity bill, and shared revolting sanitary facilities with other residents. Even when she visited Harry and his family, she preferred to use a candle rather than their electricity.

Although domestic service was dominated by women, men worked as butlers and grooms (before cars, and chauffeurs later on) for wealthy families. Typically, only very wealthy people could afford full-time male staff in the house, with male domestic servants offering both status and practical assistance. Robbie's father was a very early holder of a driving license after serving an apprenticeship as a motor mechanic, which allowed him to work as a chauffeur. His employer was a wealthy woman who wanted a driver to take her around Europe, so Robbie's father was well-travelled when war broke out in 1914. With the skills he had learned as a driver and as a mechanic, Robbie's father returned to Dublin to work as a bus driver and, later, for the Dún Laoghaire fire brigade. Gardeners were typically self-employed men with a roster of clients, but very wealthy families might, until the mid-twentieth century, employ men

Jimmy Howe, chauffeur, accompanying his employer on a tour of Europe, c.1915, during the First World War. Kind permission of Jimmy Howe.

full-time to work in their gardens and provide some janitorial services: 'we had Austin the gardener,' remembered Harry, 'he lived in a sort of a little house in part of the garden, and he looked after the garden and he looked after the dog, Rover'.

Although domestic service remained an important employment sector for women and girls throughout much of the twentieth century, it was also in steady decline. There were over 135,000 domestic servants in 1911 (on the whole island), mostly girls and women; 88,000 (in independent Ireland) in 1926; and 60,000 in 1951. The numbers employed in domestic service declined rapidly in the 1940s and 1950s,[65] while remaining higher in the Dún Laoghaire borough relative to other parts of Dublin; domestic servants accounted for 14.8 per cent of the total official workforce in 1946.[66] The decline gathered pace in the second half of the twentieth century because of the growing use of modern conveniences that made housekeeping easier, rising female education and higher levels of industrial mechanisation, giving women more opportunities. By the mid-twentieth century, many could aspire to work as secretaries, book-keepers or civil servants, in factories and other industrial settings, and in professional occupations (at least until marriage). It became much rarer for a woman to enter service young and stay with the family for an extended period, and wealthier families increasingly resorted to casual labour or to young women working for them for briefer periods, as the salaries for domestic servants were higher than before. It also gradually became easier for working-class women to devote themselves entirely to their families and eschew poorly paid casual cleaning work. The children's allowance (initially for third and subsequent children only) introduced in 1944 was paid to fathers at first, despite some opposition, but it still contributed to making it easier for working-class families to live on one income. By 1961, 93.1 per cent of all married women described themselves as engaged in home duties (although it is important to note that a census does not capture details of all those engaged in the informal economy, where many married working-class women worked).[67] Women who had started their working lives in domestic service also became increasingly reluctant to discuss their experiences, especially if they and their families had moved into the middle classes. Sarah-Jane remembered her mother and her mother's cousin as speaking little of their time as maids: 'they maybe regarded it as a demeaning job'. The vast army of domestic servants who were such an important part of the workforce for so long are often seen only as ghosts in the census, their experiences rarely recounted.

* * *

Retail was a major employer throughout the nineteenth and twentieth centuries, from ambulant sellers, such as fishmongers with barrows, to upmarket grocery and fashion shops. Graham's grandmother dealt directly with trawlers in Dún Laoghaire, stocking her barrow from which she sold directly 'like Molly Malone', while well-established suburbs like Dún Laoghaire, Blackrock and Dalkey were noted centres for retail from the mid-nineteenth century, featuring family-run businesses serving a wide community and training apprentices from around the country.

Renowned family-run businesses like Findlater's, Lee's and McGovern's were significant employers for generations, with managers, sales assistants, apprentices and deliverers. Their shops were prominent local landmarks, and their businesses were not just places where locals did their shopping,

Right: Davy Stephens selling *The Winning Post*. Stephens is described in James Joyce's *Ulysses* as 'Davy Stephens, minute in a large capecoat, a small felt hat crowning his ringlets, passed out with a roll of papers under his cape, a king's courier.' He was a well-known local seller of newspapers and magazines at Kingstown Harbour. Lexicon Library Postcard Collection.

Below: Items for sale in Crock of Gold, Blackrock, 1980. Urban Folklore Project, Dublin City. Kind permission of National Folklore Collection.

but sites of extensive social interaction. But by the 1960s, many well-known retailers were struggling, as the growth in car use and refrigeration in the home, a gradual increase in the number of married women engaged in paid work outside the home, and the concomitant decline in daily grocery shopping all took a toll. From this period, most retail outlets shifted towards self-service, relinquishing messenger boys, as customers who arrived in cars that could transport their 'big shop' increasingly selected their own items and brought them to the check-out counter. Consequently, large businesses could operate with the same number of staff as small grocery and other outlets, and they could operate with more attractive profit margins than smaller, family-owned businesses. Dunnes Stores opened a large supermarket at Cornelscourt in 1966, serving suburbanites across areas including Blackrock, Stillorgan and Sallynoggin, and facilitating further suburban development. Stillorgan Shopping Centre opened in 1974,[68] following compulsory purchase orders against homes that, as Eva recalled, left at least some locals, with local family histories dating back generations, 'absolutely distraught'. Also that year, the long-established family-run Lee's store closed its Dún Laoghaire and other retail outlets.

By the mid-to-late 1970s, many family-run businesses were closing, being acquired by supermarkets or facing dramatic change. Many small business owners, like Dorothy's father, became bankrupt. They responded by changing their business practice, winding up their business and retiring, or going to work for one of the new supermarket or other retail chains. Many were pragmatic, recognising that the supermarkets offered cheaper products that enabled poorer families to have better diets, and everyone to enjoy more variety.

* * *

State bodies were important employers across a range of sectors, including janitorial work, cleaning and park maintenance, along with a wide array of clerical and administrative positions. Kevin's great-grandfather, a gardener, worked in Blackrock Park in the 1890s. Graham's grandfather – a veteran of the First World War – was the town sweeper in Dún Laoghaire in the 1920s and 1930s, expected to dress formally with a hat and a dickie bow for this back-breaking work. Dubliners singer Ronnie Drew, a local, recalled his grandfather – a carpenter for the Corporation – as being quite formally dressed, in a three-piece blue serge suit, with a new one provided each year.[69] In the 1950s, when Howard was growing up, his father worked as the park ranger at Killiney Hill, also quite formally dressed in a uniform with brass buttons requiring polishing.

State-owned transport systems were important local employers, offering regular employment and often access to healthcare and other benefits. Rob remembered the importance of the 'CIÉ doctors' to his family – his father worked for the railways.

The Free State army was an important employer for men, particularly working-class men, in the 1920s and 1930s. Sinéad's grandfather did a stint of two years despite coming from a family that, just a few years before, were 'out and out IRA' and furiously opposed to the Treaty that would end the War of Independence (discussed in 'Fighting and Fighting Back'). In the army, he learned the painting and decorating skills that would give him employment for the rest of his working life.

Noreen started working for Dún Laoghaire Corporation in 1949, aged eighteen. The Corporation had just changed the way it recruited new staff, and one result of this was an influx of women. Previously, women were only hired on temporary contracts; if they stayed for years, they would have a succession of such contracts. Noreen worked in the planning department while Sallynoggin, as it is known today, was being built.

* * *

Until the latter part of the twentieth century, many skilled trades and professions remained predominately or exclusively male, with exceptions in areas like professional dress-making and primary and secondary school teaching. Men dominated senior roles in the civil service and other public-sector positions. Many women worked in support roles, particularly in areas like office administration, bookkeeping and secretarial work,[70] and in family businesses, albeit usually without any of the benefits of ownership of physical or intellectual property. The most significant barrier to women's progression in many professions was the marriage bar, which applied in most public-sector roles and was also adopted in many private businesses. Isobel remembered women employees of Guinness (where Isobel's husband worked) keeping their engagements a secret for as long as possible to delay being laid off. Sandra worked in the clerical sector until her marriage in 1965. She recalled an official from the local social welfare office who kept an eye on local married women, 'to see if you were working'. Breda was working in the civil service in the early 1970s, and remembered colleagues having to leave when they married. They were often 'very cross'. The marriage bar made marriage a big decision, particularly for women earning good salaries. Hannah had a good clerical job with Guinness in the late 1960s, and continued to work there after her marriage, until the birth of her first child in 1974: 'And then,' she said, 'I was obliged to leave, because they didn't take back mothers or pregnant women.' A year later, Guinness changed their policy and Hannah was invited back, but neither her husband nor her mother was available to help with childcare, so she ended up staying at home, although she would have preferred to be out working.

After doing her Leaving Cert in 1958, Sally decided to study medicine in UCD, where she was one of just ten women students in a class of about 100. Only fifty years before that, it was commonplace to think that 'the whole position of women in the social currency of the world – passive as opposed to the active male – makes it extremely undesirable that a woman should engage in ordinary general practice, or should include men among her patients'.[71] Five of Sally's female co-students were nuns, destined for the missions. Sally loved student life, but felt pressure when socialising not to admit to studying medicine; it put the boys off, so most female medical students pretended to be studying nursing when they went to a 'hop'. By and large, however, they were accepted by their fellow students: 'they'd always say, "You only got your exams because you smiled at the doctor", but mostly, you were accepted as an equal'.

The biggest resistance to women doctors, she recalled, were nurses, who hoped to marry doctors and did not like women medical students getting in their way. The nurses were thought to conspire to give female medical students the least-desirable night shifts to punish them for stepping out of line. Sally's classmate Rebecca, a doctor's daughter, faced a battle when she told her father she wanted to study medicine. He felt that it was a waste of time for a woman. Eventually, she prevailed: 'Fine,' her father said. 'I know it's a waste of money... but you can do it.' Both Rebecca and Sally had long careers in medicine. They married other doctors while also working as doctors themselves and caring for their families. Both were keenly aware that their careers depended not just on their husbands' understanding but also on the paid help of other local women whom they could hire to assist with housework and childcare.

* * *

The unpaid domestic work involved in running a home and family has traditionally largely been done by women and is often overlooked in discussions of the economy, but no economy could function without it. Through the nineteenth and twentieth centuries, middle-class and bet-ter-off working-class women who could not afford full-time or any help in the home, but whose husbands' incomes were sufficient to support a family, were the group most likely to retain sole responsibility for unpaid domestic and family work. By the mid-twentieth century, in many socially upwardly mobile families from the working and lower middle classes, it was considered shameful for women to have to work outside the home. Men were proud of supporting their wives and families, espe-cially if they came from backgrounds in which financial necessity had forced their mothers into poorly paid, back-breaking casual work. 'If you didn't need to work', was Jennifer's father's attitude, you should be at home with the children, cooking your husband's dinner. 'My father never came in to a note saying, "Your dinner is in the fridge."' Noelle

Lily Howe with her children at the sea in the 1940s. Kind permission of Jimmy Howe.

remembered. 'He didn't have a key to his own door, because [Mum] was expected to be there.'

Domestic appliances became more common and more affordable as the twentieth century progressed and, for many women, made more tangible and positive differences to the quality of their life than women's suffrage or later women's political movements. Before the mid-twentieth century, cleaning of the house and of laundry was generally done by hand. Laundry, typically done in a bathtub, perhaps with the help of a heavy mangle to extract some of the water, was heavy work. Families who could afford it had maids and/or sent their clothing to laundries, but in poorer families it was done by the woman of the house, with her daughters' help as they got older and more capable. Most women with the resources to do so embraced technological innovations like the vacuum cleaners rented out by local branches of Findlater's, which required two people to operate them – one to turn the handle, as they did not use

Pat and Michael Howe at their home in Booterstown. The washboard in the background hints at the heavy work involved in washing and drying all the clothes of large families. Kind permission of Jimmy Howe.

electricity, and another to use the brush.[72] Harry remembered a man who drove around Sallynoggin in the 1950s in a van with four or five washing machines that women could rent for the afternoon to get their 'big wash' done. Edward's mother and a friend rented a washing machine between them for an afternoon to keep costs down.

A significant proportion of women's domestic work traditionally includes procuring, processing and preparing food – feeding the family. While wealthier families ate well, even lavishly, even in the late nineteenth and early twentieth centuries, others lived on very modest incomes and often found it difficult to obtain an adequate diet. Refrigeration was not the norm in many homes until the 1960s, so women shopped daily for ingredients and used external mesh-fronted meat safes to keep meat and butter cool.

Throughout the late nineteenth and early to mid-twentieth century, middle-class women who enjoyed working and wanted to supplement the family income, and families aspiring to the middle classes who could manage on just the husband's salary but wanted a supplementary income, found employment they could balance with their duties at home. In the 1930s and 1940s, Phillip's mother worked as a model – a 'mannequin' – in a boutique and in fashion shows. From home, she also ran classes in deportment and style for girls interested in modelling. When Terence married in 1952, his wife was compelled to stop working as a tailoress, which she was very unhappy about. She continued to work from home while raising a family, contributing substantially to the family income. Clodagh's father was often unemployed so the family frequently relied on the income that her mother earned with her small baking business. Debbie, a young married woman in the 1950s, relinquished the hairdressing salon she ran in Sandyford before her marriage, but continued to work from home on a freelance basis. Charlotte's mother had trained and worked as an upholsterer before her marriage, and continued to work from her home in Churchtown afterwards. Lily, a press photographer, had to stop working when she married in 1961, but established a child-photography business. Ita left her job to raise her children in the late 1960s, but continued to earn money from home by investing in a knitting machine and taking in knitting.

The wives of professionals like doctors and lawyers – such as Terry's mother, a doctor's wife – frequently did administrative and bookkeeping work for their husbands. Nicola, who had graduated from a technical school and had experience in bookkeeping and in running a bed and breakfast, did all the administration and bookkeeping for her husband's watchmaking enterprise. Rosie's mother, similarly, provided administration and bookkeeping for her husband's building business. Many women often invested considerable time in administrative work for their husbands, but as they generally had no formal contract, pay or pension arrangements in place, they are all but invisible from the historical record.

While many have fond memories of caring fathers, until recent decades childcare was primarily the remit of women, both those with no paid work outside the home and those who also worked for money.

Working-class men particularly often also worked such long hours at demanding jobs that they were often very physically tired when they got home, and not always in the mood to play or provide childcare. Rob's family enjoyed recounting a famous story of his grandfather, who came home one day indignantly carrying a small, filthy child whom he placed on the floor. 'Look at the state of that child,' he said to his wife. 'It's a disgrace.' 'It is,' his wife said. 'Whose is it?' He spent so little time with his children that he didn't always recognise them.

* * *

Tourism, particularly local tourism in the form of day trippers, was an important aspect of the economy of the coastal areas from the nineteenth century. By the mid-twentieth century, working- and middle-class British tourists could travel to Dún Laoghaire on the mailboat and enjoy some of the thrill of a foreign holiday while remaining in an English-speaking location with a familiar appearance. The Urban Council promoted Dún Laoghaire as the Golden Gate to Ireland[73] and its attractions, including the local Baths, Dublin Bay and the Dublin/Wicklow Mountains, and activities including sailing, fishing, golf and horse racing. Winston's parents, who inherited quite a large house in Dún Laoghaire, ran a bed and breakfast. The family still has the visitors' book, which shows that almost half their visitors came from the greater Manchester and Liverpool area, and that many had Irish surnames. Fintan's mother, whose husband died when Séamus was thirteen, ran a bed and breakfast from their home during the summer. As Séamus recalled, the British – still enduring rationing well into the 1950s – came to Ireland primarily to eat. For a modest sum, they could stay with a local family and eat all they wanted. Séamus's mother prepared them huge meat-heavy meals, mostly corned beef with potatoes and cabbage. Finbar's mother was widowed in 1950 when her children were still young, so she sold the family farm in Kildare and moved to Dalkey, where she ran a boarding house, largely catering to English tourists coming for holidays and to have 'a good feed of meat'.

Holiday postcard, early 1900s.
Lexicon Library Postcard
Collection.

They also, according to Gerald of Killiney, returned to England with large quantities of cigarettes, which were still subject to severe rationing in Britain. Sarah-Jane's mother ran a busy lodging house, offering bed and breakfast to tourists. Most were couples from Britain paying for a week's summer holiday, with three meals served every day. They often returned year after year. Sarah-Jane's mother was an early adopter of domestic technologies to assist with the work. James remembered working on Dún Laoghaire pier as a teenager 'before Spain was invented' in the 1950s, setting out deckchairs for the English tourists, and moving them around so that they were consistently facing the sun, or so as to see and hear performances at the bandstand. A teenaged Jimmy worked for one of the local hotels at much the same time, taking men's shoes from outside their rooms and polishing them overnight, and washing pots and pans in the kitchen.

Women who were widowed or abandoned, but with sufficient resources to own their homes, often ran small bed and breakfasts or took in lodgers during the tourist season, and married women often supplemented the family income in this way, too. As a young married woman in Dalkey, Nicola took in guests during the summer and provided bed and breakfast; she and her husband vacated their own bedroom and slept on a roll-out mattress in the living room to accommodate their guests. Poorer women, whose homes were too small to rent a room to tourists, frequently supplemented their family's incomes by doing seasonal cleaning and catering work in these small establishments. Increasing prosperity and improved workers' rights meant that, by the mid-twentieth century, going on holiday was more accessible to families on lower incomes. Inner-city families might be able to afford a week at the seaside in Shankill. Audrey remembered Shankill families in the 1950s moving into simple lean-tos at the back of their homes, so that they could rent out the main body of their house. Yvette remembered local families erecting wooden huts from which they served tea, or sold hot water to holidaymakers so they could make their own. Gerald recalled local families making a little money selling boiling water and treats like Tayto crisps from huts on the beach. While tourism was predominately located in the coastal areas, smaller numbers of people living in inland areas also partook, for example by collecting tourists in 'jaunting cars' and bringing them to the mountainous areas of Dublin and north County Wicklow to see the sights.

For those whose family's incomes did not depend on tourism or retail, the presence of many holidaymakers locally could be irritating. 'English people came over from Lancashire and Yorkshire,' Keith remembered. 'They took the mailboat over from Holyhead... on a nice summer's day in Dún Laoghaire there were *hundreds* of these people.' Meanwhile, according to Hugh Leonard's biography, *Out After Dark*, Dalkey's parish priest blamed young Englishmen on holiday for out-of-wedlock births,

Central Tea Room owned by William Mullen, Killiney Strand, 1920s, Collection of Catherine Mullen. Kind permission of Anna Scudds.

and devised local amateur dramatics intended to showcase the perils of consorting with foreigners.[74]

In the 1960s, the introduction of the car ferry, and the fact that many tourists now travelled in their own cars, resulted in a decline in British tourism locally, and a quick, dramatic decline in the number of hotels and other hospitality businesses.[75] This occurred just as housebuilding in the inland regions of the county was expanding rapidly, transforming much of south County Dublin into a series of commuter suburbs, and transforming the green hinterland of the coastal towns and suburbs into a landscape dominated by bricks and cement. Some bed and breakfasts switched to providing accommodations for longer-term lodgers, who might be older single women or widows, or young men and women moving to the Dublin area to study or work in the civil service. Some effectively became nursing homes, in which older people (more often women) lived until they died or became too infirm for this arrangement. Eimear's mother, who had run a lodging house for tourists, segued – as did so many – into providing accommodations and meals for the elderly.

Running a lodging house, or hosting a small number of lodgers in a family home, was a common way for women to earn money throughout the nineteenth and much of the twentieth century, while also attending to childcare and domestic duties. In 1911, 5 per cent of the residents of Dublin were lodgers, and taking in lodgers was common among the working classes. It was also common among women from wealthier backgrounds, in reduced circumstances, who tended to use the term 'paying guests' to differentiate themselves from poorer landladies.[76] For women lacking the protection and income of a male relation (including widows), offering lodgings was a safe, respectable way to earn money, and compatible with child-rearing. Taking in lodgers was associated with both upward and downward social mobility; poorer families might invest the funds in their children's education, whereas those descended from wealth, now in reduced circumstances, might rent out parts of a large inherited house as a way to manage when things got harder. In the early twentieth century, following her husband's death, Molly's grandmother was left with a family to raise and a farm to run in Kilternan. She took in lodgers: 'quite a few staying in various huts… Somebody lived in what was called "the potato shed". Somebody else… in a hut up the field.' Denny's grandmother, from Dún Laoghaire, took in lodgers, young men from all over the country: 'They were working in the post office and the police and insurance companies around the place.' She played an almost maternal role in their lives, feeding them, washing their clothes and insisting that they kneel every evening for a decade of the Rosary. In 1980, Dún Laoghaire resident Elizabeth Rushby recalled a lodging house in the town that rented rooms to 'blacks' during an unspecified period in the early to mid-twentieth century, whom she remembered as playing organs and dancing on the street: 'they were all over in this big lodging house sleeping on mattresses on the floor and everything'.[77] For the few black people living in Dublin then – generally university students from ex-British colonies – it could be difficult to find lodging houses, and they often had many doors 'closed in their faces'.[78]

Despite the considerable labour involved in having lodgers, it was often viewed as 'non work' because it was done at home (thus a housewife who both took care of her family and her lodgers was likely to say that she was not engaged in work, despite spending much of her time looking after lodgers). For some whose incomes depended on lodgers – largely women – among the advantages of this work was that it often passed under the radar of the tax authorities, at least while it remained at a fairly modest scale. Jim's grandmother ran a lodging house and tea rooms in Sandyford through the 1940s and 1950s, with up to twenty lodgers at a time: 'My grandfather never had to give her any money.' Eventually, in the 1960s, the taxman came. 'You're getting no money off me!' she told him, and closed the business down.

* * *

Travellers' work also occurred largely outside of the formal economy throughout the nineteenth and twentieth centuries, despite state efforts to formalise casual commerce. Whereas before, many Travellers had bought and sold items from and to householders, from 1926, ambulant vendors had to apply for a license to sell goods on the streets, affecting everyone who had previously supplemented their income in this way, including many Travellers and many settled working-class women.[79] While relations between Travellers and settled people deteriorated significantly from the mid-twentieth century, before that Travellers were typically poor, marginalised and with little to no formal education, but accepted as part of society and integrated into local work and labour systems. Men typically offered services like knife sharpening and selling and repairing household goods like pots and pans, while women often solicited alms. Many settled families had ongoing relationships with Travelling families that were seen in broadly positive, if unequal, terms. Terence grew up on a farm in Sandyford in the 1930s and remembered Travellers staying for quite long periods on the nearby Ballyogan Road, a traditional halting area. They were welcomed by local farmers, for whom they provided useful services:

'They would mend buckets and pots... and they would do work as well if you wanted help.' Travellers were also quite welcome in suburban areas until the second half of the twentieth century. Liam remembered a particular man who visited once every fortnight or so, with a special bicycle equipped to sharpen knives and garden tools. Cecilia, who grew up in Shankill in the 1930s and 1940s, recalled a Traveller man who played the fiddle, 'Jimmy the Fiddler'; he performed for the locals – who, presumably, gave him some money in exchange. Rob was growing up in Sallynoggin in the 1960s when Travellers were a frequent local presence as temporary residents in their brightly coloured drays and barrel-top wagons at halting sites and camps on the side of the road, and as door-to-door traders in second-hand clothing and other items, as well as sharpening knives, repairing household objects and giving balloons to the children of the house.

But by the 1960s and 1970s, increasingly Travellers' traditional occupations were becoming obsolete, while hostility towards them was rising. Aidan, a teenager living on a halting site in the Nutgrove area in the 1970s, when many housing estates there were under construction, knew well how difficult it was for most Travellers to find employment. Aidan was a strong young man, not afraid of hard work. Despite considerable discrimination and disadvantage, he was offered labouring work by the boss of a well-known Dublin building firm. His employer paid him fairly and protected his interests when some subcontractors tried to take advantage of him. With the money he earned, Aidan could buy two new trailers for his mother. He would go on to spend most of his working life in the building industry.

* * *

Begging was an unquantifiable but non-negligible element of the local economy throughout the nineteenth and much of the twentieth century, declining (but not disappearing) as social welfare payments became more common and more generous. It was associated with the poorest members of the settled working classes and with Travellers. It was also associated with those with mental illness or physical or mental disability, including many First World War veterans. Specific areas often had particular residents who were well-known beggars. In 1937–8, Neans Ní Loingsigh, a student at St Brigid's in Foxrock, described a well-known local character who begged in Cornelscourt, Cabinteely and Carrickmines, known as 'Daddy Moses' or 'Holy Souls'.[80] In 1980, James Nolan recalled local 'characters' and their nicknames, and how local children sometimes teased them by calling rhymes after them.* When she was a child in Newtown Park in the 1930s and 1940s, Polly's mother had an ongoing relationship with a woman she referred to as 'the decent tinker-woman', who visited every week for a meal, which she ate perched on a step outside Polly's home. 'She was grey-haired,' Polly reminisced, 'brought back in a bun... a black shawl, a white apron and a long skirt, and she was very, very respectful.' Caroline remembered Travellers begging in Sallynoggin when she was growing up in the 1950s: 'you'd be afraid not to give them something in case they put a curse on you... and if you gave them something they'd be grateful and, "I'll say a prayer for you"'. Also growing up in Sallynoggin in the 1940s and 1950s, Harvey knew a man who appeared at around the same time every year. 'We used to call him "Johnny Forty-Coats",' Harvey remembered. 'He had loads of coats on him... every year a certain time he'd arrive at my mother's, and she'd feed him, and he'd sit on the step. Jug of tea and sandwiches and all. She'd give him a few pennies.' Racquelle remembered a man in Dún Laoghaire who appeared to have no legs, and who begged around the town in the 1950s and 1960s: 'He had a board with wheels, and he just scooted around Patrick Street.'

While begging was relatively common among the very poor working classes and Travellers for many years, by the 1960s, begging among settled people had become much rarer, there was more financial provision for people with long-term health issues that prevented them from working, and it was increasingly associated with Travellers alone, contributing to their growing marginalisation, as they moved through a period of

---

* For example, from Dundrum: 'Old Daddy Aiken / Stole a piece of bacon / he put it up his overcoat / in case it would be taken.' NFC UFP, 1980, 30.

profound economic and cultural crisis.[81] Mick remembered begging in Dalkey with his mother as a child in the 1970s: 'she had to make sure that the family was looked after. And there was always food on the table and clothes on their back.' Over time, she and her children got to know the local families who were inclined to help. 'Christmas used to be a beautiful time,' Mick remembered, when the family begged around areas such as Blackrock and Booterstown; 'because it was the Christmas time… you were brought into some of the houses and… you were given a little treat… made you that little bit more special'.

* * *

In early independence, Ireland scrambled to industrialise, as it was significantly behind other western European nations in this respect. Still, despite being more 'traditional' than many other countries, new technologies and industries were coming into play. From the 1930s, creative and journalistic professionals, including considerable numbers of highly educated Irish-speakers, found a home in Irish radio. From 1961, Irish television broadcasting was another relatively significant employer, with many producers, directors, presenters and technical and support staff living in Dún Laoghaire-Rathdown. In the very early days, there were not enough experienced television professionals in Dublin, and personnel like Margot were recruited from the BBC. Margot remembered the very idea of Irish television programming not being taken very seriously in England: 'the sort of lackadaisical Irish… there was a joke going round the BBC that, "Oh, the presenters who will be seen on the television announcing the programmes are going to be nuns".' In fact, among the most recognisable presenters, from 1965, was local woman Marguerite, who started working for RTÉ as a presenter when she was still in her teens. Initially taken aback with her sudden celebrity status, she would have a long career there.

The first transatlantic flight landed in Roundstone, County Galway, in 1919, marking the start of Ireland's aviation history. Rosie's mother, who grew up in Dalkey in the 1920s, related the story of when she and her siblings saw a plane flying overhead for the first time. Excitedly, they fetched a wheelbarrow to collect it from the beach where they thought it had landed, as it had looked so small in the sky. On the fringes of Europe, Ireland was in a strategic position for the development of the industry, and a useful stopping-off point for refuelling; the first commercial passenger flight on a direct route between the United States and Europe landed at Foynes in 1939,[82] three years after the registration of Aer Lingus as an airline. Aer Lingus, founded in 1936, was increasingly an employer of young people with more formal education than their parents. By the 1950s, air travel was more common, but the sight of a plane overhead was still exciting enough for people to stop work or go into the garden to watch it. Bella, who grew up in Sandyford, was among many well-educated young women who interviewed for a position as an air hostess in the 1960s. For women employees, being considered pretty, as well as having a good education, was a prerequisite. During her second interview, Bella was asked how she would feel if one of her siblings married a 'coloured person' – presumably to assess how comfortable she would be providing customer service to travellers from diverse backgrounds. After three years on the Atlantic route, Bella married and had to give up her work, as Aer Lingus did not employ married women, although they would take her back on a more casual, part-time basis. Sarah-Jane, from Dún Laoghaire, worked as an air hostess in the 1970s, a time she remembered fondly: 'we were treated much better than the girls are now'.

As Ireland became wealthier, the banking and finance sectors became progressively more important, and as Irish people became more educated, they also became more accessible to educated people from a wider range of backgrounds. Larry was originally from rural Meath and was among the first in his family to complete a second-level education, after which he went to England for work. By the 1980s, having had a successful finance career in London, he was living in Cabinteely and working in banking. By the time he had reached a senior level, the staff increasingly included women who wanted to work on a par with male colleagues, rather than just in support roles. There was still some resistance to this in the 1980s, but Larry liked managing women employees because, he said, they tended to be 'more disciplined' and 'better judges of people'. 'It's just… genetic,' he explained, 'women are the procreators of the race. They have to be able to pick the right people.'

Lily's husband, who worked for Guinness at a senior level, was sent to England to study computers and learn how information technology could be applied to the brewing industry. It was an exciting time for the technologically minded, as growing numbers of businesses and state bodies were starting to see how information technology could be used in the workplace. Emer got her start in the computer industry as a punch-card operator for CIÉ in the late 1960s, feeding information into an IBM 360. From there, she worked as a developer providing technical support to customers beginning to integrate computers into their workplaces. She would spend all her working life in information technology. Having grown up with brothers, she says, Emer was happy to work in an environment dominated by men. Moreover, the company was generous in offering her flexible hours when she had children. There was no statutory maternity leave then, so she had to leave work, but when she was ready to return, 'I would just ring… and say, "OK, I'm ready to come back now."' The industry was quite stratified at the time, with women dominating the lower and men the higher levels, but Emer was paid on a par with her male colleagues and treated with equal respect, indicative of a growing need for employees with IT skills.

During the latter decades of the twentieth century, in parallel with growing numbers of women engaged in paid work outside the home and the dramatic decline in the numbers of women in full-time, live-in domestic service positions, there was a growth in the provision of child-care outside the home in the form of crèches and day-care centres, of women with Montessori or other training in childcare, and modest growth in the amount of domestic work undertaken by men. In the early 1960s, with a demanding job at RTÉ, Margot was one of a grow-ing cohort of university-educated women who wanted demanding careers but struggled to deal with childcare. She tried to arrange a sort of cooperative with other mothers in Monkstown ('You take all eight of the children today, and I'll take them tomorrow') but it floundered. Ultimately, she worked part-time, and cobbled together childcare with the help of au pairs. The feeling that paid childcare was bad for children, or that it reflected badly on mothers, was persistent in the 1960s and 1970s. While many mothers were happy to be based at home, or to work part-time outside the home, those who wished to pursue a career could feel judged and ashamed for needing childcare. Sometimes their husbands said they did not want their children to attend a crèche or kindergarten, that it was the mother's responsibility to provide arrangements if they wanted to work outside the home, and that they did not feel they should be expected to participate in what they viewed as women's work.

Nonetheless, while women tended to remain primarily or solely responsible for domestic work in the home, the numbers of women also working outside the home grew steadily throughout the latter decades of the twentieth century, increasing from 8 per cent in 1971 to 17.4 per cent in 1981,[83] as the marriage bar was repealed, as the standard of women's education grew and as social mores shifted. By the end of the 1980s and into the 1990s, it was increasingly the norm for families, especially middle-class and wealthy families, to be dual income. More than half of the women in Larry's Cabinteely housing estate, he estimated, were engaged in paid work outside the home by the mid-1980s. The trend for married women to work outside the home continued to grow, and by the 1990s, the childcare sector was a significant employer.

* * *

Countless emigrants started their journey to England, and often from there to the rest of the world, from Dún Laoghaire. In the early twentieth century, emigrants typically were less skilled – often strong young men looking for labouring jobs on building sites and young women going into domestic service. Many of those who went further afield, most frequently the United States, were rarely, if ever, seen again, but their presence was felt in the form of the packages sent to their families at home. Rosie remembered that her family, and many others, received packages of clothing from relatives in America. At Mass on Sunday, those who had just got clothes from America smelled strongly of the camphor mothballs they had been packed with.

The Second World War and the period following offered work opportunities overseas to many men. Nicky's father – whose building business had failed to thrive because of the conflict – found work in aeroplane manufacture in Belfast and England. His memories of that time have remained keen for Nicky, who wrote a poem about his feelings then, as a little boy of six or seven in Stillorgan: 'How I hate the sleepless restless nights in that dank and dusty room / Wallpaper with damp mildew patches, home for apparitions / Beating my face into the pillow, asking Mathew, Mark, Luke and John / To keep my Daddy safe in that aircraft factory in Derbyshire, in England'.

After the war, there was still plenty of work in Britain for strong Irishmen, as the damaged cities were rebuilt. The 1946 census returns for Dún Laoghaire show that 7,340 married women but only 6,474 married men were present that night, hinting that many men may have been working overseas.[84] Many – including several of Graham's uncles, and later Graham himself – travelled to Coventry and worked in the rebuilding of the city, which had been almost completely destroyed by German bombers. It was easy for any young man prepared to work hard to pick up this work. 'Even on the boat,' Graham remembered, 'there were agents… "Where are you going?" "Coventry". "You want a job?" [They were] giving out jobs.' Feargal remembered that it seemed like half of Shankill was emigrating in the 1950s, to Coventry or elsewhere. 'It was the hungry 1950s,' he remarked. Some stayed in England and built lives there, and others returned with enough money to give themselves a start in life. At that time rates of emigration and migration were extremely high – in 1955 alone, about 50,000 Irish citizens emigrated.[85]

Passengers on the mailboat. Lexicon Library Postcard Collection.

The comings and goings of the Dún Laoghaire mailboat were a constant reminder of these sad and hopeful journeys. 'I used to always find [the departure of the mailboat] was very momentous,' remembered Nora, 'emotional, too… seeing it gradually gliding out, and there'd be people waving, waving, waving… and watching it going.' Remembered Niamh: 'The Carlisle Pier [in Dún Laoghaire] is where over a million men, women and children left this country… they were just like the wind, blowing away.' 'I'll never forget,' said Terry, speaking of the emigrants from the west, on their way through 1950s Dún Laoghaire: 'they were in their tweeds and the *crios* belts, and the suitcase with the strap around the middle… Oh Jesus, it was very forlorn, and then come the boat-time, little by little, the pub would empty.' Sandra remembered: 'it was sad to watch men and young boys going off. And the men were normally in suits. And they didn't even have a suitcase. Their stuff was wrapped in brown paper and tied with twine.' Another interviewee remembered being brought down to the pier for a walk in the evenings: 'and we used to see people crying [at the mailboat] and we'd say to [Mammy], "Why are they crying?" and she'd say "Well, maybe they don't feel they'll get back.'"

Many emigrants sent money back home to family members: 'Everybody did,' said Harvey, who spent years living in England. 'What you could afford, you know, because you had to live as well… Post office-registered… fold it up nice and new.' Some emigrants ultimately returned and settled in Ireland and many families worked hard to maintain a link with loved ones overseas, whether permanently or temporarily. Sandra remembered her mother sending freshly slaughtered, cleaned turkeys, carefully wrapped in sacking, to siblings in England. When there was enough money, a bottle of Paddy's whiskey might be pushed inside the turkey, too. But with time, many emigrants lost all contact with their families. Maria remembered what she had heard of a great-uncle who emigrated in the early twentieth century: '[at] sixteen, he went to sea. And my grandmother used to write to him care of the Seamen's Mission in San Francisco… she corresponded with him for years and years and years, and then suddenly it stopped.'

For Irish people from the poorest-off parts of the country, Dún Laoghaire-Rathdown itself could be both a place to migrate to in its own right, and a halting spot on their way to a greater migration overseas. These movements were often facilitated by family members and friends who had already migrated to the east coast. Sarah-Jane's mother was originally from Kerry – she had moved to Dalkey to work in domestic service – and Sarah-Jane remembered her childhood home as 'a halfway house' filled with relatives from Kerry, many on their way to new lives overseas, and others hoping to get good jobs for the council. Mairéad recalled that 'our house became one of those… where you stayed for the night and then you walked… down to the mailboat. And I often saw people just literally waving from the top of the mailboat.' It was a melancholy sight, she remembered, 'and you'd hear the boat going off, you know, and that was it and people just walked back up home'. Sally, growing up in Mount Merrion, remembered how her family frequently accommodated young-sters from her mother's native Kerry, in the 1940s and 1950s, on the eve of their departure: 'Poor people who would be going to the States, and their clothes would be in a brown box tied up with string. And these kids would have to have an X-ray before they went... They were only about 14 or 15.' Joseph, growing up in Glencullen in the 1940s and 1950s, a time of dreadful poverty there, remembered 'walking down the field and I'd be looking at the auld mailboat going out [in the distance], wishing I'd be old enough to go on it. Because there was no money, you'd no nothing, you know?'

Seasonal economic migration and temporary emigration were also an important feature of life. Many young people enjoyed going overseas – often to England – for a few years, or travelling over and back for seasonal work. Many developed skills they used on their return, like Eddie, a scaffold builder on the building sites in London in the early 1960s, who put his skills to good use in Dún Laoghaire-Rathdown as the area saw extraordinary levels of development in the 1960s and 1970s and beyond. Edward emigrated from Glasthule to Liverpool, where he had relatives, in 1958. He remained 'eternally grateful' for the plumbing skills he learned in England. When he returned in the mid-1960s, the building industry was very active, and men like him were in demand. Liz's father relied on periodic episodes of work in Britain in the 1950s. He found it almost impossible to find work at home, but in England and Wales he did short contracts for a building company, McAlpine's. While he was away, the family waited, 'with bated breath' for the 'wire' to come in its little green envelope. Philo's boyfriend was a builder, and there was no work in Ireland in 1957, so he and Philo's brother went to England together. He missed Philo so much that she decided to go too. 'And my mother said,' Philo recalled, '"Well, all I can say, Phil, is come home the way you went,"' by which she meant that Philo should not get pregnant.

As educational standards steadily rose from the mid-twentieth century, increasingly emigrants were leaving to assume skilled positions in London and elsewhere and, often, returning with experience to take up good jobs in Irish professions and the civil service. In the 1970s and 1980s, many found homes in the new middle-class developments increasingly occupying the swathe of what had once been farmland between the settled coastal area and the Dublin/Wicklow Mountains.

* * *

Despite considerable local wealth, high rates of poverty, before and after independence, made various forms of philanthropy and money-lending crucial elements of the economy, including support from charitable and philanthropic organisations such as St Vincent de Paul and the St John Ambulance Brigade, and diverse privately run organisations. Local ventures included shoe clubs providing needy families with a way to save for their children's shoes and purchase them affordably, and systems to help poor families get respectable clothing and other essentials for living. In Glasthule, for example, Howard remembered that, in the 1950s, many families relied on the Vincent de Paul during difficult periods. Comfortably off local women who wanted to help also established a system whereby good-quality clothes were donated for and distributed to families in need. But although poverty was common, considerable stigma could also be attached to needing help, and needy families often avoided asking for it until a difficult situation had become a crisis: 'you'd be watching,' commented Gerry, speaking of his grandmother's life as a widow, 'what the neighbours would say or look or think... you'd be afraid to be honest about your own poverty, so you'd put a good face on it'. 'There were many stories,' added Francis, 'about what people used to do... for the sake of keeping up appearances... The mother would come to the door to call in the son for his tea, and she'd say, "Come in for your tea, toast and two eggs". In other words, "We can afford two eggs for you".' 'It was a real disgrace if you had to go for that kind of help,' Caroline said. 'It was the lowest of the low... you done anything rather than go on social. That was just a no-go in our family. The shame of it.'

But when things were really bad, sometimes there was no other option. Graham remembered his mother relying heavily on coupons that could be exchanged for food while his father was unable to work. There was, he said, almost enough to eat. As a young adult, he was invited to eat at a friend's home. On being told, 'I'm afraid there's nothing but leftovers,' he said, 'What's that?' Nothing had ever been left over in his family home, as there had never been enough. Nicky's family experienced a difficult period when his father was sick with tuberculosis, still a dreadful scourge in the 1950s. They relied on the Vincent de Paul ('every week there was a pound of butter, a half dozen eggs and... a docket to get milk.') Although they were extremely grateful, it was also mortifying: 'the embarrassment of seeing these men in suits, everyone knew who they were... The embarrassment of them coming to the house.'

By the mid-twentieth century, with a growing middle class, and more secure pension arrangements for many, reasonably comfortably off retirees, often from the public sector, had the skills, time and availability to become involved in organisations like the Dún Laoghaire Borough Old Folks' Association, providing services such as meals on wheels and opportunities for older people to socialise and attend adult education courses, and so forth. Active retirees from the civil service (like Simon, who volunteered for this group) and their wives were often the backbone of these local volunteer organisations. They could retire earlier than many others, and often had useful management skills to apply in the voluntary sector.

Historically, many charities were associated with denominational groups, both Catholic and Protestant. Well-placed businessmen often served on a range of committees with philanthropic aims, while wealthy women, who could afford domestic staff to run their households and help raise their children, often put their education to use in unpaid managerial and administrative positions in charities, philanthropies and women's organisations. Lily, who married in the 1960s, cites, as a major reason why she became involved in philanthropy and fundraising, the fact that she had to give up work. Andrew's mother worked tirelessly to raise funds for Protestant children's homes such as the Bird's Nest in Dún Laoghaire, and was involved in the Infant Clothing Fund for the Rotunda Maternity Hospital in the city centre, which made basic clothing for the new babies of needy mothers. Nicola remembered that, in the

1950s, the Bullock Boat Owners' Association in Dalkey held an annual event for children from the Bird's Nest, providing them with boat trips, a 'slap-up tea' and a singsong. Many of these organisations did wonderful work in various ways, but the religious aspect was not always welcome, particularly in the case of evangelical Protestant charities. In independent Ireland, anxiety about proselytism (the Church of Ireland and other denominations had a long history of combining social activism with evangelism, and in this area, with its large Protestant population and several institutions with an evangelical ethos, this was quite a reasonable concern) prompted Church and other authority figures to strive to ensure that Catholics in need were catered to by Catholic charitable and philanthropic organisations, leaving Protestant charities to cater for their own. In 1929, the Catholic Protection and Rescue Society, which intervened to return pregnant Irish girls to Ireland from Britain, among other things, warned of 'soul snatchers' who 'prowled' around hospitals, capturing 'large numbers of Catholic children' with the aim of teaching them to 'hate and revile the Catholic religion'.[86] At the same time, the Catholic Church, and therefore the state, was reluctant for the public sector to intervene heavily in social activism, lest this make it easier for socialism or, worse, communism, to get a foothold in Ireland.

* * *

From 1908, the Old Age Pensions Act 1908 introduced a non-contributory pension for 'eligible' people aged seventy and over, coming into law in January 1909. A means test was applied, and applicants could be rejected if they were not 'of good character'. They had to provide proof of age in the form of a document such as a certificate of birth or of baptism, while not already being in receipt of any poor relief.[87] By 1911, 68 per cent of all Irish people aged over seventy were in receipt of the pension,[88] which excluded 'habitual drunkards, convicts, malingerers, and pauper lunatics'.[89] 'It was not the intention of the legislature,' a guide to the new law pontificated, 'that loafers and n'er-do-weels [*sic*] should receive the benefit of this new Act.'[90] Because poverty was higher in Ireland than elsewhere in the United Kingdom, and because of higher levels of fraud, the relative proportion of applicants was higher than anticipated. Some applicants appeared not to need such financial support; in Kingstown – one of the fourteen urban districts deemed qualified to appoint a local pension committee[91] – one elderly lady initially refused to queue for the pension alongside others whom she considered her social inferiors. While the pension was an improvement in social welfare – the numbers resorting to the workhouse, although they remained high, dropped by 17.5 percent between the 1901 and the 1911 census[92] – many still lived in extremely straitened circumstances. For those engaged in very heavy physical work, like domestic service or building, seventy was also quite an advanced age to reach with no pension assistance.

Various measures to expand social welfare were gradually introduced post-independence. The widows' and orphans' pensions scheme was introduced in 1935, providing for contributory and non-contributory pensions.[93] In 1944, the Children's Allowance Bill was passed to provide financial assistance to families with at least three children. The allowance, very small initially, was paid to fathers at first, and to mothers from 1974.[94] The Traveller community, previously excluded from claiming unemployment insurance, could do so from 1967,[95] at a time when the community was reeling from the rapid loss of their traditional means of livelihood. The Social Welfare Act was passed in 1975, providing a legal right for assistance in case of need for the first time, heralding the start of an era in which social assistance would be viewed from a rights-based perspective.[96]

* * *

For families on limited incomes, working in a largely cash economy, credit was rarely available, and formal and informal modes of moneylending helped people through difficult times, or provided ready funds for special occasions. McManus's operated as a successful pawnbroking business in

Dún Laoghaire until the late twentieth century, when it became easier to obtain credit from banks and credit unions.[97] Many have clear memories of family possessions – often Dad's formal suit – being pawned regularly when the family was short of cash. Denny remembered his mother talking about her own childhood in the 1920s: 'every Monday morning, my grandfather's suit would be pawned. And on Friday evening, it'd be taken out of the pawn shop.' Moneylending was also available. If people didn't have money to give the moneylender, remembered Clodagh, they hid when he came around. She recalled an episode when one Blackrock family was said to have pretended that their grandmother had died and even showed the moneylender her body 'laid out' for viewing. The next time he came, the same woman answered the door.

The credit union movement in Ireland was preceded in some areas by local Tontine Societies,* like that founded in Sandyford by Elinor's father in the mid-twentieth century. Tontines offer a sort of life insurance whereby each subscriber pays into a trust and receives a periodical payment, with capital reverting to the scheme as each subscriber dies. Elinor remembered that, 'every Sunday, the locals would come, and [Dad] had these big ledgers, and you'd pay a shilling… and then, if anybody died, [they] were buried [with collective funds]. And if there was money left over at the end of the year, it was done… a divvy was given out to everybody.' Another Tontine Society operated in Dún Laoghaire, where it was known as the 'Pig [short for 'piggy'] Bank'.

The Irish credit union movement began in the 1950s. The first credit unions were formed at Donore Avenue in Dublin and in Dún Laoghaire in 1958, and in 1960 the Credit Union League of Ireland was established to encourage the movement's growth. The number of branches grew rapidly throughout the 1960s, and by 1984 there were 389 credit unions in Ireland, with over half a million members. While they provided similar services to banks, they also had more expansive social objectives,

---

* This type of investment plan is named after the Neapolitan banker Lorenzo de Tonti, who is said to have invented it in France in 1653, although he may just have modified existing Italian investment schemes. Jennings and Trout, 1988, 107.

including supporting education and community development, and providing a more welcoming environment to women members and employees.[98] Catherine, who served on the committee for over twenty years, remembered how the Dún Laoghaire Credit Union helped families on modest incomes: 'It was a very necessary service… Once Christmas was over, it'd be Confirmations. Then it'd be First Communions. And then it might be holidays, and then it might be back to school. And then Christmas.'

* * *

Until the advent of modern supermarkets from the late 1960s/early 1970s, many families used their gardens to grow vegetables to consume at home. Wealthier families often had a gardener to help, while families on lower incomes used their gardens to supplement the family diet. The poorest families often had no outdoor space at all, and often struggled to eat adequate quantities of fruit and vegetables.

Lina's parents had both grown up in the countryside in the early Free State, and when they moved into a new council house in Monkstown Farm in about 1941, they used their garden to grow fresh fruits and vegetables. 'My father grew everything,' Lina remembered, 'gooseberries, loganberries, potatoes… cauliflower… Brussels sprouts for Christmas, carrots, onions, lettuce.' The family's healthy diet was supplemented by rabbits and eggs sent in the post by Lina's aunt in the countryside.

Until the mid-twentieth century and even beyond, those in rural areas and suburbanites on low incomes frequently supplemented their diet and/or their incomes with wild rabbits.* The nature of development, initially primarily along the coast or centred around small villages and

---

* Whereas most local hunting was for rabbits, for consumption at home or for sale, game hunting of other species not considered edible, like badgers and foxes, was also known. Jacinta's grandfather, a kind man and a veteran of the Boer War, hunted badgers in Kilternan for his hobby of taxidermy, and lovingly presented her, as a small, sick child, with a stuffed and mounted badger to cheer her up. While somewhat bemused by the unusual gift, Jacinta appreciated it in the spirit in which it was meant.

Pat and Jimmy Howe and Sunny Clare on their way to their allotment in the Dublin/ Wicklow Mountains in the 1940s. Kind permission of Jimmy Howe Jr.

towns, meant that locals had easy access not only to the countryside, but also to rural knowledge and skills, including knowing how to set a rabbit snare, how to go hunting with lamps and so on. Rural migrants to the area arrived with the skills they had learned in the countryside, and could apply them in their new environment. Writing in 2006, Seánie Wallace recalled of his childhood that he and his father hunted for rabbits with ferrets. They brought the rabbits home both alive and dead, selling the live ones to greyhound owners for training the dogs, and making the dead ones into stew.[99] Terence, growing up in Sandyford in the 1930s, often enjoyed eating the rabbits hunted by his uncle with his little terrier and his ferret (the ferret a friendly animal doubling as a pet, resting cosily inside little Terence's shirt). Hunters used ferrets in the Kilternan area in the 1920s and 1930s, Pádraic remembered: 'they'd got a little bell on them. When you'd put them into the hole in the wall… you'd hear the bell ringing.'

The ferret chased the rabbit from its hole, and the hunter's dog would swiftly kill it. One Glencullen man, Brian recalled, managed to make a living hunting rabbits and selling them in Dublin. Joseph remembered a Glencullen man who hunted for rabbits after the early Mass on Sundays; to save time, the ferret accompanied him to Mass and the bell around the animal's neck could be heard tinkling throughout the proceedings. Also in the Kilternan area, Gene's father, a local farmer, hunted rabbits during the Emergency – catching up to sixty at a time – and sold them at markets in the city centre. Feargal and his brothers hunted rabbits with their dogs and sold them locally, particularly to large families for whom rabbit meat was more affordable than what was at the butcher's. Dishes like rabbit stew were widely eaten by families that could otherwise not afford to eat meat or other proteins very often. Pádraic's mother made delicious roast rabbit, and he also remembered a man who supplied hospitals with food coming to Kilternan to buy rabbits for the patients, many of whom suffered from malnourishment. Farmers and other landowners harboured mixed feelings towards rabbit hunters on their land. Any reduction in the numbers of rabbits was welcome, as they could cause terrible damage, but the noise of the hunters, and the damage caused to stone walls when ferrets got stuck and had to be dug out, were trying.

The widespread hunting and consumption of rabbits ended when myxomatosis was introduced to Ireland. The man responsible, Pádraic said, 'should be shot!' for taking away 'the poor man's dinner'.* 'I wouldn't touch a rabbit now, not since the myxomatosis,' said Lina, who relished rabbit stews when she was growing up in the 1940s and 1950s. Rabbits were so abundant in rural Ireland, however, that many farmers were happy that their population could be controlled with myxomatosis. For several decades, the vast and sudden reduction in the number of rabbits

---

* The French scientist (Paul-Félix Armand-Delille) responsible for introducing myxomatosis to Europe, claimed Pádraic, subsequently 'went mad', perhaps, he suggested, a divine punishment for meddling with nature and destroying the 'poor man's dinner'. See Kerr et al. for a discussion of Armand-Delille and his introduction of the disease. Armand-Delille died aged eighty-nine in 1963, having been both excoriated and praised for eradicating most of the rabbits of western Europe.

had a deleterious effect on the diets of the poorest people in rural areas, and in urban or suburban areas with access to open spaces, including Travellers, for whom this became one more incentive among many then to migrate towards urban areas.[100] By the late 1970s and 1980s, the rabbit population had partly recovered, and although many families had completely ceased hunting for and consuming rabbits, there were exceptions. Sinéad's father came home to Blackrock with a rabbit that someone had given him at work once a month or so, and the family would enjoy rabbit stew. Mick from Dalkey remembered numerous trips to Killiney Hill late at night in the 1970s and 1980s to catch rabbits. He was not himself a keen hunter ('What... the eff are we doing in the field... looking for a *rabbit*? I'm freezing.') but the resulting stews were delicious.

Unsurprisingly, given the extent of the coastline, fishing is traditionally, and has remained, popular. Although some families fished at least partly from need, families in all sorts of socioeconomic circumstances engaged in fishing as a leisure activity and a source of food. Families in coastal areas like Booterstown had access to a wide variety of fish, if they had the patience and time to spend catching them: 'salmon, bass,' remembered Gerry, 'plaice, turbot, some dogfish, a small shark once'. They threw out the ones they didn't want, and – surrounded by avaricious, clamouring seagulls – gutted and cleaned the rest in the water. Back at the house, there was 'an orgy of cooking... the neighbours would come together... four or five frying pans on the go, fish, fish, fish frying away.' Flatfish could be caught at low tide in rockpools using an interesting technique, remembered Conor, who said that fishermen used long poles topped with 'a sharpened piece of clothes hanger'. They placed the spike between their toes and walked through the pools, 'stabbing dabs, flounders, plaice'. Using this technique, they could catch up to thirty flatfish. Kate's father fished for mackerel when she was growing up in the 1950s, and brought home 'buckets' of fish for his wife to pot – quickly, because mackerel goes rancid and there was no refrigeration. She cooked them in vinegar with an onion and bottled them to keep. The result was delicious ('you'd lick your ears after them'). Janet, also a child of the 1950s, remembered fishing for mackerel from Dún Laoghaire's West Pier, near a large black shed where the fishermen hung their nets. They ate huge amounts of fish, then considered the 'poor man's dinner' by those in her community, who ate a lot of it, fresh in season and pickled (with a bay leaf for flavour in Ann's house) in the winter. Children in the coastal areas could earn a little money by catching crabs and selling them to local establishments. Winston remembered, 'we would go down there at low tide… You learnt how to keep your hands safe… and pull the crabs out… and we would bring those up to the hotels… It could be a fresh crab on the menu.'

Those living in areas with easy access to countryside and parks often engaged in foraging for wild fruits like blackberries. Blackberry picking was even a community activity in some areas. Marty, from Shankill, remembered the annual blackberry picking as a 'real community get-together', and 'ritualistic… like the May procession'. Other forms of foraging included gathering mushrooms in grassy areas; Pat O'Neill recalled collecting mushrooms in the area now covered by Clonkeen Road: 'we'd bring them home on a string and have them cooked for breakfast'.[101] Some families in the uplands supplemented their incomes by selling foraged *fraughans* to English buyers (who knew them as 'bilberries'). The berries were taken away on the mailboat, apparently for use as 'vitamins' in England.

'Orchard robbing' (sometimes known as 'boxing the foxes'[102]) was common, with private orchards widely considered fair game and, as discussed in 'Who's Who', a forum where social tensions could be expressed. Much less frequently, domestic animals were stolen from landowners and slaughtered for consumption. It was relatively easy to steal a hen, which could be quickly killed and hidden under a coat, but larger animals were occasionally taken. Robbie's mother related a story of a local man who stole a sheep from a local convent's land, slaughtered it and dispensed the meat to friends and neighbours in a working-class neighbourhood where lamb was often too expensive to buy.

Generally, a family's socioeconomic status determined their diet. In an area where vast amounts of pork was consumed, the bodies of the slaughtered pigs were divvied up according to the consumers' social class, with the 'worst', cheapest parts consumed by the working classes. As Nicky remembered: 'we used to eat an awful lot of offal. That was the cheapest food, the pig's head, the pig's feet, tripe.' Sandra, growing up in Dún Laoghaire in the mid-century, was often sent with her friend to the slaughterhouse where her friend's uncle worked. The little girls would return home with a bucket full of sweetbreads (the internal parts of cattle or sheep, typically the thymus and the pancreas) for their mothers to cook for the family.

Many rural residents with lower incomes were still cooking in the old-school way, in or over an open fire, perhaps with a cast-iron crane, until into the 1950s and early 1960s. Doreen remembered older people in the Glencullen area making bread the traditional way in a pot in the embers of the fire in around the 1940s: 'a lid on top of the pot and they would put maybe bits of coal or bits of heat on the top of that as well'.

The wealthier classes of the nineteenth and early twentieth centuries had long enjoyed access to not just locally produced foods but also a wide range of luxury imported items, available in businesses like Findlater's, including exotic foods such as *foie gras*, olives and so on.[103] Lily's father, from a noted grocery retail family, was sent to France in the 1920s to study wine; clearly there was local demand not just for wine but for knowledgeable vendors. Other factors also broadened the palate of the locals, notably the presence of Italian immigrants, who predominantly worked in the food industry, operating cafés, ice cream parlours and fish-and-chip shops. Hugh Leonard spoke fondly of Dún Laoghaire's 'Roman Café' and its owners serving the locals in broken English.[104] Sam Blackmore, recorded in 1980, recalled an Italian man selling ice cream at Dún Laoghaire's seafront, and another selling fish and chips.[105]

From the 1960s onwards, local eating habits started to change dramatically. A decline in absolute poverty, supermarkets and higher levels of education and foreign travel contributed to a more varied, adventurous and gastronomically sophisticated approach to food as the first part of the twentieth century gave way to the second. As the numbers

Shopping in Dún Laoghaire as viewed from the roof of the Dún Laoghaire Shopping Centre in the early 1980s. From the late 1960s onwards, large supermarkets and shopping centres posed an existential threat to smaller, more traditional retail outlets, and would dramatically change shopping habits and the urban and suburban landscapes. Kind permission of Michael McCarthy.

of women in full-time paid work rose, convenience foods became more attractive to busy working families and, as incomes and foreign travel also rose, a varied menu gradually became the norm. Eating out became more common, with being seen in fashionable restaurants important to the well-off and those who aspired to be, while off licences responded to the growing demand for wine – by 1977, McGowan's of Blackrock stocked 1,000 labels, including luxury brands.[106]

* * *

Learning how to work, working, resting after working, getting ready to work again – it sounds exhausting, but this is how most of us spend most of our lives, whether the work we do is paid or unpaid, and whether it is experienced as a joy or as a source of stress, or indeed both. For many, the work they do is not just an essential means of making a living but also of feeding themselves and their families, an important source of identity, self-esteem and a sense of purpose. It intersects in many fascinating ways with every other aspect of life too, including individual and collective relationships with concepts of divinity, and with religious and civic authorities alike.

EARTH AND HEAVEN

Dún Laoghaire-Rathdown has historically been one of the most denominationally diverse areas of Ireland. Religion and faith, in all their aspects, have played a fundamental role in the area's evolution before and within independent Ireland. Religious architecture and sacred spaces, ancient and modern, are an important element of the built landscape and of local psychogeography. In early modern and modern history, ethno-religious differences have marked every aspect of life, from industry and commerce to recreation.

Throughout prehistory, local inhabitants left their mark on the landscape in the form of the many dolmens, tombs and other sites associated with ritual. We can only guess at the specific details of their thoughts and rites regarding the spiritual realm, but clearly religious behaviour here dates to antiquity. From the early Christian period we start to find Christian architecture and artefacts. The area is remarkably rich in ecclesiastical sites from the middle ages, at least some of which have also been loci of ritual behaviour in both folk and formal religious practice throughout the centuries.

As elsewhere, Catholicism has historically been the majority religion and has been enormously influential in many ways. Since the seventeenth century, however, Dún Laoghaire-Rathdown was notably a place where the Church of Ireland, with its favoured position under British rule, had a substantial presence. Writing in 1907, a time of great nationalist fervour, N. Donnelly stated that, under the reign of Queen

Elizabeth I, and subsequently until the repeal of the Penal Laws and the advent of Catholic triumphalism, the area was marked 'with the blood of martyrs, the sighs and groans of innumerable confessors, and by its sweeping confiscations, destructive of all Catholic landmarks'.[1] The Church of Ireland remains an important part of the local religious landscape. Other Protestant faiths are also well-represented. From 1828, Kingstown had a Presbyterian church – the engineers supervising the harbour works were Scottish Presbyterians – and from 1836 there was also a Methodist congregation. The Quaker community, largely descended from farmers and tradespeople who settled in Ireland from the seventeenth century, now included prosperous business families. Like other well-to-do Dubliners of the nineteenth century, many moved from the inner city to south Dublin. By the 1830s, the Quaker community was big enough to warrant a local Meeting House; from 1832, they had a permanent Meeting House in Monkstown and from 1860, a burial ground at Temple Hill, Blackrock.[2]

From the mid-nineteenth century, the Catholic Church – gaining strength since the repeal of the Penal Laws, amid growing affluent Catholic middle classes – was increasingly wealthy and influential, and many fine church buildings were erected. The Sacred Heart Sisters, a French order, purchased Mount Anville in 1865, and many other Big Houses were acquired as the nineteenth century marched on. For example, Stillorgan Castle, Riversdale and Obelisk Park were all purchased by the St John of God Brothers, a French order established in Ireland from the 1870s.[3] There were so many religious orders locally that South Dublin was sometimes jocularly known as 'the Holy Land'. Many were largely self-sufficient, using their ample grounds as farms. By the late nineteenth century, the Catholic Church was in a strong position, with vocations higher than ever, and religious orders located here were continuing to purchase stately homes for use as religious houses, schools, hospitals and other institutions. Dublin at the time was effectively encircled by large estates and villas that could be purchased relatively cheaply, as the economy was stagnant. 'They suited institutional use,'

Whelan points out, 'once you could endure or impose a high toler-ance for cold and draughts'.[4] Given the many links between political nationalism and Catholicism in Ireland in this era, it must have been satisfying for many to see religious orders occupying homes that had been such powerful symbols of the Protestant ascendancy.

Catholicism gained further influence when the 1932 Eucharistic Congress was held in Dublin – the biggest yet, since the first in Lille, France, in 1881[5] – officially to mark the 1,500th anniversary of the mis-sionary activities of St Patrick, Ireland's patron saint, while the Free State was immersed in nation building. For the Catholic majority, this was a thrilling recognition of Ireland's place in the world as a Catholic society, an astounding counterpoint to the final visit of Queen Victoria just thirty-two years before, and a way to underline how the Irish, who had suffered so terribly, were part of a huge, important, international faith community.[6] For the government, the religious authorities, and the citizens of an emerging nation, the Congress seemed to be a vote of confidence in the very idea of independent, Catholic Ireland.

For Dún Laoghaire, where the Papal Legate, Cardinal Lorenzo Lauri, first stepped onto Irish soil, the Congress was amazing: an affirmation of Irishness in Ireland's most 'British' area, a jubilant expression of piety and, perhaps for some, a pointed display of faith and unity in an area with a large, well-to-do, influential Protestant minority. The arrival of the Papal Nuncio occurred in the only electoral district to have returned unionist TDs after the first election in newly independent Ireland. The Organising Committee urged the Irish to give the Congress their all: 'it is for us to see that we make it possible for the historian to record a Congress not less devout and prayerful; not less worthy than any of the Congresses which have already taken place'.*

The weather was beautiful in the summer of 1932, and the atmosphere in Dún Laoghaire was riotously joyful on 22 June when Lauri and the

---

* The Organising Committee of the 31st Eucharistic Congress, Dublin 1932, 1. The com-mercially produced pilgrim's guide struck a more optimistic note, stating that 'Now Dublin! All Ireland is in readiness to make this, the thirty-first Eucharistic Congress, the most inspiring of all.' *The Pilgrim's Guide to the Eucharistic Congress*, 1932.

31st International Eucharistic Congress: People on board ship and on the quayside, Dún Laoghaire. The Independent Newspapers (Ireland) Collection, National Library of Ireland.

papal entourage, including bishops and other senior Church figures from all over the world, arrived on the SS *Cumbria* with incredible pomp and ceremony: a nineteen-gun artillery salute; a squadron of Irish Air Corps planes flying in cross formation to accompany the Papal Legate's boat from the Kish Lightvessel to the shore; convoys of decorated boats to accompany him by sea; guards of honour and the Army No. 1 Band playing as he walked down the red-carpeted gangway to be greeted by the Archbishop of Dublin, Reverend Edward Joseph Byrne, and the leader of the seventh Dáil, Éamon de Valera,[7] on what the *Irish Times* described as 'the greatest day of ritual Ireland has ever known'.[8] The Borough Council of Dún Laoghaire was in attendance, dressed in top hats and frock coats.[9] The crowd of about 50,000 onlookers went wild – the Catholic Boy Scouts provided crowd-control services – as the Papal Legate walked the short distance to his car, raising his hand repeatedly in blessing, while the Garda Band played the '*Inno Pontificio*' (Pontifical Hymn). As the entourage travelled into Dublin, spectators were impressed to see bishops and priests who looked very exotic to them, including men from Asia and Father Philip Gordon, a Native American from the Chippewa tribe, in a traditional feather headdress.[10] Regina, eleven then, remembered the day well: 'The Papal Nuncio… was in a big car, went along by the Crofton Road into town. *Crowds* of people! We never knew there was so many people in Dún Laoghaire… Oh, everyone decorated the houses… signs and flags and everything.' Regina and her friends from school, the Dominican Convent, had to wear special hats – 'white with black around the edges, and a little Dominican Convent badge on the front' – so they could be easily spotted in the crowd. 'Religion was a great thing then, you see,' Regina said, 'and it was very Catholic, Dún Laoghaire.' But her most vivid memory of that day is the shiny sixpence her father gave her to spend – a lot of money for a little girl – that she lost in the excitement. Pádraic was also in attendance as a child – he was seven – and wildly excited about the big trip from his home near Kilternan to see Cardinal Lauri: 'I never saw anything like it,' Pádraic recalled. 'The whole countryside here was a mass of colour. Of papal flags and tricolours.' The parish priest of Sandyford went up the mountain of Barnacullia to look down, and remarked that the countryside below was 'nothing only papal flags and tricolours'. Many years later, Pádraic's memories of the day remained vivid: 'It was one of the greatest sights that I ever seen,' he said. 'There was about 200 horsemen... I don't know how many brass or reed bands... a line of cars from here to, I suppose from here to Dundrum.'

Other local events included a huge garden party at Blackrock College, hosted by John Charles McQuaid (then president of the college),[11] while Stillorgan village – like every town and village in Ireland – was lavishly decorated, with a street altar outside the local church.[12] The whole city was decorated with flowers, plants, religious iconography and Vatican flags, under the guidance of the City Decorations Committee; the poorest areas tended to have the most lavish decorations. An official crest, based on the Cross of Cong, was designed, and badges displaying it were sold in huge numbers.[13] A new housing development in Glasthule was named 'Congress Gardens' in honour of the event.[14] Readers of the *Sacred Heart Messenger* were reassured that Ireland was truly unique and great in its spirituality: 'In some lands,' the paper asserted, 'patriotic and religious feelings seem to clash, while in others which were once distinguished for their Catholicity, irreligion has crept in, but Ireland's greatness in the past and her hopes for the future are indissolubly joined to the Faith.'[15] Speaking at a reception for the Papal Legate, de Valera also stressed that Ireland was, by definition, Catholic: 'Repeatedly,' he said, 'over more than three hundred years, our people, ever firm in their allegiance to our ancestral Faith, and unswerving even to death in their devotion to the See of Peter, endured in full measure unmerited trials by war, by devastation, and by confiscation.'[16] The congress lasted until 26 June and was magnificent, with Mass held in the city centre – music provided by Count John McCormack – and numerous festivities.

There were many visitors to the congress from overseas, some of whom were accommodated on ships and boats in Dublin Bay, ferried around by hobblers and other local seafarers, who made good money.[17] Nicola's family were Methodists and did not participate in the religious events, but they were also seafarers, who took the opportunity to earn extra money, bringing visitors to and from the ships being used as hotels, and delivering newspapers and other items to them. There were many other opportunities for money to be made too, including making and selling commemorative souvenirs and providing food and drink to those attending the festivities. Emer's grandfather, who grew flowers, provided many for the decorations.

For the Catholic people of Dún Laoghaire-Rathdown, undoubtedly the highlight of the whole affair was the arrival of the Papal Legate, who saw them first. For Protestants in the area, the Eucharistic Congress evoked a range of emotions. There was a sense of national pride that Ireland could host such a big celebration with aplomb, but also sometimes anger that the state was spending so much public money on a religious event, and submitting state authority to religious. Rather pointedly, that June, the Church of Ireland – which also claimed St Patrick as its founder – held its own celebrations of the saint's life in Ireland, featuring a slide show, the distribution of pamphlets, lectures and other events;[18] these may have been a convenient refuge for the many non-Catholics of Dún Laoghaire-Rathdown (like Ernest Bateman, rector of Booterstown, who wrote lengthily about the role of St Patrick in the Church of Ireland[19]), many of whom may have felt ambivalent about, or even hostile towards, the politicised Catholicism on display for the duration of the Congress.

The influence of the Eucharistic Congress persisted long after it ended, partly because of people's vivid memories, but also because of the huge number of photographs taken. These served not just as mementoes of an exciting time but as advertising, or even propaganda, for the new state, as they showed a happy people unified by their common faith.[20] In many homes, photographs of the Congress hung in pride of place for decades. In Eva's Stillorgan home, a Congress photograph still jostled for space with a red-lit image of the Sacred Heart when she was growing up in the 1960s.

In 1937, five years after the congress, the Irish Constitution was written. It reflected to a large extent the teachings of the Catholic Church and solidified yet further the idea that to be truly Irish, one should also be Catholic. 'Catholicism,' wrote Brian Girvin almost fifty years later, 'gave to Ireland a sense of identity which reinforced its separateness from Britain and gave to the Irish a strong sense of self-confidence and mission in a secularizing world.'[21] Catholicism had already had a profound influence on nation building and on expressions of Irishness. It had, in Ireland, acquired a particularly puritanical bent, which was accepted and resisted to varying degrees.

* * *

Those who remember the years of John Charles McQuaid, Catholic Primate of Ireland and Archbishop of Dublin from 1940 to 1972, recall an oppressive religious culture permeating every aspect of life. Regina's aunt, a nun, was terrified one evening when the family was in Dublin, lest she should be seen on the streets after eight, sure that she would be 'reported', as she had been instructed that McQuaid did not want nuns or brothers out in public in the evenings. Carmel was herself a member of the Daughters of Mary order, which ran St Joseph's orphanage and school in Dún Laoghaire. She was told that 'if [McQuaid] saw a sister walking around Dublin late in the evening, he'd stop his car and bring her home' (a moot issue for Daughters of Mary, who did not wear habits). Honorah remembered that, when her father suffered a heart attack, the doctor attending refused to give him painkillers until the priest had visited and administered the Rites of Absolution. John's father, a politician from a Protestant background in the 1940s and 1950s, worked in an atmosphere in which the affairs of church and state were deeply intertwined. It could be a tricky environment for politicians not of the majority faith. At one stage, John recalled, it came to McQuaid's attention that a young Catholic had been awarded a County Council Scholarship to attend Trinity College (from which Catholics were then banned), and the churchman attempted to intervene, citing the 'danger' to the would-be student's faith and morals.

John Charles McQuaid had a strong personal connection to Dún Laoghaire-Rathdown. He served as Dean of Studies in Blackrock College from 1925 to 1931 and as President from 1931 to 1939. From 1945, he lived in neo-Gothic splendour in Killiney in his home Notre Dame de Bois (originally Ashurst), which he preferred to the archbishop's residence in Drumcondra. Among other luxuries, it boasted thirteen bedrooms and a well-cultivated garden. McQuaid pottered in the garden, and he had a shooting range installed and a lift in the sixty-foot belfry tower, which he periodically ascended to view the stars through his telescope (or, according to some locals, to keep an eye on the students at the nearby Holy Child convent school, 'to make sure they stayed holy').[22] McQuaid was often seen locally in his chauffeur-driven car. Seán, who grew up in nearby Ballybrack, was on his way home one evening when McQuaid passed. The driver stopped, rolled down his window, and said: 'His Grace would like to give you a lift.' Seán sat nervously into the back as McQuaid extended his hand across the frosted glass divider so that Seán could kiss the archbishop's ring.*

Even ordinary parish priests were still often given remarkable powers of authority and subject to extraordinary deference, persisting to some degree into the late twentieth century. As a child growing up in Glasthule in the 1940s, Edward and his friends stepped into the gutter when a priest passed, saluting him deferentially. A full generation later, Mick, growing up in Dalkey in the 1970s, was hauled before the priest by his father whenever he misbehaved: 'if you ever did something wrong… as small as robbing an orchard, you were brought up to the priest'.

While priests (and to a lesser extent nuns and brothers) were respected authority figures, behaviour in ritual contexts was also managed at grass-roots level by community members. As a child at Mass in the 1950s, one

---

* Given how many have very negative memories of and opinions on McQuaid and his influence on Ireland in the 1950s, it is a relief to know that sometimes he showed a kinder side. Rosie – who was openly involved in a women's rights movement in the 1960s – recalled his great generosity in funding the higher education of a young man who had grown up in institutional care, and that McQuaid even set up an account at Arnott's department store in the city centre, where the student could buy clothes for college.

interviewee recalled how a bored, wriggly child could be admonished by a complete stranger with a hard 'puck in the back'.

* * *

Regular 'missions', when visiting priests preached, provided Mass and heard confessions, and items associated with religious devotion were sold, were a feature of religious life all over Dún Laoghaire-Rathdown, but perhaps particularly in Dún Laoghaire. Many attended from devotion, but there were other reasons, too. Jacinta, a teenager in the late 1940s and early 1950s, who described her family as 'not overly religious', went in the hope of 'meeting altar boys'. (Many boys served time as altar boys in their local parishes, a duty that some regarded as a perk. Although there was work involved, they also got time off school and could make the most of it by walking as slowly as possible on their way back.)

Missions occurred less frequently in more sparsely populated areas. In Glencullen, Joseph and Davy remembered them occurring every three years. The priests seem to have given sermons tending towards the lurid: 'You'd nearly feel the flames coming up around your arse in the seat,' remembered Joseph. 'You'd be afraid of your life,' agreed Davy. A tent outside sold religious items: Rosary beads, scapulars, holy medals. The expectation was that everybody would buy something, and on the last night of the mission, they would all be blessed by a priest.

Public religious processions were a frequent sight until the latter decades of the twentieth century. Regina remembered the May processions as wonderful: 'the walking of the blessed sacrament through the streets… every little girl – anyone that had a veil – walked… the men with their armbands and the houses would put out little altars at the gates'.

In this atmosphere of heightened religious emotion, sacred buildings were not just important, beautiful elements of the built environment but constant visual reminders of social structures and the importance of faith and religion. People often had a strong sense of attachment to particular buildings. This must have made the burning of St Michael's

Church in Dún Laoghaire in 1965 particularly shocking for locals who had spent many of the important moments of their lives within its walls. Margaret remembered her mother returning from Mass saying that she had smelled smoke in the church: 'we ran down to that block between Mulgrave Street and Patrick Street… out of the rose window was a flame about two inches… a huge breeze came down Patrick Street… and the roof just took off like a tinderbox'.

* * *

Religious organisations for laypeople were a feature of the Irish religious landscape since at least the middle ages.[23] In the late eighteenth and nineteenth centuries they increasingly became a prominent feature of religious, charitable and philanthropic endeavour, operating schools, orphanages and other institutions.[24] Membership of religious organisations like sodalities, the Legion of Mary, the Society of St Vincent de Paul and so on was a central element of society until well into the second half of the twentieth century, with broadly analogous organisations like the Mothers' Union (the Irish branch established in 1888) and Christian Endeavour (founded in America in 1881) for Protestants. This was the 'golden age' of such organisations. They were a source of identity and meaning, a public, performative expression of faith, and a means through which social activism and philanthropy could occur within socially and ecclesiastically approved norms.[25] Confraternities and sodalities were often primarily concerned with spirituality, providing faith formation and encouraging prayer, self-mortification and abstinence, and moderation with alcohol as well as retreats and monthly meetings. (Hugh Leonard recalled that Thursday was the day on which immorality and immodest behaviour were discussed at Dalkey retreats, as it was when domestic servants – 'ripe fruit, helpless on the bough and palpitating for damnation' – had their evening off and were expected to attend.[26]) The Children of Mary, which many children joined at school, encouraged prayer and contemplation. Dorothy remembered: 'once a month you'd dress in a blue cape and a little veil, and you'd go up to the top of the church... kneel at the altar or sit. And you'd pray there for an hour... when the hour was up, somebody would walk up behind you and they'd take over.' Lifelong members could be buried in their blue capes, their final garments.

Organisations like the Vincent de Paul were firmly focused on providing for the poor, and were a lifeline to many needy families. Parallel organisations for Protestant denominations served similar functions; in the early to mid-nineteenth century, many also attempted to evangelise and win converts from among the Catholic population,[27] generally with relatively little success. In 1980, Elizabeth Rushby recalled the 'penny dinners' available on York Road in Dún Laoghaire in her childhood, run by 'Protestant ladies': 'if you went in with a big bowl, you'd get meat... turnips or cabbage, potatoes... everything in that bowl for a penny'.[28]

* * *

As the Catholic Church gained power and wealth during the nineteenth century, the number of vocations rose dramatically. In 1800, for example, there were 120 nuns in Ireland; in 1900, there were 8,000.[29] By 1871, in Dublin city, there were forty-eight convents, housing 1,200 nuns.[30] Vocations remained high in early independence, with many nuns working at home and abroad, and a spike in vocations in 1954, the 'Marian Year' decreed by Pius XII following the 1950 promulgation of the dogma of Mary's assumption into heaven.[31]

The huge surge in religious vocations was due to multiple factors. For families from modest backgrounds, one was access to education. Until at least the mid-twentieth century, entering religious life – or a secondary school preparing young people for a potential vocation – was an affordable way for talented young people to get an education. In many Catholic schools, students were urged to seriously consider if they had a vocation. Barry remembered being instructed that he should examine his conscience and warned, 'If you have a vocation, and you

New statue for Marian Year at Oliver Plunkett Avenue, Monkstown. Courtesy of Jimmy Howe.

don't join, it's a mortal sin.' Across Ireland a network of specialised boarding secondary schools, often known as 'junior seminaries', had been established to foster vocations. While many of their students ultimately decided they did not, after all, wish to become priests, many of them did. Reg attended one and remembered that, of a class of twenty-four, eleven were ordained. Tom would have a long, fulfilling career as a parish priest, including long periods in Shankill, Foxrock and Cabinteely, and a rewarding experience of being called to the Church. He also, however, referenced the term 'mothers' vocations', referring to boys believed to have been pressured by their mothers to enter the priesthood, even if they were wavering. Cormac was also drawn to religious life from an early age, when many girls and boys who thought they might have a vocation attended secondary school, 'in the environment of the order or congregation that they were aspiring to'. Aged fourteen, he entered a religious order. While Cormac has had a very

fulfilling and happy life and career, as a brother and as a health professional, he noted that, today, a young person entering religious life
at such an early might be seen as having been 'kidnapped'. Eva also
entered religious life at an early age; she was sixteen. A couple years
later, she realised it was a mistake, and returned home to Stillorgan. It
was 1965 and the changes introduced by the Second Vatican Council
were just beginning to take effect, but the old stigma of 'failed' nuns or
priests lingered. Venturing out on her third day home, Eva encountered
one of the neighbours, and 'she swished up her skirts and went, "Can't
understand how anybody could enter the religious life and walk out
the way you did! You're a disgrace."' Lloyd, a teenager in the 1980s, also
attended a secondary school with a reputation for fostering vocations,
a holdout in a rapidly changing religious environment. His family lived
in Blackrock, but he boarded at this midlands school. Only one boy
from his year ultimately went forward for the priesthood, as Lloyd's
cohort graduated into an adult world where the religious environment
was in rapid flux.

Rob's father, from a long-established Dún Laoghaire family, felt that
he had a vocation, although he trained as a plumber, 'to have something
to fall back on'. In about 1947, aged about twenty-one, he entered a
Cistercian monastery in Collon, County Louth. It had taken him five
attempts to be accepted: 'I suppose you'd say they were awash with hope-
fuls,' said Rob. 'They could choose.' He embarked on the studies required
before ordination and took his first vows. Then he learned that one of his
sisters had become pregnant outside marriage and was in a mother and
baby home. He requested and received permission from his abbot to go
home, because only a male family member could get his sister out, and
their parents were dead. When the baby was born, he returned to the
monastery, where the abbot informed him that ordination was now out
of the question, because of his sister's situation.

Stevie commented on a view that was apparently quite widely held,
that greater levels of violence were experienced at the hands of teachers
who were Christian Brothers than religious teachers from other orders at

last partly because of resentments relating to social class. People felt that Christian Brothers were often men who had wanted to be priests or teachers, but whose parents could not afford to send them to a seminary or a university. When Denny was a teenager in the late 1950s, he wanted to be a teacher, but he narrowly missed winning a scholarship to secondary school, which was fee-paying then. Becoming a Christian Brother offered another route into education, so at fifteen he entered the Christian Brothers on Kill Avenue. He attended as a boarder and completed his first year, after which he was sent to St Helen's Christian Brothers in Booterstown as a novice. At sixteen, he was already having doubts, and 'when they... initiated the self-inflicted kind of flagellation, that was it for me!'

For women, a vocation was one of the few ways to avoid having a large family and instead to experience an academic education and/or a rewarding and demanding career in areas such as teaching, nursing or medicine, or domestic economy.[32] Nora entered the Loreto order at eighteen to pursue a religious life, to teach and to live according to the philosophy of Mary Ward, the Englishwoman who founded the order in 1609. Ward placed huge emphasis on the education of women and girls, and she had been fiercely opposed in her time. Nora explained that the Loreto sisters were, 'named derogatively as "Jesuitesses" ... as "galloping girls"'. A philosophy stressing academic rigour as well as faith continued to characterise the Loreto order many years later, when Nora joined.

* * *

In 1960, under the government of Seán Lemass, and on the cusp of a dramatic surge in economic modernisation and improving educational standards, Ireland was remarkable in its religiosity, with Mass attendance in Catholic parishes at or near 100 per cent in rural and urban areas, and most happy with the large role played by the Church in political and social life.[33] In many parishes, priests were revered or feared – sometimes both. Henry remembered that, in Shankill, the priests were 'a hard people. Priests always felt they were above you... Their word was law. Whatever they said was gospel.' But through the 1960s, observations of faith gradually relaxed, and younger priests became more approachable. From the 1960s, religious observance and faith were increasingly influenced by external influences and new media such as television – RTÉ, the Irish national broadcaster, was on the air from 1961, although many people in the greater Dublin area had been watching the BBC on their own TV sets for years before that.

The Second Vatican Council (which began in 1962, with the first Masses given in the vernacular in Ireland in 1965),[34] rapid growth in education, a general shift towards liberalisation and the modern women's rights movement[35] all began to impact on expressions of faith. Nuala's mother lamented the loss of the Latin Mass. She felt that it was 'more deeply religious' before and that in English people just 'babbled'. But Jim thought it was 'great': 'I thought it was the height of arrogance of the priest to be up there [before], with his back to you, muttering away in Latin.' One Cabinteely priest, locally renowned for his old-fashioned ways, resisted many of the changes into the 1970s and 1980s. While he said Mass in English, he refused to give parishioners Communion into their hands, and continued to say Mass with his back to the congregation. Generally, the locals were unimpressed. Remembered Adrian: 'I never crossed the door of the church again as long as he was there.'

After the Second Vatican Council, younger priests, nuns and brothers and actively involved laypeople were increasingly interested in approaches such as liberation theology* and in the pastoral and social aspects of religious life. Reg attended training courses in Berkeley, California, where he acquired knowledge, skills and ideas that he could apply to his ministry at home. There was a growing emphasis on the importance of the laity and on the idea of the Church as a faith community of equals. For young people with religious vocations, this was a challenging and exciting time, as long-established norms were questioned and new opportunities

---

* A form of Catholic theology that emerged from Latin America in the 1960s, combining Catholic teaching with the fundamentals of socialism, with a focus on helping the oppressed. Liberation theology became extremely influential in the years following the Second Vatican Council. See Barger, 2018, for a general discussion of liberation theology and its influence on Catholic thinking.

became apparent, even as the growing secularisation of society also became more evident. Debbie, a woman with a deep faith and a keen social conscience, welcomed the changes that Vatican II introduced. She commented that some priests seemed to struggle to accept the new status quo, whereas she saw the Church as consisting of the people. She would train in lay ministry and play an active role in her parish, one of many laywomen taking increasingly important, if not leadership, roles in the Church.

* * *

The visit of Pope John Paul II to Ireland in 1979 was the biggest public display of faith and allegiance since the Eucharistic Congress. John Paul, appointed in 1978 amid high drama – his predecessor dying after just weeks in office – broke the mould as a relative outsider from Poland. A theological conservative with an exceptional gift for communication and public outreach, his visit was a new opportunity for Ireland to

Members of the Ryan family from Booterstown with friends at the Papal Mass in Phoenix Park in 1979. The Papal Visit was a huge affair. Over a million people attended Mass in Phoenix Park, among them an enormous number of the residents of Dún Laoghaire-Rathdown, anxious to participate in one of the biggest Mass events of the twentieth century and to catch a glimpse of the new, relatively young and extremely charismatic John Paul II. Note the Vatican colours – yellow and white – which were worn by many of the spectators on the day. Kind permission of Rebecca Ryan.

showcase itself to the world as a devout, traditional Catholic country, notwithstanding the dramatic social change already well underway. Of the million who attended Mass in Dublin's Phoenix Park, many came from Dún Laoghaire-Rathdown, bussed in and shepherded about with impressive enthusiasm and organisation and variable levels of devotion. Lloyd from Blackrock, who was nine, remembered viewing the pope through one of the thousands of special pope-spying periscopes that people bought that day. Eoin, from the same area, was nine too. He remembered 'a huge level of excitement… [and] a lot of drinking! … Black Label vodka'.

Pope John Paul II advised Irish women and girls to focus on the 'vocation' of having babies and caring for them.[36] Although the birth rate increased briefly in Ireland in the year following (with one in ten baby boys born that year named John Paul),[37] the impact of the pope's visit on social change was brief. It may, however, have contributed to the success of conservative elements in politics in inserting the 'right to life' amendment in the constitution in 1983, and to the defeat of the government proposal to remove the ban on divorce from the constitution in 1986.[38] Remembering the visit, and the social change that continued to accelerate subsequently, Margie recalled that Pope John Paul was 'very charismatic' but that he was 'with the birds, of course, but even then we knew that'. 'I think,' she said, 'people were making up their own minds quite a bit at the time.' In fact, the social changes that were already taking place in Ireland generally were most firmly embedded in the Dún Laoghaire area, where 58.8 per cent of those who voted in the 1986 referendum favoured the removal of the constitutional ban on divorce: by far the biggest favourable response in the country and a sign of things to come.

The Catholic Church in Ireland had begun to participate in the ecumenical movement following the Second Vatican Council. The Irish School of Ecumenics was founded in 1970 by Father Michael Hurley, a Jesuit priest.[39] The movement was further given impetus by the Troubles in the north, which some feared might trickle south.

Above: A group of young people leaving Glasthule to cycle to Rome to see the Pope in 1980. Courtesy of Peter O'Brien.

Left: The same young people from Glasthule. meeting the Pope at Castel Gondolfo. Courtesy of Peter O'Brien.

Among the most intriguing aspects of this cultural shift in the religious life of Dún Laoghaire-Rathdown are the 'Sonrise' events held in several locations on Easter Sunday as interest in the ecumenical movement gathered pace. Terence, from Sandyford, was involved in setting up a 'Sonrise' event meeting at the nearby Leadmines chimney at about six on Easter Sunday morning. Attendees from diverse religious denominations greeted the morning sun, said prayers and sang hymns, and sometimes lit a fire. Easter sunrise or 'Sonrise' events have obvious parallels to pre- and non-Christian rituals but, in the Christian content, apparently the first Easter sunrise service recorded was that of a Moravian congregation in 1732 in Saxony. Over the years that followed, the tradition spread around the world with Moravian missionaries, becoming integrated into the liturgy of diverse religious communities and ecumenical groups.[40] In Dún Laoghaire-Rathdown, however, it primarily has been associated with ecumenical groups who, annually, worship on hilltops that were once the ritual sites of people who lived millennia before Christianity. Theresa, a former lay missionary with a long history of ecumenical involvement, explained: 'lots of races [of people]... have seen the sun as a god... as a life-giver, because it gives light, and things grow because of it... as Christians, we believe that Christ raised himself from the dead... the sun, every day, gives the whole world a new beginning – light, heat and then growth'. Harold, a retired Church of Ireland rector, pointed out the Biblical tradition of spiritual events occurring on mountaintops: 'Mount Sinai, Moses, the Commandments, the Hill of the Transfiguration, the Mount of Transfiguration, the... Hill of Calvary... Mount of Ascension ... that's where the activity of God is most active.' In the Sonrise services, he sees a local reflection of this relationship between spirituality and the mountains – which, it appears, was also shared by people in the area's very remote past, linking present generations to some of the earliest residents, who lived and worshipped here thousands of years ago.

* * *

From the 1960s, Irish society was increasingly modern in outlook, but remained relatively conservative with respect to faith and cultural norms. This conservativism was also reflected in the absence of legal abortion and divorce, and the late, restrictive legislation permitting contraception (discussed in '(Before the) Cradle to (Beyond the) Grave'). However, a small but steadily growing number was questioning how things were done, some regarding how the Church might become more open-minded, and some just becoming increasingly disassociated from it. In the early 1960s, Robbie, then in his late teens and living in Monkstown Farm, began to question Church authority, prompted by the 'churching' of his sister following the birth of her first child. 'On the Sunday morning we walked down… to Mass,' he remembered, 'and as we approached the church my sister says, "I'll see youse in a few minutes", and goes straight into the sacristy.' When Robbie asked why, he learned that a woman who has just given birth was considered ritually unclean. He was horrified: 'Well, I nearly hit the roof. I cursed, actually… I said, "She's done the most beautiful thing any woman can do… she brought a little baby into the world, and she's unclean?"' The churching of women ceased shortly after that, but Robbie had already started to question doctrine. Throughout the 1970s and 1980s, Georgie and his wife, who lived in Killiney, also became gradually disenchanted. His wife, he said, was shocked when she was twelve, and her mother had to be churched after giving birth: 'She said her mother was one of the cleanest persons you ever met.' That memory stayed with her and contributed later to her decision to disengage from formal religion.

From the early 1970s, a vast array of progressive Catholic interest groups appeared, organised and led by laypeople. In counterpoint, conservative groups, like the Knights of Columbanus, dedicated to promoting traditional Catholic values, were also active. Both, in their different ways, impacted on the religious landscape, albeit not necessarily as intended; short-term gains on the part of the conservative elements, for example, are likely to have contributed to the decline in formal religion that had already commenced, as younger people were increasingly detached from Church doctrine, and ignoring conservative messages about issues such as contraception. By 1977, while levels of church attendance remained high (but had dropped to 75 per cent in Dublin), people were increasingly likely to query or openly disagree with Church teaching on matters including contraception, homosexuality and clerical celibacy.[41] Ireland remained, however, unusually pious by western

European standards. Darragh, growing up in the Blackrock area, remembered saying the Rosary every evening: 'a twenty-minute affair after tea'.

The divisive referendum of 1983, when a majority voted to insert a clause in the constitution intended to guarantee that abortion would never be legalised, can be recognised retrospectively as representing a dramatic shift;[42] although the anti-abortion legislation passed, a gulf opened between more and less traditional elements in society, amid growing unease about the influence of the Church in state affairs. One doctor working in the area remembered the time as 'horrific', the medical profession divided. Some doctors who had been friends stopped speaking to one another because they disagreed so strongly. She tried to see both sides: 'Nobody likes abortion… But things go wrong in people's lives.' As a doctor, she had seen the health consequences for women who had taken the mailboat from Dún Laoghaire to Britain for abortions and had had to return hastily. There were times when she had 'written notes' for young women who needed time off to travel for an abortion. A note saying they were suffering from glandular fever gave them just enough time to terminate an unwanted pregnancy.

The 1980s was a time of cultural stress and anxiety in Ireland, much of which tended to coalesce around religious matters. Young people increasingly saw the Church (generally assumed to be the Catholic Church) as oppositional to how they wanted to live. Darragh, a university student then, remembered that 'history was telling me… that church and churches… are constructs between secular power and religious powers and they divide and conquer among themselves as it suits them, to organise society… it reinforced my view… we've let them away with absolute murder'. The cultural shifts occurring also led to changes like shops opening on Sundays from 1994. Reg, a parish priest, remembered a divergence of opinions among the clergy at the time. An older priest he knew was horrified by Sunday opening, and had given an angry sermon on the subject: '[He] threatened them with damnation, almost'. Shortly afterwards, Reg met fellow parishioners one Sunday morning at the local Dunnes Stores. 'We'll be with you in hell,' they joked.

From the early 1990s, a series of scandals erupted in the Catholic Church.[43] In Dún Laoghaire-Rathdown, with higher-than-average levels of disengagement from formal religion, there had already been a marked decline in religious engagement. From the 1990s, religious observance and expressions of faith generally declined quickly and dramatically. The Church, attending Mass (or service) and participating in a faith community remained at the core of many locals' lives, but the profound and even shocking changes to religious sentiments and observance had multiple and complex impacts on every aspect of life. Terence, born in the 1920s and married in 1952, during the era of McQuaid's reign, reflected on the impact of the scandals on his generation. For many, it was absolutely devastating. In some cases, he felt, 'it probably brought up some recollections of people who might have seen or heard but didn't, wouldn't accept it'. Others refused to accept that any of the stories of abuse within the Church were real. Ultimately, he said, 'it did damage to everybody'. Many, he said, 'kept their faith' but stopped attending Mass. By the late twentieth century, many of the large properties that belonged to the Catholic Church (often having previously belonged to members of the Protestant ascendancy) had become offices and hotels, notably the Radisson Blu St Helen's Hotel in Booterstown, purchased by the Christian Brothers order in 1925, sold by them in 1988, and operating as a five-star hotel from 1998.

* * *

Folk religion is often considered a primarily rural phenomenon, and as belonging to the past. It is also often thought of as something that 'other' people do. The death of folk religion in urban and suburban areas is certainly exaggerated. Lack of evidence of folk religion in these areas is largely because of a lack of research. Numerous folk religious practices were observed until recent times in Dún Laoghaire-Rathdown, and in both urban and rural areas alike, while others never died out. For example, the physical presence and use of holy objects

– statues, representations of the Sacred Heart of Jesus and so on –
encompass elements of both folk and formal religion. Iconography,
which can include 'plaster statues of Our Lady of Lourdes, Our Lady
of Fatima, St Anne, The Infant of Prague, images of the Sacred Heart,
the Immaculate Heart of Mary, framed papal blessings, Rosary beads,
reproductions of canonical Italian religious paintings, prayer books,
pious medals and leaflets',[44] served both as mnemonics to elements
of formal religious worship and as elements in folk religious practice,
with icons and associated prayer evoked in cases of special need, and
sometimes used in the context of folk healing and other popular rituals. Mick, from a Traveller background, remembered the importance of
St Brigid and the various artefacts associated with her in his extended
family: 'the making of the crosses, the rushes and everything... you'd
have two or three of them up in the house. And you just wouldn't
have it there for the day. You could have it up for about three or four
months.' The use of holy water in the Catholic faith also occurs on a
spectrum encompassing official Church teaching and numerous folk
religious practices. Mick remembered how important holy water – particularly from Knock or from Holy Island in Wexford – was in his
community when he was a child growing up in Dalkey in the 1970s.
The same, of course, was true of many settled people, with the holy
water font inside the front door a common feature in many homes, and
holy water used in many contexts.

Numerous churches, cemeteries and other sites of religious importance are located in Dún Laoghaire-Rathdown. Less obvious at first
glance are the other sacred sites that, despite being increasingly subsumed by building over the years, can still be seen and that have been
the foci of ritual behaviours. A sacred geography[45] can still be perceived
among and on the outskirts of the housing estates, the meaning of
the sacred sites shifting as political, social and religious contexts also
change.[46]

Notably, there are at least 100 holy wells in County Dublin,[47] many
probably having been in use since the period of the Reformation, when

religious observances at wells were not subject to the same repressive rigour as other forms of Catholic worship,* despite proximity to what folklorist Ó Danachair describes as 'the centre of power which looked upon them as the height of papish superstition and… took active steps to destroy them'.[48] In 1902, Patrick O'Reilly described the holy well of Tobernea in Monkstown/Blackrock (still visible today just under Tobernea Terrace). Then, the well was the site of religious observance, and its waters considered curative,[49] particularly regarding problems with eyesight.[50] The well is apparently associated with Saint Nathi, considered the founder of Taney Church near Dundrum.[51] Brian Mac Aonghusa describes coming across the well in the 1940s, when, he says, it was 'almost forgotten'.[52] 'Jacob's Well', alleged in 1887 to contain a sacred trout,[53] was located at the junction of Pakenham Road and the Hill in Dún Laoghaire.[54] Grumley's Well, thought to have curative properties relating to the eyes, was in at least sporadic use in Ticknock until the 1940s.[55] In 1938, a primary school student from Ticknock recorded that their family land contained a 'blessed well', where people bathed their eyes in the early twentieth century, leaving rags tied onto an adjacent bush.[56] The same year, B.L. Edwards described ongoing interest in a well in Dalkey, historically associated with St Begnet, where people still prayed and drank the water, and left votive offerings including 'coins, sacred cards, and beads'.[57] Also in 1938, Mrs Dunne of Dalkey, then 101, contributed to the Schools' Folklore Collection the information that the well was said to have 'a cure' and that people who had injured their hands or legs washed their wounds in its water and were better the next day.[58] A holy well also dedicated to St Begnet, once resorted to by sufferers of scurvy,[59] can still be seen on Dalkey Island. Séamus remembered St Begnet's Well on Dalkey Island being known as 'the scurvy well'. Pat O'Neill recalled his family's observance, mid-twentieth century, at a holy well located on the current site of

---

* Whelan (2018, 51) asserts that 'Holy wells should be regarded as an active response to the Protestant Reformation rather than as a passive residue left over from an earlier period.'

Clonkeen Park. His mother used it for both religious and healing purposes: 'She would bring us to Toberbawn well, dip a piece of cloth in the water and make the sign of the cross three times on our eyes. She would then leave the cloth tied to a nearby bush.'[60] Holy wells are also present in Jamestown, Kilgobbin, Kill o' the Grange, Ticknock and Kilternan.[61] St Patrick's Well, between Stepaside and Kilternan, was widely used for a range of cures, with rites including the deposition

A girl with a bottle of holy water at St Columcille's Well, Ballycullen, Rathfarnham. Religious observance at holy wells has been a remarkably persistent tradition. While many of the holy wells in Dún Laoghaire-Rathdown are now disused (and/or subsumed by development), there are still quite a few in the broader area, some of which remain in use. St Columcille's Well was visited by large numbers for ritual purposes in the mid-twentieth century, and it is still the subject of religious rites today.

Praying at St Columcille's Well. National Library of Ireland.

of votive offerings such as personal items and Rosary beads, etc. but described as no longer being in use in 1938.[62] Tim from Kilmashogue remembered being taken to festivities around Colmcille's well, located on the Ballycullen Road in Oldcourt, on 'happy Sundays' in the 1960s, with a big crowd in attendance, balloons for the children and dancing in the fields. They all drank the water from the well too, 'and we had great faith in that'.

Wells could serve both practical and more esoteric purposes. A well in Kilternan known as the Butter Well was used to keep butter cool, and also believed to have a cure for stomach-ache; Eustace remembered it in use in the 1930s and 1940s for both purposes. Into the mid-twentieth century and possibly beyond, the water from this well was also thought by some to ward away the fairies, traditionally viewed as agents of chaos. Pádraic remembered the local practice during his young days in the 1930s and 1940s: 'women would go down, and churn there to make the butter down there. Lovely water... I always went down to get a sup... after churning there, they would bring... a can of water and they would spray the barn so that the fairies wouldn't take the butter away.'

* * *

Belief in fairies persisted into the twentieth century, at least in some of the more rural parts of Dún Laoghaire-Rathdown. During the War of Independence, when a few IRA men found themselves lost along a familiar uplands route, locals informed them that this was because they had disturbed the 'good people'.[63] The National Folklore Collection also testifies to the persistence of traditions about fairies into the late 1930s, even in areas that were already quite urban. Writing in the Schools' Collection of 1937–8, Seán Kelly stated that a mysterious light often seen 'rising at the road at Clonskeagh' was said locally to be a 'fairy light guarding a treasure',[64] and Séamus Leary, a student at Harold's Boys' School, recorded that older locals described Dalkey Hill as 'a fairy playground' and that at times laughter and the sound of 'a ball bouncing' came from the hill late at night.[65] Gerald Reilly, from the same school, reported an account of a local man who cut down a tree said to belong to the fairies, and Paddy Keyes contributed that, years before, a local man was on his way home late at night near the purported location of a fairy ring on Dalkey Hill when he encountered fairies playing ball, and was only able to escape from them after an hour or so by shouting, 'Good men on both sides'.[66] A legendary narrative relating to the Widow Gambol's Hill, connecting Dún Laoghaire and Monkstown, was also submitted, collected by Joseph Goggins, a student at the Christian Brothers School in Dún Laoghaire, from his neighbour Joseph Mullen of Glasthule, stating that an area from 'McBrien's River'* to Covenger's Pond was haunted by the fairies, once seen by a man called Hugh Brannan. 'They had the headless coach as a hearse, and were carrying a coffin,' the story related. 'They gave him the coffin to carry, and then they sang, "Who will get the keys of the cemetery / Who will but Hugh Brannan / Who will carry the corpse / Who will but Hugh Brannan."' Another named individual was purported to have once been led astray by fairies in the same area: 'he was walking all night, and when daylight came he was in the same place as the night before'.[67] Speaking of an unnamed 'rath' (generally the remains of an Iron Age fort, traditionally associated in folklore with the fairies or little people), a schoolchild participating in 1937–8 explained that a local farmer interfered with it, and the next day he found two of his horses dead in their stable,[68] while builders working a few years later attempted to construct a new suburban house on the site of a fairy rath only to find each morning that the newly constructed walls had been knocked down overnight (people felt that either the fairies or the local historical society might have been involved).[69] Recorded in 1980, May McConville provided a detailed description of her parents' alleged encounter with fairies on Sallynoggin Hill in the latter part of

---

* McBrien's River, also known as Mickey Bryan's River, was a popular place for children to play; interviewees remembered sailing paper boats and playing with the bullrushes that grew there.

Up the airy mountain,
    Down the rushy glen,
We daren't go a-hunting
    For fear of little men.

During the Celtic Revival in the nineteenth and early twentieth centuries, artists often drew on Irish folklore and tradition. This greeting card by Eileen C. Booth was commissioned by the Cuala Press, which was established (initially as Dun Emer Press) by Elizabeth Yeats in 1908. It published work by a range of important writers and artists of the day, including Lady Gregory and W.B. Yeats. National Library of Ireland.

the nineteenth or early twentieth century. Her parents were coming up the hill, she said, when 'my mother seen [the fairies], that height, and he was dressed in a swallowtail coat, striped trousers and a bowler hat, and there was a woman with him'. May's parents described the fairies as walking to the top of Sallynoggin Hill, crossing the road and disappearing.[70] Growing up in the 1930s in the Sandyford area – then still very rural – Terence remembered a blackthorn bush associated with fairies growing on the family's farm, 'which wouldn't be touched, because they were afraid of what could happen if they interfered'. Henry also remembered belief in the fairies as still quite widespread when he was growing up in Shankill in the 1940s, mostly taking the form of warning children to stay away from the 'fairy trees' that the farmers still carefully avoided.

Pádraig was a young postman in June 1951, working in the Kilternan and Glencullen areas, when he had a very strange experience. 'I was finished [work] around about quarter to twelve,' Pádraic remembered. He had just over an hour to go before he had to collect the post from a pillar box. Then, he recalled, 'As I crossed the road… there was a black-thorn hedge on the right-hand side … I saw this *thing*.' Pádraic jumped off his bike to look closer. 'It was a little man,' he remembered, 'And he didn't see me… I pulled the peaked cap down over me. My eyes nearly jumped out of my head. And it jumped up… there's a long thorn, and it went in behind the thorn.' Pádraic jumped up on the bank to look – 'it was dressed in green,' he said, 'and the shoes were pointy, and they come up like little leggings, and they come into a V, like that'. The little man was holding something in his hand, but Pádraic didn't know what it was. Later, describing it to someone, they told him it must have been 'the golden hammer'. This event occurred at an extremely stressful point in Pádraic's life. His father was terminally ill with tuberculosis and had been sent home to die. Pádraic wondered if the strange experience might be a sign of his father's impending death: 'I said to my mother when I went in – he was in bed – I said, "How is he today?" "He's okay," she said. "He's all right."' Still troubled, Pádraic sought advice from a local woman, who told him it had been a 'privilege' to see the fairy, which other people had also seen, and agreed with his view that he should consult the priest. The priest took a philosophical view: 'What can be seen by night can be seen by day, there's the amount of spirits on earth as in heaven.' Although the experience with the fairy was alarming, Pádraic opted to view these experiences not as frightening but as a 'gift'.

Derek and Harry grew up hearing stories about fairies from their aunt, who was originally from Offaly but had worked in Dalkey for many years. They remembered one about a man with a hump on his back: 'he fell asleep in a field and woke up and a fairy was there. And he says, "When you wake up… you'll have no hump on your back". So your man was cured and off he went. So this other guy came along and he lay down as well and he started abusing the fairies. So when he woke up, he had two humps on his back.' Stacia, a Traveller whose family had many ties to Dún Laoghaire-Rathdown, also recounted another, longer and more detailed, version of this story, related to her by her father when she was a child. This narrative connects Derek, Harry and their family, and Stacia and hers, to countless generations of storytellers from all across Europe, if not the world. Scholars of traditional culture have often pointed out that the same stories, with regional and personal variations, are told everywhere. In 1910, Finnish folklorist Antti Aarne compiled an index of folktale types.[71] It was expanded by American folklorist Stith Thompson in 1961,[72] and by German folklorist Hans-Jörg Uther in 2004.[73] Today, it is known as the Aarne–Thompson–Uther Index. One of the stories it contains is catalogued as 'AT 503, Gifts of the Fairies', a story of the man who ended up with two humps, told over the centuries by countless narrators in their respective languages.

Many Traveller families were extremely knowledgeable about diverse aspects of tradition, including maintaining elements of the fairy faith and stories about the otherworld that many might associate with Gaeltacht areas and/or with the increasingly remote past rather than a modern Dublin suburb. When Stacia was a child, in the 1960s, her mother related to her how, as a young wife a generation earlier, she had been advised never to leave clothes drying outside overnight, in case the fairies came around. Aidan's family was originally from the west. After spending time in various places, they stayed for a period in the 1970s in Rathfarnham, where Aidan had a horse. One day, Aidan and his horse were on a thorny piece of land – roughly where the Nutgrove Shopping Centre stands at the time of writing – when they encountered a tiny man, about knee height, with dark, curly hair, dressed like a countryman. Dumbfounded, Aidan could not move, although he had no sense of danger. He concluded afterwards that he had encountered one of the Little People. Nellie grew up largely in the Monkstown area in the 1980s and 1990s and remembered fairy faith in her family at that time. 'The women would go to throw water out,' she remembered, 'and you'd see them making sure that it was in certain areas... "Don't throw it on top of the fairies... or you're going to bring us bad luck on the camp"... or if you were leaving a camp you'd... get it blessed and say, "Thanks for allowing us live on your land".' Nellie also recounted stories once told about a patch of land near Monkstown Railway Station where nothing ever seemed to grow: 'it looked like it had been scorched earth... the old tale was that it used to be the entry point for... the fairies to go back into the hills'. Other interviewees from rural areas used the term 'fairy' as a euphemism to describe mental illness or disability, hinting at the changeling lore once common throughout Ireland and that may have prevailed here into the early twentieth century, when infant mortality was still very high.

Will grew up in Glencullen and the family farm had a rath – a fairy ring – on it, probably one of the numerous megalithic tombs or Iron Age constructions found in many locations in the Dublin/Wicklow Mountains. For years, Will said, his father, Matthew, was aware of the local belief that it would be bad luck to interfere with it because of its association with the fairies. Will's grandfather, who had bought the land, had left the rath undisturbed. But by c.1980, few were taking stories about the rath seriously, and Matthew destroyed it. Matthew himself also remembered this episode clearly. 'So... we got on and ploughed,' Matthew remembered, 'and there was a big stone in it, and it had to be quarried out of it... And I didn't see any fairies!'

* * *

The banshee (*bean sí*) is a well-known Irish tradition, referring to a supernatural death messenger about whom stories have been told for centuries, perhaps since as long ago as the eighth century. There are thriving traditions about the banshee in areas including down-town Dún Laoghaire, Shankill, certain rural parts of the county and among Travellers connected to the broader area, with many having grown up hearing stories of the banshee, and some – from diverse backgrounds – even having had strange encounters themselves. Local accounts typically focus on the idea that the banshee was seen combing her hair, and that 'found' combs should be avoided, as they are the banshee's property. One of the most widespread legends is the story of her annoyance with anyone who picks up or disturbs her comb.[74] Ann Burns, recorded in 1980, remembered a personal encounter with a banshee, appearing in the form of a very small woman.[75] Mr and Mrs Malone of Barnacullia also remembered a local site that people avoided because it was associated with the banshee.[76] May McConville, from Sallynoggin, remembered when she and her brother heard the banshee wailing behind their house and their mother explained that she was an unhappy spirit being punished for the sin of pride, and that she 'followed' their family. Three weeks afterwards, May said, their grandmother died.[77] 'When we were kids,' Clodagh remembered of her mid-twentieth-century childhood in Dún Laoghaire, 'we believed that the banshee had very long hair and that she combed her hair... if you saw her, she threw the comb at you and you would die.' Henry remembered a woman dying in Shankill, 'and we heard this cry out on the road, and we were told not to look out, it was the banshee... we were terrified to go out... The little woman out there, sitting and she combing her hair.' Charlotte often visited her grandparents' home in Barnacullia when she was growing up in the 1950s, and she lives there now. She remembered the many stories she heard about the banshee, reputed to haunt the area around the gate on Charlotte's own land: 'The banshee sits out there... combing her hair.' As a child, Charlotte longed to see the banshee for herself: 'I'd love to have seen this lady sitting on the pier combing this long hair.' Peter, growing up in Sallynoggin in the 1960s and 1970s, often heard his father, from Dún Laoghaire, telling stories of the banshee there, which he associated with the Widow Gambol's Hill. 'He loved that particular area,' Peter recalled. 'That meant a lot to him because of the story of the banshee in the castle...

The banshee lived, I think, around the back of the castle... she was banished from the castle, and you could hear her wailing... I was always told that if you look out and found a comb on the ground, never pick it up... because it was the banshee's comb.' Mick grew up, mostly in Dalkey, hearing about the banshee: 'the old thing was if you found a comb, that's the banshee. She was here last night and she left it.' Other stories demonstrate a synthesis of banshee stories and other inspirations, including imagery from popular culture. Ingrid, who grew up in the 1940s, reported her mother's assertion that the banshee was a 'shapeshifter' who could take many forms to announce a death. Eoin grew up in Blackrock in the 1970s, where he was regaled by his grandfather with his enormous trove of wonderful, but often terrifying, stories. The banshee figured frequently – so much so that Eoin has perfect visual recall of how he imagined her as a child: 'the long hair, the pale skin, the dark eyes, with a trench coat! ... a dismembered body nearly... and the feet were hooves, right!'

Several also related accounts of alleged sightings of the banshee, either their own or others'. Barry grew up in Dún Laoghaire in the 1950s and 1960s. There was less lighting then, and the parks were quite heavily forested. Young people often tried to scare one another with spooky stories. When Barry was about seventeen, he decided to walk home through a local park, and 'about halfway up a figure came up out of the ground'. 'Have you never heard of the banshee?' his grandmother said when he got home. 'The laneway is meant to be haunted.' Eva's father was in the army reserves as a young man. One evening, returning to his home in Stillorgan he and his colleagues 'heard and saw the banshee'. To the day he died, Eva said, 'he would still say, "Heard and saw, don't want it to ever happen again."' Nellie's mother came home one day upset, as she had seen the banshee. The next day the Gardaí came to the family's camp in Monkstown, with the dreadful news of a tragic death in the family.

Ingrid's family often related the story of when their father was afraid he was being followed by the banshee. On his way home one night from his fishing trawler, he became aware of a disturbing noise right behind him. It was dark and he was carrying a heavy bucket of fish, but he started to walk as quickly as possible. To his consternation, the noise continued to follow him. When he reached his street someone said, 'Don't tell me you're bringing that dog home!' It turned out that a dog had been following him, licking the fish, while he had been afraid to turn around in case he saw a banshee.

Notably, stories about the banshee appear to have thrived in the modern era principally in areas where customs and traditions around funerals and death involved the community, with lavish wakes, numerous traditions and beliefs relating to death and dying, large funerals, and great attention given to matters like the Last Rites and prayers for the dead. This 'atmosphere of intimacy with death'[78] was fertile ground for banshee stories and experiences.

* * *

Religious beliefs and rituals are found in every human society in the world, shaped by history, cultural contact, experience and balances of power, as are ex-canonical beliefs and ideas about the supernatural, which can intersect with and diverge from religion in a complex web of ideas and behaviours. Religion is such a complex topic, impacting on people in so very many ways, from the intimate to the world of state politics, from the most theologically based formal observation of faith to the plethora of traditional practices that can cohabit the same psychic space, that one chapter in a book about a particular area certainly cannot do the topic justice. It is clear, though, that religion in all of its forms has had a huge role to play here, as elsewhere in Ireland, and that no history would be complete without a discussion of it.

Ideas, beliefs and stories about other elements of the supernatural exist largely beyond the parameters of formal religious thinking, and clearly lack the infrastructure, formal academic philosophy and structures of authority that are central to religious thought and practice. However, they share with religion the function of helping us to think about some of the great mysteries of life, as we try to make sense of them, as well as hinting at ancient beliefs that may linger into modern times. For these reasons, accounts of the fairies, the banshee and other elements of folk tradition which are so often dismissed as old ways or superstition are an essential element of the story of this place.

FIGHTING AND
FIGHTING BACK

The landscape and memories of Dún Laoghaire-Rathdown are marked by its history, including conflicts, tensions and personal and social responses to these. We have already referenced the profound impact of the consolidation of British power over Ireland during the sixteenth and seventeenth centuries; the many Big Houses and former estates here are a vivid testimony to the long-lasting impacts of this era. While much of Ireland was devastated by the Great Famine of the 1840s, with populations collapsing in some rural areas, it had relatively little effect on Dún Laoghaire-Rathdown. The region continued to develop,[1] with people of all social classes and occupations steadily moving into coastal and inland areas throughout the nineteenth and twentieth century, where they – like everyone else – experienced the vicissitudes of history in ways informed by where, and among whom, they lived.

* * *

The Great Dublin Lockout of 1913, a workers' response to dreadful working conditions and low pay spearheaded by union leaders Jim Larkin and James Connolly, was a pivotal urban conflict in modern Ireland. Approximately 400 of Dublin's employers excluded around 20,000 workers to punish them for belonging to or supporting the Irish

Transport and General Workers' Union.[2] In the Kingstown area, the clash of interests between workers and employees was particularly complex, because so many of the local wealthy classes were both Protestant and Unionist, when the independence movement was also rapidly gathering pace, and where boundaries between rich and poor competed with local identity, with the latter often prevailing. Among major Dublin employers, a noteworthy exception to the norm of opposing the workers was Edward Lee, a Kingstown Methodist with a major retail business who believed in workers' rights. Lee had shortened the working week for his own employees, introduced a bonus system, and was involved in providing social housing. During the lockout, Lee tried fruitlessly to persuade fellow employers to stop requiring that their workers leave unions and sought to find points of compromise.

The local Catholic hierarchy was also aghast at the lockout, seeing socialist ideals as antithetical to Catholicism, at a time when it saw the global growth in communism as an existential threat. In Kingstown, Father Patrick Flavin established an Independent Workers' Union based on the Sodality of the Sacred Heart that he already ran for working men.[3] Despite Catholic opposition, many workers persisted. Local activist James Byrne, Branch Secretary of the ITGWU for Bray and Kingstown, died in Monkstown Hospital after his arrest on 23 October 1913 and a period in custody in poor conditions. Thousands attended his funeral and burial in Deansgrange Cemetery.[4]

The lockout attracted attention overseas. Some socialists, notably Dora Montafiore – an English-Australian veteran of the women's suffrage movement – decided to help the workers. Supported by local union leaders, she devised a scheme for Irish children whose families were struggling, to transport them to Britain to be cared for by the British labour movement. The Catholic authorities were outraged to think of Catholic children being brought to England, where their carers would be socialists and generally non-Catholics (Montafiore herself was married to a Jew). The Archbishop of Dublin issued a public letter addressing the mothers of Dublin, stating that 'they can no longer be held worthy of the name of Catholic mothers if they so far forget their duty as to send away their children to be cared for in a strange land, without any security of any kind that those to whom the poor children are to be handed over are Catholics, or indeed, are persons of any faith at all'. Montafiore attempted to evacuate from Kingstown with a group of starving children on 22 October 1913, but was prevented from doing so.[5] By January 1914, the workers of Dublin had no choice but to return to work. The workers of Kingstown would, however, remember that Lee had done what he could to help.

* * *

The First World War started on 28 July 1914, when Austria-Hungary declared war on Serbia. Many young (and some not so young) Irishmen enlisted, for various reasons – economic necessity, loyalty to the British Empire, peer pressure, a desire for adventure, and more. About 210,000 men from the island of Ireland enlisted, of whom about 57 per cent were Catholics.[6] Despite the lack of conscription, the proportionate number enlisting was about two-thirds that in Britain.[7] In Dublin, widespread poverty was a significant contributing factor; about 26,000 lived in tenements, while the soldiers' pay was significantly higher than that of most working-class men.[8]

While many Catholics enlisted, Protestants tended to enlist in higher numbers, relative to their population (across the whole island, 43 per cent of recruits were Protestants),[9] partly because Protestant social organisations like the Boys' Brigade proselytised heavily for participation in the war,[10] sometimes because of a greater sense of loyalty to Britain, and possibly also, in the case of wealthier, more educated recruits, because they were more likely to assume officer positions rather than joining the rank and file, and would face less risk. Dún Laoghaire-Rathdown, with a significantly larger-than-average Protestant population, saw many enlisting for all these reasons. Propaganda posters encouraging men to join the war were displayed all over Ireland; one displaying a beautiful maiden and a legend querying whether the men had any women worth defending is set against a background thought to represent Kingstown Harbour, from which so many departed.[11] Regina's father and grandfather both fought in the war; her father altered his papers to pass as eighteen, when he was just sixteen, while her grandfather was among the older to sign up. And they were among many. Despite burgeoning nationalism, initially there was much public support for the war – the soldiers' departures were often marked by cheering crowds, sure that most would return soon, as heroes.[12] The number enlisted in the Dún Laoghaire-Rathdown area – about 900 from the Kingstown area alone by August 1915 – was such that the proportion of women drinking in pubs was notably increased. In December 1915, Michael O'Leary from Macroom, County Cork, who had been awarded the Victoria Cross, spoke at a recruiting meeting in Kingstown. His likeness also featured on a poster stating, '1 Irishman defeats 10 Germans'. Michael invited local boys to follow him into battle.[13] Social pressure was also

Volunteers serving soldiers at the Kingstown Refreshment Buffet during the First World War. Lexicon Library Postcard Collection.

applied by young sporting heroes, who could make war look glamorous. Lieutenant Colonel Geoffrey Downing, a former Monkstown rugby player, appealed to the Irish Rugby Football Union, urging them to join the army.[14] Rugby was then strongly associated with elite classes, who in turn tended to be loyalist, and rugby clubs, serving as unofficial army recruitment agencies, often encouraged members to adopt a spirit of sacrifice and express their willingness to die for their country. Blackrock College, a strong rugby school, would lose fifty-one former students in the war.[15]

As the war progressed, casualties and trauma increased. On 23 October 1914, Ned Richardson from Dalkey was killed with his own bayonet by German soldiers. Fighting in Gallipoli in 1915, Jasper Brett from Kingstown recounted: 'When one hears a shell screaming one falls flat; well, I fell flat several times, and then one time when I did not, the ground was torn up in front of me; the man in front was wounded in the neck.' Henry McCrombie of Monkstown, a veteran of the Boer War,* was shot at the Ugandan front in 1915.[16] Christine's uncle joined up as a young man in his late teens or early twenties. When he was killed, the officer in charge sent a letter to his mother: 'The poor boy didn't suffer at all,' he said, providing the purported location of his grave. Many years later, Anne learned that there was no grave: whatever had happened to him, there was no body left to bury. The family still had a framed photo of her uncle on the wall when Anne was a little girl in the early 1950s. 'I found it very creepy,' she said, knowing that he had died in such a dreadful way. 'I felt that wherever I went the eyes were following me.' Kate's great-uncle was killed in 1916 aged twenty-eight, leaving a young widow with two small children. Graham's grandfather was seriously injured

---

* While the impact of trauma on soldiers returning from the First World War, known as shellshock, was apparent, previously similar symptoms were noted among veterans of the Boer War. Ann Espie, recorded in 1980 speaking of the Ringsend and Dún Laoghaire areas, recalled a man locally known as 'Born Drunk', of whom she said: 'He was from the Boer War, maybe it was the poor man might have been shellshocked or something', NFC UFP, vol. 1984, 244.

early in the war, patched up and sent home with a special white badge to wear in public so that people would know that he was not shirking his duty. Two of Benjamin's uncles fought in the war – despite being Quakers – and survived.

Many wealthy women volunteered for the war effort. They were substantially over-represented in organisations like the British Red Cross Society, of which over 90 per cent of members were women, as poorer soldiers' wives were too busy caring for and supporting their families on the modest 'separation allowance' they received, as well as whatever they could earn through their own labour.[17] Wealthy women, without these pressing concerns, and with plenty of domestic help, could offer their services. Doris Findlater, from a prominent family with various well-known businesses, made war munitions,[18] while many women served as nurses and cooks, and provided entertainment and craft activities for wounded soldiers convalescing locally. Benjamin's grandmother, a member of the Monkstown Quaker Meeting House, had an aid station where she and others made bandages and dressings for the front. Monica Roberts from Stillorgan organised a group called 'Band of Helpers to the Soldiers' that sent essentials like socks and bootlaces, and luxuries like chocolate and tobacco, to Dubliners at war. Monica corresponded regularly with many soldiers, giving them news from Ireland and responding to their letters.[19] Fundraising efforts, or events that hosted wounded soldiers, also typically organised by wealthy women, were held in the grounds of local stately homes. In February 1915, for example, a sale of work was held at Rhos-y-Gar in Monkstown, the home of a Mrs Orpen, raising 'necessities and comforts' for soldiers and sailors.[20] Various local Big Houses, including Cabinteely House and Corrig Castle, were used as military hospitals and depots and others, including Killiney Castle and Clonskeagh Castle, were occupied by the British military. Cabinteely House was used primarily for collecting and preparing medical equipment, including dressings made of sphagnum moss.[21] Many of the owners of these homes were both Protestant and

An unknown man with Tiger the dog in a rental rowboat owned by William Mullen, who had a tearoom and boat rental on Killiney Strand in the 1920s. He founded this small business with his earnings from the munitions factory where he worked during the war. Collection of Catherine Mullen, kind permission of Anna Scudds.

unionist, and wished to show their support for the British war effort, while supporting local boys and men.[22]

As so many young men were fighting, there were opportunities in Britain in a range of industrial and agricultural sectors. Some took advantage of this to earn good money. Maria's grandfather, from Killiney, worked in a munitions factory in Britain. When it was all over, he would use his savings to invest in a small seaside business catering to tourists and day trippers: rowing boats for hire and a tea tent.

* * *

Oisín's grandmother, Kitty – from Drumcondra – was in Cumann na mBan and was a personal friend of Pádraic Pearse; Kitty would relate how the two of them went boating in Kingstown, partly so that he could speak about his activities where he would not be heard. Later, she referenced these boating trips in her deposition to the Military Archives.[23] Doubtless many other conversations about the impending uprising were also held, but for many of the residents of Dún Laoghaire-Rathdown, the Easter Rising initially seemed small and distant. The first most heard was when their regular commuter service was interrupted. Timothy's aunt told him about going to the train station in Dalkey only to be told: 'No trains! No trains! Revolution in the city!'

While huge numbers of locals were involved in the First World War, considerable numbers also participated in the Rising. Members of the E and F sections of the Volunteers, including insurgents from Sandyford, Dundrum, Kingstown and Glasthule, participated, as did members of Cumann na mBan, like Máire Walker, founder of a branch in Glasthule.[24] Janet's grandmother – still remembered when Janet was a child as a 'tall, stately woman' – often related her exploits as a gun runner. Her baby (Janet's father) was born in 1916, and she was said to have used a perambulator with the baby inside to transport weapons, the guns tucked under the child. She would die in 1922, but stories were told of her for years after that.

Despite considerable republican activity locally, many were horrified and baffled as the Rising unfolded. While large numbers were risking their lives overseas, it seemed like dreadful timing, even to numerous nationalists. Most of the Anglo-Irish, and many of the professional classes from diverse backgrounds, were opposed to the Rising. Opposition was also common among the working classes. Kate's great-uncle was known in the family to have flown a British flag from his window in a work-ing-class neighbourhood, demonstrating his contempt for the Rising. For families – like Kate's – who had fought with the British, and whose livelihoods were intimately entwined with British enterprises and ser-vices, the Rising was unwelcome. Some residents of the coastal areas provided breakfast to the British soldiers arriving at Kingstown pier, grateful they had come to put it down.[25]

Many remember their parents or grandparents describing encoun-ters with the British soldiers – 'kids in uniform, brought over by the English,' Niamh's grandmother described them as – several with the detail that some soldiers seem to have initially believed themselves to

Soldiers looking for rebels or
ammunition in a hay cart during the
period of the 1916 Rising. Lexicon
Library Postcard Collection.

be in France. Benjamin's mother and grandmother were riding horses
near Seapoint when they saw a line of recently landed British troops. 'As
they approached,' he was told, 'the officer broke away and he talked in
French.' Both women spoke French and answered him in that language
as he asked what direction the city centre was in. Clearly, the officer
knew exactly where he was, but the women were left with the impression
that he did not want the troops to know much about where they were or
what was happening. Christopher's mother and grandmother directed
them towards the city centre via Ballsbridge, and would hear later that
many of those men were killed in the hostilities.

By 26 April 1916, so many British soldiers had arrived that the seafront was 'a seething mass of khaki'.[26] The Battle of Mount Street, on
that day, was one of the bloodiest exchanges of the Rising. Philo's father
told her that he – a teenager from Blackrock at the time – had been

with the rebels in Mount Street before the hostilities began, but that because of his young age, he was sent away before shots were fired. Fred Dietrichsen, from Nottingham, was one of the soldiers of the Sherwood Foresters troop sent to quell the Rising. They landed at Kingstown on 26 April. While many of the others were disoriented and confused, it was familiar territory to Fred, whose wife, Beatrice Mitchell, was a Dubliner. Thinking that Fred was fighting in France, Beatrice and her children were among the supporters lining the streets of Blackrock to welcome the soldiers. When Fred saw them in the crowd, he broke formation to give them all a hug. Fred was one of the first British soldiers to die at the Battle of Mount Street.[27] In Stillorgan that day, Eva's grandmother gave birth to a little girl six weeks before her due date – shock, the family thought, because she had just realised that her brother was in danger in the General Post Office, which had been seized by the rebels. Eva's great-grandmother lived in Stillorgan with her husband, an English ex-army man who had converted to Catholicism to marry her. Despite the English connection, the family was extremely republican. Family lore related that Eva's great-grandmother, whose son was in the GPO, walked from Stillorgan to O'Connell Street, where she knocked on the door of the GPO, and asked to speak to her son to see if he needed anything. When he said that he needed more ammunition she was said to have collected ammunition from an IRA detachment in Clontarf, hid it in her petticoats, and delivered it.

The presence of so many British soldiers was very disruptive even when they were not engaged in hostilities. Roy's grandfather, who owned a dairy in Glasthule, sought compensation from the army for the damage done to his grazing field when the artillery occupied it, reducing it to mud (the family still has the solicitor's letter). Members of the British Secret Service, stationed locally in considerable numbers, were rumoured to cross dress to mingle unnoticed in pubs and other public places to gather information.[28] By 28 April it was increasingly clear that the British had won. When they looked across Dublin Bay, or down from the uplands, suburbanites in the south could see smoke hanging over Dublin. The Blackrock Company of insurgents, led by Tim Finn, had been in position at Stillorgan Grove for several days; by 28 April, all but one of Finn's men had deserted, and he concluded that the battle was lost and went home. The next day, 29 April, Mary Martin of Monkstown wrote: 'Fighting still continuing as fierce as ever in Dublin & fires were seen during the night & one could hear the big guns going. We hear great rumours of the damage that is being done to the city by the cannonade.'[29] Sam's family were well-to-do landlords and Catholics ('Castle Catholics') in the Glencullen area. Despite their mixed loyalties ('they felt all kinds of ways… In a strange way [my grandmother] was a monarchist, and when she went to London she loved to applaud the queen'), they allowed Constance Markievicz to have a house on their land, from which she trained young insurgents in the use of firearms. It was an awkward situation, as Sam's grandfather was 'Justice of the Peace under the British Crown', but the family was also fond of 'Con'. They decided to simply look the other way. When a warrant was sent out for her arrest, they helped her to escape by arranging for her to travel steerage on the mailboat, assuming that the authorities would search for her in first class.[30]

Wherever their loyalties lay, people were very inquisitive. Many families still relate stories they have heard about their parents' or grandparents' experiences of the Rising. Roberta's grandmother and her younger sister, from Kingstown, tried to get into the city centre to see what was happening: 'They walked in as far as they could… they won't have got in too far before they were witnessing gunfire.' After Easter Week, said Jennifer, her grandmother was so curious that she and her daughter – Jennifer's mother – went into the city centre. Exploring the Rotunda Gardens at the top of O'Connell Street, she tripped and fell, and immediately a crowd gathered, thinking that a woman had been shot.

From 3 May, the British authorities executed the leaders of the Rising, including the seven signatories of the Proclamation. Public opinion started to shift, one sign of which was that fewer wrote supportive letters to soldiers at war.[31] Rachel's grandmother was an Englishwoman living with her Irish husband and their family in Dalkey. Despite her pride in being English, she was shocked by decisions taken by the British government. Reflecting later on the events of 1916, she would say, 'We [the English] were very wrong. We were very wrong in doing that.' She was, her granddaughter remembered, '[still] upset. She was speaking about the 1916 men, and she said, "*We* were very wrong"; I do remember her saying that. "We". To her, that was England.'

Just over a year after the Rising, the British released the remaining 118 insurgents convicted of offences. Some were released from life sentences. They had all been serving time in Britain and were greeted by rapturous crowds at Kingstown Harbour,[32] a scene oddly reminiscent of that which had greeted the British soldiers a year before. Eva's great-uncle was one of the men imprisoned. The story that has stayed with her is his description of Michael Collins as a 'cute hoor' who grabbed his shorts during a match in jail, preventing him from scoring a goal.

* * *

After 1916, the number of Irishmen joining the army dwindled to a trickle, at least partly because of the huge public anger at how Britain had dealt with the Rising.[33] Republican sentiments also grew and sharpened among Irish soldiers. Returning soldiers were increasingly likely to express sympathies for the fallen rebels and their cause; in 1917, Irish soldiers in Dublin were discovered giving army rifles to contacts in Sinn Féin.[34] The British army increasingly demobilised Irish soldiers outside Ireland, largely to avoid the risk of British weapons being handed over.[35]

Irish casualties mounted, as did war-induced mental and physical disability. In April 1916, Jasper Brett, mentioned earlier in the chapter, was diagnosed with 'neurasthenia' (now known as post-traumatic stress disorder). After several periods of treatment, he was discharged and returned to Kingstown in January 1917. On 4 February, the former rugby player, aged twenty-one, lay himself on the train rails in time for the ten past ten train from Dalkey to sever his head. Jasper's sorrowing parents laid him to rest in Deansgrange Cemetery. On 8 August 1916, Charles Goff of Killiney died aged twenty-seven, apparently because of a shell explosion, although his body was never recovered. His mother, a widow, finally accepted the reality of his death in November, when she placed an '*In Memoriam*' notice in the *Evening Mail*. On 23 October 1916 Herbert Lemass of Monkstown was killed, aged nineteen (his relative Seán was involved in the Rising and would serve as Taoiseach from 1959 to 1966). The three Cruess-Callaghan brothers of Blackrock – Eugene, Stanislaus and Joseph – were killed, respectively, in 1916, 1917 and 1918.[36]

Ordinary families with loved ones fighting in the trenches were increasingly exhausted, and communication was limited. When Kevin's mother was born in 1917, nobody knew exactly where her soldier father (an Englishman and veteran of the Boer War) was. The birth certificate recorded him as 'somewhere in France'. The next baby, a son conceived during the soldier's brief leave of absence, died before his father got home. Some soldiers were more fortunate than others. Richard's father, Eric, joined the British air force in 1917, aged just 17. He survived, returned with an aeroplane propeller as a souvenir, went to Trinity College, and proceeded with the rest of his life. The war had disillusioned him: 'terribly sorry for poor God. Because the Germans were all praying to God... and the English were all praying to God. And he said he thought God had a terrible time.' Both of Michael's parents were from pro-British backgrounds; this disillusionment may, Michael feels, have contributed to Eric's drift away from a loyalist and towards a more republican viewpoint.

The many injured Irishmen needing treatment required extra hospital provision. In 1917, Gertrude Dunning loaned Leopardstown Park Hospital to the Ministry of Pensions for the treatment of wounded soldiers. It became the principal treatment centre for neurasthenic soldiers in southern Ireland. The facilities were good but insufficient to cope with huge numbers of traumatised soldiers as the war progressed, and after the hostilities had ended. Among the treatments available, they were encouraged to garden in the hospital's attractive grounds.[37] (The hospital would operate until 1931, when it amalgamated with the hospital in Blackrock.[38]) Linden Convalescent Home in Blackrock was used as a military hospital, and the Protestant Meath Industrial School, also in

Blackrock, was acquired for military use.[39] By then, forty-six hospital ships had arrived since the war started, bringing about 19,255 patients, most of whom were taken to treatment centres by the Red Cross and the St John Ambulance Brigade.[40]

Because of soaring food prices, malnutrition – already a serious problem for the poor before the war – became much worse. Food shortages* led to the provision of allotments for growing vegetables in city-adjacent areas including Kingstown, Glasthule and Sallynoggin.[41] Leopardstown Racecourse provided twenty acres that were used to grow oats. Foxrock Golf Club was asked to provide land for allotments, but chose not to.[42]

The German offensive of 1918 demonstrated that more soldiers were required to fight for the Allied Forces. There were demands to extend conscription to Ireland where, so far, joining the army had been voluntary. The House of Commons in London passed the Military Service Bill on 19 April, followed by a huge wave of anti-conscription sentiment across Ireland, including from the Catholic Church. Éamon de Valera drafted a pledge of resistance to compulsory service, and thousands signed it from 21 April. In Dundrum, Dalkey and Kingstown, religious authorities addressed huge crowds, urging them to remain firm against conscription.[43]

On 5 October 1918, the *Leinster* mailboat was struck by a torpedo from a German submarine on its way from Kingstown to Holyhead. The mailboats were contractually obliged to sail during the war, and to carry military personnel onboard, despite German U-boats operating in the Irish Sea.[44] One of the survivors described her experience: 'Pieces of

---

* Food shortages and anxiety about food would have contributed to the telling of stories like one related by Victor: 'the two spinster sisters in Sandycove who received a biscuit tin from the frontline... inside was soup. They couldn't make out what it was. So they put it into their tea or their soup... ghastly stuff... it was the ashes of their brother... the letter that accompanied the biscuit tin went astray... only subsequently they discovered that they had been trying to consume the remains of their brother.' Intriguing as this story is, in fact it is a rather well-known migratory narrative of the type often referred to as an 'urban legend' and has been much-studied by folklorists. See for example de Vos, 1996, 88; 149. While the story is untrue, the account of food shortages lend it veracity.

A naval cutter in Kingstown Harbour, c.1897–1904. Clarke Photographic Collection, National Library of Ireland.

iron and wood flew about, hitting various people, many of whom were wounded, blood flowing freely… The boat immediately listed, and the deck went perpendicular… I jumped off into the water, and was sucked under the sinking vessel. On coming to the surface I swam away until I got hold of an upturned boat.'[45] Other ships passed but were ordered not to assist, for fear of further torpedoes. Over 500 died. About 200 survived by climbing onto lifeboats or holding onto flotsam until the rescue boats arrived, hours later.[46] Bríd's grandfather, a chef on board who had survived an attack on the *Connaught* mailboat on 3 March 1917, survived; he still had the keys to the galley in his pocket when he was taken to hospital. Many of the dead were civilians, including twenty-one post office sorters.[47] Many were also locals, like Sophia Barrett of Carrickmines, a nurse who had served in the war and was returning to the front after her leave. Sophia is buried in the Kilternan Parish Churchyard.[48] Robert Ernest Lee, a member of a locally famous retail family, was a doctor who had survived active service to die within sight of home. Harry's grandfather, who worked in the port, told Harry about the awful sight of the bodies lined up for identification on the Carlisle Pier: 'a horrific experience'. The British authorities refused to hold a public inquest into the disaster, the worst ever in the Irish Sea.[49]

The war ended on 11 November 1918. Of the approximately 200,000 Irishmen resident in Ireland who served, about 27,000 died, about 100,000 returned, and the rest stayed in Britain, emigrated or had left the forces due to injury before the war ended.[50] After fighting in and surviving the war, three of Gareth's uncles, from Barnacullia, went to New Zealand – perhaps partly, the family speculated, because they were concerned about how they would be received as former British soldiers (although they did return later on). Harvey's father was a teenager during the war. By fifteen, he was out of school and delivering telegrams, some of which informed parents that their sons had been killed. Nonetheless, he had decided to sign up. Thankfully, he survived unhurt. After the war, still serving in the British Army, he fell for a pretty girl working behind the counter in Woolworths in Dún Laoghaire: 'Come off on leave once and he went in… with a bunch of flowers to her and asked her out.' But her family were republicans, so she said, 'I'm not going out with no British soldier.' (He eventually managed to talk her into going out with him, and they would go on to get married; he was demobbed in 1922.)

The end of the war was greeted with jubilation and weariness. In the first days of 1919, a German submarine bedecked with a white surrender flag and a German ensign at half-mast were displayed in Kingstown Harbour – a dramatic war trophy.[51] Many families celebrated the return of their loved ones, or mourned their slaughtered sons with grief and pride. Many also questioned why so many Irish boys were sent to die for a country that did not see Ireland as an equal partner in its union, while poverty and all of its associated problems remained rife.

Inevitably, written material on the long-term impact of the war on the returned soldiers and their families gives more insight into the experiences of the wealthier social classes. With lower levels of literacy, and more pressing financial issues, working-class families were much less likely to leave a written record of their sorrows and hardships.

Regarding material culture and tangible memorials, Protestant soldiers also tended to leave a bigger footprint than their Catholic colleagues. While Protestant communities memorialised their dead in the form of plaques displayed on the walls of churches and other community buildings – like the Connemara marble plaque at St Patrick's Church in Dalkey[52] – Catholic communities usually did not; not in churches, which were reserved as sacred spaces and rarely, as the nationalist movement mounted, in other public areas. An exception is a memorial in the side porch of St Brigid's Church in Cabinteely, a holy water font erected in memory of Second Lieutenant Hugh O'Farrell of the Irish Guards, who died in France on 27 September 1918, six weeks before the end of the war, aged nineteen.[53]

Relative to the size of the sacrifice, there are few public memorials to fallen soldiers in Dún Laoghaire-Rathdown. Generally, the Free State would opt to avoid significant commemoration.* Ireland was the only country in the British Commonwealth, of which it was still a member, not to contribute to the Imperial War Graves Commission, responsible for maintaining the graves of the war dead, including the Irish.[54] One monument can, however, be seen in Kilgobbin, where the local community erected a Celtic cross, created by local stonemasons, in the old cemetery.[55]

Surviving soldiers returned to a country in turmoil, the public mood increasingly shifting towards a desire for independence. On 6 March 1918, John Redmond, who had campaigned for Home Rule, died in London. His body arrived at Kingstown to a reception by the National Volunteers and a guard of honour from the Royal Irish Regiment. His death symbolised the demise of hope that the Irish quest for independence could be peacefully resolved.

Many ordinary families suffered the after effects of the war for decades. Kimberly's grandfather, in Dún Laoghaire, had severe shellshock

---

* The Islandbridge Memorial in Dublin city centre is the notable exception to this rule. Work began on the park in 1931 but it was no longer maintained from 1940 and was only restored in 1988.

and other health issues. He had difficulty breathing and speaking, and was almost confined to bed for years. His wife – mother of a large family – worked as a cleaner and in a local launderette, leaving her husband to care for the house and family as best he could.* While soldiers from poorer backgrounds were more likely to struggle with reintegration, soldiers from all social classes had difficulties, including poor mental health and physical disability and illness. Even relatively fortunate survivors could be left with permanent challenges. Lettie's uncle, a doctor, had lost every hair on his body after being gassed. 'I remember Mummy saying,' Lettie remembered, 'he was very confused then… visiting the patients, would he be less frightening with a wig on or a wig off.'

The aftermath of war was complicated by the 1918–20 influenza pandemic – Kingstown was one of the first areas where many sickened[56] – and by ongoing shortages of food and fuel.[57] Dennis Kenny, who grew up in Stillorgan and served time in prison in Belfast because of his republican activities, recalled that, when he returned, he found 'a terrible lot of the population gone'.[58] Kevin's grandmother, from Blackrock, lost seven of her (adult) siblings over a period of three and a half years, thought by the family to have been victims of the pandemic (although the records do not relate their causes of death). Janet's family, from the same tight-knit community in downtown Dún Laoghaire for generations, often spoke of local children who had been orphaned by the pandemic but, rather than being given to orphanages, were absorbed into other local families, even acquiring their surnames in the absence of a formal adoption process.

Noreen and Gladys's father fought in the war and was sent home on leave in 1916 when he married their mother in Dún Laoghaire. In 1918, he was wounded and sent home for good; he would receive a small war pension for the rest of his life. Gladys was born in 1924 and remembered how, throughout her childhood, her father chatted about his war

---

* In later years, one of her clients was Jack Doyle, a Cork native known as the 'Gorgeous Gael' who was a famous boxer married to an actress, Movita Castaneda, who would become Marlon Brando's second wife. Jack and Movita stayed at a private house called Rocklands in Dalkey in the 1940s whenever they were not on tour. Taub, 2007, 277.

memories with a local friend who was a Boer War veteran. The family always marked Armistice Day on 11 November. Gladys and Noreen were unsure how the family, Dún Laoghaire Catholics, felt about Irish independence. When they were little, in the 1930s, people tended to be 'careful what they talked about'. Gladys and Noreen's father was quite fortunate after the war: he got a good job for the Armistice Commission, a British Civil Service position, and he was transferred in independence to the Irish Land Registry. One day, Noreen and her father were in the city centre when he encountered a man who had fought alongside him in the trenches. The two men embraced silently, with great emotion. Reflecting, Noreen felt that they had formed a close bond through all they had endured.

* * *

Elections were held on 14 December 1918, as part of the General Election in the United Kingdom. Sinn Féin had a landslide victory in most of Ireland. Kingstown Town Hall was the count centre for the South Dublin constituency, and the Sinn Féin candidate, George Gavan Duffy, was returned with 5,139 votes (contrasting with 3,819 for Sir Thomas Robinson, the unionist candidate).[59] The War of Independence began on 21 January 1919. Many ex-servicemen joined the IRA at a time of high unemployment among veterans (about 46 per cent by 1920).[60] Speaking in 1980 of the Dundrum area decades before, James Nolan stated that the locals 'had great respect for law and order'. They were, he said, 'for the establishment', and most of them were 'contented with their lot, with no 'rebellious feelings'.[61] But many had plenty of rebellious feelings. Dennis Kenny, of Stillorgan, served with the IRA, spent six months in prison because of his activities, and dedicated years of his young life to the cause of independence. Remembering this period from the distance of 1980, he said that 'most of my travelling was done at night cross-country… crossin' main roads, over one wall into another. You'd become used to it like that. Sometimes I was armed.'[62]

From September 1919, all the republican units in south County Dublin became part of the new Sixth Battalion of the Dublin Brigade, with active companies in areas including Dundrum, Ticknock, Barnacullia, Sandyford, Glencullen and Stepaside. The Sixth Battalion operated in a challenging environment: the good infrastructure facilitated the British forces, the Royal Irish Constabulary Barracks were generally in built-up areas, and there were high levels of loyalism locally. Whereas local resentments around inequality fuelled some of the violence in Ireland, apparently in Dún Laoghaire-Rathdown this was less of an issue, despite vast socioeconomic inequality, presumably at least partly because the wealthy were significant local employers, and many were individually liked. While many of the larger houses were raided by the IRA for weapons or vehicles, generally their inhabitants were left unharmed. Local IRA organiser Ernie O'Malley was something of an outsider when he encouraged training on the demesne grounds, hoping this would help the insurgents to lose respect for the elite.[63]

Many families retain quite detailed stories about their recent ancestors' IRA involvement, or other ways in which they were involved in the push for independence. Peter's grandfather, from Kingstown, was with an IRA unit and told stories later of hiding in the Dublin/ Wicklow Mountains and walking for hours to reach and attack British garrisons. Barbara's uncle, who had served in France, joined the IRA, as did his brother. Jennifer's grandfather was a First World War veteran who lived in Rosary Gardens – a development for ex-servicemen – and worked as a delivery driver. He recounted a story of giving Michael Collins a lift while delivering items in County Wicklow, saying that his war service made him a good man for the job, as the authorities would have let him pass on seeing his papers. Ellen's father joined the Fianna, a youth organisation, as he was too young for the IRA. Sarah-Jane's aunt, working in service in Dalkey, stated that she had been involved in bringing supplies to Seán MacBride when he was hiding in the mountains. Terence's uncle, who was in the IRA, recounted how the Guinness family, residing at Burton Hall in Sandyford, left out their car with a full tank of fuel for the IRA's use, and that they took it out for the night and returned it in the morning. Another uncle of Terence's was interned in Frongoch in Wales for a period because of his IRA involvement. Relatives of Gladys and Noreen had to emigrate because they had – apparently unawares – rented a basement flat to IRA members, resulting in the loss of business from their predominately unionist clientele. Regina remembered her mother and uncle's stories about delivering messages for the IRA: 'Well,' Regina said, 'my mother's stepbrother was running with messages in the evenings, and he would use my mother's room in Patrick Street to hide there and to pick up messages… they'd bring messages to her and someone else collected the messages. So I used to say to her, "You were a spy, Mam!"' Jacinta's father, from Kingstown, served with the IRA and spent a considerable period in prison. It was terribly difficult for the whole family. His own father was a former solider with the British Army, and a veteran of the Boer War. His mother suffered agonies when he was in prison, and later related her account of visiting him in Kilmainham. He asked her to take a set of Rosary beads that he had made, and then spilled a number of bullets into her hand, for her to take away and dispose of.* In May 1919, the IRA raided a British field kitchen at Ticknock, stealing two mules.[64] Austin's father's family had a grocery shop and post office, as well as a public telephone, in the uplands community of Kilternan. His father was in his teens, minding the shop, when an IRA man came in to take the telephone apart (presumably to make it more difficult to alert the authorities to local manoeuvres): 'Dad said he was a bit nervous and shaky and the gun went off and luckily missed Dad by two inches.'

The new recruits to the RIC in 1920 and 1921, who initially wore improvised uniforms in combinations of military khaki and police black and dark green, were nicknamed the Black and Tans. They

---

* Years later, in 1966, celebrating the fiftieth anniversary of the Rising, Eugene marched on O'Connell Street with many other IRA veterans. He had a heart attack that day, and de Valera himself – Eugene's idol – visited him in hospital.

started to arrive on 25 March 1920, instilling terror in many locals but – at first – relief in others. Kate's grandmother, a working-class lady from Kingstown, was very pro-British and, later, she would recount how she had initially entertained the Black and Tans in her home. But soon most regarded them with terror. Catherine's grandmother was a much sought-after midwife in Kingstown, who told stories of the many babies she delivered during the unrest. She would take a local cab to the labouring woman's address, but many of the births occurred late at night, and she would have to return after dark, alone, hiding under bushes in gardens for safety if the Black and Tans roared past. Christine's father was a teenager then, and he and the rest of his football team were returning home to Dalkey when the Black and Tans intercepted the tram at Monkstown and made them get off for inspection – presumably, they felt, because they were dressed in green football kits and might have looked 'suspicious'. While nobody was harmed, the lads were terrified they would be shot. Harvey's mother, a teenager in Kingstown, delivered food to safe houses where IRA men were hiding. At one stage, she was arrested by the Black and Tans, 'because she had food hanging out of the crossbar of her bike, supplies for the guys'. She was briefly held in Mountjoy, but was released to her father's custody on the understanding that he would not allow her to reoffend. Harvey's mother added the detail that women carried firearms and weapons 'in their knickers' for the fighting men (back when knickers were voluminous). Visiting a couple horses he liked to feed in a local stable, Christine's father went in and said, 'Up lads' (to the horses), whereupon three local members of the IRA leapt from the straw and ran off.

Jennifer's mother often told her about the Black and Tans roaring through Kingstown on their trucks. Jennifer's great-uncle, a railway worker, was apprehended by them one evening, coming home from work after curfew, and felt that he was lucky to escape with his life. A family that had been quite apolitical, with rather pro-monarchy views, became pro-independence, and Johnny would go on to be involved in the local nationalist movement. A relative of Janet's, also from Kingstown, was known in the family as 'Speed' because of the swiftness with which he had fled Ireland after shooting a Black and Tan.

In April 1920, about 150 houses were raided by the IRA for guns and ammunition, and in May 1920, telephone and telegram equipment were destroyed in post offices in Dundrum, Kilternan, Dalkey, Kingstown, Blackrock, Sandyford and Foxrock.[65] Kingstown's name was changed to Dún Laoghaire in July 1920. Council Minutes from the Urban District of Kingstown reveal that the change was proposed by Seán Ó hUadhaigh from the Kingstown Township on 6 July 1920, confirmed by Dublin County Council on 24 July 1920, and acted upon a month later, on 5 August 1920.[66] In the context of the ongoing hostilities, this was a pointed change.

On 11 December 1920, Eden's uncle, from Shankill, was shot in the head and died during a Black and Tan raid on the Sinn Féin premises in Little Bray, after which the family was granted permission to hold a funeral, provided there were no protests or demonstrations.[67] 'I do remember,' Eden said, 'growing up, seeing a photo of him and his head was all bandaged up.'

Philo's mother was working in domestic service in Blackrock. She was on the tram one day when it was stopped: 'The men were sent upstairs and then they searched [them].' As one passed her, he slipped something heavy into her pocket. After the soldiers left, she found that it was a gun. Later, they would start searching women too. Rob related an account of a man local to Kilternan who had a small 'jaunting car' taking tourists from the coastal areas to the uplands on day trips. He had recently bought his first motorcar when the Black and Tans seized and set fire to it – terrible damage to a very significant investment. Another local story recounts a pitched battle between the Black and Tans and the IRA, with the gruesome detail of a Black and Tan's body left lying on a wall for four full days before anyone claimed it, everyone simply too scared to get involved.

Brian's father was in his early forties during the War of Independence. He related what happened after an 'English lorry' was taken to Glencullen and abandoned, after the wheels were removed: 'the Tans got to know where it was and they went up and got the lorry,' Brian said. The next Friday, the Black and Tans arrived, collected the local men and lined them up. One of the men was apparently just two or three places away from Brian's father: '[Dad] could see him getting paler and paler'. When the officer come down to search him, Brian's father 'kept interrupting him'. The Black and Tan turned to Brian's father and said, 'You've enough to do to answer your own questions when they come to you', and Brian's father retorted, 'That man has… to milk the cows down the yard and they're roaring down there with the pain of the milk and he should be down there… instead of being interrogated by you.' Exasperated, the Black and Tan let the man go. When the Black and Tans had gone, Brian recounted, 'Daddy went out to this fella and he asked, "What the hell was wrong with you that you were so pale?" And he says, "He was putting his hand in the inside pocket and if he had pulled out the papers I had, it would have incriminated half the lads in Glencullen."'

IRA men often stayed in Foxrock while on the run, and the Black and Tans, who had a base in Cabinteely, made frequent raids.[68] The family of Cabinteely resident Mary Brennan was evacuated by the Black and Tans and provided with emergency accommodation in the local Carnegie Library during a period of particular local violence.[69] Ailish, who moved to Cabinteely in 1948 and married a local, heard stories from her in-laws about the days of the Black and Tans. Everyone had to be home by ten o'clock at night, or they would be shot at. There were still physical reminders in the form of the bullet holes in the walls. Some who had been in the IRA or affiliated organisations left Ireland when things got too dangerous, and many never returned. An uncle of Howard's left for Australia after a few days in hiding in a safe house in the Dalkey area and settled there, returning only many years later, in his sixties or seventies, to see his family and reunite with his former comrades-in-arms.

While some families were deeply involved in the struggle for independence and the civil war that followed, many others just hoped for things to go 'back to normal'. Rachel's Quaker family, based in Dalkey, were resolutely pacifist. Her grandfather was an engineer who serviced boilers in laundries, and his work continued as normal. His wife, an Englishwoman who had been happy to settle in Dalkey because it was the part of Ireland that reminded her most of England, would remember the troubles as a 'worry'. 'It was a *worry* to us,' she would say, 'because we had to take the tram into Kingstown and sometimes soldiers would get on, and then there might be disagreements, and everybody would have to get off the tram. And then you were put about.' The family had various minor encounters with the hostilities: '[the children] went to their playhouse… and they discovered all their precious things had been turned upside down, and there were these boxes… [their father] went out and looked at it… it was gelignite'. All they and many others wanted was for it all just to go away.

The War of Independence officially ended on 22 July 1921, the Anglo-Irish Treaty was signed on 6 December and, after a transitional period overseen by a provisional government, the Free State became a self-governing dominion on 6 December 1922. Reactions in Dún Laoghaire-Rathdown were mixed. Barbara's family were staunch republicans – her uncles and father were involved with the IRA – and delightedly flew the Irish tricolour from their home, but the family of one of her employers, a comfortably off Catholic family from Blackrock, 'weren't too happy, so they put out the British flag'.

The Civil War broke out on 28 June 1922, between pro- and anti-Treaty factions (the Treaty agreed that the twenty-six counties in the south would become independent, while six counties of Ulster would remain part of the United Kingdom). Noteworthy hostilities in Dún Laoghaire-Rathdown included an attempt on the life of Michael Collins in Stillorgan,[70] and the burning of a barracks in Dundrum.[71] In the summer of 1922, Leopardstown Hospital, still caring for mentally ill veterans of the First World War, was raided by anti-Treaty forces, who removed clothing and a van for their own use.[72] Of course, the Civil War was painfully difficult for many families. Maria's family often recounted the 'legend' of her grandfather's encounter with his brother. Anna's grandfather was in the Free State Army, and his brother was in the IRA. At one point, apparently the IRA attempted to hold up a train, and 'my grandfather… looked out of one of the carriages… and hopping out of the train was his brother… and my grandfather said to him, "Get out of here, quickly!" he said, "otherwise I'm going to have to shoot you! … I can't go home to my mother and tell her that I've killed you."' Anna's uncle would later die of pneumonia, contracted on the run in the Dublin/Wicklow Mountains. Cecilia's father, a mechanic from Shankill, supported de Valera and could often help by providing cars at short notice. When the *Irish Press* newspaper, offering news with a slant consistent with Fianna Fáil policy,* was founded by de Valera in 1931, he was given work there.

The Civil War ended not with an absolute victory, but with ceasefire. The fighting between the Free State forces and the anti-Treaty IRA gradually descended into a series of affrays and on 30 April 1923 the IRA leadership ordered their forces to stand down. The Civil War had ended the lives of many of the most prominent fighters for independence and would impact on many for years. Dennis Kenny, who had been in the IRA and had taken the 'wrong side' during the Civil War, was interned for about fifteen months and, on his return, found himself 'more or less shut out of any sort of local employment or anything like that'.[73]

* * *

Ireland had been at war of one kind or another for over nine years. There were fewer physical reminders of the violence in Dún Laoghaire-Rathdown than in many areas. During both the War of Independence and the Civil War, stately homes and other symbols of the elite and of British colonialism were often targeted for attack, such as destruction by burning. Various properties in Dún Laoghaire-Rathdown were attacked,

---

* The *Irish Press* was published from 1931 to 1995. One of its strong selling points, particularly in the earlier years, was ample coverage of Gaelic sports and of the Irish language. The first editor was Frank Gallagher, a comrade of de Valera's during the War of Independence. It would feature writing by some of Ireland's foremost journalists and writers.

but only one, Kilteragh House in Foxrock, was destroyed, on 30 January 1923 (it was reconstructed in 1925).

The institutions that continued to care for veterans of the First World War remained a feature of Dún Laoghaire-Rathdown for decades. When Gertrude Dunning, owner of Leopardstown Park Hospital, died in 1926, her husband relinquished ownership and gave it to the Ministry of Pensions for the continued care of mentally ill veterans.[74] There were still some elderly men in residence in the 1960s, when Margie and her husband moved into a new-built adjacent housing estate. Other mentally ill soldiers were even less fortunate, as there were never enough places in hospital for them all.[75] Homeless, mentally ill war veterans remained visible in rural and urban areas of Dún Laoghaire-Rathdown and were helped with varying degrees of graciousness and generosity by locals. Joseph remembered that the 'knockabout lads', as tramps were known in Glencullen, were 'usually ex-army men', whose circumstances rendered them homeless and unsuited for regular work. His mother gave them whatever she could share: 'tea and that'. But Joseph's family was not wealthy. At the end of the evening, the only place for these now-aging former soldiers was 'an old coal shed. Rats and everything in it, you know?' People in Glencullen pitied them, but one of the main reasons they helped these former soldiers was the entertainment they provided: 'they'd start to tell you a story about the front. Describing maybe horses and someone they met that they never seen after. They'd go on, but they'd never finish it.' The only currency these veterans had were their war stories. To encourage their hosts to invite them in for a second night, 'they'd leave a bit [of the story] for the next night to get in'. Brian, also from Glencullen, remembered the knockabout lads too, particularly one – now an aging alcoholic, but a hard worker and a gifted man – who said that he had spent time with the British Army in China before being discharged, and that it had taken him a year to get home. Oisín, who grew up in Mount Merrion in the 1940s and 1950s, also recalled an aging 'shellshocked' veteran, whom he knew as John. John lived rough in a ramshackle hut in the Mount Merrion Woods. He received support from some of the local families, and from the Little Sisters of the Poor, but others, frightened by his evident madness, shunned him. One day, John showed Oisín a large paper bag on which he had done detailed drawings of masonry work. He had grown up in a stonecutting community, and could still remember the work he had helped his father with before the war.

Some physically disabled veterans remained in hospital for years; the Industrial School for Protestant Boys on Carysfort Avenue was taken over by the British Army in 1917 and operated until the 1930s, when the remaining patients were transferred to Leopardstown Park Hospital.[76] Organisations such as the Red Cross did their best to help sick and disabled veterans. By 1927, the Red Cross was assisting 6,212 cases per year, at vast cost. In Dublin, 76 per cent of the sick and disabled veterans had worked as labourers before the hostilities, and now they were unable to do the work they had done before and untrained for anything else.[77] Amid the ongoing after effects of the war, some people – notably members of the Quaker community – were involved in pacifist organisations working to avoid any further wars. Isobel's father, an Englishman, came to Ireland in the 1920s, for reasons that she believed were linked to his involvement with the Fellowship of Reconciliation, an ecumenical anti-war organisation, founded in 1914 by Quaker Henry Hodgkin.

Victor's grandparents were a young couple living in Belfast in the 1920s, his grandmother an active member of Cumann na mBan, and his grandfather – despite being Catholic – a teacher at a well-known Protestant school. As it became progressively more difficult for them to stay in Northern Ireland, they found a new home in Dún Laoghaire (where, in old age, his grandmother would regularly meet with other Cumann na mBan veterans, all wearing their uniform berets).

On the evening of 9 July 1927, a man knocked at the door of Cyril's grandfather's home. He declared that the family's car was going to be 'borrowed', that it would be returned the following morning, and that the family would not be harmed provided they did not tell anyone. The next day, the car was indeed returned, shortly after the assassination of Kevin O'Higgins – then Minister for External Affairs, who as Minister for Justice in 1922 and 1923 had confirmed the sentences for execution for seventy-seven republican prisoners of war – on nearby Booterstown Avenue by anti-Treaty IRA men. While there is no way to know for sure, the family believed their car was used in the assassination. On 16 July, the *Dublin Leader* mourned O'Higgins, describing him as 'one of the cleverest and most forcible leaders of his time'.[78]

Tim, from the Kilmashogue area, remembered that, as late as the 1960s, there were still bad feelings between some older local men because they were on different sides in the Civil War. Marty, from Shankill, recalled how apparently minor incidents, like someone's hens wandering into someone else's garden, occasionally provoked such strong reactions that he surmised that old enmities relating to the Civil War were being brought to the fore, a generation or two later.

Considering how bitter the Civil War was, it is extraordinary how some of those who were key actors in the hostilities apparently settled down and could live in close proximity with former rivals with no problems at all. Éamon de Valera and Seán Collins, Michael Collins's brother, lived in Booterstown with their respective families. To onlookers, they appeared to be on very good terms and both families were quite integrated locally. Ellen Devine was recorded in 1980 discussing how Mrs de Valera knew all the local children, and frequently socialised with local woman,[79] and others remembered hearing about or seeing the families engaging with one another happily.

* * *

Injured First World War soldiers often depended on pensions from the British government, which it provided before independence partly from obligation, and partly because of concern that unsupported veterans were more likely to bring hard-won battle skills to the republican cause.[80] Post-independence, as part of the Anglo-Irish Treaty, the Irish government undertook to protect those who had previously been loyal to the British crown, extending some legal protection to war veterans. But although some significant employers in the Dublin, notably Protestant-run businesses like Guinness and Jacobs,[81] strove to employ former soldiers, unemployment levels among them were high. Veterans worried they might not be as well-treated as others by state organisations supposed to help working-class men to work. Increasingly, returned soldiers were seen as turncoats or traitors, while many, including those now ill or disabled, depended on support from Britain. Rather than being hailed as heroes, many were now viewed with distaste; some even had to deal with taunts, jeers and even assault.[82] Some avoided Ireland completely, or delayed their return until – they hoped – tensions had declined. Kevin's maternal grandfather, an English soldier who had met and married his Irish wife while stationed in Ireland before the war, did not return to the family home in Blackrock until 1923.

Approximately 37,500 former soldiers, about 16,000 of whom in the Dublin area, received a disability pension.[83] Many others worked while living with injury or disability. Graham's grandfather, for example, was the street sweeper in Dún Laoghaire despite having been seriously injured. His skull was 'held together' with metal plates that had to be replaced every two years or so, and he suffered from chronic, debilitating headaches. Fortunately for both the veterans and a cash-strapped new Irish state, the British Exchequer treated Irish veterans the same as the British, paying a range of pensions, allowances and grants, estimated to have amounted to at least £2 million by 1926.[84] It also provided subsidised treatment for ongoing issues with injuries or disease contracted while in the service of the British Army (although former soldiers with mental health problems were less likely to be supported than those with physical disability).[85] Emer's grandmother was widowed young when her husband died from a heart condition resulting from his war experiences. She could manage reasonably well on the war widow's pension she received from the British government, supplemented by her earnings as a housekeeper for a wealthy local family.

But it could be hard for veterans and war widows with low standards of literacy to learn about and apply for the assistance they were entitled to. Kate's great-uncle, an educated man, was kept busy helping other veterans to apply, and was also deeply involved with a local chapter of the British Legion.

Former IRA soldiers were considered heroes in early independence and they often also needed financial and other forms of support. In 1923, the Dáil decided to compensate soldiers wounded in 1916 or the War of Independence.[86] The Army Pensions Act required applicants to prove they were involved in active service, that they (or the relevant family member) had been wounded or killed, and that they had not been involved in serious misconduct. From 1924, 18,186 military service pensions were awarded across Ireland to veterans of the War of Independence. The initial criteria were restrictive, and because of the exclusion of Cumann na mBan, only one female veteran was eligible.[87] The Army Pensions Act of 1932 extended provision further to include not just those active in military roles but also members of ancillary organisations, like Cumann na mBan. Further legislation in 1937, 1941 and 1943 extended the time limit for applications for former soldiers and their widows and dependents,[88] and expanded provisions to include Na Fianna Éireann (a youth organisation), the Hibernian Rifles, and widows and other dependants.[89] Generous pensions were awarded to immediate family members of the 1916 Proclamation signatories.[90] Pensions were awarded to veterans from both sides of the Civil War, contributing to the easing of tensions.[91]

The bureaucracy involved in applying for a pension could be considerable. The authorities could reject applicants or award them pensions for lower ranks and grades than they had actually held.[92] Clearly, the criteria and burden of proof required for determining who was entitled to a pension was much more complicated in the case of veterans of a guerrilla war, particularly when it came to determining rank, as positions in the revolutionary army did not always neatly correlate to those of an official state army.[93] Those with proven IRA track records were often asked to corroborate others' applications, and were sometimes placed under considerable duress. 'You'd be surprised the men that came down,' Jacinta remembered of her father, a recognised IRA veteran. '"I was out with you… wasn't I?"… But they were all looking for pensions.' This could be stressful for Jacinta's dad, who sometimes vocally wondered, 'did he think he was right or was he wrong'. It was generally believed that former IRA soldiers were rewarded with steady jobs in the public sector. Catherine remembered her father and his friends saying, 'He's in Dalkey… he's working on the trams', as shorthand for discussing a friend who had been active in the War of Independence, and on the pro-Treaty side during the Civil War that followed.

For women involved in the War of Independence, obtaining an IRA pension was often very difficult, often because they were involved in areas like espionage, and had maintained low profiles. Sinéad, from Blackrock, knew about her grandmother's republican views, but had not realised that she was active in the War of Independence until her grandmother died, when 'all these men turned up and did a six-gun salute, turned up in their masks and then walked off!' Many women republicans had little or no paperwork and few witnesses to their efforts. Bob's aunt, who worked in the propaganda department of Sinn Féin, subsequently as a personal secretary to Arthur Griffith during the 1921 Anglo-Irish Treaty negotiations, and in the Department of External Affairs post-independence, strove for years to obtain a pension for her involvement in the War of Independence, but never succeeded.[94]

The British Legion provided huge support to ex-servicemen in Britain, but in Ireland relatively few ex-servicemen were involved with them, probably because of the imperialistic tone of their events, which continued to feature renditions of 'God Save the King'. Nonetheless, the Legion continued to actively lobby on behalf of former soldiers and their families, and in 1934 there were 119 men's branches and twenty-three women's branches in independent Ireland.[95] As a Blackrock teen in the 1950s, Kevin brought his grandmother, whose husband had fought in the First World War, to British Legion meetings. Kate remembered attending parties thrown by the British Legion as a child in the 1950s: 'I hated going... you'd think you'd be delighted going to a party, because you got nice parcels and all. I hated going. But my granny used to say, "Go up there now!"'

As the twentieth century progressed, even people whose family backgrounds might have suggested a certain loyalty towards Britain often tended to drift away from British symbols and celebrations. Timmy, whose parents were both born into educated, comfortably off Church of Ireland families in the early twentieth century, stated that by the mid-twentieth century they both found events like Remembrance Day, with its associated symbology, distasteful: 'they quietly but firmly disassociated themselves... very symbolically once a year'. They were, Timmy said, 'committed to the idea of working for the new state and building up... the country', and increasingly inclined to disassociate themselves from the colonial past.

Frequently, veterans of the First World War and the War of Independence lived close to one another in similar housing. Inevitably, tensions sometimes emerged. By the mid-to-late 1920s, the symbolic poppy of Armistice Day celebrations had become indelibly associated with British rule, and it became increasingly difficult for Irish war veterans to discuss their experiences publicly.[96] Jacinta's father was an IRA veteran. One of his neighbours was a woman with a fierce devotion to the IRA and another was a widow whose husband had died in the First World War. The latter esteemed the British Legion and pointedly wore a poppy for Remembrance Day. The other neighbour would 'give out yards'. Roy remembered a veteran from Glasthule who attended Remembrance Day ceremonies in Clarinda Park, wearing a borrowed bowler hat and a poppy, removing the poppy before he returned, for the sake of good neighbourly relations. Kate's mother, from a working-class, Catholic, unionist family, worked as a young girl in domestic service for a comfortably off local family with a strong republican identity; the woman of the house had served with Cumann na mBan. 'I remember,' said Kate, 'my mother telling me that she quite innocently bought a poppy one day… and [her employer] was very rude to her when she arrived… And she said she was very upset, because she didn't know.'

* * *

From the mid-1920s, the IRA in the Free State shifted from its previous stance of protecting employers towards identifying with poorer members of the population. By the 1930s, *An Phoblacht*, the organisation's newspaper, stressed its allegiance with the working classes and small farmers, and the IRA tended to support workers on strike, although awkward situations arose when workers were represented by British unions.[97] A new Fianna Fáil government, under Éamon de Valera, came into power in 1932. De Valera sought to end Irish repayments to Britain of land annuities originating from (British) government loans to Irish tenant farmers. The British authorities countered by imposing steep import duties on Irish products. (The UK at the time represented 90 per cent of the Irish export market.) De Valera in turn placed a similar duty on British imports. The Irish economy was very badly affected, while the much larger British economy was not. IRA activity was boosted by the message that one should 'burn everything British but their coal'. Roberta's father owned a pub in Dún Laoghaire, and although he was advised not to sell Bass beer, an English brand, he continued doing so, to the ire of the local IRA, which decided to act: 'A bunch of fifty people started marching up and down with cudgels and with hammers… five of them went into our pub, and they took out adverts and things like that, and smashed them on the ground… whether [Dad] was exaggerating or not, I don't know, but [the story was] that they had beaten him up.'

* * *

Germany invaded Poland on 1 September 1939, and on 3 September Britain and France, closely followed by Australia, New Zealand, South Africa and Canada, declared war on Germany. Despite Ireland's

The German battleship the *Schleswig-Holstein* visited Dún Laoghaire in 1937. Austin Mullin, centre, was one of many children who met sailors. The *Schleswig-Holstein* fought in both world wars. It was hit by a large-calibre shell in the Battle of Jutland in 1916 and decommissioned in 1917, but it returned to service in the 1920s. In 1935, it became a training ship for naval cadets. It fired the first cannon shots of the Second World War on 1 September 1939, when it bombarded the Polish base at Danzig's Westerplatte. Used as a training vessel for most of the war, it was sunk by British bombers in Gotenhafen in December 1944. Collection of Catherine Mullen, kind permission of Anna Scudds.

neutrality, there were many impacts on society, notably a marked decline in the quantity and quality of food available, particularly to those on limited incomes.[98] 'Tea,' recalled Hugh Leonard from Dalkey, 'was the champagne of the poor, and my mother would spread the used leaves on the window sill to dry in the sun and be employed again and perhaps a third time, until what finally dribbled from the teapot was the colour of diluted lime juice.'[99] The decline in food quality contributed to a dramatic rise in gastrointestinal disease among infants and small children, particularly children from poor families.[100] Richard's family had no food shortage, but during his primary school days in the 1940s his teacher stopped using dried beans to teach the children maths, as was her habit, and started using seashells instead, as it seemed tactless to use beans when so many were hungry. Fuel shortages became a challenge too, leading those in more rural areas to seek out trees to chop down or to harvest their own turf even if they had not done so before.[101] Residents from areas such as Dundrum acquired plots that they used until the war ended.[102] Most private car owners could not use their cars during this time, and the 'glimmer man' who could call unannounced to homes at any time to ensure that people were not using gas when they were not supposed to became a dreaded figure: 'He'd even come and feel your saucepans,' remembered Ellen Devine of Booterstown in 1980, 'a dreaded person to have around the place.'[103] Bigger farmers in areas like Glencullen and Kilternan, who depended on hired-in labour for the busy times, remembered Brian, found labour harder to get, as so many young men had gone to Britain to work in munitions factories. However, for those whose incomes were unaffected, life carried on much as before. British visitors noted that those who could afford it could still eat as much meat and other types of food scarce in Britain as they wanted.[104]

The mailboat was operated by British Rail during the war years, and as there were staffing shortages in Britain – because so many personnel were fighting or otherwise involved in the war effort – some of the Irish staff were relocated there. Barbara's father was sent from Dún Laoghaire, where he worked as a porter, to Birmingham, where he worked at a railway station. He stayed in digs, hating every minute of it. One of Barbara's earliest memories being quite nervous of him on his return, as she had no memory of him.

Despite its neutrality, there was great concern that Ireland might be attacked. Locals organised groups of wardens who distributed gas masks and explained how to use them, and inspected homes to ensure that blackout blinds were being used properly. Air-raid shelters were constructed, like one on the grounds of Blackrock College, to which locals were supposed to flock when air-raid sirens sounded.[105] The reduced street and public lighting, and ambient lighting from homes, made Dublin generally much darker. In around 1942, when Nicola was about ten, her mother got her out of bed and they walked down to Bullock Harbour in Dalkey to watch the aurora borealis, which is rarely seen in

Ireland, and was possibly only visible then because of the exceptional darkness.

A small number of bombs fell on Dublin, including two on Rosmeen Gardens in Glasthule on 20 December 1940, injuring three and damaging over 100 homes.[106] Marianne's father was en route to meet his girlfriend for a date when a bomb fell, 'and when he woke up, he was at the bottom of the crater'. Shaken, he crawled from the crater and went to a chemist's and then St Michael's Hospital. Meanwhile, his angry girlfriend assumed she had been stood up. The next morning a neighbour said, 'I hear a bomb fell on your [boyfriend] last night.' His story had been covered by the newspapers, and his girlfriend forgave him.[107] Richard, then eleven, remembered the bombs that fell on East Wall, across Dublin Bay: 'we stood at the kitchen door, which faced Dublin, and you could see the searchlights and you could hear the bang'. Michael's mother and the children sheltered under the stairs: 'Everybody who hadn't got a shelter outside [was] told to make provisions under the stairs, because… the staircase usually survives.' Isobel, nine when war broke out, remembered a bomb shelter on Temple Hill, near her home. 'Nobody ever bothered going there,' she said. Local families, including her parents, cleared a space under their stairs to use if bombs started to fall on south Dublin. In 1980, Elizabeth Rushby remembered how her husband – a British demobbed solider who had converted to Catholicism to marry her – died alongside five other employees of Irish Lights when their lightship, the *Isolda*, was bombed on 19 December 1940.[108]

Belfast was bombed in four German air raids on important targets. A small attack occurred on the night of 7–8 April 1941. On 15 April, 200 German aircraft attacked military and industrial targets. About 900 were killed and many wounded. Robbie's father was working for the Dún Laoghaire Fire Station, and his was one of the brigades sent to the north to help extinguish the fires following the bombing of 15 April. He often described the crowds that waved at them as they drove through towns and villages on the way, and the hordes he saw travelling south from Belfast towards safety. Robbie's father and his colleagues were each given ten shillings by the British government as a gesture of thanks, but very little fuss was made of the brigades by the Irish government, which – understandably – did not want Germany to think that neutral Ireland was helping with the British war effort.

Some felt called to fight alongside the British. 'Somebody had to go to war,' said Timothy of the attitude he recalled towards these returned soldiers, whose name and rank were pointed out to him by his father, 'and somebody did go to war.' Douglas's father went, although he talked about it very little afterwards: 'he got through it unscathed. He served on a couple of destroyers. Sort of convoy duty and stuff like that. Nothing exceptional about his war.' Others were less lucky. Matthew's uncle joined the RAF. He was shot down and his body never recovered; this loss would affect Matthew's mother badly all her life. Karen's husband, whom she married in the late 1940s, had served in the war, having joined the British Navy in his late teens (he had been an experienced sailor of Dublin Bay since childhood, allegedly 'tied to the mast' as a little boy by his mother, determined not to miss a day of sailing). He saw a lot of action and earned several medals, but survived unscathed, while several of his former class-mates from Kingstown Grammar were less fortunate. Cyril's family were Quakers and helped the war effort by joining the Quaker Ambulance Unit. Benjamin's mother, also a Quaker, took the unusual step of moving from Dublin to London during the Second World War, to provide her services as a nurse. She brought Benjamin with her, so his very earliest memories – he was born in 1942 – are of wartime London.

Local opinion of Irishmen fighting in the war varied. Certainly, there was admiration for those whose consciences prompted them to join the fight against Hitler – but there was also approbation from those who saw them as turncoats, fighting with the enemy. Pádraic's father, a staunch nationalist living in the Kilternan area, 'had no time' for Irishmen who served with the British, regarding them as traitors and 'soup drinkers'!*

---

* A reference to the trope of Irish Catholics said to have converted to Protestantism during the Famine in exchange for food in response to Protestant evangelism and, more broadly, to those considered to have sold out to the British. Nuttall, 2020, 45–56.

Following the war, locals who had served in the British Army returned and, according to some, could easily be spotted when they walked on Dún Laoghaire pier, or in other popular areas to promenade, by their military bearing. Sometimes seen as 'West Brits' who had joined because of a lingering sense of loyalty to Britain, they were also often objects of admiration, heroes who had fought against a dreadful foe.

Before the war, the Irish state had been more inclined to accept requests from Catholic rather than Jewish refugees, who were regarded with suspicion. The Department of Justice delegated the vetting of refugees to a voluntary group, the Irish Co-ordinating Committee for the Relief of Christian Refugees, which focused largely on Austrian refugees classified by the Nuremberg Laws as Jewish, but who had converted to Catholicism. The committee initially capped the number of refugees it would admit at seventy. Irish Jews who tried to help Jewish refugees come to Ireland were fiercely opposed by two officials in particular: Peter Barry, a senior civil servant in the Department of Justice, and Charles Bewley, Ireland's envoy to Berlin from 1933 to 1939. As late as September 1945, the Department of Justice stated that its policy was to restrict Jewish immigration, saying that 'the murmurs against Jewish wealth and influence are frequently heard', and that a large Jewish population 'might create a social problem'.[109] One of the few Jewish refugees in Ireland, an Austrian woman, lived with Isobel's family in Monkstown during the war years. Isobel's family were Quakers, and she believed the woman arrived via a Quaker organisation helping to place Jewish refugees with families in safe places. The day she came, all of Isobel's schoolfriends rushed to see her, excited because they assumed that she would be black, and none of them had ever met a black woman before. Of course, being Austrian, the new arrival was as white as they were, and the children were disappointed. One day laundry was delivered to Isobel's home by the Swastika Laundry, which was based in Ballsbridge. When the family's guest opened the door, she saw their logo and thought for an awful moment that the Nazis came to collect her. She studied medicine during her time in Ireland, and qualified as a doctor.

In May 1940, Frank Aiken, the Minister for the Coordination of Defensive Measures, recommended that the Irish Red Cross Society establish a 'refugee reception committee' and one was duly founded, also including representatives from the St Vincent de Paul, the Legion of Mary, the Quakers and the Great Southern Railway Company. Refugees fleeing Britain started to arrive from September 1940, and were met by volunteers at various ports along the east coast. In December 1940, a group of about 700 – mostly women and children – arrived following the bombing of Coventry. By this point, so many refugees were arriving that the pier service at Dún Laoghaire was struggling to cope, and the members of Red Cross branches in Mount Merrion, Cabinteely, Dalkey and Blackrock stepped in to help. Rebecca's aunt was with the Red Cross, and she wore her uniform and greeted refugees arriving on the mailboat. Many of the new arrivals had friends or relatives in Ireland, but they still needed at least short-term accommodation.

Chloe's maternal grandparents were Hungarian and her grandmother was Jewish. In the years leading to the Second World War they were increasingly concerned about the future, so they arranged through the International Red Cross for their only child, a daughter, to come to Ireland, where she worked as an au pair. After the war, their daughter now married to an Irishman, they moved to Ireland too, and settled in Blackrock.*

As well as refugees per se, some English families who opted to ride out the war in Ireland settled temporarily in Dún Laoghaire-Rathdown. Oisín, who grew up in Mount Merrion, remembered several English families in Ireland for the war years, the children seeming 'different' because they were Protestants, had English accents and – it seemed to him as a small boy – had enviably fancier toys. ('I mean, the guy next door to me had an *electric car* – a battery-driven car!') Some local residents were staunch republicans, and some of those had actually been

---

* A small influx of Hungarians some years later, after the Hungarian Revolution of 1956, would provide them with a set of compatriot friends. This latter group could travel to Ireland because it had joined the United Nations and become a signatory to its 1951 convention, so, for the first time, the Irish government was required under international law to recognise the rights of those seeking asylum in Ireland. Lehane, 2019, 85–6.

involved in the War of Independence, just two decades before. The presence of these temporary British residents must have made for some interesting juxtapositions. At one stage, Oisín's father brought home two German prisoners of war, apparently day tripping in Dublin from their internment camp in the Curragh. 'He brought them home on the bus for tea,' Oisín remembered. 'One had a big leather coat... he had a big scar on his face because he had been injured. They were sailors and they'd been picked up by the Irish Navy.' When the war was over, Oisín's parents also hosted some Bretons who had fled France, where they were suspected of having cooperated with the Germans.

The German Ambassador, Eduard Hempel, was appointed in June 1937, and lived in Gortleitragh House, Monkstown. In 1938, Hempel presented the National Folklore Commission – then headed by Séamus Ó Duilearga – with an impressive collection of 250 volumes of folklore in German, with 'Geschenk des Deutschen Reichs' (Gift of the German Reich) on each flyleaf.[110] The same year, the Hempels' son was born in their new home.[111] Germans in Ireland (considerable numbers of Germans had come to Ireland in early independence to work on various infrastructural projects, including the construction of the Ardnacrusha hydroelectricity station on the Shannon river) were concerned that British troops might invade Ireland and intern them. With de Valera's help, they obtained safe passage back to Germany via Britain. On 11 September, many boarded the mailboat in Dún Laoghaire, with shouts of 'Auf Wiedersehen'. A Professor Herkner told the *Irish Times* that they were 'returning to Germany to join the colours', and Heinz Mecking, who had been involved with the Turf Development Board, gave a Nazi salute on the quay.[112]

During the Emergency, the Hempels were in a delicate situation. They were officially tolerated, because of Irish neutrality, but many around them were ideologically aligned with the Allies, including families who had loved ones fighting in the British forces. Following Hitler's death by suicide on 30 April 1945, Éamon de Valera and the Secretary of the Department of External Affairs visited Hempel to give their condolences, and the swastika flag at the German Legation on Northumberland Road was flown at half-mast.[113] Richard, a classmate of Eduard Hempel's son, remembered that the

Hempel family had no income following Hitler's death, and that nobody was prepared to visit the embassy, even those who had been friendly with the Hempels before. Eva Hempel, the ambassador's wife, had to bake and attempt to sell cakes in the local area so as to feed her family.

Hermann Görtz, a German veteran of the First World War, had been visiting Ireland since 1927, and had developed a fondness for the country at a time when there was an active group of the overseas branch of the Nazi Party in Dublin. He also developed a relationship with groups opposing the Anglo-Irish Treaty. After a period as a sort of freelance spy in Britain in the 1930s, he served time in prison there, being deported to Germany in 1939. In the summer of 1940, Görtz was parachuted into Ballivor, County Meath, to liaise with the IRA, hoping that they would cooperate if Germany occupied Britain. He made his way to Dublin, apparently dressed in his Luftwaffe uniform. He would remain at liberty in Dublin for nineteen months, staying in various safe houses connected to the IRA, including houses in Glenageary, Dún Laoghaire, Dalkey and Shankill, while the Irish authorities possibly half-heartedly looked for him, or perhaps left him at liberty hoping that he would lead them to active IRA members.[114] The property in Glenageary, at Spencer Villas, was the home of a family friend of Gladys and Noreen. Gladys was in her teens then, and heard how, when the authorities eventually decided to arrest Görtz, his hosts rushed to their bakery in Dún Laoghaire ('a lovely shop beside Woolworths') and burned his German uniform, after which the Irish Special Branch raided the bakery and poked the metal uniform buttons – clearly important evidence – from the hot ashes. Görtz had hoped to be collected by a submarine from the Wicklow coast, and had spent hours on a beach waiting for one in the company of two of the women from the household where he was staying. Instead, he was arrested in Clontarf on 27 November 1941 and detained for the remainder of the war. Afterwards, he lived in Glenageary, where he became secretary of the Save the German Children Society, founded on 16 October 1945 to find foster homes in Ireland for destitute German children.[115] Apparently, he hoped to stay in Ireland, but on 23 May 1947, Görtz was informed by the authorities that he would be deported the next day. Fearing that he might be handed over to the Soviets – although the government had requested this not happen – he killed himself, biting down on a glass phial containing poison. He was buried in Deansgrange Cemetery three days later with a swastika flag draped over his coffin, and several Irish mourners, some of whom raised their hands in the Nazi salute.[116] Among the mourners were the daughters of Gladys and Noreen's family friend, who had become very close to Görtz during his time with them. This outraged Gladys and Noreen's aunt: 'They're up there,' she scoffed, 'they're thinking which of them will be… in the grave beside him first!' But neither of them was, because his remains were disinterred and moved to the German Military Cemetery in Glencree in 1974.

* * *

Armistice Day celebrations, tolerated by the government in the 1920s and 1930s, were restricted during the Emergency because of Ireland's neutrality.[117] This important, if symbolic, severing of further cultural ties with Britain would lead seamlessly to Ireland's departure from the Commonwealth of Nations in 1949. The actual departure of Ireland from the Commonwealth was largely greeted, and subsequently remembered, with indifference. An exception was Liam's father, a senior civil servant, who was unimpressed: he saw leaving the Commonwealth as 'silly', an empty gesture. Still, there were ceremonies in Dublin city centre and elsewhere. Kevin, a boy of eight then, remembered the local pipe band in Blackrock marching triumphantly to Deansgrange Cemetery, the resting place of many nationalist heroes, alongside the Sixth Battalion of the old IRA. A little further down the coast, in Dún Laoghaire Harbour, boats were strewn with flags, public buildings were decorated and twenty-one guns on the East Pier fired a welcome to the Republic at a minute past midnight.[118]

* * *

By the late 1960s, the Troubles in Northern Ireland were underway. In theory, the IRA was forbidden by its General Order No. 8 from military operations in the twenty-six counties, but they did occur. The IRA was involved, for example, in two attempts to blow up the King George IV monument in Dún Laoghaire in late 1970.[119] One local man served time in Mountjoy for his involvement in IRA activity, to the discomfort of his mother ('mortified about the whole thing'). Andy, working for the Special Branch then, was distinctly aware of IRA activity in Dún Laoghaire-Rathdown. Many young men, from various rural locations, working in the building industry – booming as housing estates were constructed – were also involved in the IRA. At around this time, Aidan remembered, his family was approached by Sinn Féin at their Travellers' halting site in Rathfarnham and asked if a few Northern Irish families could be housed in trailers beside them – Catholic families from the Bogside in Belfast looking for a safe place to stay.

For some other activists, including trade unions, the discrimination faced by Northern Irish Catholics seemed to resonate with the issues they were campaigning for in Ireland. Protests could turn violent. On 31 January 1972, following the Bloody Sunday massacre in Derry, when peaceful protesters were murdered by British paratroopers, about 20,000 gathered at the British Embassy in Merrion Square. On 1 February, with protests all over the country, 150 'Foxrock housewives' protested outside the Sandyford home of the British ambassador, decrying the 'new Black and Tans'. Many churches, including those of diverse Protestant denominations and Jewish synagogues, held commemorations for the fallen. On 2 February, among the protesters chanting outside the embassy, 'If you hate the British Army clap your hands', were the Trinity College friends of the British ambassador's son, who was studying there.[120] By the end of the night, the crowds had set the British embassy alight and its interior was gutted. In Dún Laoghaire that night, Kevin was working with the fire brigade when the local branch of the Royal Liver Assurance Company was bombed, presumably because it was an English company: 'the office cleaning lady was in cleaning the office... two fellas walked in and said, "Right, love, you've a minute to get out."' As she ran away, 'she looked back and she saw one of the fellas holding something in his hand with smoke coming from it, and he threw it in to the office... what they had been sprinkling in the office was petrol, and what they were throwing in was a stick of dynamite'. The shop was badly damaged, but nobody was hurt.[121] In Dún Laoghaire on 3 February a crowd of 700 marched to the local British Legion offices in protest.[122]

Throughout this era, republican sympathies continued to clash with some families' pride in their historical involvement with the British forces. Kate's aunt cherished photographs of family members in their British Army uniforms, and was devastated when burglars broke into her home and destroyed them by tearing them and burning them in her grate, presumably because they objected to the visual reminders of Irish involvement with the British forces, or with British colonialism. Also in Kate's family, more than a generation after the War of Independence, there was now some anxiety about things that had happened before. Kate's grandfather had served in the First World War and received a commendation certificate with a picture of the British queen, which he had proudly framed and mounted on the wall. Now, following the parish priest's annual visit, newly self-conscious amid current affairs, he wondered if he should take it down.

As the situation deteriorated in Northern Ireland, a network of IRA safe houses in Ireland offered protection to IRA operatives. There were apparently many safe houses in Dún Laoghaire-Rathdown. Sometimes the visiting IRA members were injured and needed medical treatment. A local GP treated one woman delivered to her clinic presenting with dreadful headaches, who had a bullet lodged in her brain following a violent encounter with the British forces.

While many protested against the excesses of the British forces in the north, many others worried about what impact the Troubles might have on them and on Ireland's future stability and development. One woman, identified only as a Foxrock mother of small children, said, 'We fear for our families... We fear so much for them that we sometimes feel the north should be left alone to get on with its own destruction.'[123] Terror visited Dublin on 17 May 1974, when bombs set by loyalists from the north killed thirty-three innocent civilians, including a pregnant woman.

On 26 July 1976, the newly appointed British ambassador Christopher Ewart-Biggs, and civil servant Judith Cooke, were murdered in a landmine explosion in Sandyford just two weeks after Ewart-Biggs's arrival with his young family.[124] Taoiseach Liam Cosgrave stated that 'this atrocity fills all decent Irish people with a sense of shame'.[125] Years later, Ewart-Biggs's daughter Kate, eight then, remembered, '[Mummy] picked me up and took me inside where we were greeted by a line of staff, all of them crying, and I knew in that moment… my father had died.'[126] A few days later, Kate's mother Jane did a broadcast from the residence's sitting room, introduced her children, and pleaded for peace and reconciliation. On 30 July 1976, Jane published a notice in the *Irish Times* thanking the people of Ireland for the thousands of messages of support she had received,[127] and the following year she established a literature prize in her husband's name. In December that year, a detective was critically wounded by gunshot fired by IRA members during a robbery at Cornelscourt.[128]

The family of British ambassador Christopher Ewart-Biggs at his funeral following his murder in Sandyford in 1976. His widow, Jane Ewart-Biggs, became a Life Peer in the House of Lords. She campaigned to improve Anglo-Irish relations and set up the Christopher Ewart-Biggs Memorial Prize for Literature. Getty Images.

By the late 1970s, the Sinn Féin newspaper *An Phoblacht* was quite widely sold in many areas of Dún Laoghaire-Rathdown, chiefly in pubs, with minor scuffles erupting occasionally over refusals to purchase a copy. While the Troubles stayed generally in Northern Ireland, by 1980 nearly 100 people in the twenty-six counties had been killed because of the conflict, and hundreds injured. Some Protestants in independent Ireland were concerned that anger towards northern unionists would spill over to them. In May 1972, over 100 southern Protestants had attempted to calm northern unionist ire by assuring in the form of an open letter that, in independent Ireland, they played a full part and were not at all marginalised.[129] Indeed, while the Protestant experience of independence was varied – with the greatest tensions felt in border areas and areas with substantial Protestant working-class populations – the experiences of a family in a comfortable suburb in south Dublin, like Dalkey, Monkstown or Foxrock, where many well-to-do Protestants lived and were active locally, were in the main extremely positive. Many Protestant families in Dún Laoghaire-Rathdown were affluent or comfortably off and, even if they had declined in relative privilege, they generally still had pleasant lives. Against the backdrop of the looming Troubles, sectarian incidents did occur, however, such as the smashing of the windows of the Methodist Church in Blackrock,[130] an unwelcome suggestion that the Troubles had the potential to come south.

* * *

Those who were young adults in the early 1960s often remember a sense of frustration, a feeling of being left behind. Educational standards were rising quickly, and it was easier than before to get decent work locally, but emigration levels remained relatively high. It often seemed that everywhere else was more exciting. Members of this generation often comment, wistfully, that 'everybody else' seemed to be having a lot more sex than young Irish people. Timmy remembered thinking, 'This is the swinging 1960s, so why are we not swinging?' and assuming, when he visited London, that young men and women there were all enjoying a much more liberated youth than he experienced in Dublin. In 1967, the smash hit West German documentary film *Helga, the Intimate Life of a Young Woman*, directed by Erich F. Bender, following a young woman from pregnancy through to childbirth, was shown in cinemas; it had been passed by the film censor for viewing by Irish audiences with two cuts, one of which removed a section dealing with abortion.[131] There was a certain amount of 'hullaballoo' about it, Bríd remembered, but ultimately many of the young people who wanted to see it managed to persuade their parents to let them go (not Bríd, unfortunately – a neighbour was working in the local box office and refused to sell her a ticket). Increasingly liberal views among young people about relationships and sex could alarm older generations, who could be moralistic, or worry that the younger people had not really considered the potential consequences. Austin remembered his mother fretting that liberal trends might be nice for young men, but could be to women's detriment: 'The girl could be used and dumped and… and lose her reputation… it suited young men, but it didn't necessarily suit young women.'

In 1972, the Irish electorate voted decisively to join the EEC, which would later become the EU. The implications for the future evolution of the Irish workplace, and the culture of the whole country, would be vast. This was an important step towards the development of a more autonomous economy and an impetus to the dramatic economic, social and cultural shifts already underway. By now, too, censorship of printed materials was increasingly controversial. The custom officers in Dún Laoghaire frequently intercepted items, including pornographic magazines, and impounded them in a shed on the Carlisle Pier that was the object of great local curiosity and an emblem of the sort of Ireland that fewer people wanted.

* * *

The modern women's rights movement descends from many different groups of women who were active in various ways, including activists for women's education and financial autonomy, certain religious orders that promoted higher education for women (at least women from more comfortably off backgrounds, notably the Loreto and Dominican orders), and women activists focusing on issues of concern to women and families, including targeting alcoholism (identified as a major contributor to domestic abuse). Early women's rights activism tended to be dominated by well-to-do women with more formal education, more free time and more resources than working-class women. One focus of nineteenth-century activism was legislation passed in the 1860s creating the Contagious Diseases Act, providing for the incarceration and forcible treatment of women suspected of having venereal disease and for the compulsory medical inspection of prostituted women.[132] These laws were intended mainly to reduce infection among prostitutes' clients, and not among the women themselves,[133] and they attracted protests from early women's rights activists. The act was repealed in 1886.

The Irish women's suffrage movement of the late nineteenth and early twentieth century included nationalist and unionist women. From 1898, well before universal suffrage, women could stand for election to municipal authorities.[134] Interest in women's suffrage grew rapidly in the early twentieth century until, between 1912 and 1914, membership of official organisations dedicated to the cause – and to related issues, including concerns about prostitution, alcoholism, domestic and child abuse, and the right of women to act on juries – grew to over 3,000. Many small groups, with members from varied social, economic and political backgrounds (with affluent women still over-represented), gathered under an umbrella group, the Irish Women's Suffrage Federation – of which Louie Bennett, from Killiney, was a co-founder with Helen Chevenix, born in Blackrock – which became increasingly militant.[135] On 13 June 1912, twelve women were arrested for breaking government building windows in Dublin and were sentenced to a month in prison.[136] Isobel's mother, a Quaker, was involved in the women's suffrage movement as a non-violent protestor, and travelled to England to attend a meeting in Hyde Park. Women ratepayers (and wives of ratepayers) over thirty were granted the vote in 1918, alongside men over twenty-one who did not own property, swelling the voting franchise from 25 to 75 per cent of the population,[137] and clarifying that, despite decisive gains for women, men were still on top.

The local elections of 1920, held on 15 January, saw various women from Dún Laoghaire-Rathdown running for office, including Ellen Barry from Dún Laoghaire, Charlotte Brazil and Louie Bennett from Dalkey, Helen Rose Gibbings from Military Road and Margaret Dockrell from Blackrock. Josephine Cantwell was the first woman to be elected to Kingstown Urban District Council, when she won a seat for Sinn Féin in the Glasthule Ward. These candidates came from diverse political and socioeconomic backgrounds, and several had long, distinguished records in campaigning for women's suffrage, particularly Margaret Dockrell, from an Irish unionist perspective,* and Louie Bennett, a trade unionist and founding member of the Irish Women's Workers' Union.[138]

Alongside these dramatic cultural shifts, many other women in the early decades of the twentieth century were uninterested in, or even hostile towards, the women's suffrage movement. Of her grandmother from Dalkey, Rachel remembered that 'she would have felt that they were very wrongheaded… she absolutely believed men were definitely leaders. And the woman should always do what their husband tells them.' In early independence, it quickly became evident that there was little appetite for the advancement of women's rights in most sectors. Although the new state's laws guaranteed women's right to vote from twenty-one, like men, and although five women were elected as TDs in 1923,[139] legislation that

---

* Margaret Dockrell expected to be elected as chair of the Urban District Council, but the position was given to a man. Claiming the high moral ground, she stated that she viewed her opponents with 'infinite compassion', hoping that 'their poor restricted outlook might be enlarged'. Ó Maitiú, 2003, 130.

would impact disproportionally on women who were, or wanted to be, in the public sphere was quickly enacted.[140]

While many women may have been quite apolitical at the time, many others were keenly aware of the importance of their vote, and of the fragility of modest gains made for women's rights. Eden, born in 1924, remembered how adamant her mother – born in the nineteenth century, long before women could vote – felt about the political process. No matter how busy she was, she would 'drag herself out to vote', and she told her daughter that 'she was in it to fight for women to have a vote'. Eden's mother's example has stayed with her always: 'Today, this day,' she said, 'if I had to *crawl*, I'd go out to vote. I've never missed a vote. Because women fought for it.'

In 1924, women were given the right to exempt themselves from jury duty, and most did.[141] In 1926, a conference of women's societies met in Dublin and rejected the idea of women jurors having only a voluntary panel, stressing the importance of mixed panels, particularly for cases including 'infanticide, seduction [often a euphemism for rape], or assault'.[142] In 1927, despite opposition from organisations including the Irish Women's Citizens' and Local Government Association and the National University Women Graduates' Association, the government proposed removing women from juries completely, but finally agreed they could serve, but could be exempted. In Dáil debates Kevin O'Higgins – Minister for Justice from 1922 until his (previously mentioned) assassination in Booterstown in 1927 – argued against women jurors because a woman's 'normal and natural' function was motherhood.[143] As so few women served on juries, legal cases of particular concern to women, notably regarding rape and other sexual offences, sexually motivated murders of women and infanticide, were generally tried before all-male juries.[144]

In the 1920s and 1930s, growing numbers of middle- and upper-class women were accessing higher levels of education – at least a good second-level education, and increasingly also university education. Among this cohort, who would often marry professional men and have domestic help, it could be frustrating not to be able to pursue careers. In 1935, women activists succeeded in preventing the passing of legislation intended to bar all women from holding certain high-ranking civil service positions, but the marriage bar, requiring women to leave most public-sector jobs on marriage, remained firmly in place. In 1937, the Irish constitution made divorce constitutionally illegal. Women whose husbands abandoned them or did not support them had nowhere to go.

Despite a rise in educational standards generally, even in the 1940s, 1950s and beyond, some families felt that higher education was not just a waste of time for girls, but also bad for them, making them feel frustrated and less likely to have happy marriages. Arthur, who grew up in a comfortably off home near Sallynoggin, remembered his father's strong feelings about his daughters' education: 'the girls never went to third level because they were never intended to. He wanted to bring them up as good wives so that they would marry well. And that's what was good for them.' But growing numbers of girls from middle-class and wealthy backgrounds were getting excellent educations. Theresa remembered not realising that women were often treated as second-class citizens in the 1940s and 1950s, when she was growing up. This was partly because her father was prepared to pay as much for her education as for her brothers', and also because her education, at Sion Hill in Blackrock, was provided by nuns whom she described as 'extremely forward-looking'. Still, at university in the early 1950s, when one of her classmates declared her ambition to become the president of Ireland, 'we all laughed, including the tutor. Like, the *absurdity* of a woman becoming president of Ireland.'

In early independence, diverse organisations worked for women's rights in various ways. Some of the most effective were good at avoiding appearing overtly political, such that certain groups that made important gains for women's rights have not received the recognition they deserve, sometimes because they were working within power structures retrospectively considered oppressive *per se*. The foundation of the Legion of Mary by Frank Duff in 1921, on the eve of independence, with a focus on compassionate conservatism, was a positive step for women within the Catholic Church. The Legion of Mary was notably different in some ways to other religious organisations. It focused on the empowerment of the laity, including women. While the legion spread throughout the Catholic world – and throughout the parishes of Dún Laoghaire-Rathdown – it was not always regarded with favour by religious authorities, who could be alarmed by some of their initiatives, including outreach programmes to prostituted women that focused on compassion and practical help rather than condemnation. Duff was, as his memoirist noted, 'an innovator in his notions of care for the unmarried mother'. When unmarried mothers were frequently coerced or forced to place their children in orphanages, 'Frank… insisted on taking mother and child into the Regina Coeli Hostel', a hostel (mentioned in 'A Roof Over Their Heads') run by the Legion of Mary in north Dublin for female 'down and outs'.[145] It welcomed among its first residents an unmarried mother and her child.[146] Duff's approach was seen then as 'radical', as he believed that 'the natural thing was that the [unmarried] mother rear the child'.[147] By 1950, the Regina Coeli Hostel offered accommodation to a hundred families headed by unmarried mothers.[148]

Secular women's organisations continued to work for women's rights. In 1935, the Joint Committee of Women's Societies and Social Workers demanded, among other things, that the laws for solicitation should be the same for men as for women. Under Irish legislation, only women could be arrested for prostitution.[149] In 1938, the Women's Social and Progressive League noted that the condition of Irish women had deteriorated following independence, and urged women to consider carefully for whom they should vote.[150] The Irish Countrywomen's Association (ICA), founded in 1910, had branches in various locations across Dún Laoghaire-Rathdown, including Shankill and Kilternan. It was a non-denominational organisation providing women with opportunities to socialise, engage in crafts and other creative activities, pursue further education and acquire business knowhow, enabling them to monetise their skills and work. It attracted women from all social classes and grew rapidly in early independence. In its early days, it benefited from the free labour of educated, comfortably off women like Timmy's mother, who worked alongside founder Muriel Gahan and others on areas like governance and administration, and Lily's aunt – a member of a well-known retail family – who travelled the country as a judge in vegetable growing and other contests, among other things. Many women attended training courses at the association's headquarters, An Grianán in County Louth. The ICA also successfully lobbied the government to provide rural areas with better services, including electrification and running water.[151] As a young mother in the early 1960s, Philo started an ICA guild in Ballybrack. The ICA was a lifeline to her, and she loved the opportunities for further education. One of the points of the ICA, she said, was always 'to empower women', and she noted that many women in political life started their careers in local ICA guilds. Emily, whose poultry business in Ballycorus is discussed in 'Mouths to Feed', was enabled to run her enterprise thanks partly to the ICA. The Country Market in Kilternan, founded in 1964, was inspired by a lecture that Muriel Gahan gave at the local vocational school. After that, locals – mostly women – started a market, selling farm produce, baked goods and more. The Country Market, one of many such businesses around the country, became a way for women excluded from many jobs to earn a living, and to gather, organise, socialise and develop business skills.

The more overtly political Irish Housewives Association (IHA), founded by Hilda Tweedy in 1942, was dominated by educated, middle-class women.[152] It campaigned for various causes, including adequate nutrition for children, school meals and the equitable distribution of life essentials, including food, fuel for the home and electricity.[153] Some religious authorities argued that feeding children at school, as the IHA proposed, would interfere with the sanctity of the home.[154] Tweedy and her colleagues maintained that Irish women needed and deserved a place in public life, and that Irish women should be educated to understand how politics impacted on their lives.[155]

Throughout the 1940s and 1950s, while relatively few women were involved in women's rights activism, many Irish women, accessing higher average levels of education than before – were simply immigrating to countries offering them more work opportunities and greater independence.[156] By the late 1960s/early 1970s, although Ireland remained unusually conservative by western European standards, societal norms were changing. The ban on married women working in the public sector would be repealed in 1973, but was gradually eased from about 1970, although concurrent developments in childcare facilities did not keep pace.[157]

While many women were happy to devote themselves to home and family, many others – especially those with professional qualifications and better-paid, rewarding work – were devastated to be fired when they married. Emily did clerical work for Associated British Cinema, which ran several cinemas in Dublin. When she married in 1962, she lost her job because the company would not employ married women. She felt, she said, 'very sore, because I did a good job'. She wrote to her boss saying that she 'felt it was very unfair'. He did not respond. Phil deeply resented having to relinquish her job with the *Irish Times* when she married, so she was 'very interested in the feminist movement… it was so male-dominated, and women were kind of really treated as second-class citizens'. Most of her women friends were extremely interested in contraception and many would have liked to continue paid work, at least until their children were born. She saw them struggle when they dealt with unwanted pregnancies, and when they had to give up work despite needing a job.

Noelle started working for Guinness in the early 1970s. At that time, 'boys could start at the same age as girls, but boys instantly went on to a higher grade'. While Guinness was considered a good employer, men were treated differently to women: 'there was a ladies' staff, and there was a men's staff, and then there was kind of a brewing staff… women could reach a certain level, but that was pretty well it'. Chloe was a young full-time mother when she and her husband settled in Stillorgan in the mid-1970s, and she remembered feeling frustrated when women like her seemed to be completely overlooked at a dinner party: 'They were all professionals. And people [were] interested in what [my husband] did…

and that I almost didn't have opinions… I remember… being *not* asked my opinion about things, because I mightn't *have* an opinion.'

Women's bodies have always been a battlefield. Long before independence, women's bodies and fertility were often treated as commodities. Many women's rights activists in the 1960s and early 1970s felt that voting rights and other political gains were meaningless when women had no bodily autonomy. Rosie was involved with the Dalkey Women's Action Group, having become interested in the idea of access to contraception as an essential women's right, partly because of her own difficult experiences with Irish maternity healthcare. Priscilla was one of the founding members of the Women's Political Association in 1970. They focused on access to education for women, and on getting more women actively involved in politics. Priscilla was one of the first women to serve on the board of the Rotunda Maternity Hospital. Her job, she felt, was to stand up for what the patients needed, because the consultants were all men, who 'made all the decisions and did what suited them'. But what suited them, she said, did not always suit women: 'some of these male consultants were too big for their boots… [they] weren't particularly keen to communicate with women'. Priscilla was also concerned about access to contraception, especially for working-class women, who still often had huge families. She was in hospital recovering from the birth of her daughter when Mary Robinson – president of Ireland from 1990 to 1997– arrived with a bunch of flowers and a request for Priscilla's support in her campaign to stand for the Seanad (Robinson would take a seat previously occupied by Priscilla's father).

In 1974, the Women's Representative Committee was founded by the Minister for Labour to officially represent women's interests.[158] Irishwomen United was founded in 1975.[159] Other important organisations included Cherish, a group of single mothers, and Women's Aid, representing women subjected to domestic violence.[160] In May 1974, giving an address in Foxrock, activists Nuala Fennell, Susan Donnelly and Kevin Quinn wrote to the *Irish Independent*, announcing plans to open a refuge for battered women, and requested help.[161]

In 1976, the Contraception Action Programme was founded by various women's and family planning organisations working together. In Ballinteer, a local group was formed in 1977, as a new health centre was planned, and activists wanted it to include a family planning clinic. Women from one in five households in Ballinteer were surveyed, the results showing massive support for the provision of contraception and advice about how to use it.[162] 'We suburban mothers,' read a letter to the newspaper by an angry group of women, 'are growing increasingly sick of male medic misogynists holding forth... We believe it is our right to make a free and adult choice from a comprehensive range of family planning methods. [They] have no understanding of the strain bearing and rearing numerous children, nor the anxiety of playing "Vatican Roulette" every month.'[163] In 1978, Irish Women United opened a shop on Harcourt Road in Dublin, selling contraceptives. Unchallenged by the police, they had sold everything after just a few hours.[164]

While most women were not active in feminist organisations – and some were even hostile to them – contraception and reproductive rights were increasingly commonplace topics in everyday conversation. One interviewee remembered discussions about contraception, and the interest that she took then: 'Nell McCafferty and... contraceptives ... you'd read about it, and you'd say, "Yeah, well, you can't go on having children forever".' Grassroots women's organisations, including organisations that were not obviously political in any way – even some religious organisations – provided women with opportunities to discreetly exchange useful information, such as which local doctors were more likely to prescribe 'the pill' to 'regulate their menstrual cycle'.[165] New legislation introduced in 1985 allowed condoms and spermicides to be sold without prescription. The birth rate continued to fall.

* * *

Throughout much of history, quite significant levels of domestic violence, generally involving husbands beating their wives and/or children, and sometimes parents of either sex beating their children, was not just tolerated but considered entirely unexceptional. For many women, their husbands' moods and forays into violence were almost like tempestuous weather; steps could be taken to mitigate against it, but it could not be prevented. When Ann Burn's husband asked her how she would feel if he hit her (in the context of criticising her treatment of their children), she threatened him: "'You wouldn't dare", says I. "Raise your hand to me, would you? By God, you might raise it once, but you'd never raise it a second time, for I wouldn't be here.'"[166] The reality was that most women experiencing violence in the home had very little choice but to stay and hope for the best.

Edward recalled that when he was growing up in Glasthule in the 1930s and 1940s, the sight of a woman fleeing her drunk, violent husband was relatively common. It was rare, as he recalled, for people to intervene, because 'the man was the lord master'. Barry remembered, in the 1960s, helping a friend of his and the boy's mother to barricade the door of their Dún Laoghaire home to keep her husband out. On Sundays, he routinely got drunk, came home and beat his wife. The women's rights movement transformed issues like domestic violence, which had (despite activists' efforts since the nineteenth century) previously been generally treated as a private family matter, into a topic for public discussion and legislation.[167]

People who encountered domestic violence in an official capacity, like the Gardaí, struggled before training was offered in this area. By the 1960s and 1970s, however, younger Gardaí were increasingly likely to see domestic violence as a crime. Vinnie came to Dún Laoghaire-Rathdown as a young guard in the mid-1960s. In his earlier years in the force, he encountered many women seeking help with the violence they experienced at home, and witnessed the often unhelpful attitudes of the older Gardaí, who were untrained in the area and not always inclined to be sympathetic: "'There's an old wan in there,'" a senior colleague told him, "'she got a few clips from the husband… she's there all night, will you take her home?'" Women rarely wanted to make an official statement, largely – Vinnie felt – because of their financial dependence on their husbands and the lack of a safety net. Women today have jobs, Vinnie said, 'but... a woman with four or five children, she had no job, no support, apart from the measly money she got from the husband... [if she made] the statement, she wouldn't have any support at all'. Well into the 1970s and even the 1980s, women who suffered domestic violence were expected to remain married and not complain too much; such women infrequently testified against their husbands in those rare cases that came to trial.[168] There were no organisations for women in violent marriages then so, as a young guard, Vinnie did his best: 'I would go back to the husband, and I had to call a number of them aside, and say, "Lookit, being honest about it now... this is the second time I'm back, your wife is badly beaten up – by *you*. Are you ashamed of yourself?"' Sometimes all he could do was offer a beaten woman a cup of tea at the station and give her some time away from her husband, leaving him to cool off and sober up.

Systems for dealing with children and women suffering sexual or other physical violence at home were also almost non-existent in the early 1960s. Vinnie recalled a girl of fourteen who came to the station to complain that her father was molesting her. At that time, Vinnie said, there appeared to be no specific police protocol for cases of this sort. Ultimately, he had to intervene in a personal capacity.

The first women to enter the Garda Síochána did so in 1959, after relevant legislation was passed in 1958. In the course of the Dáil debates, one TD commented that, 'while recruits should not actually be horse-faced, they should not be too good-looking; they should just be plain women and not targets for marriage'.[169] The greater physical vulnerability of women was one reason against having women in the police force. Another was the view that, 'if a woman were investigating a crime, she would not be considered credible in court'.[170] Only well into the 1980s, according to Vinnie, did a significant cultural shift start to occur. Domestic violence and sexual assault were taken more seriously and, with more women in the Gardaí, it was a little easier to handle crimes of this nature. 'Well,' Vinnie remembered, 'it was definitely easier for women colleagues with regards to allegations of rape... guys found it awful hard to handle the rape situation.'

* * *

Throughout the nineteenth and much of the twentieth century, women whose husbands were abusive, died (and until recent decades, people died at younger ages in much greater numbers than now) or became unwell and unable to work were in a dreadful situation, a world in which women on their own were still less likely to get 'good' jobs and to be paid well, even as the family's sole breadwinner. Widows who had worked in the civil service, although they generally had to give up work before the marriage bar was repealed, were in a better position than most, as they could return to work. For women during most of the twentieth century, there were often many pragmatic reasons not to leave even extremely unhappy marriages. It was difficult for most women to find work that paid well enough to support them and their children, and those who were married were excluded from many occupations. Wealthier women in unhappy marriages faced the prospect of a dramatic decline in their standard of living, while poor women faced absolute poverty. Both had to consider the stigma associated with separation. Rosario remembered her mother and her mother's friends discussing, in the 1970s and 1980s, the difficulties women faced when their marriages broke down: 'there would have been a kind of fear with women... if they didn't feel their marriages were going the way they wanted... "Well, how would you survive?"' Women whose husbands were unfaithful had often left the paid labour force years before, and dreaded the loss of income and status that accompanied marriage to a good provider.

Whereas widowhood and marriage breakdown both posed practical dilemmas to women, in some ways marriage breakdown was worse. Marital separation was still heavily stigmatised throughout most of the twentieth century, particularly for women. When Bella and her husband separated, she removed her wedding ring, only to be approached at an event at her children's school by a woman who said, 'Bella, I'd advise you to put your wedding ring on, it just doesn't look good.' Another no longer let her children play with Bella's, 'just in case'. Lloyd remembered a woman whose husband left her in the early 1980s. Whereas their suburban community gathered supportively around widows, this was not the case for her. People felt that she 'wasn't able to keep her man' and, as he recalled, 'I don't think she stayed there much longer after. She was quite shunned.' He remembered another local woman telling her friend that she wanted to leave her husband, and being advised 'to cop herself on, go home, cook the dinner'.

* * *

Mags started working for a bank in the mid-1940s, when she was in her late teens. For much of her career, women employees were paid less than male colleagues, and were much less likely to be promoted. Even more aggravatingly, Mags remembered, men were given time off to attend rugby matches, while women were not given time off for equivalent activities, or for issues relating to women's health, and workplace bullying was common, but difficult to complain about, as women were expected to 'tolerate' teasing from the male staff. Grace worked as a saleswoman in Lee's in Dún Laoghaire in the 1960s. Lee's was considered a good employer, but it followed norms regarding women's and men's pay, and Grace remembered annoyance when her male colleagues were routinely paid more than her. She felt this was appropriate when a man had to support a wife and family on his salary, but was resentful when single male colleagues, performing the same tasks as her, outearned her. Women rarely complained, though: 'in those days, women were glad to have a job'.

In 1966, children's allowances were still given to fathers, when many married women did not work outside the home (Rob remembered his wife needing 'a piece of paper' from him stating that he had 'no bans on her getting the children's allowance' from the post office). Men were entitled to receive rebates from income on which their wives were taxed, and women required their husband's signature to obtain a mortgage or purchase goods by hire purchase.[171] Even opening an account at a local library could be tricky for a married woman. Elaine went to her local library in Stillorgan in the 1970s and was informed that she could not join without her husband's signature. Rebecca tried to buy a small house in Dún Laoghaire and was refused a mortgage as a single woman; she managed to buy with her parents as co-signatory, a little humiliation. Later, when she wanted the electricity and gas connected, she was asked for her husband's details; she nearly wept in frustration. Bea, a few years later, could not buy a car without her husband's permission, and needed his signature to carry out normal banking activities. The year 1970 saw the founding of the Irish Women's Liberation Movement, which focused on these issues.[172]

Noreen worked for Dún Laoghaire Borough Corporation from 1949. Her experience there was generally positive, but she was infuriated to see women being treated differently to their male colleagues. Many of her male colleagues seemed to find it difficult when women did not behave submissively around them. In the early 1960s, Noreen got involved in trades unions to fight for women's rights from that context, and she started to attend the Jesuit-run College of Industrial Relations in Milltown. One of the priests in the college commented that he could clearly see discrimination against women in the workforce. 'Every fella that comes up here… drives up in a car,' he said. 'Every woman that comes up, comes up on her bike.' One of the problems facing women then, Noreen said, was that the few who did get promoted to senior positions rarely supported campaigns to change the law, because they were afraid of drawing negative attention to themselves and damaging their careers. Noreen and her fellow campaigners used every weapon in their arsenal, including an encyclical from Pope Pius XII regarding women's rights* and some unlikely support from John Charles McQuaid, the Catholic Primate of Ireland and Archbishop of Dublin, who met them, listened to their concerns and introduced them to a Monsignor who was an expert on industrial relations. 'I was always sorry,' Noreen reflected, 'that I didn't just pay… one tribute to McQuaid because he got so much criticism… *justified* criticism. But he did take the women seriously.'

* * *

While many women's organisations worked quite quietly, periodic dramatic public protests captured media attention and tend to dominate official memory of women's activism in the 1960s and 1970s. For example, women swimmers' anger at being barred from swimming at Sandycove's famous Forty Foot bathing spot, an all-male bathing area, was a perfect story for journalists to cover, as it involved angry and/or bemused naked men and defiant 'girls in bikinis'.[173] On 22 July 1974, the Dublin City Women's Invasionary Force went to the Forty Foot with placards bearing messages like, 'We will fight them on the beaches, we will win between the sheets', and 'In Ireland private property means men's property'.[174] Mr Frank Robinson, one of the committee members of the Forty Foot, stated that the committee was going to 'have a meeting', but conceded that there appeared to be no legal way to stop women swimming there.[175] On 7 August some of the male bathers grumbled to journalists, stating that they had built the toilet themselves, that there was no toilet for women and nowhere for women to dress, and that – anyway – the water was too cold and too dangerous for women. Another suggested that the

---

* Among other things, in his encyclical in 1947, Pius XII said, 'But now you [women] appear abroad, you enter the arena to take part in the battle: you have not sought to do so, but courageously you accept your new duties; not as resigned victims nor merely in a defensive spirit; you are determined to pass to the counter-attack and conquer.' He went on to say that while 'most' women would be devoted to home and family, others 'who have more leisure and are suitably prepared, will take up the burden of public life'. https://www.papalencyclicals.net/pius12/p12woman.htm, retrieved 12 July 2023.

Sign at the Forty Foot, 1974. Courtesy RTÉ archives.

Women protesting at the Forty Foot in 1974. Veteran campaigner and journalist Nell McCafferty would later recall that 'There was loads of sexist abuse from the men ... The women were told, although in cruder terms, that what they all needed was sexual intercourse.' Courtesy RTÉ archives.

A swimmer being interviewed during a protest by women at the Forty Foot in 1974. Courtesy RTÉ archives.

men scare the women away by swimming nude.[176] Ultimately, however, the women prevailed.

* * *

Women's activism in the 1960s and 1970s has been much discussed, and has contributed to some of the biggest social changes in modern history, but only a very small minority of women was ever active in women's rights organisations. Many were so busy with their work (paid and unpaid) and family lives that they did not give them much thought, at least at the time. As the socioeconomic environment gradually improved during the twentieth century, young couples from working-class backgrounds who could afford for the wife to stay at home took great pride in it. Many had grown up in families in which their mothers endured up to twenty pregnancies and cared for vast families, while also undertaking cleaning work, laundry, farm labouring or other arduous physical work outside the home. For them, being affluent enough on one income to focus on their children and families was often more than reward enough. Kimberly remembered her parents' attitude: 'My mother didn't work. I think my father's thing would've been, no, he's the provider… he always had decent jobs… he brought his wages home to her… there was never a week where my mother wouldn't have had her wages.'

Most interviewees who lived as adults through the period when second-wave feminism was in the ascendant reported that they took little interest in the movement then. Many said it seemed irrelevant to their lives, or that they feel now, with hindsight, that most of the changes women activists sought were inevitable and would have come anyway, with growing modernisation and membership of what was then the EEC; equal pay for equal work and other changes relating to female employment were among the prerequisites for Ireland joining the EEC in 1973.[177] Many women, especially from working-class backgrounds, viewed women activists as 'students' and 'university types', out of touch with most working women and mothers in the home. Catherine, a wife and mother of a young family of four children in the late 1960s and early 1970s, was aware of the women's rights movement then, but not terribly interested: 'you wouldn't have had time to worry about things like that. You know, they were all politicians, and they'd plenty time to do nothing else.' Isobel, whose ten children were born in the 1950s and 1960s, and were growing up by the mid-1970s, remembered her reaction to the women's liberation movement. 'At first,' she said, 'I was a little bit shocked.' She struggled with the idea that it was better for women to work outside the home, and have their children cared for by someone else. 'I didn't really approve of women working [outside the home, for pay],' she said, referring especially to the formative years of early child-hood. On reflection, she decided that, despite this difference of opinion, she was in favour of many of the changes that women activists sought. She noted, however, that while more women were working outside the home, not all of them found this liberating. One friend got a good job that she expected to enjoy, but now found that she was doing two jobs, as all the domestic tasks she no longer had time for Monday to Friday were waiting for her at the weekend.

Some women were positively hostile towards the women's liberation movement, feeling that it was not just unnecessary, but wrong. Jennifer, who had a good job in a travel agency, was one such. '[I] didn't sympathise with it at all!' she remembered: 'it clashed with my very orthodox Catholic ideas... I really couldn't see why they would want contraception or anything of that. It was a sin, and that was it.' Jennifer said that she 'really sort of bought into the idea that women *shouldn't* be paid as much as men because they weren't as important... We were only there to prop up the boss. Never mind that we [secretaries]... put their letters into good English and made them look good... we were... only there to support... a man should be the breadwinner.'

Generally, women's activism in the 1960s and 1970s encouraged women to limit births and increase participation in the formal, paid workforce, which it saw as offering access to the corridors of power. In the process, women who were happy as full-time housewives often felt excluded from the conversation, while many working-class women felt they were not really being addressed at all. Inadvertently, women's activism at the time often undervalued the mostly unpaid work that so many women did at home. Many interviewees have memories of women – mothers, grandmothers – whose lives appeared joyful and fulfilling as they cared for their children, husbands and homes. Others can testify themselves to the satisfaction they found in caring for their families and homes.

Women from middle-class and upwardly mobile working families found the southside suburbs comfortable, friendly, supportive places in which to raise their children. Cora was 'delighted' to dedicate herself to her family in Shankill in the 1950s and 1960s: 'I loved being at home,' she remembered; '[in] the summer holidays… we went down to the sea every morning at 10'. (Although she also remembered a sense of feeling disrespected sometimes, because her husband was the breadwinner: 'Oh my God, is she spending all your money?' someone might comment. 'And I would say to them, no matter where I was,' Cora said, 'excuse me, it's not his money, it's *our* money.') Eve recalled how much she loved being at home with her children in the 1960s and 1970s: 'I was quite content… surrounded by other women… I was proud as punch wheeling my pram around… we'd be in and out of one another's houses, and having the cups of tea, helping one another out with babysitting for one another.'

Women dedicated to home making could utilise the skills they had learned at home from their own mothers and in school. Middle-class and wealthy women who expected to play a supportive role in their husbands' careers by being able to entertain and cater lavish dinners might attend additional classes in cuisine. Lily's mother, the wife of a prominent businessman who did a lot of entertaining, travelled to the UK in the 1940s and 1950s to attend cookery classes with Constance Spry, a notable proponent of *cordon bleu* cookery, then an important signifier of social status as well as an important influence on fine dining in Ireland. With the skills she acquired she could present her guests with dishes like *galantine* (boned, stuffed meat). Finghin recalled with appreciation his wife and many of her friends attending such classes in Dublin in the 1960s and 1970s: 'the standard of cooking in this house... was very, very high'.

The happiness and satisfaction of women working exclusively in the home depended heavily on the quality of their relationship with their husband, who was in some respects their employer as well as their life partner. A woman whose husband was kind, fair and faithful could have a very happy life. Kate remembered her grandmother, a warm and open woman with a rich social life, and her many friends: 'they all had very good husbands, and consequently.... they were liberated before the term "liberation" ever came in. They could go off to the theatre... and the cinema, and always had friends in, and went out socially... I often thought of the contrast there, when you have a good husband... compared to [women] who don't.'

A mother with young children in 1967, Yvette and her women friends in their Dundrum suburb were all at home with their children and, generally, happy to be so. They established a mother and toddler group, and shared the joys and trials of young motherhood. Many became involved in voluntary work in various capacities in and beyond the community; Yvette was involved with the National Women's Council, founded in 1973 to pursue women's rights. Women in the home who were religiously active were frequently engaged with the ecumenical movement (for example, the Women's World Day of Prayer), as it gathered steam in the 1970s and into the 1980s, and with other volunteer and philanthropic organisations, as well as performing unpaid elder-care duties for their own and their husbands' relatives. Of course, some housewives were concerned about their complete financial dependence on their husbands – but for many, this was only a problem if their marriage broke down, or if their husbands died, which, at a time of decreased and decreasing mortality among younger adults, seemed less of an issue than it had before.

Although many women engaged full-time in the home did not feel represented by women's rights activists, many others were interested in

Bernie Mac Giolla Phádraig and sons, c.1969, in the Blackrock area, photographed by a local milkman. For many families, the 1960s was an era of growing prosperity. The suburbs were expanding, with comfortable homes with nice gardens for middle-class and upwardly mobile young families. Fewer working-class women had to take on casual work outside the home, as it was easier to survive on one salary, while women in general were increasingly engaged in debate about their role in society and public life. Kind permission of the Mac Giolla Phádraig family.

what they were doing, and admired at least some of their aims. Cora was never involved, but she felt they were 'great' to support women who wanted careers outside the home as well as children. Margie, who spent time as a stay-at-home mother and subsequently re-entered the formal workforce, felt that most of the women in her middle-class neighbourhood admired women's rights activists. 'I felt they were a voice for good,' recalled Anne, 'and I was very happy that women were beginning to move on.' Liz gave no thought to issues of women's rights as a young woman working in an industrial sector, or when she was a young mother, busy with her children and home. While she provided accommodation to students and supplemented the family income, she did not work outside the home until her children had grown up and she returned to an office job. Nearly thirty years after leaving paid employment for the first time, she was struck by how much things had changed. When she was young, all the managers were men, and women support staff had addressed them deferentially. Now there were women in management and that deference had gone. Only retrospectively did she understand what women's rights activists of her generation had wanted. Kate agreed:

'I didn't take them seriously. I didn't take what they were doing seriously. It's only retrospectively, I realise that they were pioneers.'

The Anti-Discrimination (Pay) Act was enacted in 1974 and the first Employment Equality Act in 1977. Educational levels among both women and men continued to rise and the gap between women's and men's educational attainment continued to narrow. By the 1980s, working outside the home was becoming common for middle-class women, growing numbers of whom had university or other forms of further education or training. Attitudes were starting to shift among men with regard to their female colleagues and staff, as women entering the workforce were increasingly as educated as men, if not more. Jimmy worked in an industrial sector. He remembered that, in the 1980s, when he was in quite a senior position, all the 'girls' in his business were in the typing pool. Many of the women staff were doing secretarial work, which was of course essential, but the system did not accommodate women who wanted to do something else, and certainly not those who aspired to management roles. At one stage in the 1980s, a sales position opened up, and one young woman nervously approached Jimmy and asked for permission to apply. Until now, sales positions – offering opportunities for advancement – had only been available to male staff. This was a Damascus moment for Jimmy, who gave her the job 'because she was brilliant'. He realised that 'for too many years, this country, and most countries, had disregarded [women in the workplace]… young girls were subjected to that crap'. Sinéad was a young woman, coming of age, in 1986. She wanted to work in finance, but when she joined the bank 'they put the girls into the secretarial pool and boys as clerks'. She was outraged. 'I mean,' she thought, 'how *dare* they… why am I doing that? Why is it all men?' The difference for Sinéad, compared to women from earlier generations, is that when she objected, she was put into the department she wanted, where she learned the skills she needed to advance.

The latter decades of the twentieth century continued to see enormous changes for women and families. Births declined by a third between 1980 and 1994.[178] Rape within marriage was criminalised in 1990, the year Mary Robinson became Ireland's first female president. Bea, a young married woman in Cabinteely from the 1970s, remembered Robinson's election as 'a big milestone… the start of women having a better life in this country'. Divorce became legal in 1996, the result of a narrow referendum margin. Even views on the extremely contentious issue of abortion had shifted dramatically; by 1992, 33 per cent of those surveyed agreed that there were circumstances where abortion might be necessary.[179] While some issues, notably domestic and sexual violence, remained a significant challenge, in many ways women's – especially wealthier, educated women's – lives had been transformed, while women who preferred a traditional role in the home started to feel overlooked.

* * *

Trade unionism, while it has an important history in Ireland, has historically been less developed here than in many other nations, primarily because of significantly lower levels of industrialisation and the persistence of agriculture as the core of the economy until far later than in most of western Europe, and partly because oppositional relationships predicated around Fianna Fáil versus Fine Gael supporters replaced those between workers and employers, and possibly also high levels of emigration. Trade unions served multiple functions – striving to protect workers from exploitation, but also, sometimes, restricting access to certain professions to those whose fathers or other male relatives already worked in the field. Trade union membership increased significantly, particularly among male workers, in the 1940s and 1950s (some employers cut corners by hiring teenaged boys, paid less than adult men, for less-skilled jobs and fired them when they turned eighteen). Industrial action also steadily became more common as the twentieth century progressed. Under a new government led by Seán Lemass, from 1959 to 1966, Ireland's industrial base grew, and the government met with more union resistance, with frequent strikes.

Peter entered the workforce at fifteen in 1979. Shortly afterwards, postmen went on strike, seeking higher wages. Peter's contract was only temporary, so in theory he could have worked, but as his father – a seasoned postman – was a union official, they felt it would not look good. The strike lasted for nineteen weeks, during which the family managed on what Peter's father could earn mowing lawns while not on picket duty. Eoin's father was once on strike for months, eking out a meagre living with odd jobs until it was resolved. Until then, Eoin said, his father could provide for the family quite well: 'I'd never tasted margarine in my life.' The strike persisted so long they had to make cutback after cutback at home, including replacing butter with margarine, and eventually having to ask the neighbours in their housing estate for help. Finally, Eoin's father broke the picket and returned to work, tolerating the insult of 'black leg' thrown at him by some of his colleagues.

With the notable exception of the Irish National Teachers' Organisation, which allowed women to join from 1868, hardly any women were members of the earlier trade unions; craft unions excluded women from apprenticeships and trades and resisted the mechanisation of trade, partly because of fears this would open them up to women workers. The Irish Women Workers' Union was formed in 1911 when trade unions were concerned that a significant influx of women into the workplace would result in an overall decline in wages, as women would probably be prepared to work for less. Throughout the 1930s, against the backdrop of the global economic depression, laws were introduced to limit married women's access to formally paid work. A famous strike at Downey's pub in Dún Laoghaire occurred from 1939, when the Vintners' Union objected to the employment of non-unionised women staff (presumably largely on the basis that women workers would drive down wages). In response, the publican fired all the union staff and replaced them with non-union labour. The ensuing industrial action lasted for fourteen years, continuing even after Mr Downey's death.[180]

Some unions, notably those representing teachers, in which more women were represented, were increasingly inclined to listen to women among their ranks. Before the General Election of 1948, the Irish National Teachers' Organisation argued, among other things, against the compulsory retirement of female teachers upon marriage. Women workers started to join trade unions in much larger numbers in the 1960s and 1970s, and by the end of the 1970s, they were as likely to be union members as were men. By this point, things were changing dramatically in the skilled professions, amid a general rapid improvement in educational standards. Whereas before many professions had been restricted to the male offspring of men already in the trade, now schools and colleges were offering other routes into the skilled trades. Social changes in wider society were changing things too. Julian, who followed his father into the metalwork industry, recalled that, when he was starting out in the 1960s, 'the older craftsmen would still wear collar and tie to work. You know, they were so proud of their status… they had a proper collar and tie. They thought us apprentices were scruffy little buggers.'

* * *

From the early to mid-1960s, Traveller activists and their allies were increasingly political in their goal to improve Travellers' living conditions.[181] Growing numbers of Travellers were accessing formal education, and had started to develop a keener political sense of their role in society, their challenges and the changes they wanted. Their demands often conflicted with government policy and the general attitude among settled people, that Travellers should be absorbed into mainstream society. In 1963, the Commission on Itinerancy, which informed government policy, stressed that all organisations intended to support Travellers 'must always have as their aim the eventual absorption of the itinerants'.[182] In 1969, the Irish Council for Itinerant Settlement (later the National Council for Travelling People) was founded, with the goal of improving the quality of life and opportunities for Travellers, then generally 'existing in caravans – if they are lucky – otherwise under canvas, without heating, cooking, or toilet facilities'.[183] The council saw

Travellers' nomadism as intrinsically troublesome and *per se* a barrier to integration. Also in 1969, John Charles McQuaid, then Archbishop of Dublin, described Travellers as 'these good people' who 'retained their love of the Faith' despite challenging circumstances. He stated that their nomadism had prevented them from benefitting from 'systematic education and the normal amenities of society', asserting that it was 'amply evident' that Travellers wanted to settle.[184] In Foxrock, a group of locals formed the Foxrock Itinerants' Settlement Committee in the mid-1960s (there were various 'settlement committees' around the country, the first of which was founded in 1965[185]). Timmy's parents were among the members, and as they had quite large grounds they volunteered space to provide a site for a Traveller family, who stayed for several years. On 8 April 1973, Victor Bewley – who was on the Council for Itinerant Settlement – told the *Irish Times* that there were fifty homeless Traveller families in an area of south Dublin/north Wicklow from Milltown to Bray. Considering the large sizes of Traveller families prevalent at the time, this is likely to have amounted to several hundred people.[186] Aidan, a Traveller who knew Victor, remembered him as a 'great man' who did his best to help, although the Council's work is retrospectively regarded as flawed.

By the 1980s, Traveller activists were increasingly critical of earlier efforts to secure greater rights for Travellers. They had generally been led by settled people, who often assumed that the best outcome for Travellers was for them to become settled people too. These had grown to be criticised for not having sufficient understanding of Travellers' culture and concerns. Lawrence, a young Traveller activist in the 1980s, remembered the Vincent de Paul and a Settlement Committee trying to help. Their intentions, he said, were good, but insufficient: 'They were interested in helping people to alleviate the poverty… But they weren't prepared to challenge the injustice or the racism or the discrimination… or the inequality.' Traveller activists increasingly pointed out that, for many, nomadism was seen as essential to their identity and way of life, and they felt that it should be accommodated. In Dún Laoghaire-Rathdown, the

Southside Travellers Action Group was established in 1984, operating from Blackrock Library for a time. Lawrence, who was involved with the group, noted the lack of attention paid not just to Travellers but to people living in poverty in the area generally, describing local poverty as 'kind of invisible' because the area was generally seen as affluent. While various governing bodies attended meetings with the group, Lawrence remembered some of them as being quite unwilling to engage, inter-rupting with comments like: 'I don't have to listen to this horseshit.' The authorities wanted Travellers to settle, but apparently not in the south-side suburbs. Even Travellers who did want to settle found it extremely difficult to get housed in council estates. Money allocated to a budget supposed to deal with Travellers' housing was largely spent on evictions. In various developments locals formed groups dedicated to ensuring that no Travellers halted or settled in or near their housing estates or sports facilities. These residents' protests could be successful in preventing the construction of halting sites. Feargal remembered a would-be site in the Shankill area blockaded for months, after which the council decided to build one elsewhere. Motivated partly by reasonable concerns about the impact of non-serviced unofficial halting sites on local communities, with the inevitable accumulation of uncollected rubbish, much uglier views also prevailed and were widely accepted. Halting sites, remem-bered Austin, were sometimes referred to with names like 'Fort Apache', referencing tension between Traveller and settled communities, and the idea that these were places apart from the rest of the world. At one point in 1969, some Foxrock residents used and/or threatened physical vio-lence to induce Travellers to leave. Local curate Father Malachy Mahon denounced this behaviour from the pulpit. Around this time, Stacia's family was camping in Ballybrack. Previously, they could access drinking water from pumps and wells, but now they had to ask householders and garages for water, and were often refused: 'we'd go for a can of water... and they wouldn't give it. They'd shut the door in your face.' Thankfully, a local couple attached a hose to their kitchen tap and left it outside their window so that the Travellers could get the water they needed.

The situation deteriorated throughout the 1970s. In 1978, a reader's letter to the *Irish Press* said of Travellers that, 'They should all be sterilised and the kids taken up the motorway and thrown under lorries.'[187] Darragh, who grew up in a suburb near the N11, remembered anti-Traveller activism at a local housing estate. A group of Travellers had been moved on, and residents wanted to prevent their return, so some used timber, old furniture and cars to barricade a junction staffed by local men who allowed only certain people in and out and maintained it until the Travellers had left definitively. 'I have,' Darragh said, 'a clear visual memory of, "Oh, look at that! Look at what they are doing, that looks very illegal!"'

At around the same time, conflicts were breaking out along the Ballyogan Road. This had been a traditional halting area for Travellers for as long as anyone could remember. For generations they had provided services for local farmers and had enjoyed a broadly positive relationship with them. When the area was developed with council and other estates, Travellers continued to camp there, although there was now much less demand for their services and many fewer opportunities for casual labour. Representatives of the settled community protested by picketing the local dump, preventing movement in or out. Ultimately, the council moved the Travellers on. On 1 December 1981, residents of Carrickmines-Foxrock protested plans to settle up to thirty Traveller families in the Ballyogan Road area, from where Traveller children could travel to a 'Special National School' in Bray (one of several schools in the greater Dublin area established specifically for the education of Traveller children).[188] In June 1986, a Traveller couple was moved on the Ballyogan Road, and then Rathfarnham, by the county council. A letter to the *Irish Independent* highlighting their plight pointed out that they had been living in the area for a long time – far longer than most of the settled people who had 'flooded in' in recent years.[189] Around this time, remembered Rebecca of Dún Laoghaire, a Traveller family who were friends of hers was given a council house, only for certain locals to burn them out: 'I found the house burnt out and one of the kids' toys on a bonfire, a few teddy bears and books and things.' In the late 1980s, when Travellers were moved from a site in Foxrock, residents organised groups of volunteers to create and staff road blocks to prevent them from setting up camp.[190] From 1990, the Irish Traveller Movement represented Travellers and settled people working together.[191] However, despite some positive alliances, the relationship between Travellers and many settled people remained fraught.

* * *

The Criminal Amendment Act 1885, Section 11, condemned 'any male person' who committed 'gross indecency with another male person' to imprisonment or hard labour. Thus, men who had sex with, or were attracted to, other men were singled out for particularly harsh treatment, while lesbians were not recognised at all.[192] Fear and loathing of same-sex attraction had pervasive societal impacts. Even children's innocent games could be interpreted as suspect by a teacher with a horror of any sort of intimacy between males.

While invoked relatively rarely, the Criminal Amendment Act had a deeply chilling effect on the lives of gay men throughout much of the twentieth century, when sexuality generally was heavily policed. They were prosecuted into the 1940s and 1950s and, while the sentences were often quite light,[193] the stigma and shame associated with being convicted for 'gross indecency' were generally devastating. Almost all gay men remained firmly in the closet, although sometimes their close friends knew. Karen remembered attending her first dinner-dance in 1943, when she was just fifteen. She was surprised that her mother was so happy to let her go out with her date, who was older at twenty-one. Years later she realised that her mother was unconcerned, because she knew that Karen's date did not find girls attractive.

Arguably, if surprisingly, the modern Irish gay rights movement started – inadvertently – with the Legion of Mary. The Legion of Mary, founded in 1921, is retrospectively acknowledged as having anticipated many of the social and pastoral changes introduced following the Second Vatican Council of the 1960s,[194] and was a vanguard of the more compassionate Catholicism that characterised many social outreach programmes of the 1970s and 1980s. While certainly not at all progressive by today's standards – indeed, today it would be considered shockingly retrogressive – it needs to be understood from the perspective of the day, when same-sex sexual activity was a crime in Ireland and condemnation was the norm. From 1965, the Legion of Mary in Ireland hosted discussion groups for same-sex-attracted men which, while they advocated for chastity (as they did for all unmarried people) and presented same-sex attraction as a problem to be solved and as sinful and immoral, at least provided space for dialogue. Unintentionally, it unified some earlier Irish campaigners for gay rights.[195] The Irish gay rights movement became more political, and more focused on sexual freedoms, from the mid-1970s. The law was still punitive: between 1962 and 1972 there were 455 prosecutions for 'indecency with males' and 'gross indecency'.[196] The Irish Gay Rights Movement was founded in 1974[197] and held its first march, to the Department of Justice, brandishing banners stating, 'Homosexuals are Revolting'.[198] From the late 1970s, although same-sex intimate relationships remained illegal, gay rights organisations held events like weekly discos, and activists increasingly worked towards legislative change.[199] Inspired by active gay rights movements in other countries, gay men and lesbians were becoming more visible.

Dangers to the same-sex attracted were also growing. Peter remembered a park in Dún Laoghaire known, in the late 1970s and early 1980s, for 'gay bashing' and 'queer bashing'. In 1983, in Fairview, on the other side of the city, Declan Flynn was beaten to death in a 'queer bashing' incident. The suspended sentences the aggressors received did nothing to dissuade similar attacks elsewhere. A young man who had been a classmate of Peter's killed himself in his early twenties, apparently at least partly because of the bullying he had lived with as a young gay man. In 1988, playwright Aodhán Madden's play *Sea Urchins* had its world premiere at the Hawkswell Theatre in Sligo. Based loosely on the murder of Declan Flynn, the play was set on Dún Laoghaire pier, portraying a group of young men engaged in 'queer bashing' and illustrated the 'acceptable social prejudice' that 'a homosexual is Fair Game'.[200]

Inevitably, throughout much of the 1980s, gay rights activism, particularly regarding same-sex attracted men, was deeply concerned with the AIDS epidemic, which initially impacted above all on gay men, while health services were overwhelmingly provided by hospital and other care providers under the control of the Catholic Church. From 1985, the Gay Health Action Group provided education and information about AIDS.[201] By 1989, intravenous drug users of any sexuality were the most likely demographic to have AIDS.[202]

Young men who came out or were revealed to their parents to be gay were sometimes still kicked out of the home and estranged from their families. Some found supportive friends – perhaps a friend's parents – while others did not. Bullying in school and the social contexts of young people perceived to be gay was common. Parents of sons who were young gay men in the 1980s and before often indicate their relief at the decriminalisation of homosexuality in 1993 and now query why this could not have taken place years before.

Although, ostensibly, the lesbian and gay rights movements had much in common, the relationship between the two groups (or rather between the many groups under the two rather large, overlapping umbrellas) could be testy, and the issues they faced were more different than appeared at first glance. At the 1981 Gay Liberation Conference, a women's workshop accused male gay rights activists of being more sexist than heterosexual men. Exasperated, many lesbians opted to campaign in association with women's rights activists, most of whom were not lesbians, rather than gay men. In 1981, the Women's Centre opened in Dublin, and although many lesbians were involved in running it, they agreed to feature nothing on their noticeboard that might 'alarm straight women'. One of the issues that lesbians faced was that they were often mothers supporting children, with less economic clout than gay men, who were also less likely to be parents. Lesbians Operating Together was

Dún Laoghaire Dykes and supporters, including Marie Mulholland and Jane Pilkington, demonstrating in Dublin city centre, 2004. Christopher Robson Photographic Collection, National Library of Ireland.

founded in 1992, invited to an audience with President Mary Robinson in 1992, and worked to ensure that matters affecting lesbians were covered in the *Gay Community News* newspaper.[203]

Public attitudes towards same-sex attraction had started to shift, although it was still difficult to come out as gay in many Irish families, and shunning and ostracisation remained common responses to a son or a daughter coming out. In 1990, the Irish Council for Civil Liberties called for the decriminalisation of homosexuality and the Catholic Church labelled homosexuality an 'objective disorder'.[204] It was decriminalised in 1993.[205] By then, acceptance of same-sex attraction was growing. Parents whose children came out to them often found it hard at first – largely because of concerns about AIDS – but increasingly most came to terms with their child's news.

* * *

Hard drugs like heroin started to arrive in Ireland in the 1970s. Like everywhere else, Ireland was unprepared for how rapidly many would become addicted. Eimear, in her mid-teens then, remembered feeling afraid to grow up. Drug use was becoming more visible, and she was afraid that someone might 'force' her to take drugs. As social and health workers struggled to understand and deal with the situation, drug abuse continued to escalate.

The 1980s were a period of economic crisis, with high levels of unemployment (rising by 77 per cent nationally between 1979 and 1982), and almost 25 per cent of the entire population of workers employed in the public sector and therefore not directly involved in wealth creation. By 1983, a million were at least partly dependent on a social welfare payment. When heroin was introduced into this already difficult situation in a culture in which substance dependency (generally alcohol) was a long-established problem, a perfect storm was created. Things deteriorated further when HIV/AIDS, then a devastating illness with no effective treatment, entered the population of intravenous drug users. In Dublin, inner-city areas were particularly badly impacted,[206] but the suburbs were affected too. Dún Laoghaire and surrounding areas – near a major port through which drugs were trafficked – experienced high levels of addiction, together with associated rises in crime and drug-related disease. Josie remembered the drug epidemic having a sudden, dramatic impact on Dún Laoghaire: 'it just turned into scumbag town'. Some areas became so well-known for criminality that people feared going there: 'the police didn't even go down there because they just got battered and pelted'. Some of Josie's friends were affected by drugs, and some even died. Peter, who grew up in Sallynoggin, also saw the havoc that the new drugs wreaked. Some of his friends and former classmates died from their addiction; although many did not have a lot of extra money, drugs were getting easier and easier to get, young people were bored, and medical and social work professionals were struggling to cope. Conor remembered the arrival of heroin into the Dún Laoghaire area, and its sudden and devastating impact on vulnerable families: 'overnight they got access to heroin, and they flipped [from drinking cider]… very quickly, some of the lads started getting sick [with hepatitis and AIDS]'. Derek knew several people who contracted AIDS around this time. Several of them died. One, a 'really handsome guy, well got', ended up dying 'screaming in a nappy'. Kimberly, in her teens in the early 1980s, remembered the devastation. One particular gang of young people left their homes and slept rough around Dún Laoghaire: 'one of them died a couple of years ago that I know lasted longer than most of them'. A study conducted in the Dún Laoghaire area in 1983–4 confirmed that heroin abuse was a significant local problem, and that anti-drug activism tended to result in addicts moving into and out of different homes, making it difficult to keep track of them. Treatment centres were located far away, in the city centre, making it more difficult for addicts from the southern suburbs who wished to quit to get help.[207] Sinéad grew up in a housing estate in Blackrock that was also home to several major drug dealers. Ironically, she said, their presence made the estate safer than others, 'Because they never… shit on their own doorstep.' Still, locals were keenly aware of the problems: 'if [people] were being chased by the police,' she remembered, they often just dashed through the nearest front door, 'and out through the house and out the back door and over the back wall and they'd be gone… and when the police came through and they'd ask you "who was it?", you'd say, "I don't know".'

Locals in badly affected areas, including Dún Laoghaire, Sallynoggin and Ballybrack, were increasingly involved in grassroots organisations targeting drug dealers. A Dún Laoghaire organisation, Concerned Parents, arranged marches to known dealers' homes, hoping to highlight the problem, shame the dealers and focus the attention of the Gardaí. Peter remembered 'hundreds' attending these marches, intended to intimidate known (or sometimes suspected) drug dealers into leaving. Protestors also gathered outside the clinics of local politicians like Barry Desmond, Minister of Health from 1982 to 1987, feeling that the government was not doing enough. One alleged local drug dealer, Derek remembered, denied that he and his family knew anything about it, and even drove through the centre of Dún Laoghaire in the back of a transporter van to make his public denial in response to the marches held outside his house.

New and established suburbs for the middle classes, like Cabinteely and Foxrock, were increasingly seen as safer for families to live in, away from the worst impacts of the drugs. Previously, suburbs in these areas had been marketed for their clean air, contrasted with the miasma in the city centre, and promoted as being good for one's physical and mental health. Now the perception that these were places where one could raise a family away from the drugs epidemic was an important selling point. While no social class was immune, the crisis was far worse in working-class than in affluent areas, and the differences between the haves and the have-nots were stark.

* * *

The nineteenth and twentieth centuries were an era of remarkable technological, educational and social change, punctuated in most places – and no less in Ireland – by outbreaks of violence and of counter-efforts against it. In many ways, we are still living through the consequences of those changes, and – as cultural shifts can take years to fully manifest and can only really be understood retrospectively – we are continuing to adapt to and learn about them as we participate in a story that is still being told.

GETTING AHEAD

Formal education, apprenticeships and learning in the home are all time-honoured ways of getting 'a start' in life, and historically Dún Laoghaire-Rathdown has offered opportunities in all these fields. Whereas in the late nineteenth and early twentieth century, one could work as a manual labourer or domestic servant with little formal education, gradually high standards of literacy became the norm, and those without fell ever further behind. The period from the late nineteenth century onwards was one in which extraordinary advances in education occurred, particularly from the mid-twentieth century, with the working classes and particularly Travellers the least likely to receive a good educational foundation throughout most of that time.

Those with poor literacy skills often depended on others when they needed to communicate in writing, apply for pensions or benefits, or inform themselves. An aunt of Janet's, born in the late nineteenth century, visited the Carmelite convent in her native Blackrock in the early twentieth century,[1] where she dictated letters to her brother in San Francisco to a helpful nun. At around the same time, Maria's grandfather, from Killiney, 'used to buy the newspaper and read to the men of the village, because obviously he could read and write, not an awful lot of them could'. While those with limited literacy skills could be very creative in accessing information and writing support, it was increasingly clear by the early twentieth century that formal education was ever more essential. Successive governments in independent

Ireland took various initiatives to improve the country's educational profile.

As elsewhere, in nineteenth-century Dún Laoghaire-Rathdown education was largely provided by religious bodies, and separated along denominational lines. Even before the state provided free second-level education, some religious bodies had already started doing so,[2] and many private schools of various religious adherences came and went over the years. Independent Ireland thus inherited an education system already heavily dominated by the churches. It did nothing to challenge this status quo – understandably, as the system was already working quite well, when the fledgling state was cash poor, and when all the major religious denominations and their adherents not only accepted the status quo, but insisted on it. Simultaneously, the dramatic growth in vocations in the late nineteenth century (for example, an eightfold increase in the number of nuns)[3] meant that there were plenty of suitably qualified religious to teach.

Following the 1932 General Election, when de Valera led Fianna Fáil to power, the Catholic Church became even more powerful. De Valera's government had a reverential attitude towards the Church and

Nellie Sharp (centre) and friends at the teacher training college in Carysfort, c.1935. Kind permission of Noreen Kerins.

its leaders. Church and state effectively 'closed ranks' to ensure that only two authorities influenced the provision of education (particularly of the Catholic majority) – the state, which controlled the national curriculum, and the Church, which controlled the hiring and firing of teachers and the interpretation of the curriculum.[4] Generally, parents were expected to have little to no input into their children's education.[5] Lay teachers complained bitterly about poor salaries, and lack of support and promotion opportunities. They could be summarily dismissed to make way for members of the religious qualified to teach. At this time, the Catholic Church had a great interest in, in its own words, the 'salvation of souls'.[6] Protestant and other minority schools were, of course, also required to teach the national curriculum, and in other respects they generally ceded similar levels of power to their own religious authorities, which were also in the business of saving souls. All of the churches had no doubt that their approach to education was the singularly right one. Douglas was attending a Church of Ireland school in Dalkey in 1960 or 1961, when a local Catholic child was enrolled. 'The next thing,' he remembered, '[the local parish priest] arrived…. and the child was… removed… it was a bit traumatic for the rest of us…. we didn't understand.'

In Dún Laoghaire-Rathdown, an area of notable economic and educational inequality, educational establishments were further subdivided by social class, with wealthier students attending fee-paying schools like Blackrock College or Wesley College, while students from more modest backgrounds went to schools run by organisations like the Christian Brothers, which started educating children in Kingstown in 1863,[7] with a plethora of small private schools in between, catering for girls and boys from varied socioeconomic circumstances. Despite numerous challenges, the young Free State strove to ensure that education reached a broader proportion of the population. The Education Act of 1892 had required children to attend school for just seventy-five days a year, and was haphazardly enforced, but from 1926 school was compulsory from the ages of six to fourteen, and children were expected to attend on every day of the school year, with parents potentially liable for legal action for absences. Children who were habitually absent could be sentenced to the dreaded industrial schools.[8]

St Joseph's Orphanage in Dún Laoghaire, founded in 1861 to care for orphaned or otherwise needy children, was recognised as a National School from 1929. It opened as a day school for local children, as the nuns caring for the orphans wanted them to mix with other young-sters, to minimise the impacts of growing up in care.[9] St Joseph's had an excellent reputation. People noted that the children who lived at the orphanage appeared very well cared for, particularly in comparison with those in other local institutions, and the school was noted for the high quality of its education. Eden, who started school in c.1930, remembered being known as one of the 'outdoors children' as opposed to the 'house children', cared for by the nuns. Eden's parents paid a fee of about half a crown per term for her to attend. Because her father worked at the Dún Laoghaire dispensary, providing healthcare to the poor, he could send nutritional supplements like Parrish's Food* and cod liver oil directly to the orphanage. Eden was very happy at St Joseph's. Gladys started attending St Joseph's in c.1932, when she was about eight. She had a wonderfully happy education and retained vague memories of a visit in 1934 by Madame Montessori, whose pioneering educational philosophy was being introduced by the sisters, who had adopted a child-centred approach to education and childcare. It was '[a] most wonderful place to go to school,' agreed Maria, who attended a generation or so later.

But many who attended school in the early to mid-twentieth cen-tury had a very difficult experience, one consistent with the teachings of Father Timothy Corcoran, a Jesuit priest and professor of education at University College Dublin. Corcoran was the main adviser on education to the Free State. He advocated for children to be taught in a strict atmos-phere involving corporal punishment and authoritarianism. Although

---

* Parrish's Food was a popular, widely used supplement used from the mid-nineteenth century, often together with cod liver oil. Named after Professor Edward Parrish, a Philadelphian pharmacist, it was listed in the *Extra Pharmacopoeia of Unofficial Drugs and Chemicals and Pharmaceutical Chemicals* in all editions up to 1982. Reed, 1998, 212.

The Harold School in Glasthule, an important local educational establishment that was viewed with dread by many local children in the early and mid-twentieth century. Photograph by Robert French, c.1865–1915. National Library of Ireland.

Maria Montessori's teaching methods had been adopted by some education providers, including the Ursuline and Dominican orders, and Quaker school patrons, during her visit in 1934 her approach was fiercely attacked by Corcoran, who described her methods as 'an astonishing specimen of braggart blasphemy'.[10] Corporal punishment was common in most schools for generations, backed by the societal consensus that it was an appropriate response to children misbehaving or failing to grasp academic concepts and would help them to grow up with a respect for authority and as good citizens.[11] Laws enacted in 1907 and 1931 attempted to restrict corporal punishment to certain school employees, and only in the case of serious transgressions,[12] but it remained widespread. Dalkey native Hugh Leonard's memoir, among others, records the violence he experienced in primary school.[13] In 1980, Elizabeth Rushby recalled how, in her school in the early twentieth century, children had their 'brains bet out of them' with a ruler for toasting bread on the classroom fire.[14]

While growing up in a comfortably off or affluent background was certainly not a guarantee of a happy experience of education, or of the absence of abuse or violence in the educational context, on average poor children were much more likely to experience extreme levels of violence at school and much less likely to retain happy memories of their schooldays. Deborah mostly attended private schools for her primary education, but she spent a brief period in a National School in an area with a large intake of poor children. Even as a child, she was deeply shocked by the difference in the way the children were treated, being hit, slapped and beaten. 'And I was *sickened* by it,' she remembered. 'I'd never seen anyone hit [in the private school], and I'd never come across such meanness.' Many of the interviewees who contributed to this book stated that sixty, seventy, eighty or even ninety years later, it remains deeply distressing to remember the violence they experienced as children. Some were unable to discuss their education without getting upset. Others described levels of violence that seem utterly extraordinary now. Francis's father, for example, often related how he lost the sight in one eye as a schoolboy in the early twentieth century. In response to some general classroom mischief: 'the priest drew around and gave my father a left hook to the side of the head, and burst his optic nerve and blinded him in his right eye'. The loss of his eye had a long-lasting impact on him. When his children were small, 'we didn't know that he had a false eye, and it was kept very quiet, and you couldn't talk about what was wrong with Daddy's eye'. He lived with the constant fear that he would be sacked from his van-driving job if his employers learned that he had a prosthetic eye. Gareth attended a small Church of Ireland National School in Kilternan in the 1930s and 1940s. The Church of Ireland at the time was anxious to improve students' knowledge of the Irish language, a prerequisite for many higher-level public-sector jobs, but many Protestant teachers had a poor command of Irish and Church of Ireland schools had tended to lag behind. As a result, said Gareth, in his school they attempted to 'beat it into us'. 'When you got your hands walloped, you couldn't hold the bloody pen or pencil afterwards,' he remembered. This method of teaching Irish left him with a lifelong hatred of the language. Peter's father attended Harold's Boys' School in Glasthule in the mid-1940s. Even in his later years, his memories of school were very painful: 'He wouldn't talk about it too much. He used to hate it. He used to leave... his mother's house, walk around the corner... the longest walk of his life... to school. And it was only maybe from here to the door. But they were so afraid.' Also growing up in Glasthule in the 1940s, Ingrid remembered how terrified she often was as a child, so much so that she would become ill, faint and have to be sent home. Edward still remembered his joy when the family moved away from the catchment area of a school that had the reputation locally for 'throwing children against the wall'. Stephen remembered extraordinary violence in the two-teacher school he attended in Kilmashogue in the 1950s, and a teacher with 'froth coming out of the side of his mouth' who could compose himself instantly if an adult arrived. Georgie, attending a Christian Brothers school in the 1950s, remembered the apparent pleasure with which one of the brothers beat the children: 'he'd say, "God help the last three",' he remembered. 'We all had to stand up. He'd go around and ask you a question. If you answered the question, you could sit down... When you were in the last three... they got twelve on each hand... he'd put every ounce of energy into it. You'd see the sweat pouring out of him when he'd be finished... He was enjoying it.' Kevin grew up in Cabinteely and remembered particularly severe violence meted out to children struggling academically: 'if you couldn't add one and one, or you didn't know your Latin grammar or your Irish grammar, oh Jaysus. And actually what hurt me the most... well, it hurt me that *I* was getting clattered, but me watching *you* getting clattered... fellas going home with a blue mark across the face there, because they didn't know their Latin grammar.' Provision for less academically able children was poor. Anthony attended primary school in Glasthule in the 1950s. The children were divided into an A and a B stream; those in the B stream were known as 'MD', for 'mentally deficient'. Anthony felt that most of the attention was given to the brighter children, with the result that the others learned little.

Most children's families tolerated or approved of high levels of violence in the classroom, but some reached their limits. Janet's father had
lost the sight in one eye in an accident, but it remained sensitive to light,
so at school in the 1920s he needed to keep his head away from light
coming from the window. His teacher took exception to his lowered
head, so he 'threw a slate at him and gave him nine stitches over his good
eye'. After his treatment at St Michael's Hospital in Dún Laoghaire, his
aunt ('four foot tall and four foot wide') went to the school and 'she
got [the master] and she hit him with the blackboard' and he 'never
rose his hand to another man or woman after'. This remarkable woman
knocked on every door of the school and warned each of the masters
never again to lay a hand on a member of her family. Graham recalled
being taught that 'God made the stars so that Peter and the Apostles,
fishermen, would be out on the Sea of Galilee and it would take some
time to fill their nets, and the stars are there at night to show them the
way home.' When he asked what they would have done on a cloudy
night, the teacher knocked him unconscious. Many parents would have
done nothing in this situation, but Graham's father was tough. He went
to the school and punched the Christian Brother in question so hard that
he passed out. Then he went to the school principal and, Graham said,
told him that he could call the police or the ambulance: 'But if you call
the police I'm having them charge him with assaulting a junior.'

Children in private schools catering to middle-class and affluent families could also be hit or beaten by teachers, but beatings tended to be
less frequent and less severe, and their parents were more likely to object
– and to be listened to – in the case of serious violence. Liam's father
was determined not to send his sons to a Christian Brothers school: 'he
said that even as an adult, when he saw a Christian Brother, fear ran
through him'. Instead, in the 1940s and 1950s, they attended Willow
Park, where corporal punishment was 'not meted out randomly'. When a
teacher wanted a child to be beaten, a note was written and the child and
the note both dispatched to the school dean, the only person allowed to
administer corporal punishment, which he often chose not to. One day,

a misbehaving Liam was sent to the dean. 'And he said, "Hold your hand out,"' Liam recalled. He did what he was told and closed his eyes. When he heard a 'a loud *thwack*' he realised that he had felt nothing. The dean was hitting the banisters instead of him. 'And then he said, "Right, there's your punishment"... "if you speak a word of this to anybody, especially your teacher, I will *really* thwack you the next time."' George grew up in an extremely well-to-do family in Dalkey, and remembered attending in Carraig na Gréine, the junior school for Loreto Abbey in Dalkey from 1948 to 1952. 'You had very nice nuns,' he recalled. 'Mother Cyril was a nice little nun, because she very often kept a sweet apple in her pocket and she'd say, "Would you like a sweet apple?"... You changed your shoes from your leather shoes into little canvas shoes for going around the class.'

There were also other marked differences between the educational experiences of poor and better-off children. Brian, who attended National School in Glencullen in the 1940s, recalled the quite primitive conditions typical of rural schools then, as well as the poverty of some local schoolchildren, expected to scour the hillside for fuel in the form of furze sticks, for the smoky fireplace heating the classroom. It was difficult, he remembered, to persuade teachers to stay in a rural area like Glencullen, so they came and went quite often, and the learning environment was far from ideal. In this context, the child-centred education offered by the Daughters of Mary at St Joseph's Orphanage, and the other schools educating the children of ordinary families that eschewed high levels of corporal punishment, seems remarkable. Although the level of violence in schools tended to decline from the 1950s, with childhood memories of primary education gradually becoming less harrowing, it remained legal for Irish teachers to chastise children physically until 1982, while the act of a teacher beating a student was not formally criminalised until 1997.[15]

* * *

In 1930, the Vocational Education Act established vocational schools around the country. They charged modest fees for a secondary education and provided a curriculum largely predicated around practical skills, often divided into 'boys'' and 'girls'' materials.[16] Ireland lagged behind most European countries educationally, particularly in progression from primary to secondary, and from there to higher education. The social class into which children were born often determined whether they would progress to secondary school, while factors like the availability of public transport had a huge impact on access. The Glencullen bus, for example, which provided public transport in the 1940s, enabled those who wished to to continue to secondary or technical schools nearer Dublin.

Until the 1960s, many young people did not progress to secondary school, with most leaving education at thirteen or fourteen, and then either starting work or an apprenticeship or performing duties in the home or in a family business, such as a shop or a farm. Among those who progressed to secondary school, many attended a vocational school that taught them practical skills and did not equip them for university or the professions.[17] One pupil at the 'Tech' in Dún Laoghaire in the 1950s, Barbara, remembered that, 'My ambition was to be a dancer on a ship, but… we were being prepared for good, pensionable jobs in the county council, ESB, civil service and Aer Lingus.' Technical schools also offered night classes and educational opportunities to for those who had started work young. Fintan worked from thirteen and a half following his father's early death, but as he progressed through a career in retail, he attended night school at Dún Laoghaire Tech and a school of retail distribution in Parnell Square in the city centre. 'The learning,' he said, 'was fantastic.' Academically bright young people whose parents could not afford to pay secondary school fees could attend a 'secondary top', where they could stay on for their Intermediate Certificate, with which they could get a better job or do further training at, for example, a secretarial or bookkeeping college.

Secondary schools other than technical schools, particularly those preparing young people for university or a career in the professions, were usually single-sex. Many saw these as offering social and educational benefits. For girls, opportunities to achieve academically in an all-female environment were often prized. Schools that catered primarily to wealthier girls often offered rigorous academic standards and opportunities to excel in an all-female environment before entering a world where they would not be competing with men on an equal footing. Boys from wealthy backgrounds often attended schools that offered networking opportunities that would help them win in the future. However, for both girls and boys whose interests were not those typically associated with their sex, single-sex education also had drawbacks. Emer, for example, 'would have preferred to have done science-type subjects'. Emer was talented at maths, but the girls' school she attended in the early 1960s did not offer higher-level maths or the hard sciences. She would have a career in information technology, but has always regretted not having had the opportunity to study advanced maths.

As the decades advanced, parents were increasingly ambitious for their children, second-level education was increasingly important for those aspiring to the middle classes, and educational standards rose steadily throughout the mid-twentieth century, and dramatically from the 1960s. Larry, who had a successful career in banking and settled in the Cabinteely area, commented on the vast difference that a good second-level education made to so many of his generation, attending secondary school in the late 1950s and early 1960s. The huge surge in education then was, he said, 'the best thing that ever happened'. For many young people of Larry's generation, a vast educational and cultural gulf opened between them and their parents, as more and more young people reached levels of education that their parents had never even dreamed of.

Until 1967, fees were payable for any young person wishing to progress to secondary school. While fees were often quite modest, they were a significant barrier to educational progression. Bright children from poorer backgrounds could, if they were encouraged, apply for County Council Scholarships, but the very existence of fees indicated to many families on modest incomes that further education was not for them. In some predominately working-class areas there was sometimes social pressure on young people not to pursue academic education at all, and not to pursue the sort of work that might follow a higher level of formal education. Rob remembered a Christian Brother who taught him and encouraged him to apply for 'the scholarship', which he won: 'It was a wonderful sum of 30 pounds, but it was an important 30 pounds.' Despite scholarships for high achievers, there could be social barriers between students with scholarships and students from wealthier backgrounds. Roberta remembered: 'Mother Enda took our class... she said, "Now girls, tomorrow, there are going to be three new girls"... she explained that they were the ones that got the grant... she made it *absolutely clear* that we didn't need to associate with them outside school!'

In 1967, Fianna Fáil Minister for Education Donagh O'Malley introduced free second-level education. The numbers progressing to secondary school soared. From 1972, the school-leaving age was raised to fifteen. The number remaining in education after the age of fifteen continued to rise,[18] until it was difficult to find sufficient qualified teachers. Yet even after abolishing fees for secondary school, the cost of educating young people was difficult for many working-class families: 'Like, it was supposed to be free,' said Caroline, 'but by the time you'd buy a uniform and books and all the rest, for working-class people it might as well not have existed.' Nonetheless, most parents could now see how important education was in an increasingly industrial economy, and educational levels continued to rise.

While most education continued to be provided by religious organisations, through the 1950s and 1960s the state also supported the development of comprehensive and technical schools for both girls and boys. These remained under a degree of supervision by religious authorities. In 1972, Newpark Comprehensive opened in Blackrock, with a Church of Ireland ethos, but for girls and boys from all denominational backgrounds. The Catholic Church expressed concern about the state-sponsored comprehensives, and was reassured that the boards of management would feature bishops' nominees, who could exercise vetoes on religious or moral grounds.[19]

Various attempts to open multidenominational schools occurred as Ireland became increasingly liberal, but even in the 1970s, multi-denominational education was considered controversial. Efforts to establish a school for all in Ballinteer, for example, foundered in the mid-1970s, largely because of fierce opposition from Catholic authorities.[20] In 1978, the Dalkey School Project opened, following considerable activism on the part of a group of local parents, making it the first multidenominational school recognised since the foundation of the state in 1922.[21]

Young people from working-class backgrounds sometimes felt social pressure not to push themselves too far academically, which could be a barrier to completing secondary education. Rob remembered a man from his area of Ballybrack who had a white-collar job in the 1950s and was known, disparagingly, as 'the lady' because – unlike other local men – his job did not involve getting his hands dirty. Audrey completed secondary school in the 1960s, a time when many in her native Shankill did not. Some locals, she remembered, 'were saying, "That one's more than her status"'. Even as late as the 1970s and 1980s, after two decades of free secondary education, amid a steadily improving educational environment, some working-class parents still counselled their children to do something practical and not to aim too high academically, for fear of disappointment. Remembered Kimberly: 'you felt none of that was possible for you... The disappointment would've been overwhelming. So it was better not to... look for anything because then you can't be disappointed.' Yet when Kimberly was accepted into third-level education, her mother was 'over the moon'.

* * *

In early independence, the Free State enacted and enforced legislation intended to preserve the use of Irish in Gaeltacht areas, and to promote its use among the general population. Irish became a prerequisite for senior public-sector jobs, making a good knowledge of Irish a significant form of social capital. The first Irish-language school in Dún Laoghaire-Rathdown was Coláiste Moibhí. The school was founded in 1926, and moved to Rathmichael in 1948. The boarding school was established to educate future Church of Ireland teachers through Irish. In the first decades of its existence, many young Protestants who were academically gifted, and often from modest backgrounds, received a good education there, and they would go on to improve the quality of Irish taught in Protestant schools, and thereby facilitate Protestant integration into the new state and into the civil service, where a good standard of Irish was considered essential.[22]

Arthur's grandfather, a Department of Education employee, and a fluent Irish speaker, was one of several people forming a committee to establish an all-Irish-speaking preparatory school. Scoil Lorcáin, the area's first primary-level Gaelscoil, opened in Blackrock in 1952 with just thirty-nine pupils. It quickly became an important element of the local educational sector, with 441 students by the academic year 1968–9. Liam's father, a senior civil servant, was a fluent Irish speaker, and was pleased to be able to send his youngest children to a Gaelscoil in the 1950s. Odhrán's parents had both migrated to Dún Laoghaire from rural areas. Although they were not themselves fluent Irish-speakers, they felt strongly about an Irish-language education for their children, sending them to Scoil Lorcáin in the 1970s and encouraging them to speak Irish at home: 'Dad didn't want us speaking any other language.' For Odhrán's father, his love of Irish sprang from his strong nationalism, at a time of the Troubles in Northern Ireland and considerable local interest in the IRA and the armed struggle. The family also attended parades and events in Deansgrange Cemetery in honour of the fallen insurgents interred there. Mairéad attended Scoil Lorcáin too, and she commented, '*Bhí an-spéis ag Daid go háirithe i gcúrsaí stair na hÉireann agus is dócha ó san, spreag sé an teanga agus an cultúr ionainne agus sin an fáth go ndeachaigh muid chuig Scoil Lorcáin, is dócha.'* [Dad was particularly interested in Irish history and probably from that, he encouraged the language and culture in us and that's probably why we went to Scoil Lorcáin.] Coláiste Eoin, an Irish-language secondary school for boys, opened in 1969, and Scoil Íosagáin for girls opened in 1971. The Irish language sector was an increasingly important element of local education in the decades that followed, also catering to the children of people originally from Gaeltacht areas and to families eager for their children to have access to good jobs in the civil service. As time passed, Gaelscoils tended to decouple from overt political and cultural nationalism, and parents who were interested in the Irish language and in linguistic diversity, as well as the benefits of bilingualism, but who were not necessarily particularly political, were increasingly likely to seek a good education through Irish for their children. In general, the Gaelscoils have played an extremely important role not just in preserving the use of Irish among those families who already spoke it well, but in promulgating the use of Irish as a second language among the broader population. *'Agus sílim go n-imríonn siad siúd tionchar ar líon na ndaoine atá líofa sa Ghaeilge agus a theastaíonn uathu an Ghaeilge a labhairt ar bhonn laethúil'* [And I think that they influence the number of people who are fluent in Irish and who want to speak Irish on a daily basis], commented Tadhg.

* * *

While young people typically left school aged fourteen for much of the twentieth century, many exited into apprenticeships and other forms of training designed to prepare them for adult life. They could work in retail and learn, in the process, how to run a business of their own, or serve an apprenticeship for a trade. Kieran's father died when Kieran was thirteen and a half. Staying on in school was no longer an option. One Friday, he said, he left school in 'a pair of shorts, because that's what you wore at that time'. On Monday, 'I was in my first pair of long trousers in a job in a hardware shop in Glasthule.' He quite enjoyed the work, and his employers treated him kindly, but he missed school and his friends. The first thing he had to do every morning was clean the front of the shop. He didn't want his friends to see him from the bus they took to school, so he hid until it had passed.

Very few attended university in the early twentieth century and in early independence, while the new state struggled to adequately fund higher education, which therefore remained largely attainable only to the wealthier or the few with scholarships.[23] University College Dublin (UCD) was the obvious choice for Catholic young people from the growing middle and elite classes of the twentieth century, as well-educated ambitious families, featuring fathers with good jobs in the civil service or in the professions, sought higher education. Trinity College was banned for Catholics ('under pain of mortal sin'), unless they could obtain an exemption;[24] it had long been educating the sons and, since 1904, the daughters of middle-class and elite Protestant families, of whom there were many in Dún Laoghaire-Rathdown. In practice, students from elite Catholic families from Britain, and from affluent Dublin suburbs who had attended fee-paying schools in Britain, often attended Trinity too. As they had never studied Irish, which was necessary to attend the National University (UCD being the Dublin branch), they found themselves in a loophole that apparently satisfied the religious authorities. Vera, a Catholic from Northern Ireland who settled in Booterstown near her husband's home of origin, could attend Trinity because she did not know Irish; her husband, whom she met there, was also exempt from the ban, having attended boarding school in England.

The National University of Ireland was greatly influenced by Church authorities. UCD, particularly, was in the sights of Archbishop John Charles McQuaid, maintaining influence there through his own authority, and through the large number of Catholic priests and lay allies who worked at UCD and ensured that subjects like philosophy and the social sciences maintained a Catholic ethos.[25] From the 1950s, there was a gradual decline in Church influence and growing numbers of students from somewhat more diversified social and economic backgrounds, although young people from better-off backgrounds continued to be represented at university in much higher numbers than their poorer peers. The number of full-time university students increased by more than 55 per cent between 1951 and 1961.[26] Terribly overcrowded in its premises in the city centre, UCD was moved to Belfield, becoming Dún Laoghaire-Rathdown's first university. The first buildings were completed in 1964, and the various faculties moved to Belfield on a phased basis from 1972. This contributed to the ongoing dramatic transformation of the south Dublin suburbs, then already in a period of rapid expansion into what had been agricultural or estate land.

By the 1970s and 1980s, university attendance had become the norm for young people from middle-class and wealthy families, and increasingly also for upwardly mobile families from working-class or rural backgrounds that aspired for their children to acquire university and professional qualifications to give them the skills they needed in Ireland's increasingly industrial economy. 'My mother,' remembered Darragh, who graduated from secondary school in the 1980s, 'was absolutely firmly of the view that we were all going to get a third-level education because it was the step up that she intended we all would have.' Numbers attending university full-time had grown dramatically in the two decades before Darragh's college days, expanding from about 9,000 in 1960 to 51,000 in 1984.[27] Many of the young people studying at university then were the first in their families to do so. Universities were also no longer primarily male, at least in terms of student enrolment. In the first half of the twentieth century, female university students had been generally a small minority, subject to stricter regulations regarding personal conduct.[28] This too would start to change from the mid-century, with the number of female students steadily rising throughout the second part of the twentieth century, boosted yet further in the 1990s when nursing – traditionally an overwhelmingly female profession – was increasingly taught in universities. Sometimes the experience of seeing their children graduate and move into a very different cultural and social milieu could be bittersweet, as parents felt both proud of their achievements and estranged from the very different worldview that sometimes accompanied them.

* * *

In the 1960s, for the first time, the state began to pay serious attention to the issue of formal education for Traveller children who hithertofore had acquired traditional skills through observation and practice, but were generally illiterate. Until the early twentieth century, the educational difference between Travellers and the poorest settled working-class people was much less marked, with high levels of illiteracy or sub-literacy among both groups. But by the mid-twentieth century, being illiterate had become a serious disadvantage in practically every area of life and illiteracy was rare among settled people. By contrast, in 1963, the Report of the Government Commission on Itinerancy reported that 'almost all itinerants are completely illiterate', and that only 160 'itinerant' children were on school rolls, while only 114 were attending school regularly.[29] Previously, while parents from settled backgrounds could be prosecuted if they failed to ensure their children attended school, the authorities did not enforce school attendance laws for Travellers, while Travellers' nomadism also made regular school attendance difficult.

Growing numbers of Traveller children started to attend school from the 1960s onwards. Experiences varied, but for many, attending school was not a happy time, and many did not attend for very long. In 1975, of about 6,500 Traveller children of school-going age, only 2,719 were in school, most did not start until they were eight or nine and few remained after the age of twelve (Confirmation was considered a rite of passage, after which children generally left). Illiteracy among Traveller teenagers and adults remained extraordinarily high, at 95 per cent.[30] Lawrence remembered attending school in a prefab set aside for Traveller children in the early 1970s and that the general attitude towards Travellers in school was 'seen more as containment… rather than education. I don't think there was any expectation. That's why a lot of Travellers left school not being able to read and write.' Subsequently,

Lawrence attended a mainstream school, where Traveller children sat at the back of the class and were exempt from homework. 'I remember sitting at the back of the class,' Lawrence remembered. 'I'd a pencil and a piece of paper and that was it… people would be getting on with their lessons. I wouldn't be part of that at all. I wouldn't be part of the discussion.'

Mick's parents moved into a permanent home in Dalkey in the 1970s largely because they wanted their children to have the opportunity to get a decent education. Previously, Mick had attended an all-Traveller school, but now that his family lived in a house, he and his siblings went to a local National School. From an early age, he knew that many of the other children disliked him ('knacker', they called him) because of who he was. 'We were easily targeted,' Mick remembered, 'even in high infants.' Traveller children were kept physically apart, at a special desk behind the teacher rather than among the other children, singling them out even further. There was much aggression towards the Traveller children and, as Mick remembered, teachers rarely intervened. As Mick got older, the aggression he faced worsened: 'I wasn't fighting one. I was fighting armies.' A rare black student, a year or two older, seemed to have to deal with similar treatment.

As late as 1985, only 50 per cent of Traveller children were regularly attending school, of whom only 10 per cent progressed to secondary school.[31] Government policy was still to maintain separation between Traveller and other children. For example, if more than twelve Traveller children attended a mainstream school, a special class was established for them, and they were also taught a different, less academically rigorous curriculum, with an emphasis on subjects like woodwork and metalwork for boys, and knitting, cooking, sewing and domestic work for girls.[32] The 'special classes' were founded with good intentions, but seem often to have served to marginalise Traveller children yet further within the school population, while failing to challenge Traveller students who were not struggling academically, or who were academically gifted and needed much more support to develop their talents.

Sometimes settled people were opposed to offering Travellers education locally, fearing this would encourage them to stay where they were unwelcome. Caroline remembered Sister Colette Dwyer, who worked with Travellers in the Sallynoggin area. Writing in 1988, Dwyer recalled how she had 'become involved with the education needs of travellers in a fortuitous way, when a group of adult travellers... asked me to teach them how to read'.[33] As Caroline recalled, there was local opposition to the establishment of classes for the Traveller women. 'Nobody would have really wanted [them] staying around,' she said. 'They didn't mind them moving on from place to place.' Nonetheless, Sister Colette prevailed and a class was established.

By the late 1980s and '90s, young Travellers were increasingly remaining in school for longer. While their experiences of education and of being accepted were extremely variable, with many children dealing with bullying and other issues, at least some had a more positive experience of school than the older generation. In the mid-1980s, the authorities wanted Sheelagh's children to attend a special school for Travellers, but she felt they would learn more at her local National School, and wanted them to be part of the local community. After Mary Robinson, then a member of the Seanad and a well-known legal expert with an interest in progressive causes, wrote a letter on Sheelagh's behalf, her children were enrolled. The headmaster was a supportive, friendly man. Nellie was an academically gifted child who, in the 1980s and '90s, attended a school where her talents were nurtured and the challenges she faced in getting ready for school and doing her homework in a cold tent or caravan were recognised: 'there was never a problem with me turning up at school with no uniform or no bag... They were just glad to have me actually attend... [the teachers] all instilled a kind of confidence in me that was never lost... to want something better, and always try for something different.'

* * *

Schools offered one arena where girls were prepared for the future work in the home. Home economics was studied by most girls, and almost never by boys. But many girls, of all social classes, learned most of the skills they would use in their working lives at home by observing and helping their own mothers, grandmothers, aunts and sisters. In the nineteenth and throughout at least the first six decades of the twentieth century, many – if not most – families from all social classes prioritised boys' education, with the view that, as girls were largely destined to be wives and mothers, it was less important for them to receive formal instruction. Girls were also more likely to be responsible for one or more younger siblings or cousins, particularly in large working-class families. While some resented this, others loved having a younger child to treat like a doll. Sandra remembered she and her friends knocking on the doors of neighbours who had small babies, and asking for 'a loan of the baby' to take for a walk.

Whereas working-class women almost invariably worked for pay before they got married, and more often than not returned to the workforce – albeit often as casual, temporary workers – at various stages during their lives as mothers, until at least the end of the first half of the twentieth century, wealthy women were often prepared primarily for marriage too, albeit into a particular cultural milieu. George's mother, for example, from a very wealthy family, was sent to a 'domestic science college' to learn 'the duties of a home'. She was well-trained for her life as a mother of seven children, with a substantial staff of both live-in and casual servants to direct.

* * *

There have been lending libraries in Dún Laoghaire since the 1830s, but these early libraries were privately run. Ireland as a whole had only eight public libraries in 1900, so for people on lower incomes, access to reading material, for entertainment and self-education, was often quite limited.[34] From 1902, the Public Libraries (Ireland) Act ensured that the state paid more attention to the provision of public libraries. Because of Ireland's denominational school system, it was decided that libraries should be housed in buildings entirely separate to schools so that they would be available to people from diverse backgrounds.

Compared to other areas, Dún Laoghaire-Rathdown fared quite well regarding library provision. A large public library was founded in 1890, and was subsequently replaced by the Carnegie Library, following a donation from Andrew Carnegie,* a wealthy American philanthropist who gave away most of his vast fortune and who, in 1913, created the Britain Trust to administer grants throughout Britain and Ireland.[35] Eighty libraries were originally planned for Ireland (most, but not all were built) using funds from Carnegie,[36] of which sixty-two survive.[37] The charity funded the construction of several libraries in Dún Laoghaire-Rathdown: in Dalkey (where he paid for the purchase of a site after the community had raised money for building), Blackrock, Cabinteely, Dundrum, Glencullen, Kingstown, Sandyford and Shankill.[38] The Glencullen Library was constructed on land donated by a local landlord family, the Fitz-Simons.[39]

Particularly in poorer areas, where there were few other resources, these libraries were important venues for entertainment, community building and self-education. Charlie's uplands family was deeply involved with the Glencullen Carnegie Library, which depended heavily on community involvement, and was an invaluable local resource. From his childhood in the 1950s, he remembered gathering fuel – furze sticks from the hillside – to keep the library fire going. In some areas, the libraries also added significantly to the local architectural stock, especially in Dundrum, Cabinteely and Shankill, where they were designed by the noted architect Rudolph Butler, while the Glencullen Library – which also served as an important community hub for a rather scattered, predominantly low-income rural community – featured innovative washbasins where users could wash their hands before handling books

---

* Pearson, 1981, 115. Carnegie, Scottish by birth, emigrated to the United States at twelve, and would become the richest industrialist in the county, devoting his later years to philanthropy.

in sinks that used rainwater collected in a tank on the roof.[40] Eden's mother ran the Carnegie Library in Shankill before her marriage, and before Eden's birth in 1924. She loved the work and would remember later on how much people appreciated it, and how easy they were to please, despite a fairly limited selection of books.

In 1928, the Cumann Leabharlann na hÉireann was founded to administer and promote the use of libraries. While Church and some state authorities often regarded libraries with suspicion, fearing that they might disseminate 'immoral ideas' in the form of non-Irish literature,[41] they were quickly embedded in their communities as important sources of ideas and opportunities to learn, notwithstanding the efforts of the government censor, and of elements concerned that the libraries would contribute to the 'anglicisation' of the population, which might be able to access information about topics like birth control in them.[42] Still, state censorship of libraries, heavily influenced by the Church, thrived during the first decades of independence, and the communities that used them could engage in informal censorship too, telling the librarian if they considered a particular book unsuitable. Charlie, whose father was a community librarian in Glencullen, recalled that 'if the reader disliked some earthy bit that was in a book, it returned to the father marked, "This is a dirty book". And Dad put it into a special shelf, and the county librarian took it back.' Clara remembered of the Carnegie Library in Dún Laoghaire in the 1950s and early 1960s that she was only allowed to borrow 'suitable books', excluding 'art books in glass cases that contained far too many pictures of nudes'. But the contribution of the Carnegie libraries to the people of Dún Laoghaire-Rathdown is incalculable. Francis's family was far from wealthy at a time when working families rarely had more than a basic primary education. They deeply valued the Carnegie Library in Dún Laoghaire – their local – as a means of self-education and personal improvement: '[We made] frequent visits… we had lots of books… they were all well-read… even though they finished school at kind of seventh class… and they educated themselves from then on through the library service.'

Some libraries, including those in Blackrock and Kingstown, had separate reading rooms for ladies, who apparently could feel 'out of place' in the special newspaper rooms, where men often gathered to discuss horse racing and such matters. Many libraries were also used as *de facto* community halls. For example, the upper room in Dundrum Library had a stage, and was used for 'concerts, dances, plays, and even jumble sales',[43] while the libraries in Glencullen, Shankill and Cabinteely often hosted card games, dances and other recreational pursuits.

* * *

Various social, professional and sporting clubs and organisations offered adults opportunities to socialise, learn from one another and forge relationships that could be professionally helpful. Macra na Feirme ('Stalwarts of the Land'), for example, was founded in 1944 by a rural science teacher, Stephen Cullinan, to provide educational and social opportunities to young people working in agriculture. For Brian, who had hated National School, the opportunity to learn was much appreciated. All talk of politics and religion was banned in his local chapter – a good idea, less than a generation after the War of Independence.

Austin remembered the Rotary Club as an important networking opportunity for people working in transportation and tourism in the 1960s. Often, organisations like the Rotary Club were men-only, reflecting the fact that most middle- and upper-class women at that time were not engaged in paid work outside the home. It was considered that the presence of women might be a distraction from conversations about business. As more women entered the paid workforce in the 1970s and 1980s, that started to change: 'I remember the first women being brought in,' Austin mused. Other clubs and social organisations, including yacht and golf clubs, rugby clubs and GAA clubs, the Irish Countrywomen's Association and many more all offered valuable networking opportunities as well as opportunities to socialise.

* * *

The educational landscape of Ireland generally, and Dún Laoghaire-Rathdown no less, changed dramatically during the twentieth century. With a higher-than-average population of middle- and upper-class families, the area had long also had a higher-than-average population of well-educated professionals. While social and educational gulfs were not erased over this period, educational differences eroded significantly, with seismic changes in many families during just one or two generations.

FUN AND GAMES

The endless possibilities for fun in Dún Laoghaire-Rathdown have been an important contributing factor to its development. Especially in the longer-established urban and suburban areas, there was a wide variety of modes of entertainment and art forms, including sports, performance and the literary and visual arts, with a rich history reflecting changing tastes and fashions, political and cultural allegiances, and social and

Cycling, which became much more affordable in the late nineteenth century, was a popular pastime as well as an essential mode of transport. Kind permission of Mary White.

Two women with bicycles in Kingstown at a time when bicycles were growing rapidly in popularity for both leisure and general transport, c.1897–1904. Clarke Photographic Collection, National Library of Ireland.

Michael Mason and Joan Presch enjoying the snow at Stepaside, 1962. Independent Newspapers, National Library of Ireland.

economic shifts. Moreover, as we have seen, the leisure and tourism sectors have historically been important local employers, while property developers and estate agents have also focused on the area's potential for entertainment. An 1889 guide to Kingstown, for example, stressed the abundance of leisure opportunities, including lawn tennis, chess and yachting, and promoted the efforts of the Kingstown Permanent Amusements Committee, consisting of '21 local gentlemen',[1] while parts of Dún Laoghaire-Rathdown were promoted variously as a tourist destination and a playground for Dublin city throughout the twentieth century.

* * *

Throughout much of the Western world, city councils and other authorities became increasingly concerned in the mid-to-late nineteenth century with the issue of providing public green spaces to give ordinary people room to play, enjoy fresh air, and engage in sports and other healthy activities. By the late nineteenth century, Dún Laoghaire-Rathdown was well equipped with such parks, which were of benefit above all to large families living in cramped conditions, but which also created an environment where people of all social classes could mingle, representing the antithesis of the squalor in the inner city while growing numbers of middle-class people were leaving the city for the suburbs.[2] The People's Park officially opened in Kingstown in 1890,[3] the Pavilion – a beautiful timber-and-glass construction – and its elegant gardens in 1903,[4] and by 1936, there were sixty-eight acres of public space in the Borough of Dún Laoghaire, including Blackrock Park, Sandycove Gardens and Killiney Hill.[5]

Blackrock Park. Photo by Robert French, Lawrence Photograph Collection, National Library of Ireland.

Lawn, with Dún Laoghaire harbour in the background, c.1860–1883. The clothing of the man and woman on the left suggest that they may be employed as domestic and/or ground staff. The Stereo Pairs Photograph Collection, National Library of Ireland.

Parks were not just pleasant green spaces in which to have a good time, but also spaces where diverse interests competed for dominance. They were laden with symbolic meaning, as they were considered important for the physical and moral health of the people, when social issues like physical illness, overcrowding and immoral behaviour were seen as intrinsically interlinked. In many areas, they also had an important symbolic function in the clash between ethno-religious mores. By the 1880s, Dublin Corporation was increasingly dominated by nationalist Catholics, whereas the suburbs to the south of the city, albeit diverse in population, were still predominately controlled by Protestant, typically unionist, members of the wealthier classes.[6] Pre-independence, one of the various functions of parks was the assertion of Protestant cultural norms: Protestants typically did not engage in sports on Sundays, whereas Catholics did, and consequently sports were often banned from parks on Sundays. Public monuments and statuary frequently reflected the concerns of the ruling classes,[7] and asserted their supremacy; Victoria Hill in Killiney, for example, was opened to the public in 1887 to mark the Queen's golden jubilee.[8] The People's Park in Kingstown, asserts

Joanna Brück, with its roughly symmetrical layout and large, impressive architectural elements, 'demonstrated the wealth, accomplishments and cultural capital of the civic body… ostentatious forms of cultural display [were used] as a means of legitimating the newly acquired wealth and power of the middle classes', while Blackrock Park and the railway line, in their juxtaposition, represented values central to the ideals of the British imperial goals: urbanisation, the extension of capitalism and the conquest of nature.[9]

Post-independence, parks and other public spaces were quickly claimed by the new ruling classes, which renamed them, erected new monuments and statuary in honour of fallen patriots, and strove, with varying degrees of success, to erase physical traces of the previous reality of British rule. As many Big Houses were acquired by the state, their grounds were opened to the public as parks – among them Marlay, Cabinteely and Fernhill.[10] Marlay Park, for example, originally the seat of the Harold family, was purchased by David La Touche in 1764, who named it after his wife's family. The property passed through various hands and the land and house, then in very poor condition, were purchased by the state in 1972 and opened as a public leisure amenity in 1975.[11] Other parks created from the lands of former stately homes include Deerpark in Mount Merrion,[12] part of the Merrion demesne, which was opened to the public in 1971.[13]

* * *

Here as elsewhere, card playing and gambling were ever-popular activities, despite disapproval from Church and other authorities. Most locals are familiar with the most infamous account of card playing going terribly wrong, a story associated with the Hellfire Club in the Dublin/Wicklow Mountains, about which it is recounted that a card game being played by a particular dissolute group of young men was visited by the devil himself (a 'well set-up man' in a long black cloak, whose identity was revealed when a card player bent down and saw the stranger's cloven hooves).[14] Cock fighting, and the associated gambling, was a popular pastime in parts of the area until at least the mid-twentieth century, taking place in a cemetery in Dundrum, among other locations. Recorded in 1980, James Nolan recalled that participants would 'put two cocks together and they put spurs on their legs, steel spurs, the cocks would fight... until one killed the other'.[15] In other areas, often but not always those associated with stonecutting, tugs of war between rival groups of men took place – locals or men employed locally: the Windy Arbour team was composed of local 'keepers' from the Central Asylum and, occasionally, one or two inmates.

* * *

Music of various sorts was important to countless families, with recitals and dances in private homes widespread across the spectrum of the social classes in the nineteenth and early twentieth centuries. Remembering her childhood in the 1920s and 1930s, Regina said: '[Mam] played that gramophone and all the records', and that the family was raised with music and dancing: 'she had a favourite tenor, Peter Dawson*... he sang beautiful ballads... then she would put on Irish céilí music and she would make us all get up and dance to the "Walls of Limerick" and all in the kitchen'.

Formal training in music and dance, including Irish dancing, ballet, piano lessons and so forth, along with contests like the Father Mathew *Feis* [Festival],[†] when young people performed and won prizes, contributed to a lively cultural scene. Irish dancing was popular throughout the twentieth century, particularly with girls, many of whom competed for prizes and performed in venues like the Town Hall in Dún Laoghaire and assorted libraries and parish centres. Regina, among many others,

---

* Peter Dawson was a famous Australian tenor who specialised in light, popular ballads and songs from operettas.

† Named after Father Theobald Mathew, an Irish Catholic priest and teetotalist reformer, founder of the temperance movement in Ireland.

started her musical life performing in *feiseanna* [festivals]; Regina, with her beautiful voice and striking good looks, would become a well-known local performer in pantomime and musical theatre from the 1930s onwards.

Before and after independence, musical tastes could intersect with political views, to varying degrees. Throughout much of the twentieth century, interest in traditional music and/or patriotic ballads and nationalism often intersected, with a love of traditional Irish music and rousing Irish ballads often, but not always, indicative of nationalist political views. Beth's grandfather, a market gardener, loved ballads and taught her to sing lots of them, including many well-known nationalist songs like 'Boolavogue' and 'The Croppy Boy' (both relating stories from the Rebellion of 1798). 'Now, please remember,' he told Beth when she was little. 'These ballads are the history. And they were sung to keep the history alive in people's memories.' Many of the more urban parks in Dún Laoghaire-Rathdown still feature bandstands, and throughout the nineteenth and much of the twentieth centuries it was common for bands like the Blackrock Mooney Band, featuring Beth's grandfather, among many others, to be employed to play in venues like the bandstands on Dún Laoghaire pier, Sorrento Park and Killiney Hill: jaunty brass band music and céilí dance music both featured.

The rapidly growing suburbs of the region that had sprung up around the Harcourt Line and the major roads from Dublin and continued to grow throughout the first half of the twentieth century and beyond provided opportunities for entertainment as young populations looked for fun. A lively popular music and entertainment scene flourished, often despite the disapproval of authorities, which could link music and dance to 'immoral' behaviour, and claimed that 'certain forms of entertainment' led to the 'demoralisation' of young people.[16] Dancing was perennially popular before and after independence, despite the efforts of Church authorities to restrict or control it; in 1927, the Catholic authorities published their pastoral *The Evils of Modern Dancing*, railing against dance halls, women's immodest clothing and jazz as a threat to public morality, while dancing could be implicated by the media in crimes like rape and infanticide.[17] In 1935, the government passed the Public Dance Halls Act, effectively banning 'house dances', informal dances held in private homes; the Church suggested that such dances could not be effectively supervised, and that they risked introducing new, foreign dance styles that might encourage lewdness. Loss of income from the renting of parish halls may also have been a cause of concern.[18] From the mid-1950s, popular music for dancing was performed at Roebuck Hall; as the events became more popular, the local Monsignor stepped in and arranged for dances to be moved to the Parish Hall of Mount Merrion, with the exception of Lent, when dancing was not permitted.[19]

Certain types of dancing were viewed with greater favour than others. Parochial dances in the early 1950s frequently banned jiving (too sensual and 'annoying' for other dancers on the floor) and appointed committees to observe the dancers and make sure they were behaving 'respectably'. Jacinta, an enthusiastic jiver, was thrown out of one such dance. 'I was terrified,' she said, 'my mother would find out.' Boys and young men could also fall foul of strict social mores. Lenny remembered fashionable young men having their trousers measured outside dance venues, and being turned away if their trouser legs were too narrow. The young people of the area danced on in halls, parish centres and at tennis club hops. The latter tended to exclude young people from council estates, but there was usually a way to get around the rules and get in. Very good dancers might go far, figuratively and literally: James, a boat builder from Dún Laoghaire, did ballroom dancing in spectacles and competitions, often in the Olympic Ballroom in Dublin, but on occasion as far afield as Blackpool and London.

Some families, like the Blackmore and Brady families in Dún Laoghaire, were particularly well-known locally, running and per-forming in pantomimes and other forms of musical theatre, including 'Black and White' minstrel shows. Minstrels, which originated in the United States, had a long association with Irish America and were popular throughout the English-speaking world from the early nineteenth century until the 1970s, lingering in advertising until the 1980s and 1990s. American minstrel shows had visited Ireland from the early nineteenth century, while the abolitionist movement – in Ireland deeply linked with the Quaker community – was very active; they were not then seen as discriminatory. Irish minstrel performers, wearing blackface, started offering homegrown entertainments from the 1860s.[20] In the first half of the twentieth century, Dún Laoghaire was home to a popular troupe, the Borough Minstrels, led by Gillie Blackmore, a talented local performer and musical leader. The Borough Minstrels performed for many years, locally and on Radio Éireann and in well-known venues in Dublin, often raising money for charity[21] or entertaining patients in hospital.[22] Catherine was friendly with some of the group. She remembered them performing in Dún Laoghaire Town Hall, some of the men in blackface, and the women in costumes that showed their pretty legs. Barbara, who loved music and dancing, joined the Borough Minstrels in the 1950s. 'The men were blacked up,' she remembered, 'wore red jackets and red dickie bows and played banjos and sang negro spirituals. The women... wore gingham dresses, gingham turbans, black tights and red tap shoes.' No one in Ireland at the time generally had any conception of minstrels as being anything other than good fun. From the 1970s, however, growing awareness of racism, including unintentional racism, and of movements like the civil rights movement in the United States, started combining to make black and white minstrel shows unacceptable. 'We would be run out of town nowadays,' Barbara commented.

The Top Hat, which opened in 1953, was a popular venue in Dún Laoghaire. 'The Top Hat was my *life*,' Lina remembered of her teen years in the 1950s. 'Loved it, I *loved* it! Couldn't always afford it... they might be bringing Chris Barber [a well-known jazz musician and bandleader] or somebody over from England, and it would be another ten bob.' Harvey has similar fond memories: 'We used to all dance in the Top Hat. We all knew each other.' The early 1960s was the showband era, and many of the showband greats, like Dickie ('Spit on Me') Rock and the Miami

The Fountainhead, an Irish rock band founded by Steve Belton and
Pat O'Donnell in 1982, at the Top Hat in 1988. Kind permission of Pat
O'Donnell and Steve Belton.

The Three Sons, a group from Sallynoggin that performed locally at
venues including the Top Hat and Dún Laoghaire Town Hall in the 1960s.
Kind permission of Anne McGlone.

Showband, Brendan Bowyer and the Royal Showband, and Joe Dolan and the Drifters performed there;[23] Nuala's father managed the Top Hat and the Purty Kitchen pub then, and she was often allowed to listen to the performers rehearse. In 1963 Chez Mac's, also in Dún Laoghaire, featured a performance by the US artist Chubby Checker, whose 1960 single 'The Twist' was hugely popular.[24] Other popular acts included Blackrock band the Greenbeats, and Jim Farley and the Tophatters. By the late 1960s, the Top Hat was one of the top venues for showband concerts in Ireland. But musical tastes were starting to change. Trendy young people were mooching around cafés and record shops, listening to and purchasing different genres. By the late 1970s and early 1980s, venues like the Top Hat were hosting performances by emerging bands like U2, the Pogues and the Boomtown Rats,[25] and better public transport and more car ownership made it easier for young people to attend bigger venues in the city centre, posing a challenge to venues in the suburbs.

The traditional music scene was bolstered from early independence by the influx of people from areas where the tradition was stronger than in Dublin, by cultural nationalists for whom traditional music could make a political statement as well as being a pleasure to listen to, and by state support of traditional arts. It was also threatened by various factors, including the Public Dance Halls Act of 1935, which reduced small, more spontaneous performances of traditional music, pushing artists into larger, more formal venues, where audiences were bigger but opportunities for spontaneity were reduced amid the chilling atmosphere created by fears of Church, state or public disapproval.[26] The Carnegie Library at Cabinteely, among others, was a venue for *céilithe*, with traditional music and dancing in the 1950s now under the watchful eye of local grandees.

Comhaltas Ceoltóirí Éireann (CCÉ, Irish Musicians' Fellowship) was founded in 1951 and, with substantial state support, played a major role in both preserving and bringing new energy to traditional music, despite concerns that it was also contributing to the homogenisation of regional musical differences.[27] While Ireland had been independent for almost thirty years, amid huge efforts to revitalise the Irish language and build a sense of nationhood, traditional music was threatened by high levels of emigration, particularly from areas where the tradition was strongest. CCÉ established the Fleadh Cheoil na hÉireann, annual festivals of traditional music and dance. From 1968, it published a magazine, *Treoir* (*Guidance*).[28] In 1974, CCÉ established its headquarters in Monkstown, the Cultúrlann na hÉireann (Irish Cultural Institute), from where it promoted interest in traditional music both through local channels, by developing close links with schools and other community organisations, locally, nationally and internationally. The 1960s, when the strict social mores of the 1930s, 1940s and 1950s were beginning to relax, also saw the flourishing of gritty, urban music that drew heavily on both traditional and modern canons, notably The Dubliners, featuring the vocals of Ronnie Drew, a Dún Laoghaire native.

* * *

The first screening of a film in Dublin occurred in 1896, and by the second decade of the twentieth century, cinema-going was an established, respectable pastime.[29] The first cinema in the area was the Kingstown Picture House, which opened in 1913. It was known as 'the Bug House' as it was said to be infested with fleas or lice.[30] Cinema-going became ever more popular during the First World War, as people were anxious to catch up on the latest news from the front, via the Pathé newsreels. In the 1920s, the Pavilion, originally a pleasure house for day trippers and tourists, was converted into a cinema. Into the 1940s and 1950s, children could access the cheaper seats ('the woodeners') at some cinemas in exchange for refundable glass bottles. Isobel remembered the huge role played by cinemas in the social lives of young people when she was a teenager in the 1940s. They were cheap, and everybody went. 'Now for a really good film,' she recalled, 'we would queue for over an hour, no matter what the weather, out of doors… there was an awful lot of flirting.'

Dún Laoghaire-Rathdown historically was home to many amateur and professional actors and venues. Street performers of various sorts included, in the nineteenth and early twentieth centuries, organ grinders with monkeys on their shoulders and, in Dún Laoghaire, a Russian man with a performing bear: 'the bear'd dance around him and all the children'd be lookin' at him'.[31] Fixed venues in the twentieth century included the Gas Company Theatre in Dún Laoghaire.[32] Theatrical performances were lively, generally inexpensive and enjoyed by a wide range of people, particularly before most had televisions, and the founding of RTÉ in 1961. The most democratic form of theatre were the fit-ups – travelling theatrical companies. Fit-ups thrived in early independence and were an important element of the artistic and social scene in small towns, rural areas and the more distant suburbs of cities until the late 1960s.[33] Rosa's aunt ran a fit-up company, travelling with everything she needed in her van to put on shows. The company travelled during the summer, often in concert with a family-run circus like Duffy's, with which it had arranged to collaborate, arriving the same week or the week after the circus had staged its show. When weather permitted, they staged shows in tents or outdoors, but when the weather was bad, they performed in parish halls. This required permission from the local priest, who had to see the show before it was staged and decide whether it was sufficiently moral: 'if he thought that there was anything above the knee, that would have been it. They wouldn't have been allowed.'

* * *

Here, as elsewhere, sport has served not just as a healthy and fun type of recreation, but also as an important signifier of identity, social class and political allegiance. It has also provided a forum for conducting business and social networking. Prior to 1880, most sports participation was informal and locally organised, with considerable local variation in rules and regulations. By the 1880s, with a growing middle class, there were also larger numbers of people with sufficient income and leisure time

Competitors in a cycling race in the 1950s. Lexicon Library Cycling Club collection.

to engage in formally organised sports – sports clubs and facilities were becoming increasingly popular all over the country.[34] From about 1880 to 1920, in parallel with developments in Britain, and with improvements and innovations in transportation, allowing competitions to move beyond the merely local, the rules for organised sports were codified. Sports also become more democratic, with the involvement of athletes from a broader range of socioeconomic backgrounds.[35] By 1930, formally organised sports clubs had become an integral part of Irish life. Across the country, there were 'at least 365 athletics clubs, more than 160 clubs and 59 schools affiliated to rugby, more than 1,000 GAA clubs dedicated to Gaelic football and hurling, more than 200 golf clubs, and so on'.[36] Sports become more overtly political during that crucial period. While some Irish nationalists, for example, happily enjoyed sports like cricket and rugby, others eschewed them in favour of the view that Irish people should only engage in Irish sports like hurling or Gaelic football – a view that tended to harden in early independence.[37]

By the mid- to late nineteenth century, cricket was widely played across all social classes, facilitated by the fact that it was then the only sport with universally codified rules, meaning that teams could play one another with a complete set of rules that both accepted.[38] This was particularly important as it got easier to travel large distances; people generally understood the minor rules variations between local teams, but going to play with a team in far-off parts, where rules could be very different, was a bigger challenge. Cricket had grown dramatically in popularity during the nineteenth century, when hurling was in decline.[39] The Kingstown Cricket Club, which played in a field near Glenageary, was founded in 1848,[40] at a time when the game was admired by many nationalists, including the renowned Daniel O'Connell,[41] as well as those loyal to Britain. In Dublin, both Catholic and Protestant schools catering to middle- and upper-class boys routinely offered cricket as part of the sports curriculum.[42] By the 1860s, it was played by the Catholic boys at Blackrock College, among other local schools,[43] and in 1877, on the occasion of the fortieth anniversary of the reign of Queen Victoria an editorial in the *Irish Sportsman* newspaper declaimed, 'the barbarous Pastimes of other days have given place among our people to the graceful amusement of cricket'.[44] By then, however, cricket was in decline, as interest in other sports, including athletics, rugby, soccer and Gaelic games, were in the ascendant.[45] By early independence, cricket was played largely by the students and former students of Protestant schools, who competed with one another.

Hurling had suffered a serious decline in the nineteenth century, relating to early nineteenth-century disapproval of the game on the part of the Catholic Church[46] and of state authorities under British rule, emigration following the Great Famine of the 1840s and other factors. By the late nineteenth century, hurling was largely restricted to limited areas including north Tipperary and east Galway.[47] In 1883, the Gaelic Athletic Association (GAA) was founded to preserve and support indigenous sports (then unknown in parts of the country),[48] and to formalise a set of

'Irish' rules for sports like field athletics and cycling. It reflected the sort of cultural nationalism then ascendant, that would influence modern Irish sports and society for generations. The first Gaelic football match was played in 1885, the year the GAA gained control of Irish athletics, with an emphasis on traditional Irish weight-throwing and jumping.[49] The GAA ran its first All-Ireland Championship in 1887, having been given the blessing of Archbishop Croke to play on Sundays.[50] (Croke had also denounced lawn tennis, then very popular among the monied classes of Dún Laoghaire-Rathdown and elsewhere, as an 'effeminate folly'.[51]) The same year, all members of the police were banned from membership in the organisation, and from playing its sports. Also in 1887, the Geraldines Club from Cabinteely challenged a Wicklow team, the John Dillons of Monaglough, near Woodenbridge, only to leave the field in outrage at their opponents' roughness.[52] This ignominious defeat must have confirmed for many spectators the assumption that hurling was primarily a rural sport; Dublin's heyday was still far in the future.

Despite some challenges in its early years, when a growth in interest in rugby and soccer threatened the viability of many GAA clubs,[53] the first national stadium for GAA sports, Croke Park, was acquired in 1913. In the early twentieth century, the GAA banned from its membership anyone who played or attended 'foreign games' – generally interpreted as rugby, soccer, cricket and hockey[54] – and tended to portray Gaelic athletes as morally and physically superior to sports considered British, which they portrayed as being tainted by social degeneration, among other flaws.[55] The GAA did not ban golf, presumably because the high costs involved meant that it was of limited appeal to those on modest incomes – most people – and did not represent a threat to Gaelic games.[56] Gaelic sports were also used in a tactical manner to get children and young people involved in the nationalist movement.[57] As the First World War approached, the GAA was increasingly aligned with ardent nationalism and the militarisation of nationalist politics, an association it would retain for years, despite simultaneously striving to present itself as non-political.[58] The brutal murder of fourteen civilian spectators by

British forces at a match in Croke Park between Dublin and Tipperary on 21 November 1920 would cement the organisation's place forever in the national psyche as an emblem of Irishness and Irish freedom.

The GAA expanded dramatically in early independence, hosting the Tailteann Games in 1924, the biggest sporting event held in the world that year, which included water sports at Blackrock Baths. There were more than 1,600 local clubs by 1935.[59] The GAA continued to deride 'foreign games' with a creative, engaging array of insults, referring to 'Black and Tan' rugby, 'wageslave' soccer and 'sluggish' cricket. It was even suggested that teachers who promoted such sports in schools should have their diplomas confiscated.[60] Pádraic, growing up in the 1930s and 1940s, steeped in his father's republican views, learned to disdain these 'foreign' sports: 'I never saw a soccer match,' he said, 'I wouldn't have anything to do with them!' Some schools – or at least some teachers – threw themselves into GAA to the point of firmly discouraging students from playing other sports. At Walter's primary school in the 1950s, 'it was kind of bet into you,' he said, 'if you played soccer and you went to school on the Monday morning, you were in trouble'.

From the early twentieth century, sporty women from nationalist backgrounds also played camogie, a slightly modified version of hurling that included a rule against using voluminous skirts to stop the ball.[61] The first camogie club was established in Meath in 1898, and camogie would become increasingly popular in early independence, when its links with the Irish language and with cultural nationalism generally were also growing.[62] The Camogie Association was founded in 1904. Girls' teams, including school-based teams, were very active. In March 1930, for example, the Dominican College Sion Hill school from Blackrock defeated a rival Dominican College team from Eccles Street in the city centre. The Ladies' Gaelic Football Association was founded in 1974, after which women's Gaelic football was extended countrywide.[63]

GAA was played in many schools, both *Gaelscoileanna* (Irish language schools) and English-speaking, and teams from all over the country competed with each other enthusiastically. Protestant schools – and many elite Catholic schools – generally played 'foreign' games, and while some Protestants in rural areas played GAA, it was rare for them to do so in Dún Laoghaire-Rathdown, probably largely because their population was big enough that they could socialise only with one another, if they wanted, and did not need to seek community among local Gaelic games enthusiasts. For residents of Dún Laoghaire-Rathdown with roots in rural Ireland – a large and growing number throughout the mid-twentieth century – GAA sports were a way to engage with their background, by following the fortunes of teams in their home areas, and attending county matches in Croke Park. Mairéad remembered her Kerry family 'living' in Croke Park when Kerry was playing, and travelling to Kerry to attend important matches. Mairéad herself was a keen camogie player, and would grow up to be involved with the Dublin Camogie Board.

The GAA's position vis-à-vis 'foreign' sports mellowed gradually with the passing of time. The ban on GAA members playing, listening to or watching such sports was abolished in 1971, by which time radio and television had made it a moot issue anyway. Still, Odhrán, who grew up in Dún Laoghaire, recalled that in the 1970s his father, a Kerryman, still frowned on sports like soccer for reasons deeply intertwined with his nationalist views. The family often visited Croke Park to watch matches. Odhrán recalled that, during half-time, he could peek over the wall to watch rugby matches being played in a small adjacent park, much to his father's disapproval.

By the 1960s and 1970s, almost two generations had passed since the War of Independence, educational levels had risen dramatically and were continuing to rise, the industrialisation process was underway, and the GAA was poised to begin transitioning into an important tool for community integration and bonding, as well as the outlet for sports and physical activity that it had always been. In the latter decades of the twentieth century, women's Gaelic sports also started to rise in popularity, creating an environment much more favourable to female sporting achievement.

Parnell vs Cuala, 1988. Hulton Archive, Independent News and Media, Getty Images.

While the GAA contributed hugely to community and nation building in independence, one advantage possessed by both rugby and soccer was the possibility of beating the British at their own game. The Irish Rugby Football Union formed in 1875,[64] and by 1877, a few schools that had previously played cricket were now playing rugby.[65] Rugby and soccer both became increasingly popular from the 1890s, with rugby adopted enthusiastically in elite boys' schools, including Catholic boys' schools that would be strongly associated with the struggle for independence, and with the government and leadership in early independence; the sons of some of those involved at the highest levels in the 1916 Rising and the War of Independence would play rugby in assorted elite schools. Tadgh Ó Murchadha, who taught in Blackrock College in 1922–3, wrote an Irish-language book, *An Cliathán Clé (The Left Wing)*,[66] relating the story of boys in a Dublin boarding school for whom rugby exemplified the school's ethos and a robust, masculine view of Irishness. The book was pro-duced by An Gúm, a body established in 1926 as a subsection of the Department of Education to supply schoolbooks, fiction and nonfiction in Irish, with the view to creating a substantial literary canon for a society that the government hoped would soon be bilingual.[67] Rugby, clearly, would occupy an ambivalent position in the national and local psyche with its varied associations – historically, with a loyalist elite and, as the decades marched on and Irish society changed and developed in independence, with elites drawn from both Anglo-Irish loyalist or formerly loyalist and Catholic nationalist circles. Rugby, however, was played not uniformly by members of the elite, but also by many young men from quite modest backgrounds, with many of those who had fought in the war working in ordinary clerkships and office jobs during peacetime.[68]

The Irish Football Association of Ireland was formed in 1880[69] and the Football Association of Ireland was established in 1921. The Free State League of Soccer, which took shape in the 1920s, offered professional opportunities to talented players, but opportunities remained greater overseas.[70] At grassroots level, soccer was a popular sport with much enthusiastic amateur participation. A national women's soccer team was active from 1973.

Writing in 1944, T.S.C. Dagg – former player on the Three Rock Rovers team from Rathfarnham and President of the Irish Hockey Union from 1920 to 1924 and 1930 to 1931, began a discussion of hockey in Ireland with a chapter about hurling and concluded, rather defensively, that hockey and hurling (he used the term 'hurley' to refer to the game) both spring from a common origin but that 'modern hockey' is 'a scientific development of the ancient Irish pastime' and that referring to it as a 'foreign game' is 'as little reasonable as to say that our ancient Irish melodies cease to be Irish when presented in a modern setting'. Daggs then proceeds to apply quotation marks to the word 'hurley' periodically throughout the book, apparently considering hurling a poor cousin of the 'more scientific' hockey. For a hockey devotee living through a period of intense cultural nationalism that impacted on sport in many ways, Daggs's frustrations are clear. Daggs clarifies that modern hockey was introduced to Ireland in 1892 with the formation of several clubs, including clubs in

Three Rock, Dundrum and Monkstown – Monkstown (Men's) Hockey Club, for example, was founded in 1896 – spreading quickly to other locations around the country. The Irish Hockey Union was formed in 1893, and by 1908, over 100 clubs were affiliated to it.[71] The Irish Ladies' Hockey Club was founded in 1894, six months before the equivalent club in England, prompted by the enthusiasm of several clubs in the Dublin area, including one in Dundrum.[72] It would play under 'Irish rules' or the same rules as the men. The *Irish Times* and *Daily Express* covered their first match, against England, held at Alexandra College in 1886,[73] describing the players and their outfits as 'pretty', 'animating' and 'charming'; they wore long-sleeved blouses and long, flowing skirts over petticoats and stockings. After 1902, skirts six inches off the ground were introduced (but considered too immodest to wear on the street).[74] Richard's mother was a founder of the Monkstown Ladies' Hockey Club, and would remain actively involved with it until the 1940s.

Women's and men's hockey tended to be associated with both Protestant schools – for example, Avoca School in Blackrock and Kingstown Grammar (which together would become Newpark Comprehensive in 1972), which held tournaments with each other – and with areas with relatively larger Protestant populations, the generally denominational nature of the Irish education system functioning as a sort of social barrier (albeit somewhat permeable) between different types of sports. Janet's father, a Catholic from Dún Laoghaire whose best friend was Protestant, played hockey in the mid-twentieth century, cited by Janet as evidence of his open-minded nature when open-mindedness sometimes seemed to be in short supply.

Tennis thrived in Ireland, particularly urban Ireland, in the 1880s and 1890s, when it was primarily played by the upper- and middle-classes. Women fared better in tennis than they did in most sports. From 1879, the National Championship included events for both women and men.[75] Tennis clubs like Monkstown Lawn Tennis Club (founded in 1884), Sandycove Lawn Tennis Club (founded in 1886), and Glenageary and Kingstown Lawn Tennis Club (founded in 1888) became known as venues where young people could meet and court one another within spaces segregated by social class and, sometimes, religious denomination. Tennis was also a sport well-suited to the physical environment of the rapidly expanding middle-class suburbs, as it required less space to play than most team sports, with private homes with large gardens even in a position to have their own courts for practice. At Sandycove Lawn Tennis Club in the early days, would-be members were voted on anonymously by means of the committee voting with black or white beans; if one in three of the beans was black, the person was rejected. Tournaments were well-attended; on 2 July 1888, the *Daily Express* reported that over 600 attended the Sandycove Lawn Tennis Tournament, where they were entertained by not just the tennis, but also the band of the First Battalion King's Liverpool Regiment.[76] The clubs also became notable venues for dances, particularly outside the summer lawn tennis season.

Partly because of the rising tide of Irish nationalism, manifested in sports at the same time by substantial and growing interest in Gaelic games, and partly because of a growing interest in cycling (in the summer of 1890, Leopardstown Racecourse was hired to act as a 'cycling resort', which allowed young people to engage in sporting activities away from the gaze of their elders), tennis would become relatively less important from this period onward,[77] although various tennis clubs around Dún Laoghaire-Rathdown, as elsewhere, remained well-known as locations where the courting rituals of the better-off members of society were enacted, as tennis clubs could be quite exclusive, providing facilities for dances and other entertainments to 'members only'. Until the 1970s, some clubs were still further subdivided according to denomination, with certain clubs having memberships strongly aligned with the Protestant minority. The records of many clubs, however, show progressively larger numbers of members with more obviously 'Irish' names in the early decades of the twentieth century, showing the shift in relative power and influence then occurring in all areas of life, as well as the relative decline in interest in tennis, which now competed with many other sports, such that clubs could no longer afford to be socially exclusive.

A group at the Dún Laoghaire Golf Club – note the special golfing outfits. The Independent Newspapers (Ireland) Collection, National Library of Ireland.

Ireland has a long-established history of golf, the first course having been laid out in the Curragh in County Kildare in 1852.[78] The Golfing Union, established in 1891, is the oldest golf union in the world, although the game originated in Scotland. The Irish Ladies' Golf Union was established in 1893,[79] the same year that the Foxrock Golf Club was founded with a 'clubhouse and ladies' pavilion' and promoted as a local asset to potential buyers in the area. A new club was established in Carrickmines in 1900, the Stillorgan Park Club in 1909.[80] The Kingstown Golf Club was founded in 1910,[81] changing its name to the Dún Laoghaire Golf Club in 1951, over thirty years after the town's name change.[82] By now, many golf courses were catering primarily to well-to-do professional men when the landed gentry were declining, and the affluent middle classes were in the ascendant, with golf in Dublin particularly associated with those who worked in law.[83] The relative decline in wealth of the aristocracy was a contributing factor to the development of golf: they had ample lands suitable for conversion into golf courses, while the rising upper-middle classes had the social ambition to want to play a game associated with the gentry, and the money to pay golf club fees.[84] Early golf clubs sometimes introduced professional golf teachers from Scotland to improve the standards of the players' game,[85] while the particular style of (expensive) dress used to play also offered the opportunity for a certain amount of performative wealth.[86] Whereas pre-independence golf had a strong association with the Anglo-Irish and the monied classes generally, post-independence it continued to flourish and, as the twentieth century progressed, memberships diversified regarding the ethno-religious backgrounds of the players, if not their socioeconomic status, as the game continued to cater primarily to people of means. For Vickie's father, an antiques dealer, the golf course was where he 'got most of his business from' in the 1950s and 1960s. Later, as suburban estates for young, ambitious families continued to rise, golf remained an aspirational activity. Larry commented that while some golf courses only required (substantial) membership fees, others also expected would-be members to be 'socially acceptable' and that membership applications from those considered unacceptable could be rejected, even when they had plenty of money.

Swimming, the ultimate free sport and leisure activity, certainly has a history in Dublin Bay dating back to the earliest days of human activity there. As the coast became more developed in the early modern and modern period, so did facilities for swimmers, and the monetisation of swimming. From the late eighteenth century, swimmers used bathing machines in locations like Killiney Beach, women generally changing into their costumes inside the portable huts and accessing the water directly from there. In 1843, developer John Crosthwaite built baths in a corner of Scotsman's Bay. These were rebuilt in 1864, and acquired by Kingstown Urban District Council in the late 1890s. Between 1905 and 1908, the baths were relocated nearby and remodelled, with separate bathing sections for men and women, after which they became known as the Kingstown Baths and, from 1920, the Dún Laoghaire Baths. Various improvements were completed during the 1920s and 1930s. The Blackrock Baths were constructed by the railway company in 1839 following local protests about the sea having been cut off by the rail infrastructure. These were purchased in 1928 by the Urban District Council and remodelled for the upcoming Tailteann Games.[87] Honorah and her siblings – whose father ran the Dún Laoghaire Baths from the 1930s – learned to swim, as did so many, with the help of an instructor, whose technique was to use a 'long pole with a thing around it, and they'd put it around their waist, and he'd drag them along'. By the 1960s and 1970s, outdoor swimming pools were losing ground to heated, indoor facilities, at the same time as incomes had risen and travel to international locations for sun holidays had become more affordable.

Leisure swimming in Dún Laoghaire for those who could not afford to pay an entrance fee into the Baths was facilitated in 1877 by the construction of ladies' and men's bathing places in Salthill and the West Pier respectively, although both had problems relating to the discharge of sewerage into the water nearby. The Forty Foot in Sandycove was a local icon from 1863, when the Kingstown Commissioners obtained permission to construct a public bathing space at Sandycove. The Sandycove Bathers' Association was founded in 1880 to protect and develop the area.[88] The all-male swimmers using the spot traditionally bathed naked until nine in the morning, after which they were expected to don a swimsuit. As we saw in 'Fighting and Fighting Back', it would remain male-only until 1974, cited as one of the reasons for the swimming spot's great popularity.[89] Although women could swim at the Forty Foot from the mid-1970s, they were not allowed to join the Sandycove Bathers' Association or use its changing huts. The Vico Bathing Place in Dalkey was another male-only swimming area.[90] The Loreto nuns used a women-only bathing spot further down the coast, proving to astonished local children that nuns had ordinary legs beneath their habits.

The seaside was, of course, a playground to children living in coastal areas, with children given considerable freedom to play autonomously until the latter decades of the twentieth century. Kevin remembered the many hours he spent swimming at Seapoint and the names by which rocks and other prominent features were known: 'The Hillary... the Fairy... the Bull's Eye... the Dead Man's Slip... the Devil's Rock... the Swimmers' Pool'. Girls were more likely than boys to be limited by their

Left: Rosaleen and Kathleen Mullen on Killiney Strand, c.1926. Children's seaside games have not changed with the passage of time, as evidenced in this photograph. Collection of Catherine Mullen, kind permission of Anna Scudds.

Right: Cousins Jimmy and James Howe at the Blackrock Baths, c.1915. Kind permission of Jimmy Howe.

guardians in where they went to swim, largely because of concerns about sexual predation, with more isolated swimming spots sometimes considered 'off limits' for girls because, as Kate recalled, 'there were weird men hung around because [the swimming spot] was kind of secluded'. Another interviewee, also a young girl in the 1950s, remembered 'old men' who 'hung around' the Dún Laoghaire Baths offering to teach young girls how to swim, 'but to their own advantage'. You weren't allowed to talk about 'anything like that' in those days, she said, but 'you just knew it wasn't right… you just knew you didn't want a stranger having a feel, let's put it that way'.

Yachting has been an important feature of marine life in Dún Laoghaire since shortly after the construction of the pier. A regatta organised by Lord Errol took place in Kingstown in 1828; apparently the

Yachtsmen travelling out to yacht, 1948. Yachting has long been a great source of pleasure to many in the area, while also a significant provider of employment. Because of the costs involved, it has historically been largely confined to the middle and upper classes, with people living on more modest incomes more likely to be involved in service and support positions. *Dún Laoghaire Borough Civic Week Souvenir Handbook* 1948.

first.[91] The Royal Irish Yacht Club held its first regatta in 1832, becoming the Royal St George Yacht Club from 1847,[92] at which stage it had 400 members, and was a significant local employer at its premises on a site obtained from the Harbour Commissioners. Throughout much of the nineteenth century, only the very wealthy could afford yachts; by the start of the twentieth century, growing numbers of middle-class enthusiasts were getting involved and there were clubs, now including the Royal Alfred Yacht Club and the Edward Yacht Club,[93] the latter founded in 1870[94] (renamed the National Yacht Club in 1930). They tended to have a higher percentage of Catholic members in comparison to the others, which were associated with wealthy Protestants.[95] All, as discussed in 'Mouths to Feed', were significant local employers. As the first Water Wags, a style of boat indigenous to Dublin Bay, built in 1878[96] ('the ideal boat,' explains local marine historian Vincent Delaney, 'cheap and simple and suitable for everybody')* were made available, it became easier for middle-class people to own their own sailing boats and join the yacht clubs, although costs remained prohibitive to the working classes.

---

* To this day, owners of Water Wags sail them in Dún Laoghaire Harbour on Wednesdays. This is thought to date to the nineteenth century, when Dún Laoghaire shops remained closed on Wednesday afternoons.

Rowing is also an important local sport, with rowing clubs having been established in most of the harbours once associated with piloting, including Dún Laoghaire and Bullock and Coliemore Harbours in Dalkey.[97] There was huge rivalry between rowers from Dún Laoghaire and Ringsend, with competitions held annually that occasionally ended in physical conflict. Leisure boats, for hire to tourists and day trippers, were also an important part of the local marine economy during its heyday as a tourist destination in the mid-twentieth century.

Horse racing and gambling have a long history here, with horse racing having been the best-organised, most well-funded sport everywhere on the island of Ireland from the early modern period. While not everyone could afford to own or run a horse, in many respects, horse racing was one of the more democratic sports, as people from all walks of life enjoyed watching races, gambling and the socialising that accompanied both activities. Leopardstown Racecourse is the most famous in the area, but numerous locations hosted races at different points, including Ballybrack, from 1865 to 1866, Dundrum in 1842, Kingstown from 1834 to 1860 and Stillorgan in 1843. Leopardstown opened on 27 August 1888 with a course modelled on Sandown Racecourse in England, and was the brainchild of a Captain George Quin, who oversaw an inaugural meeting attended by over 50,000.[98] While other racecourses came and went, Leopardstown was a central element of the racing scene in Dublin for generations.

At the Leopardstown Races, c.1900. Mason Photographic Collection, National Library of Ireland.

A little more niche, but still a popular local sport, was pigeon racing, with clubs like the Dún Laoghaire Pigeon Club. During the season, approximately from Easter to September, pigeons were dispatched all over the country and overseas, often with the help of rail and ferry services, while their owners anxiously awaited their return. Pigeon racing was seen as a working-class sport, with afficionados primarily located in urban areas. It was also generally a sport for men, whose wives frequently regarded the pigeons with a jaundiced air, as they could take over entire back gardens, where they posed a threat to washing hung outdoors and to anyone who might want to enjoy a cup of tea outside the back door.

Hunting for food, of course, dates in Ireland to the earliest days of human habitation, but the concept of hunting as an activity associated with the upper classes dates to the Norman era. Once established in Ireland, the Normans enforced hunting rights, with certain people given rights to hunt desired species in specific areas, and others excluded from doing so, or involved only in carrying out the more menial tasks associated with the hunt. Hunting with horses and hounds spread further during the plantation period of the seventeenth century, and over the course of the eighteenth and early nineteenth centuries, hunting for foxes with horses and hounds became increasingly popular in Dublin, where it was strongly associated with the wealthier classes.[99] In 1919, following a triumphant show in the General Election of 1918, Sinn Féin held a campaign to stop blood sports, but particularly fox hunting, for as long as Irish political prisoners – including Éamon de Valera and William Cosgrave, who was interned since May 1918 under suspicion of conspiring with the Germans – were incarcerated. As fox hunting could damage land and property, and was therefore extremely annoying to smaller farmers over whose land the hunt often passed without their consent, there was already a history of opposing the hunt that dated back several decades.[100] Villages like Shankill and Cabinteely were often associated with fox hunting, and the names of some of the pubs in the area – the Galloping Green on the Stillorgan Road, and the Horse and Hound in Cabinteely, for example – continue to evoke a time when hunting was an important local pastime. In the first half of the twentieth century, in parallel with the rising numbers of socially aspirant middle classes, hunting became somewhat more socially diverse, although the expense involved was prohibitive to anyone on a lower income ('when the local butcher became master of the South County... it descended a bit,' commented Tommy Fennell, with a touch of irony, when he was recorded in 1980[101]). Feargal from Shankill remembered the local publican serving drinks on a silver tray to the Master of the Hounds, and then seeing and hearing the hunt – horses, dogs, bugles and the riders in their special hunting gear – going uphill into the country. With the expansion of the suburbs, the areas available for hunting receded ever further from Dublin, and in the latter decades of the twentieth century fox hunting declined in popularity as blood sports were increasingly seen as socially unacceptable.

In some rural areas, sport hunting – both fox hunting and hunting for grouse and other game birds – could be a source of occasional seasonal work for locals. Joseph remembered working on a 'grouse beat' in the mid-twentieth century. In September, 'ex-British soldiers and whatever... like colonels, the top brass' came to Glencullen to hunt grouse. Local lads were employed as beaters, frightening the grouse from the thick mountain vegetation.

The vast majority of sports were played by men for men. In the nineteenth and early twentieth centuries, women were often discouraged from taking part in sports amid fears that their fertility might be affected. While more women played competitive sports in the nineteenth and early twentieth century than is often assumed, throughout much of that period many nationalists and loyalists alike, as well as many medical men and men of the cloth, proposed that sports fostered manly virtues and opposed 'effeminacy', suggesting that there was little room for women athletes. Nonetheless, as the suburbs around Dublin grew, so did the number of women wishing to engage in sport, at first typically lawn tennis[102] and golf, with the gradual incursion of greater numbers of women participating in vigorous sports like camogie as athletes rather than just as spectators and purveyors of refreshments. Sporting events that held women's and men's contests in parallel, where the sexes might mingle in their sportswear, enraged some religious authorities, on the grounds of immodesty and the widely held view that sports was physically and morally 'bad' for women.[103] In 1928, the first year women athletes competed in the Olympics (albeit in just five events), Pope Pius XI stated that sport was 'irreconcilable with woman's reserve' and an *Irish Times* editorial fretted that the 'extreme exertion' required by sports might kill even the 'most robust women'. In 1934, John Charles McQuaid, then President of Blackrock College, wrote to the *Irish Press* stating that women should not attend athletic events at which men were also present, as this would be 'unIrish and uncatholic' and also both a 'social abuse' and a 'moral abuse'.[104] He was reflecting the comment issued by the Vatican in 1930 that stated: 'In athletic sports and exercises, wherein the Christian modesty of girls must be, in a special way, safeguarded, it is supremely unbecoming that they flaunt themselves and display themselves before the eyes of all.'[105] The all-female Camogie Association, perhaps anxious that such views might

Children at the Dominican Convent, Sion Hill, playing sports. Lexicon Library Postcard Collection.

threaten its future, wrote in the *Sunday Independent* that it 'would do all in its power to ensure that no girl would appear on any sports ground' in inappropriate clothing. In 1944 – incidentally the same year McQuaid, now the Archbishop of Dublin, 'strongly disapproved' of the use of tampons, even for married women – he was still exercised about women's sports, and several girls' schools catering to middle-class families were discouraged from offering hockey, on the grounds that the 'twisting movements' made during play might affect girls' fertility.[106]

While many women continued to play sports despite the views held by authority figures, and the number of women involved in sports grew, investment in sports for women and girls continued to lag throughout the twentieth century. Jimmy, reflecting on his childhood, and when he and his wife were settling in Cabinteely in the early 1980s, said, 'I think women had no rights… if you'd go down to the local parks on a Saturday, or a Sunday morning, you'd see boys playing GAA, or soccer, or rugby, or whatever. There was nothing… for young girls.'

While local social, class and sex divisions were often clearly visible in sports, at its best, sport could be a way to bring people closer together. Golf and other elite sports provided a location for innumerable business contacts to be made and deals to be struck, but some of the most important comings-together happened at humble local sportsgrounds. In the 1970s, Mick and his friends – then young boys – sneaked onto the grounds of a local convent to play football. They were trespassing and someone rang the guards. But the local detective, rather than scolding them, encouraged them to join a local team, for which he coached. For Mick, who often had been bullied for being a Traveller, this was the first time he could interact positively with other local children from settled families. He still experienced a lot of bullying, but he also became involved in both soccer and Gaelic sports, and in 1982 got to travel to Germany with the rest of the team: 'it was something that I will never forget… I had friends… that two-week period, I didn't experience any racism or any bullying whatsoever.' Sports gave Mick the chance to be not just accepted but, on one wonderful occasion when he prevented the opposing team from scoring a crucial goal, a champion: 'it was like a big celebration. I was a hero! I remember going into the class next day... everyone bowed down to me... I got them to the semi-finals.' Tug of war was a popular diversion in some uplands areas like Glencullen. The competition could be fierce between the various small communities. As well as good fun, these events were opportunities for areas largely populated by small farmers to team-build – essential in a small farming environment in which cooperation was crucial. Many of these areas also hosted many nurse children, some of whom had a chance to shine, and to truly feel part of the gang – perhaps for the first and only time in their lives – at inter-community tugs of war.

* * *

In 1888, the Kingstown Men's Christian Institute was founded to provide Protestant workers – largely young apprentices and shop assistants – with opportunities to socialise in an environment considered wholesome and suitable for self-improvement. The institute's premises was completed in 1891, and officially opened in 1892 (Protestant women could join as associate members only, with limited use of some facilities, like the reading room). More frivolous recreations were gradually introduced, with billiards tables becoming available, apparently under some duress, from 1913.[107]

Workmen's clubs became increasingly popular in the late nineteenth century, partly in response to the need for working men to have leisure space other than pubs, when excessive alcohol consumption was increasingly considered a significant social and moral problem. For men who worked long hours in demanding jobs, often returning to small, crowded houses, a club could be a welcome retreat from the demands of work and family. They sometimes also offered bathing and sanitary services to men who had difficult, dirty jobs and no running water or sanitation at home. The first Workmen's Club in Kingstown opened on Clarence Street in 1893, with a constitution stating its non-sectarian nature, and a multi-denominational board of trustees. It offered entertainments including billiards and board games.[108] The club moved to Library Road in 1915.[109] As the twentieth century progressed, events like snooker tournaments were introduced, with friendly matches held against clubs across a wide area – even in Wales. The no-alcohol rule continued to be observed, with a notable exception being made – remembered Graham – for a visit by Alex 'Hurricane' Higgins following his victory of the World Title in 1972. Workmen's clubs throughout the area would remain a significant part of the social landscape, featuring dances, card playing, sports and other entertainments, as well as organising day trips and outings for the members.

For many women, organisations including the Legion of Mary and (especially in more rural parts of the county) the Irish Countrywomen's Association (ICA) were important elements of their social life, as well as providing means by which they could engage in religious and/or charitable works (in the case of the Legion of Mary) and a further education and activism on behalf of women's rights (in the case of the ICA). Groups like the various suburban Ladies' Clubs, offering women the chance to socialise and to express themselves creatively, were also important outlets for women as the suburbs grew from the mid-twentieth century onwards.

Children's social organisations were, generally, strictly denominational throughout the nineteenth and much of the twentieth century. The popular scouting/guiding movement was seen as too Protestant or British for Catholic Irish children and, in 1928, an organisation for Catholic guides was founded.[110] Protestant children could also join the Boys' or Girls' Brigade, offering similar activities to scouts, alongside a more overtly religious activities, including prayer, scripture study and public displays of faith and allegiance. Julian was in a company that met at the Mariners' Church (now the National Maritime Museum): 'We used to have pillbox hats and a yellow bandolier. A satchel and a special belt… you wore your Sunday suit under that, with the belt and sash. And we did marching, we had a band.' Ambrose, a former scout, remembered how the Protestant scouts with whom he marched in the

1960s only ever met other Protestants: 'we only did scouting things with Protestant scouts'. The St Vincent de Paul ran youth clubs for boys from families with modest incomes, offering entertainments in a safe environment, extracurricular classes in various crafts and skills, and the opportunity to have a holiday in one of the Vincent de Paul's holiday venues.

* * *

Most feast days are and were associated with special days in the ecclesiastical calendar, but not only were they experienced as an aspect of the spiritual side of life, they also had important social aspects. For example, as elsewhere, Corpus Christi celebrations were marked with enthusiasm in towns, villages and suburbs all over the borough. Corpus Christi is a feast day that entered the Catholic liturgy in 1264, celebrated in Ireland since the middle ages. After the repeal of the Penal Laws in 1782, Corpus Christi and its processions became important community events and celebrations of faith, featuring parades, the erection of altars and the decoration of towns. They would remain so until the recent past. 'That was a great day,' remembered Maureen, of the Corpus Christi parades of her youth in the 1940s and 1950s. 'Crowds of people. All the parents came, and all the children were dressed in their First Communion clothes, or their Confirmation clothes.' Children, especially those who had just made Holy Communion, as well as many community groups, including representatives from the army and the Gardaí, participated, with women and men typically segregated in their various sodalities and other religious organisations. Obviously, non-Catholics did not participate in these parades, although they were certainly aware of them. Douglas, growing up in a Church of Ireland family, lived in Dalkey in the 1950s, and had clear memories of the Corpus Christi processions: 'Very colourful, and exotic, and totally alien things to us … my parents would say, "You can have a look. But… try not to let people see that you're looking because you're not supposed to."' In areas like Kingstown/

Dún Laoghaire, and other coastal parts of Dún Laoghaire-Rathdown, with large Protestant populations, as in parts of Northern Ireland and certain border areas, Corpus Christi could have a – largely unspoken – political edge, as representatives of state authority marched alongside bishops, priests and the faithful.

Calendar festivals like Christmas, Easter, St Patrick's Day and so on were celebrated in typical fashion. Nollaig na mBan (Women's Christmas, 6 January) was not widely observed, with some exceptions among women originally from rural areas where the tradition was strong. Odhrán's mother, originally from Kerry, always had a small group of women friends over for Nollaig na mBan, occupying the family living room and enjoying tea and scones.

* * *

Sports and leisure are often overlooked by historians, but they provide fascinating insights into society in the many, complex ways in which they intersect with political, commercial and civic life, and how they can both prompt and mirror broader social trends in society. Even when many people struggled to survive on very low incomes, and worked extremely long hours, the natural need for leisure and entertainment asserted itself here in many inventive ways.

(BEFORE THE) CRADLE TO
(BEYOND THE) GRAVE

Human experience is marked by a series of life events and rites of passage that bring us from the very start of life to the end. Each life unfurls in episodes, punctuated by major life events. Every life starts at the beginning, with conception, pregnancy and birth.

Throughout most of history, obstetric and gynaecological matters were attended to by parturient women themselves and by traditional practitioners, also generally women. The latter, using a combination of healing and herbal knowledge, folklore and magical practices, offered a range of services, including midwifery and abortion.[1] Data about the Irish experience of childbirth before general literacy is quite limited. Writing

Children outside O'Donnell Gardens, Glasthule, 1920s. Candid shots of children from this era in their everyday clothes are relatively rare, making this picture particularly special. Collection of Catherine Mullen, kind permission of Anna Scudds.

in 1846, William Wilde, a medical doctor, wrote sympathetically about traditional midwives and their work, although he wished to see traditional practices replaced with science-based medical care. Many of the traditional techniques he describes were still in use in the mid-twentieth century, before childbirth in hospital became almost ubiquitous.

The removal of childbirth from the home to a medical environment was gradual. In 1850, the year after Wilde's comments were published, the first 'lying-in' or maternity hospital in the area was opened in Dún Laoghaire-Rathdown by the Sisters of Mercy, occupying a premises first on Pakenham Road, Monkstown, and subsequently at 100 Lower George's Street, Kingstown.[2] Most women, however, continued to give birth at home. Although there was a system in place for training female midwives from the late seventeenth century, many women – especially the poor – were attended by midwives without formal training, or much formal education at all, until well into the twentieth century.[3] Sometimes known as 'handywomen', they had trained in traditional methods of midwifery through experience. Because they worked outside formal channels, and because 'women's work' was generally less observed and studied – and because researchers were usually men, with whom women generally refused to speak about matters considered delicate – references to them in the historical record are relatively sparse.[4]

By the late nineteenth century, authorities were increasingly concerned with regulating childbirth, and began to implement a policy of registering women providing these services to ensure minimum standards of care and enshrine in law the idea of midwives as being lesser than doctors, at a time when many doctors saw obstetrical care as undignified and not very interesting. In 1893, the Select Committee of the House of Commons welcomed these changes because they would relieve male doctors of 'irksome and ill-paid work'.[5] In Dublin in 1904, the Chief Medical Officer for the Guinness Brewery (providing medical care to workers and their families) noted that workers' wives generally preferred to give birth at home and described their midwives as often 'half-trained' and 'more dangerous than helpful'.[6] Midwives who required medical assistance with a difficult birth were in an impossible situation: their clients often could not afford a doctor's fees, and if a doctor was called, the midwife herself might have to pay.[7]

From 1907, Irish parents were legally required to register births,[8] an important step towards the formalisation of maternity and childbirth services, and a challenge to traditional approaches to childbirth. The early twentieth century also saw a major push to promote maternal and infant survival and health, led primarily by women activists and organisations, like the Women's National Health Association, Infant Aid and the Irish Women's Local Government Association (many of whose members were also active in the women's suffrage movement).[9] In 1918, the Midwives Act was passed, making it illegal for an untrained midwife to assist at a birth, except under the direct supervision of a doctor. Across Dublin, Lady Sanitary Officers visited mothers under the terms of the act, one of the goals of which was the elimination of the provision of childbirth services by handywomen.[10] A further act in 1931 made legal provision to give official badges to licensed midwives and to issue a substantial fine to women practising without formal training. Homebirths declined steadily; by 1925, 57 per cent of the births overseen by the National Maternity Hospital at Holles Street took place in hospital.[11]

But many women in working-class areas continued to give birth with the assistance of unlicensed local women. Many mothers preferred the care of a woman they knew personally, and did not wish to, or could not, deal with the additional expense of a qualified midwife and the items that she might request for the birth and care of the baby.[12] Sometimes they opted to be attended by a woman known locally for her expertise, at other times by a neighbour woman who just wanted to help. Kevin's grandmother was a handywoman working in Blackrock without formal training or a licence into at least the 1940s. She was aware that she was breaking the law, but many families could not afford doctors' fees. Women in labour would 'leave things to the last minute,' Kevin said, hoping for the baby to come with no need for medical intervention.

'There was a structure there for handywomen, right?' Kevin explained. 'They got two-and-six for doing this. A woman had to stay in bed for a week… the handywoman looked after [her]… She was committed for a few weeks to that woman.' For working-class women like Kevin's grandmother, holding a respected position in the community as a much-needed handywoman also elevated one's social status. At around the same time, Liz's unmarried aunt helped many Blackrock women to deliver their babies. Liz remembered when one of the neighbours was having a child: 'it was just a case of one of the children, or the husband, knocking at the door and saying, "I think the baby's on the way"… she'd come back rolling up her sleeves… She'd say, "She's another boy." Or, "She's a girl".' Women who helped labouring women often also helped the dying and prepared the dead for funerals. Clodagh's mother was often away from home, helping the local midwife, sitting with a dying person overnight or laying out the dead. She was away so often that when her husband came home to find her absent, he would say, 'Well, who's coming or who's gone?'

In 1953, new legislation introduced a degree of free healthcare for pregnant women and infants up to six weeks, and the government invested in infrastructure and facilities for maternity care. Pregnant women were entitled to a full maternity-care service, free to those on lower incomes and heavily subsidised for better-off mothers.[13] Official policy was for women to give birth to their first and their fifth and subsequent children in hospital, with other uncomplicated births overseen at home. By then, many more women were opting to give birth in hospitals or in private nursing homes, but a lack of formally trained midwives, the cost of the service and often women's own preference for a traditional approach meant that into the 1950s some women continued to opt for home births.[14] During a transitional period, when hospital births were becoming the norm but most families did not own cars, small taxi firms and haulage companies with lorries catered for women from rural areas like Sandyford and Glencullen when they needed to attend prenatal appointments and when they were in labour. Bella's father ran one such taxi firm from the Lamb's Cross area. Gareth's father owned the only lorry in Barnacullia in the 1930s and early 1940s, and brought labouring women to hospital to give birth: 'He was the main maternity transport... they went in... a two-tonne truck [that] shook the guts out of them.' By 1961, almost 80 per cent of Irish babies were born in hospital. By 1971, only 0.7 per cent of Irish babies were born at home.[15] While most women were happy to give birth in hospital – and infant mortality rates were improving – their experiences were variable, with some reporting deeply unpleasant encounters with obstetricians who seemed to view them with contempt. Remembered Ingrid, 'the way they spoke... they weren't speaking to you, to me, they were... speaking to one another'.

The extraordinary levels of prudishness present in Irish society prior to the 1960s and 1970s meant that young people often had little or no understanding of human reproduction and no idea when their mothers were pregnant with younger siblings. 'It could have been an immaculate conception for all we would have been told,' said Honorah, who grew up in Dún Laoghaire in the 1930s and 1940s. Remembered Debbie, 'we always thought [the midwife] brought the baby in the bag'. Nicola had no idea that her mother was expecting a baby in 1942, when Nicola was ten. Her father woke her in the morning with the news that a baby brother had arrived. When Edward was fifteen, his mother had a new baby: 'As I was coming up the road, one of my neighbour's daughters said, "You have a new brother."... I didn't even know my mother was pregnant.' Miscarriage was also not considered appropriate for conversation. 'If somebody lost a baby,' remembered Honorah, 'that was their business, it wasn't anybody else's, and it was never talked about.' This prudishness extended even to the agricultural sector, where children growing up on farms or in households with livestock were often deeply confused about aspects of their parents' work. A child might be dissuaded from asking why a hen was 'broody' or why a sow had to be brought to a boar in order to give birth. Nicky remembered embarrassed giggling in his family home when he returned one day with fertilised 'farm eggs' that he had purchased and planned to place under a hen.

* * *

By the late nineteenth century, people were increasingly interested in the welfare of children. In 1889, an Irish branch of the Society for the Prevention of Cruelty to Children was inaugurated.[16] Funding was raised by means of fêtes and garden parties, like that thrown by Lady Emily Arnott at Blackrock House on 25 July 1901.[17] But life for the poorest children remained both difficult and tenuous. Anthony's father, growing up in Glasthule in the early twentieth century, was one of seventeen, of whom six died as babies. Infant mortality was high in early independent Dublin, when some new mothers were so malnourished they could not breastfeed. Mortality rates were higher in Dublin than in British cities, while also higher than in rural areas of Ireland, presumably because of overcrowding and inadequate sanitation.[18] They were higher again among the babies of unmarried mothers. In 1923, the Annual Report of the Registrar General observed that one third of 'illegitimate' infants died, a rate six times higher than that of the children of married parents.[19] Until at least mid-twentieth century, the idea that children conceived outside marriage were congenitally weaker than others, because of their 'sinful' origins, was widespread, even informing public policy.[20] For children in institutions, or 'boarded out' to women who cared for them in their homes, mortality rates were appalling. In 1905, a 'boarding-out nurse', Sarah Tennant from Blackrock, was charged with having caused the death of baby Kathleen Redding, aged eleven weeks, by withholding nourishment. Kathleen was officially in the care of the Cottage Home in Kingstown, to which Sarah had been introduced as a respectable woman with a tidy home and an employed husband.[21]

Parents of children born prematurely or otherwise in delicate health strove to keep them alive in the days before intensive care in hospital. Bríd's mother, born in 1917, was a twin, much smaller than her sibling and expected to die. Her father spent as much time as possible with the baby tucked against his body, between his shirt and his flannel vest, and she started to grow and thrive. In 1922, an aunt of Janet's was a prematurely born twin. Weighing just two pounds, the prognosis for her was poor – but her family kept her warm 'in the side of the range' and, against the odds, she too survived. A combination of factors, including better maternal nutrition and the invention of antibiotics, caused the infant mortality rate to decline steadily throughout the twentieth century. Death rates, however, remained consistently higher among poorer children.[22]

Pre-independence, unmarried Irish women could not sue their children's fathers for maintenance (unlike English and Scottish unmarried mothers), resulting in numerous single mothers seeking refuge in workhouses. The only legal recourse available was for the guardian or parent of the woman in question to sue the father for 'loss of service' from the woman.[23] Long before the legalisation of abortion in Britain, unmarried pregnant Irish women and girls often fled on the mailboat.[24] Between 1926 and 1930, the Liverpool Society for the Prevention of International Traffic in Women and Children reported meeting 1,947 pregnant Irish women,[25] which can only have been a fraction of the total. Giving birth in Britain as an unmarried mother meant being away from prying eyes. They did not have to remain in an institution for so long and were more likely to be allowed to keep their children,[26] or to be able to give them up for adoption and go home without anyone realising what had happened. Some women sought help from charitable organisations like the London Crusade and Rescue Society, which in 1936 received 356 requests for help from Irish unmarried mothers, of whom at least eighty had conceived their children in Ireland.[27] In Ireland, before and after independence, unmarried mothers from lower-income backgrounds particularly were often institutionalised, separated from their children and permanently tainted with the 'stain' of pregnancy outside marriage.[28] The financial struggle of unwed mothers who tried to keep their children was unbearable. In 1930, the Free State introduced legislation requiring their fathers to pay modest rates of maintenance,[29] but many unmarried mothers had to pay maintenance fees if they wished to leave their children in institutional care, with the risk of the child being returned to them, revealing their status as unmarried mothers, if they defaulted.[30] The mortality rate then among children born outside wedlock was five times higher than for other children,[31] with many deaths occurring in institutions.[32]

* * *

In the nineteenth and early twentieth centuries, when contraception was either unavailable or unreliable, and stigma associated with unmarried motherhood (women in domestic service were generally dismissed if they became pregnant) was huge, infanticide was relatively common. Abortion rates were lower in Ireland than in England or Scotland, but rates of infanticide, concealment of childbirth and abandonment of babies were all higher.[33] While only twenty-nine women were found guilty of infanticide between 1850 and 1900, the authorities were informed of about one case every week.[34] At least 4,645 cases of infanticide, concealment or attempted infanticide occurred in Ireland from 1850 to 1900, and 900 cases of infanticide and concealment were known to the police from 1900 to 1919, according to Central Criminal Court records. In 1884, the *Irish Times* reported on the separate murders of two infant boys in Blackrock and Monkstown.[35] In 1890, a woman was found guilty of killing a baby girl at Summerhill Road, Kingstown.[36] A further 141 cases of infant murder and 858 of concealment occurred in Ireland from 1927 to 1950. In 1929, one judge described infanticide as a 'national industry'.[37] Rates are probably underestimated; at a time of generally high infant mortality, it was easy to 'allow' a child to perish through neglect or inadequate care, while evading the attention of the authorities; deceased babies and small children were often found to have no food in their digestive tracts.[38] Barbara's uncle was working as a signalman on the Dublin–Bray line in the early twentieth century. He related to his family an account of how, one evening, he saw two women crossing the railway line and heading towards the sea. They were carrying a bag, from which a whimpering sound emerged. Wondering if they were about to drown a puppy, he followed them and was on time to save the newborn baby they were intent on drowning.

Irish courts were often relatively lenient with women accused of infanticide, giving them punishments considerably less severe than the maximum penalties allowed.[39] Nonetheless, judges tended to send women convicted of these crimes to religious-run institutions,[40] and to place obstacles in the path of future efforts at rehabilitation. Many were sent to the Central Criminal Lunatic Asylum in Dundrum.[41] Many women involved in cases of infanticide were employed as domestic servants, and would have been dismissed from their positions if their pregnancies were discovered,[42] and possibly also cast out by their families. Recorded in 1980, May McCauliffe remembered a story her mother told her about her own young days (presumably mid-to-late nineteenth century, as May was elderly at the time of the recording). Speaking of unmarried mothers at the time, May's mother commented that 'if a girl had a baby… there was a red cross painted on her neck… if she wasn't married, she wasn't entitled to have a baby. They had to be exposed to the whole world.' If the girl and her boyfriend wished to marry, she was not allowed to wear a white dress, and the couple could be married not on the high altar but only in the vestry, in shame.[43] If there was nobody available to marry her, and she was poor, her prospects were appalling. This is the social context in which these tragic crimes must be considered. An Infanticide Act, allowing for these crimes to be treated differently to general murder and manslaughter, was passed in 1949.[44]

* * *

William Wilde wrote with incredible compassion in 1849 (while many of his peers were attempting to attribute the recent, devastating potato famine to God's wrath on an indolent people, and a hundred years before Irish law permitted infanticide to be viewed separately to murder in general) of the many young women who sought abortions: 'Can we

366

wonder,' he said, 'at the ignorant Irish girl wishing to conceal her shame by the destruction of her offspring, in a country acknowledged to be one of the most moral in Europe.' Through the late nineteenth and into the twentieth century, women with unwanted pregnancies frequently attempted to abort them, typically with herbal or other substances, by taking hot baths or 'mustard baths',[45] and by self-harming, such as throwing themselves off heights. Recorded in 1980 in her old age, May McCarville remembered hearing about these attempts ('terrible things') years before: 'putting [pregnant women] in a bath and give them... Gin and something with it to drink and it'd bring the [premature] birth of the baby quicker than any [surgical] abortion'.[46] More invasive attempts at termination were much more likely to result in detection and prosecution,[47] but they were available for those who could pay and were prepared to take the risk.[48] In 1944, Booterstown resident George Ian McCabe was found guilty of 'using an instrument with intent to procure the miscarriage of a woman'.[49] In 1956, Mary Anne Cadden, a well-known Dublin abortionist, was sentenced to death after dumping the body of a woman who had died during a procedure (the sentence was later commuted to life in prison).[50] Subsequent to the legalisation of abortion in Britain in 1967, and notwithstanding the abortion referendum of 1983, when 66.9 per cent of the electorate that voted passed a new amendment intended to copper fasten the illegality of abortion,[51] many Irish girls and women (about 200,000 between 1967 and the legalisation of abortion in Ireland in 2019) crossed the Irish Sea – generally on the Dún Laoghaire mailboat – to end their pregnancies. One contemporary counsellor described women getting off the boat in Britain, going straight to the nearest policeman and asking where they could go for an abortion.[52]

* * *

In 1849, William Wilde also wrote of women's attempts to 'procure barrenness' (prevent conception) by consuming milk in which a grass mouse had been boiled, or having their afterbirth 'buried under an elder tree and covered with a bowl by three old women'.[53] Many women would continue trying to limit the size of their families in the years that followed. The Free State banned contraception in early independence. Printed materials from overseas that discussed the topic or explained how contraception worked were censored.[54] In 1929, the Censorship of Publications Act banned publishing or selling any material about contraception; the work of Marie Stopes in Britain was one target, as she received letters from Irish people seeking advice on contraception, demonstrating high demand.[55] In 1930, the Censorship Board published the details of thirteen banned books; ten were about contraception.[56] Also in 1930, the Church of Ireland adopted a tolerant view of contraception, and the *Church of Ireland Gazette* published an editorial broadly supporting its use. Lower birth rates among Protestant couples suggests that many were already using it. Cyril's grandparents, non-Catholics, 'used to stock up on condoms when they went on holidays to Wales... once they got caught by customs... there was a bit of a giggle and [Grandad] said, "Well, we're not Catholic, it's nothing to do with us," and [the customs officers] said, "Fair enough. Just don't tell the boss."' The Vice-President of the Executive Council (the cabinet and *de facto* executive branch of government of the 1922–37 Free State), Seán T. O'Kelly, stated, 'the practise of contraception is contrary to Catholic doctrine and is abhorrent to the people of Saorstat Eireann', suggesting implicitly that those who used contraception were not Catholics and not even truly Irish.[57] It was also suggested that married women who used contraception were like prostitutes.[58] In 1935, the Criminal Law Amendment Act prohibited the sale or importation of contraceptives.[59] In 1951, Ireland threatened to withdraw from the World Health Organization when it adopted pro-contraception policies.[60]

Irish families, especially working-class families, continued to be large in independent Ireland, exacerbating poverty and poverty-related disease. A 1941 study demonstrated that Dublin children in very large families were typically smaller and lighter than children from smaller families, as many parents of large families were struggling to nourish

Customs men on Carlisle Pier, 1940s. Collection of Catherine Mullen, kind permission of Anna Scudds.

their children adequately.[61] The Irish birth rate remained unusually high by Western standards in the mid-twentieth century, but young couples were beginning to reduce their family sizes. In 1961, the birth rate among married women was still twice as high as in England, Wales, Belgium and Denmark, but from then it declined dramatically. Many women were using contraceptive pills and/or condoms despite the ban. Women working the Atlantic route as air hostesses often responded to their friends' requests for contraceptives, which they usually managed to get past customs. 'We didn't talk about sex,' one remembered, 'but we did talk about our lives and how our marriage affected us and like, "I don't *want* another baby!"' People going abroad on holidays were also often asked to bring contraceptives home. One recruitment agency was known for making discreet enquiries as to whether promising female candidates were Protestants, who might use contraception and be absent from work for maternity purposes less frequently. One young woman who was working in England at that time was petitioned by friends in Dún Laoghaire to bring 'French letters' home and she did, in abundance. She was also startled when her mother advised the next generation of women in the family that they no longer had to have one baby after another, but could take a contraceptive pill: '[Men] don't have to have their own way all the time, you know.' Women were getting bolder about discussing contraception publicly and challenging traditional views. 'Oh,' one of her peers remembered saying to her mother, 'the Pope hasn't got to feed a house full of children.'

In response to a *fait accompli*, Catholic-run hospitals began offering married couples advice on how to use the 'safe period' to limit family size. More people knew what to do to avoid having huge families. One young man saw his sister's calendar hanging on the wall, with lots of days ticked off. 'Mind your own business,' she said, when he asked who had so many appointments. Catholic teaching on artificial contraception remained unchanged, but the contraceptive pill was widely prescribed to married women as a 'cycle regulator', evading the ban. By 1966, 75 per cent of obstetricians were routinely prescribing it for 'social reasons', mostly to better-off women. Working-class women were much more likely than wealthier women to obey Church teaching, and also much more likely to have health problems relating to multiple births. Men's failure to cooperate with natural family-planning methods was a big problem. Doctors often refused to prescribe hormonal contraception to women who did not claim to suffer from irregular menstruation; working-class women, typically less well-read, did not always know they had to pretend to suffer with irregular periods, and generally attended state clinics, which were more likely to observe the Catholic rulings than the private doctors whom wealthier women could afford to visit.[62] In 1968, Pope Paul VI issued an encyclical reaffirming that Catholics must not use artificial contraception. In 1969, the first Family Planning Association clinic opened in Dublin, and increasingly – at least partly because of the women's rights activism discussed in 'Fighting and Fighting Back' – couples were importing contraceptives for personal use from Britain and Northern Ireland.[63] One man, in his twenties at the time, remembered women peers discussing the relative merits of different types of contraceptives, while he personally could buy contraceptives when the scout troop he led was on a visit to England. 'We actually made up our own mind,' he remembered. 'That was the beginning of the end of the Church.' The popular *Women's Way* magazine even published an advertisement for a device to help women to use the 'rhythm method' of contraception in defiance of Archbishop McQuaid, who stated that he did not approve.[64]

While most doctors were still men in the 1960s and 1970s, there were growing numbers of women GPs, some of whom are quoted in this book. Many of their women patients – like those of their male colleagues – were using the contraceptive pill ostensibly as a 'cycle regulator' long before contraception was legalised. Increasingly, young couples were having three or four children, and deciding this was enough: 'We just didn't want any more.' By the early 1970s, several Dublin hospitals and clinics were openly providing help with contraception. The Rotunda Fertility Clinic referred women on if they wanted an intra-uterine device or diaphragm,[65] and women who did not want more children and were refused contraception by the family's doctor could attend a city-centre clinic that assisted in preventing further pregnancies.

Family sizes dropped rapidly throughout the 1970s and would continue to do so thereafter. From 1979, contraceptives were legally available to married couples using them for '*bona fide*' family-planning purposes. One man who married in the early 1980s felt relaxed enough discussing contraception to approach his father, a doctor, to request a prescription for condoms. His father produced a prescription for 'a gross' (144). At the first chemist's shop he tried, he was rebuffed: '"How dare you come into this shop with that, get it out of here immediately!" And she was blessing herself as I'm going out. Throwing a bit of holy water after me.' However, he could obtain condoms at a pharmacy on George's Street in Dún Laoghaire from an embarrassed employee: 'a young lady in a white overall and she blushed. And she just indicated to me, like that, with her finger down to the back of the shop.'

* * *

Before the legalisation of adoption in Ireland in 1952, after foreign newspapers had run stories on the 'black market' in Irish babies,[66] and its implementation in 1953 – permitting the adoption of children up to the age of seven orphaned or born outside marriage[67] – adoption was arranged informally, often within families, to deal with orphans, inconvenient births or children whose parents struggled to feed them. As babies were plentiful, often little oversight was applied. Hugh Leonard described how his mother, after several stillbirths, simply procured a baby (Hugh) without even telling his father that they were going to adopt a child.[68] In 1951, a single mother placed her child in Temple Hill orphanage, under duress, but somehow managed to get him back a few months later. The baby was raised by her brother and sister-in-law as their own child, with his biological mother a frequent visitor to the home. When adoption was legalised, he was formally adopted. He would not learn the truth about his parentage until he was a grown man and his birth mother had died.

One important reason why adoption was legalised so late in Ireland was concern on the part of Catholics and non-Catholics alike, and particularly senior clerics,[69] that orphans and children born outside wedlock might be adopted by parents of the 'wrong' denomination. One desperate woman, unable to pay the maintenance fee a children's home demanded, wrote to John Charles McQuaid requesting help, stating that she might be left with no choice but to hand the care of her child over to Protestants.[70] Targeting unmarried mothers who had gone to Britain, Catholic organisations like the Catholic Protection and Rescue Society, concerned that Catholic women's babies might be adopted by Protestants, and that unmarried mothers might be vulnerable to Protestant proselytism, worked to repatriate them via the mailboat, and deposit them in mother and baby homes. The British authorities tended to cooperate, as pregnant Irish women and girls were seen as likely to be a burden on British taxpayers.[71] The work of the society contributed to the dramatic growth in births outside wedlock registered by the authorities annually between 1930 and 1943, from 1,850 to 2,574.[72] Other Irish babies were born overseas. Marianne's aunt became pregnant outside marriage and went to England to have the baby. A married sister offered to adopt the child, but the baby's mother was afraid of what her male relatives might do ('the men ruled the roost in all those poor families') and the baby was adopted abroad.

Between 1953 and 1972, 90 per cent of unmarried mothers gave their infants up for legal adoption.[73] Unmarried women who became mothers were still often represented as threats to the family and a destabilising societal influence. From the late 1960s, however, most single mothers gave birth in the same maternity hospitals as other women, rather than in special institutions, with a growing number keeping their babies, and their families increasingly unlikely to reject them. Declining hostility towards unmarried mothers related to more liberal views on sexuality generally, and was also a response to the liberalisation of abortion laws in Britain, and the fear that unmarried, pregnant Irish women would have abortions if Irish society rejected them.[74]

Women who had many children close in age, or who 'suffered from their nerves' after childbirth might give their child to be raised by grandparents or by an aunt in an informal fosterage arrangement. Marianne, for example, was raised by her maternal grandparents, who gave her a loving home and a happy childhood. Informal fosterage arrangements of this sort were common, particularly in large families. Charlotte's grandmother gave birth to twins in the early twentieth century, and gave one of them to her cousin – a childless woman – to raise, as she already had a very large family.

* * *

Before the mass adoption of infant formula, breastfeeding infants was an important element of women's work. The importance of breastfeeding was a central element to public health policy in early independence. The state recognised that breastfed infants fared better, amid high infant mortality, and that malnourished mothers were often unable to feed their infants. Therefore, public health and philanthropic organisations across Dublin strove to improve maternal and child nutrition.[75]

While women generally felt a need for modesty when they fed their babies, feeding infants in relatively public places where there were no men was unexceptional in the first decades of the twentieth century. Karen, who was born in 1928, remembered young mothers meeting at Seapoint on sunny days in the 1930s and sitting along a wall breastfeeding their babies together. At around the same time, women in Kimberly's family and their community in downtown Dún Laoghaire frequently wet-nursed one another's children when a mother had to go to work, as most of them did. It just made sense, in an area where everyone was quite poor, and the close-knit community got through life by helping one another and sharing resources. However, open breastfeeding even in all-women or intimate family circles seems to have gradually become unacceptable. Philo, growing up in Blackrock in the 1930s and 1940s, remembered all of her younger siblings being breastfed, and that her mother was extremely modest when feeding, retiring to her bedroom to feed the baby in private. Anthony recalled his mother, in the 1950s, encouraging him to come and meet his newborn sister while she was being breastfed, but he was too embarrassed to approach and left the room instead.

Levels of breastfeeding dropped from the 1950s,[76] alongside the growth in availability of alternative methods of feeding infants and the availability of clean water. In 1951, the Public Health Department of the Corporation of Dublin published a notice by James Harbison, the City Medical Officer, urging mothers to breastfeed their infants as the 'best and safest' way of feeding them and of avoiding gastrointestinal disease.[77] Guinness, a very big employer and an outlier regarding the supports available to its employees, provided free Guinness to employees' wives in the 1950s when they were breastfeeding. Isobel, whose children were born in the 1950s and 1960s, recalled that she used to be embarrassed when the 'diddy beer' was delivered. But by 1958, when Philo's first child was born, things were starting to change. She breastfed her first baby, but her subsequent children were bottle-fed. A benefit of bottle-feeding for her was that, when women were not supposed to breastfeed in public, an infant could be brought to a cinema matinee on a rainy afternoon, and kept quiet with a bottle.

By the 1960s, most women gave birth in hospitals, sometimes attended by staff with little practical knowledge of breastfeeding, while conventional medical wisdom started to stress the idea of feeding children according to a schedule, rather than on demand, as is typical for breastfed infants.[78] As breastfeeding was also used as a form of contraception, albeit unreliable,[79] the gradual increase in availability of contraception, even before legalisation, may also have been a contributing factor to its decline. The rate of breastfeeding was exceptionally low by global standards by the 1960s for reasons including anxiety about modesty, the popular association of breastfeeding with poverty, the advice of some younger medical professionals, the ready availability of formula and a feeling among many women that bottle-feeding offered them greater freedom. Older doctors and nurses typically still encouraged women to breastfeed, but young mothers often looked askance at this advice. Clodagh, whose children were born in Loughlinstown Hospital in the 1960s and 1970s, remembered one doctor being 'furious': 'going around the wards, and he said, "What do you think you have them [breasts] for?"' Younger medical staff often felt that formula was better, and advised mothers accordingly. Emily became a mother in the 1960s, and opted to bottle-feed on her doctor's advice: 'He thought it was better to bottle-feed your baby because you knew exactly what it was getting.' Eve, whose children were born from the mid-1960s to the mid-1970s, breastfed her children, because 'I was rather ahead of the times. I was reading the books.' As she was the only woman in the ward doing it, however, 'I remember it being very awkward and very stressful.' Vera gave birth to her first child in the late 1960s and found that the medical staff could not help her with breastfeeding: 'She said, "Imagine you're in the jungle, what would you do?" And I said, "Well, you know, could you help me a little bit more?" and she said, "No I can't, I have no experience."' Aileen's children were born at the same time as Vera's, and she also remembered most women opting to bottle-feed, as did she: 'They asked you which did you want to do, and I just said "bottle".' Ita, a young mother then, remembered breastfeeding as 'a taboo subject... like cancer'. By the 1970s, breastfeeding had become a minority practice, was often seen as quite exotic or old-fashioned and was even considered by some women to be bad for babies, or bad for women, while others saw breastfeeding as additional labour, and bottles and formula as modern innovations making their lives easier.[80] Emer became a mother in 1976. Of all the women on the ward, just one or two were breastfeeding. Emer was one, and she was supported in this by the matron of the hospital. Elinor also became a mother in the mid-1970s. She had stopped working outside the home and formed a group of friends with other young mothers. Very few of them breastfed their babies: 'you were almost apologetic if you breastfed,' remembered Elinor. She did, because she had a much younger sibling whom she had seen being fed by their mother, and she knew what to do.

The first Irish branch of the La Leche League, an organisation promoting breastfeeding and supporting suckling mothers, was founded by Nora Leach, a woman then resident in Ticknock.[81] Nora, a biologist and a mother of seven children, had heard about the league in the United States and wanted to address the low rates of breastfeeding in Ireland, where women were often getting poor advice and inaccurate information. The first La Leche League meeting in Ireland was held in Dún Laoghaire in 1966.[82] In 1979, it put on a seminar, 'Breastfeeding in the Modern World', at the Royal Marine Hotel.[83] By the 1990s, while breastfeeding rates remained notably low in Ireland, breastfeeding mothers were increasingly likely to feed their babies in public. For those who had grown up when this was considered a private activity, it could be startling. Edward, whose siblings were born in the 1930s and 1940s, when his own mother fed them in the privacy of her bedroom, remembered the first time he saw a woman breastfeeding her baby in public, in a small coffee shop: 'I was astonished.'

* * *

The availability of medical care in the coastal areas developed in parallel with the development of the harbour and the subsequent development of the area. Conflict between tradition and science could sometimes come to a head: in the eighteenth century, the era of 'bodysnatchers', medical students, or people working for the medical schools, visited graveyards in the areas near Dublin seeking cadavers to use in training.[84] The graveyard at Kilgobbin was said to have been the site of the exchange of gunshots between a local man protecting the grave of a recently deceased parishioner, and a group of medical students intent on removing him,[85] and those responsible for Carrickbrennan graveyard in Monkstown are said to have converted the ruined church into a watchtower in order to catch the graverobbers in action.[86]

In 1831, the Kingstown Dispensary was established, and a hospital for cholera (there was a cholera epidemic at the time) opened in Glasthule. In 1834, the Rathdown Dispensary and Hospital opened. From 1874, the Sisters of Mercy ran a hospital, St Michael's. State provision of healthcare remained inadequate in independence, with most provided by religious organisations, or in institutions with a strong religious ethos. Religious orders dominated the management of Catholic institutions and Protestants often served on the committees of Protestant-ethos hospitals, like Joyce's father, who was on the committee of the Adelaide on Peter Street in the city centre.

In 1851, the Medical Charities Act reorganised the dispensary system and set new laws and regulations. The act divided Ireland into 723 dispensary districts[87] and allowed 'any poor person' resident in the area of a dispensary to access medication and medical advice on the presentation of a 'ticket' provided by a member of the dispensary committee.

Linden Convalescent Home, c.1865–1914. The Linden was opened by the Sisters of Charity as a convalescent home in 1868. It served as an auxiliary military hospital from 1915 to 1916, and from the mid-twentieth century often employed young girls who had grown up in St Joseph's Orphanage in Dún Laoghaire. Photograph by Robert French. The Lawrence Photograph Collection, National Library of Ireland.

Different-coloured tickets indicated whether the patient would be cared for at the clinic, or if they needed care at home.[88] For many on lower incomes, their only contact with formal medical care was through the dispensary system.[89] Patients living in or near urban areas were more likely to get effective treatment quickly, as isolated rural dispensaries often catered to scattered populations over large areas, and doctors often had to order medications from Dublin.[90]

Eden, born in 1924, grew up in an apartment above the Dún Laoghaire dispensary, at 99 Patrick Street, where her father worked. The dispensary had two surgeries for doctors. Eden's father, who was employed by the Rathdown Board of Assistance – still based in the old workhouse premises – administered the dispensary. In working in healthcare, he was following in the footsteps of his own father, who had operated a horse-drawn ambulance for the Loughlinstown Workhouse, before it became a district hospital in 1920. He opened the doors at about half past nine in the morning, admitted the patients, and prepared everything for the doctors, who arrived at ten. Red tickets were given to patients who needed home visits, and black to those seen at the dispensary. He dispersed food vouchers and milk and coal dockets to the needy. Very occasionally, small sums of money were given to families in need. Births, deaths and marriages were registered, and Eden's father also had to visit the sick and needy in their homes – for which he was given one of the first local cars to use. From 1970, public and private patients were treated by the same family doctors, and public health nursing was provided by health boards. Patients with medical cards whose incomes were below a certain limit were entitled to free consultations and medicines.

* * *

Contagious diseases, particularly tuberculosis, were major sources of premature mortality. At the turn of the twentieth century, half of all deaths between the ages of fifteen and thirty-five were from tuberculosis. While the situation was improving in many countries, in Ireland it was deteriorating, leading some to wonder if the Irish might be naturally susceptible.[91] High levels of poverty and squalor were contributing factors. The Women's National Health Association, providing aftercare to patients on their release from sanatoria, reported that poor patients typically deteriorated soon after returning to 'their wretched surroundings'.[92] Tuberculosis grew even worse in the 1940s for reasons including the fuel rationing that made it harder for county tuberculosis officers and district nurses to do their work.[93] Even when patients did not die, a bout could blight their life forever. Catherine was in hospital for eight months with tubercular meningitis. When she recovered, her parents were advised to keep her out of school for three years, as the scholarship class she was in might have kept her brain 'too active', contributing to her illness. Despite being a high achiever, she never caught up. Booterstown local Paul Lyng recalled public efforts, in the 1940s, to eliminate outbreaks of scabies, and compulsory screening for tuberculosis in schools: 'There was a boy sitting beside me in school, who told me he was coughing up blood and had no intention of going in for his X-ray, so I told the nurse about him… He was taken away to Peamount [sanatorium].'[94] Tuberculosis devastated many families. Feargal's mother

Above: Little Nano O'Brien, on the right, died of tuberculosis aged twelve, shortly after her Confirmation, and was waked at the family dairy in Glasthule. In the 1930s, TB was widespread. Kind permission of the O'Brien family.

Right: Condolence letter to the family of Nano O'Brien. Courtesy of O'Brien Family.

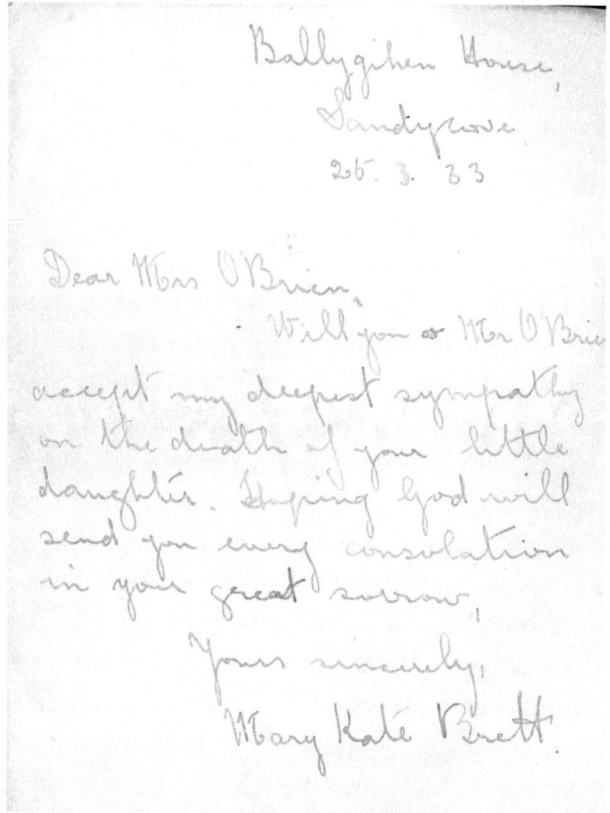

was also sent to the sanatorium in Newcastle. He was four when she left, and ten when she was sent home to die, so he barely remembered her. Her children were sent to relatives in the Barnacullia area, and later the boys were sent to an orphanage, St Dominic's, in the city centre. Their father visited once every fortnight or so. Heartbreakingly, on a day trip with the orphanage to Shankill, where his father was now living, Feargal and another little boy slipped away to look at Feargal's father's home. They peered in the window, and saw him, but did not dare to call out a greeting. Of course, they were in trouble later on for having left the group. Fortunately, the children left the orphanage after two or three years, but their mother's tragic death, and its aftermath, had changed their childhoods forever. Pádraic's father died at fifty-six, in the 1940s, after battling with tuberculosis for years. It was a trauma for Pádraic not just because he had lost his father, but also because he felt he had to relinquish his dream of immigrating to Canada – his mother would have been left all alone.

Not everyone died. Molly's parents originally met, in the 1940s, because of her father's family's experience of tuberculosis. He was a teenager from Ranelagh, near the city centre, and, as he was considered delicate, the family was advised to move him to higher ground, with cleaner air. Molly's grandmother was a farmer in Kilternan who took in lodgers, and she provided a place for him to stay during the summers, where he met and fell for the daughter of the house. Roberta's mother contracted tuberculosis in the late 1940s and, because the family had means, went to a sanatorium in Switzerland, where she was treated for several years. Sandra's father suffered from tuberculosis and was sent to a sanatorium in Newcastle, and on his return consigned to a chalet in the family garden, where he could live in the fresh air. The chalet was minimally heated, so he went to bed with 'a stone hot jar'. When he was cured, the government took the chalet back to give to someone else. When Philo's sister was diagnosed with tuberculosis, her mother 'nearly lost her reason', sure that the girl would die. She spent ten months at a sanatorium and made a good recovery. By 1955 – by when the number of beds available for tuberculosis patients had increased by 50 per cent since 1943, and hospitals and sanatoria were treating patients with effective medications – the incidence of tuberculosis was dropping. By the end of the 1950s, the BCG vaccination had dramatically reduced the incidence of the disease, and residential sanatoria were no longer necessary.[95]

Other infectious diseases were also treated as major causes for concern. Robbie came down with scarlet fever in 1951, aged seven. As soon as he was diagnosed, an ambulance was dispatched and he was taken to Clonskeagh Fever Hospital, where he would spend a month with no visitors, and his bedroom was sterilised and sealed to avoid the disease spreading in the family.

Rickets, a disease caused by vitamin D deficiency, was widespread among the poor of Dublin, particularly in the inner city, where children with the condition developed soft bones that became deformed if

Nurses promoting the Irish Sweepstakes. Lexicon Library Postcard Collection.

they were left untreated. Ella Webb, one of an emerging generation of women doctors, and a campaigner for women's suffrage and women's healthcare, founded the Children's Sunshine Home in Leopardstown in 1925 following the purchase of a premises together with Letitia Overend, a prominent philanthropist from Airfield, Dundrum. Initially caring for twenty patients, it was entirely dependent on charitable donations. In 1935, it admitted ninety-seven children, of whom fifty-nine were cured and eight improved. In 1943, 173 of out of 1,000 Dublin children suffered from rickets,[96] the health profile of Dubliners having deteriorated during the war years. After the Second World War, improved knowledge of the condition and the fortification of flour caused the incidence of rickets to fall.

Access to dental care was largely income-dependent. People of all social classes, but especially the poor, ate a lot of sugar-rich food. For people with low incomes, it often made sense to have their teeth replaced with dentures as soon as their dental health started to fail. In the early twentieth century, Eden's grandmother waited until her teeth 'went bad' and then had them all removed: 'before she went to work, she went to the dentist, and she had all her teeth pulled, and she went to work with a mouth full of cotton wool to bite on for the day'.

* * *

Until relatively recently, both physical and intellectual disability, and chronic illness and certain diseases like tuberculosis, were regarded as shameful and often seen as a stigma on a family. Disability was, of course, relatively common. Catherine commented that, in her childhood in the 1940s and 1950s, it seemed that many babies were born that 'weren't right', and usually died young. Her own mother lost four baby boys. A disabled family member might impact negatively on the rest of the family's marriage and employment prospects. There were also concerns that a particular condition might be hereditary. Until well into the twentieth century, people sometimes felt that there was something 'wrong' with a child because of the mother's behaviour during her pregnancy, that the disability was a divine judgement or punishment. Stigma could be attached even to relatively minor disabilities. Jennifer's great-aunt, living in the early twentieth century, had a leg that was 'shorter than the other' due to a congenital condition, but the family told people that she had suffered a bicycle accident, as they worried that a disability might reflect badly on the family as a whole. Also in the early twentieth century, Marianne's grandmother had a very large family whom she was raising on her husband's salary from his job with the mailboat. Money was very tight in their Glasthule home, so when Pears Soap held a 'Miss Pears' competition for the most beautiful little girl, she entered one of her daughters. There was a cash prize, and the family needed money. When the child won, Pears arranged for the girl to wear a gorgeous outfit for the publicity photograph. She died shortly afterwards, and the feeling in the extended family was that her mother had tempted fate by drawing so much attention to her: 'A curse,' said Marianne, who grew up hearing the story of her tragic aunt, 'but that's the way the men would think.' The child's mother would have to live with the guilt.

Families with sufficient resources could outsource disabled children to the better live-in institutions where they were cared for reasonably well, or hire live-in carers for them. Children living with significant levels of disability in families with low incomes had fewer options. Until the second half of the twentieth century, most disabled people and their families were left very much to cope on their own. Eva's great-uncle was born deaf, because of which he was effectively mute, as he received no special training or education. He was often referred to as 'retarded' and never had a commercial job, although he had no intellectual disability and was a talented carpenter. With no income, Jack depended on family for support.

Stigma also applied to most forms of mental illness. The most seriously mentally ill were confined to workhouses or asylums in the nineteenth and early twentieth century, and then psychiatric hospitals, but many with mental health issues suffered largely alone, well into the twentieth century. Some with severe mental illness, well-known in their communities, could be tolerated or considered figures of fun, such as the 'man who thought he was Napoleon' discussed in 1980 by James Nolan of Dundrum, who also stated that deceased mentally ill people were buried in a special part of the local graveyard, reserved for this use. Those with milder forms of mental illness, such as depression or postnatal depression, could suffer too. There was little general understanding of mental illness, and few legal protections for those afflicted.

As in other areas of healthcare, many with severe mental illness and disability were cared for in religious-run institutions. In 1882, the St John of God order, for example, purchased a large house in Stillorgan accompanied by thirty acres of land. Initially run by French brothers who spoke no English, gradually the premises grew and attracted Irish brothers. By 1899, it was caring for almost 100 patients, with impressive rates of successful treatment for a range of mental disorders. By 1926, a novitiate for Ireland was run from Stillorgan, and from 1931, the institution was run as a home, St Augustine's, for boys with intellectual disabilities (then known as 'mental defectives') and was reported in the *Irish Independent* as possessing 'every modern convenience'. By 1957, the brothers were caring for over a thousand patients around Ireland, and in the 1960s they expanded into a new premises, Dunmore House.[97]

Access to education gradually improved for young people with disabilities in the second half of the twentieth century. Debbie's daughter was partially sighted. When the government introduced free secondary education, Debbie had to grapple with the authorities to ensure that her daughter also had access to a good education rather than the typical training in basketwork available to the blind. Her daughter would be educated in England, as there was no provision then for second-level education for the blind.

* * *

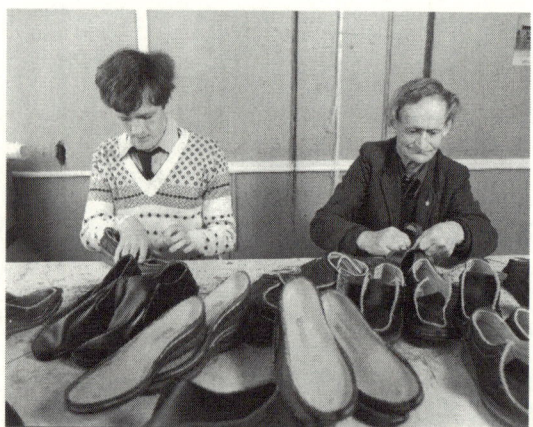

Residents of a St John of God centre engaged in hand-work, 1970s. Kind permission of Br Finnian Gallagher, St John of God Heritage Centre, Stillorgan.

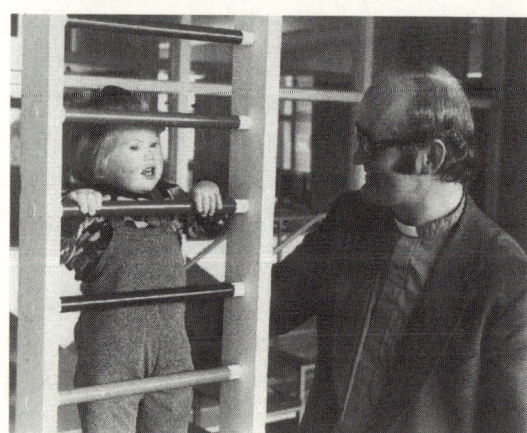

Brother Maurice O'Brien and a young resident of the St John of God centre at Dunmore House, 1970s. Kind permission of Br Finnian Gallagher, St John of God Heritage Centre, Stillorgan.

Residents of the St John of God centre in Glenageary clearing ground to prepare for horticulture, 1970s. Kind permission of Br Finnian Gallagher, St John of God Heritage Centre, Stillorgan.

For much of modern history, traditional and science-based medicine coexisted, sometimes in conflict, but more often operating in parallel. Knowledge and use of traditional remedies and cures persisted long after the availability (for those who could afford it) of science-based medicine. These include the use of medicinal plants (Dalkey Island, for example, was known for the medicinal plants that grew there),[98] moulds and other substances, as well as poultices and sacred items including holy water and holy medals. Thus, folk medicine occurred along a spectrum that incorporated actions broadly similar to science-based medicine (poultices, tonics, etc.) to those related to religious belief and practice (scapulars and so forth) and to magical practices (such as the use of special stones for treating warts). Practitioners of folk medicine might use all three approaches to an ailment in a single treatment, or at least incorporate all three into their repertoire.

Kevin's grandmother, from Blackrock, was well-known in the locality as a handywoman who helped to deliver infants, laid out the dead and sometimes administered traditional remedies. He stated his view that she may have been attracted to the work following the tragic death of most of her family over a few years encompassing the period of the influenza pandemic following the First World War. She delivered many children, including at least one of her own grandchildren. Regarding other forms of healthcare, Kevin said that her skills were perhaps not as good as she hoped. One of her own daughters lost an eye after being treated with a poultice of some sort – as was common then – rather than visiting the doctor, which was expensive. Roy remembered a family member initially being treated for ringworm by a traditional healer (and later being cured by the local doctor). Caroline's grandmother, a traditional midwife and handywoman, used many traditional cures, including bread poultices, which were widely used: 'children got boils and all years ago… you had to lance the boil or… a bread poultice that would be hot, and you'd put that onto a cloth and put it on to try and draw… out the boil'. Bread poultices were widely used generally, and many have memories of being treated with them as children. Janet's mother grew up in Limerick before moving to Dublin and marrying a man from downtown Dún Laoghaire.

Because, Janet said, she grew up among Palatines,* she had learned all their traditional cures, and used some to treat her own children. When Janet badly burned her arm as a child, she was successfully treated with a jar of ointment provided by a Palatine acquaintance from Limerick. Henry, from Shankill, reported the widespread use of nettles for the treatment of aches and pains such as arthritis. The afflicted person beat their own skin with nettles, as the stings were supposed to help with the pain. One woman he knew used to stuff an old pair of tights with young nettles and use this to sting herself all over, hoping to obtain some relief from her arthritis. Nano remembered two local men who had traditional cures, one apparently for oral thrush, and another for styes of the eye and boils. Sineád's maternal grandfather – born in 1905 – was her primary caregiver as a child in the 1970s and 1980s. Her grandfather knew how to gather nutritious nettles and wild garlic around their Blackrock estate and stew them. When Niamh and her siblings had sore throats, he scraped moss off some old leather boots that he kept in the back garden and made a tea of it for them. When the children had chilblains on their fingers or toes, they were instructed to pee on them, and when they got worms, he dosed them with turpentine. Ingrid's grandmother treated ganglion cysts by pounding them with a heavy book, ideally a Bible. Austin's father had spent most of his life in farming, moving to Shankill for a more suburban life only in his later years, when Austin was a child. He retained knowledge of some of the traditional cures he had grown up with, particularly the use of oak tree bark soaked in water for the treatment of wounds.

Warts, which until recently were notoriously difficult to treat, have often been the target of a range of folk medical practices. James Goggins from Glasthule, a student at the Christian Brothers School in Dún Laoghaire, recorded information in the academic year 1937–8 about a

---

* People of German origin who fled the Palatinate states in the early 1700s. About 200 families settled in Ireland, with many retaining a distinctive Palatine culture until into the nineteenth century.

stone cross that gathered water, believed to cure warts.[99] Gene, growing up in Kilternan in the 1960s and a young adult in the 1970s, had a neighbour who was the seventh son of a seventh son, and locally well-known for having the gift of curing warts in both animals and humans: 'he'd get a little bit of a straw, and he put a cross on the wart,' Gene remembered, 'and those warts would disappear.' Gene himself had his warts treated as a child: 'Within three months, three days, three weeks or three months, your warts will disappear.' Lina's parents, who both originated from rural areas, were knowledgeable about folk cures: 'if you have a wart, you get a sewing needle with thread in it and you dangle it around… if there were any snails around, get the snail and put it on the wart'. Rosa's grandmother, originally from Monaghan, had a traditional cure for warts, involving rubbing a snail on the wart, and then keeping the snail in a jar for a certain number of days. Opposite the White Church, a Church of Ireland church at the bottom of Kilmashogue Lane, the locally well-known Wart Stone remains. It was – and is – renowned for the supposed curative properties of the water that gathers in its concavity, traditionally used for curing warts. Tim, who grew up nearby, remembered it being used in the 1960s and 1970s.

Kate's great-grandmother was renowned in Sallynoggin for laying out the dead and assisting women giving birth, and for her knowledge of traditional cures and remedies. She was a strong character about whom stories are still told. 'They seemed to love her,' Kate recounted: 'they used to call her "nurse", but she wasn't a nurse… children used to come to the door, and they'd say, "Mother wants to know will you give us something, my brother has the whooping cough." And she'd give them a spider in a matchbox, and she'd say, "When the spider dies, the whooping cough will be gone."' Mick's father, a Traveller, had a great interest in traditional remedies. After the family settled in Dalkey, Mick's father befriended an elderly neighbour who made potions and remedies that she offered to the family for childhood complaints. By then, the 1970s and 1980s, the use of traditional remedies for most common complaints was becoming much rarer.

While the general trend throughout the twentieth century was for folk medicine to wane, while science-based medicine became the norm, the relationship between science-based and folk medicine was often more nuanced than one might imagine. While all GPs and health practitioners wanted to ensure that the sick obtained evidence-based medical care, others felt that there was a place for at least some folk-healing practices too. Rebecca worked as a GP in the Shankill area, and was aware of, and interested in, an array of folk remedies still in use in the uplands in the 1960s and 1970s. She had a patient who 'used to bring me down a marvellous mixture every year of beetroot juice and something else, nettles probably. And I was very interested, because of course, they're terrific… she would drink it solemnly every spring and dose everyone.'

The tradition of using blood to treat shingles, a common disease caused by the varicella-zoster virus, is remarkably persistent in this area, as elsewhere in Ireland.[100] Generally, families thought to have a 'cure' for shingles are Keoghs or Cahills; a tradition that has very long roots in Ireland and is thematically linked to similar folk-medical practices from all over the world, and since ancient times. Typically, the cure is thought to pass down the male line, from father to son. Tim's father 'rubbed' people with his own blood to treat shingles all his adult life.* When he was old, and Tim was a young adult, he said, 'Tim, you're going have to take over.' At first, Tim was reluctant. It seemed at odds with his modern lifestyle and education: 'I had been to London… I was into Led Zeppelin… I thought I was more scientific. I was doing science in school. My father [an older father, born in 1898] was a throwback to a different era. And I thought it could never work with me.' But Tim's father talked him through what he would need to do: remove blood from his finger, rub it on the afflicted person's rash, and say a prayer – any

---

* Blood may have been used in ritual contexts by pre-*Homo sapiens* hominids, suggesting the very deeply rooted association of the substance with magical thinking; see J.B. Hutchings, 'Blood in Anthropology and Folklore', in K. Nassau (ed.), *Colour for Science, Art and Technology* (Amsterdam: Elsevier, 1997), p. 197.

prayer – with them. Finally, he was to say, 'Storm the heavens' and recite a prayer to St Anthony.

* * *

The lives of the residents of Dún Laoghaire-Rathdown were, of course, punctuated by happy events marking a child's gradual journey to adulthood and so forth. Rites of passage such as baptism, Holy Communion and Confirmation were important elements of faith and indicators of where an individual fitted into the broader community. Baptism was, of course, essential. Until the mid-twentieth century it was common for children to be quickly baptised shortly after birth, often without the mother. Among Catholics, the idea that unbaptised infants who died were not admitted to heaven was a frequent source of sorrow and anxiety. Recorded in 1980, May McAuliffe recalled how, during a difficult birth, her son was given a 'lay baptism' even before his full body had left hers in case he died during childbirth.[101]

Children who had just made Holy Communion, for example, participated in Corpus Christi processions, alongside confraternities, sodalities, the Catholic Boys Scouts and the Children of Mary. While of course Holy Communion and Confirmation were significant events in any child's life, festivities relating to these events were generally modest until growing prosperity enabled more families to throw lavish parties.

Rites of passage also conferred certain social and legal rights. Young couples, on marriage, could freely live together without disapprobation and have a family, while marriage conferred on men the obligation of providing for a family, and on women the need to care for the children of the marriage, which in many cases also meant giving up paid work outside the home.

As well as formal liturgical rituals, rites of passage often also involved a range of folk traditions to mark the event and make it special. A tradition known as 'grushies' was observed in some areas, whereby the couple getting married would throw money in the air, resulting in all the

Members of the Ingram and Mac Giolla Phádraig families of Blackrock celebrating First Holy Communion Day in 1976. By this point, suburban housing estates as we now know them were increasingly well-established, and growing numbers of families lived in comfortable three- and four-bedroom homes with private gardens and access to shared green spaces. Courtesy Miriam Ingram.

children scrambling to retrieve the coins. Remembered Noeleen C: 'the groom would have a handful of money and he'd throw all this money towards the kids. And all the kids would rush to try and get as much money as they could. And that was called a grushie.'

For many, particularly men, the excessive consumption of alcohol was considered a crucial aspect of an active social life and an essential element of the celebration of most rites of passage. It was also, of course, identified as one of the great social scourges. Alcoholism was perceived as common among all social and cultural groups throughout the nineteenth and twentieth centuries, with alcohol at the centre of most major life events, from birth to death. Various organisations strove to reduce alcohol consumption. The Temperance Hall of Kingstown, multidenominational and non-political, was founded in 1892. Despite all these efforts, alcohol retained significant social and ritual functions at all rites of passage throughout the modern period.

Patrons in the Punchbowl, Booterstown, c.1960. Lexicon Library Postcard Collection.

* * *

Occasionally, an exceptional event, like a period of unusually bad weather, could supersede the usual course of individual and collective journeys through life. These events often stand out in oral histories, precisely because they were unusual and interesting. They become a focus around which memories can cluster – 'before' or 'after' the event occurred. In 1946, for example, an exceptionally wet and difficult summer resulted in farmers struggling to gather their harvests. As this threatened not just their livelihoods but also the Dublin food supply – while there was still rationing, following the Emergency – urbanites and suburbanites were encouraged to volunteer. With much of Dún Laoghaire-Rathdown near farmland, many young people offered their services, and trucks were provided to bring them to farms.[102] A year later, the winter of 1947 challenged rural people even further, when the Big Snow cut many of them off from towns and services and made it impossible for them to reach a doctor in case of emergency. Residents in areas like Kilternan,

Barnacullia and Glencullen were cut off for weeks, sometimes with disastrous consequences. Brian, born in the early 1930s, remembered it as if it were yesterday. The weather had already been very cold before the snow started falling, so it landed on hard, frosty ground, 'and it stayed on top of the ground for a week until the following Saturday'. Then it started to snow again. 'Not terrible heavy,' Brian recalled, 'but the ground was so hard with the light snow.' It snowed all night and right up to lunchtime the following day. By then, the roads in the uplands were blocked. Local men were employed by the county council to make tracks through the snow, but because of the strong southeast wind – 'a black wind' – the roads filled up with snow as quickly as they could clear it. 'My God,' Brian remembered, 'the snow drift! I heard someone saying, it must have been… thirty feet high going down to Glencullen.' The exceptionally bad harvest of 1946 exacerbated the hardship considerably, as farmers' stock of hay and other feed was lower than usual, and their own pantries less full. Brian's family, who owned one of the bigger local farms, fared relatively well, but a nearby farm lost twenty-seven cattle to starvation. Florrie, from the Glencullen area, remembered her family finding many cattle dead and covered with snow on the hillside. Charlie's little sister, just five years old, contracted pneumonia and died in her uplands home. The snow was so heavy it was impossible to hold a funeral and the little girl was removed from her home by a lorry, the only vehicle that could handle the conditions. 'They got a lorry onto the roads,' Charlie recalled, 'and threw her coffin in the back… I'd say my father probably went down [to the cemetery] but that's probably all. Nobody else could go near it.' Gareth was a teenager growing up in Barnacullia when the snow isolated much of the uplands. It was so cold, he remembered, that it was impossible to dig graves to bury the dead. While the terrible weather lasted, coffins were lain on galvanised iron sheets and dragged across the snow to the graveyards, where they were left to wait until the ground had defrosted. Joseph was a little boy of six, growing up in the uplands area of Glencullen, the winter of the Big Snow. His mother managed to get him out of the mountains and into the city centre to stay with relatives, as it would be easier for them to keep their home warm than for householders in rural areas. Joseph remembered it well. Many foster children, regarded as children whom nobody wanted, were raised in Glencullen, and he worried that his parents had given him away. It is a clear memory nearly eighty years later: 'it was off the South Circular Road, and I was looking at [a] little robin hopping along, and I'd start to cry'.

For families in urban areas, keeping their houses warm during the big freeze of 1947 could be a challenge, as many had no access to firewood, and coal was growing scarce. Philo, thirteen then, and her brother pushed a handcart together from their home in Blackrock to the coal yard in Dún Laoghaire to get fuel. The residents of her housing estate, many of whom worked full- or part-time for the local Vincentian nuns, were also allowed to source firewood on the convent grounds. Henry's grandfather, from Shankill, died and Henry could not attend his funeral, as he had no shoes and the weather was far too cold to go barefoot. Nicky was in his final year of primary school – Confirmation year – during the Big Snow. Most children were kept at home but, as it was considered important for the candidates for Confirmation to attend school, a trench was built all the way from Goatstown to Kilmacud so that they could get to class through the snow and they were assured they 'wouldn't get slapped' if they attended lessons. About twelve of the children made it to school, where they huddled around a 'miserable fire' studying the *Handbook of Religious Knowledge.* For those who could afford to keep their homes adequately warm, the cold weather was less of a challenge. One Booterstown resident remembered that 'It was very hard for our parents but lovely for us children. We loved the snow and ice and the slides. It was very difficult for the horses, as then all deliveries of bread, milk, turf, etc., were made by horse-drawn carts.'[103] Kevin, aged seven, enjoyed the freeze in his home area in Blackrock: 'there was... two hills... we would put water on them... and it would freeze over very quickly. So we had slides for the night... and into the next day.'

∗ ∗ ∗

Some families have stories about portents of doom; we have already mentioned the banshee, Ireland's best-known doom-crier, but there are other traditions too, which speak loudly of the central place that death and dying hold in the collective psyche. One family was said to be followed by a 'dead watch' and by a dog crying: they would hear the sound of a watch ticking and/or the sound of a dog crying whenever a member of the family had died; the interviewee herself heard the dog crying before the birth of one of her own children, a boy who only lived for three and a half months.[104] Other recorded traditions include the belief that seeing a 'headless' coach was a prediction of the viewer's own death.[105] Charlotte's family was said to experience a warning before a death in the family, generally in the form of a stopped clock or a knock on the door. Another family reported the experience of a dog becoming very upset around his owner for no apparent reason, only for the person in question to die suddenly, hours later.

Until well into the twentieth century, it was much more common for people to die young, and death was a much more quotidian affair, with its associated rites and rituals deeply embedded in everyday life. Nicky remembered checking the 'notifiable diseases' in the *Evening Mail* to see who was sick or dying as a regular ritual in most homes, and Ronnie Drew, raised by his grandparents in Dún Laoghaire, recalled that funerals were regarded as 'a big source of entertainment'.[106] In many areas, particularly working-class neighbourhoods, laying out the dead was done by local women, who performed the task from a sense of community spirit (these were often, but not always, women who also helped their neighbours to give birth). They were the custodians of an ancient tradition: the tasks involved in caring for a dead body have for centuries been the domain of women.[107] After death, various customs were widely observed: stopping the clocks in the house to note the time of death, dressing the bed in white,[108] opening the window to let the spirit of the deceased out,[109] closing the curtains and covering mirrors. As in Ireland generally, funeral customs were an important aspect of traditional culture, with working-class and rural areas in particular often observing quite exuberant practices relating to death, and various undertaking businesses thriving across the region.

Ingrid remembered how certain Glasthule women, in the 1940s and 1950s, kept white sheets and crucifixes in their homes to always be ready. When someone died, they gathered these items, went to the deceased's home, covered all the mirrors and prepared them for their final journey. When the corpse was ready, Ingrid remembered, all the local children dropped in to visit. 'It was a great thing,' she remembered, '[to] see them laid out.' Children were not generally scared of the dead then, she said. Certain people, who could be women or men, were locally known for leading prayers – typically the Rosary – at a wake. Christine's aunt laid out the dead in Dalkey, making them presentable for the wake, and preparing their rooms with a table dressed as an altar with a fresh altar cloth, a wooden crucifix and candles. Clodagh's mother did this too, and was always prepared: 'She had a suitcase kept under the bed and it contained a white sheet, beautiful pillowcases… tiny little pleats in a frill all around the pillowcase and a white quilt… a little tray with a crucifix and a little dish… a piece of palm… holy water.' Emer's grandmother was called on to carry out these services. She kept a pile of shrouds in the bottom of her wardrobe in Monkstown Farm, to be always prepared. By the time the priest and/or undertaker had arrived, she had prepared the body: 'got them all washed and dressed and cleaned them and then put the shroud on. And then the priest… said all the prayers'.

Conor remembered the approach to death in the urban area of Dún Laoghaire, where wakes and funerals were often public affairs, particularly in close-knit working-class neighbourhoods. Anyone who wanted could enter a home where a death had recently occurred to 'pay their respects to the corpse'. He often did so himself: 'I remember standing beside dead people and just wondering about their stillness, and what had happened… looking at a dead granny or something.' When Philo was growing up in Blackrock in the 1940s, a local teenaged boy died. Curious, Philo and her brother went to see him. 'That was a big thing,' she remembered, 'to go in and see the body.' Their dog went along too, and Philo remembered the kindness of the boy's mother, who let the dog in and gave him a bowl of water in the very room where the dead child lay. Denny remembered his grandmother's funeral, when he was a child of about eight in the 1950s. A local woman led the public mourning: 'She more or less cried for the whole time... she was there to lead,' Caroline remembered, as a child, being terribly curious to see a family friend's deceased baby. The bereaved family, who lived in Sallynoggin, made her very welcome: 'I was brought in to see the baby. It was a little doll. It was gorgeous. And even though I was a young child myself, I was sat down at the table and given tea and biscuits.' Generally, she recalled, in those days, wakes and funerals were big affairs in working-class neighbourhoods, with children alternating between playing in the street and running inside to 'show a bit of respect for the dead person'. She recalled the considerable expense involved in holding a wake, as traditionally nobody was turned away: 'I think strangers off the streets used to come in... The local pub would give you boxes with glasses, pint glasses, and they would also advance you the money... for the drink... there was always money for a wake. You mightn't pay for it for years, but you had to find the money.'

For little Janet and her friends, growing up in Dún Laoghaire in the 1950s and early 1960s, visiting the morgue was an integral part of their play during the school holidays. After having checked if there was a wedding on in the local hotel (because if there was, the guests would be drunk and could be persuaded to buy them lemonades), someone would say, 'C'mon and we'll see who's in the morgue.' Off they would go, 'crowds of us'. The morgue door was generally open. Often there was a nun in charge. 'Can we see the corpse, sister?' the children asked. They were admitted to say a prayer for the deceased, whom they might or might not have known: 'if we knew them, it was better, 'cause – you had every excuse to get in'. Once inside, 'we'd be tittering and laughing and picking and pushing and, "Touch it, see does it move?"' Bríd, who also lived nearby, was not quite as daring. She and her friends perched on a wall overlooking the morgue and assessed the deceased's popularity according to how many mourners there were. 'God forgive me,' she said, 'but the morgue was a great source of entertainment.'

Religious beliefs, of course, came very much into play on the occasion of someone's death, as did any allegiances they had had during life. Members of the Children of Mary were often laid out and buried in their blue robes, symbols of the religious faith that had meant so much to them in life. Gravediggers in the stonecutting community of Glencullen laid their tools in the form of a cross, protecting the deceased from interference from parties that might include the fairies.*

Funerals could be big business. As Dún Laoghaire was an important port, many bodies passed through: people who had died abroad and whose remains were repatriated, and sometimes drowning victims. Certain undertakers in the early to mid-twentieth century were known for using the rather pushy sales technique of just arriving and loading the coffined corpses that arrived into their vehicles. Some even visited the homes of the recently deceased and took the bodies away. Often the families were too upset to protest and negotiate, and they would get the business. One of these undertakers earned the nickname 'Swallow the Corpse' in this way.

---

* Pádraic provided a long explanation for this tradition with a version of an ancient legend that is often used to explain the fairies' origin, a narrative combing elements of the Book of Genesis with folklore. It is found across Europe, apparently having spread to Ireland towards the end of the Middle Ages (Ó hÓgáin, 1990, 187). According to Pádraic's account, after a war in heaven, God cast out the rebel angels, some of which remained on earth. During St Patrick's time in Ireland, Patrick clarified to a concerned sexton that 'fallen angels' or fairies will be damned on the Last Day; the sexton had heard the fairies wondering what would become of them. Patrick advised him to dig a grave, get into it, and lay his tools over it in the shape of a cross, stating that this would protect him when he broke the bad news to the fairies. Very angry and upset at the news, they duly 'went stark mad, pulling up trees, so forth, et cetera.' This, according to Pádraic, is the origin of a Glencullen tradition whereby a stonecutter's tools are placed in the shape of a cross over a grave. The tradition of protecting a grave, and the soul of the deceased, from the fairies in this manner was once common (Logan, 1981, 17).

399

* * *

Before the nineteenth century, most graveyards were simple, and the very poor dead were often only marked with an unengraved stone, or not at all. There are beautiful examples of historic graveyards in Dún Laoghaire-Rathdown, notably the evocative space around the old, ruined church of Rathmichael and the melancholy graveyard located around the medieval Kill o' the Grange church off Abbey Road, which is thought to date to the tenth or eleventh century, and to have been dedicated to St Fintan, now surrounded by former council houses constructed in the 1950s.

In nineteenth-century Ireland, as in much of the West, graveyards were reimagined. Elaborate funerary art was in vogue and there were growing numbers of people wealthy enough to pay for it, and also fashionable was the idea of the final resting place of the dead as somewhere one might visit for a day out: a pleasant, landscaped environment in which to contemplate death and enjoy life at the same time. The creation of such 'garden cemeteries' (of which Goldenbridge in Inchicore was the first in Ireland and Britain, consecrated in 1829)[110] often predated the development of large public parklands, making them green lungs in urban areas, and open spaces that even the poor could access. Deansgrange Cemetery, which opened in 1865, is an example of the sort of formally landscaped graveyard popular during the Victorian era, forming our expectations for what a graveyard should look like ever since.[111] Deansgrange was founded as a multidenominational burial place in 1861[112] and, following the events of the early twentieth century, it became an important venue for the commemoration of the fallen heroes of the War of Independence, with annual pilgrimages to the republican plot.[113] Here, the remains of the more humble citizens of the area share space with local and national grandees and with the dead of various conflicts, some of whom are remembered as heroes.

Despite social pressure to provide for one's loved ones in death with a marked grave and all of the appropriate accoutrements, in the

A flower seller at Deansgrange Cemetery, 1993. Our Own Place
Photography Project, National Library of Ireland.

late nineteenth and early twentieth century, the expense involved was
still beyond the reach of many families, perhaps particularly young,
low-income couples who had lost a child at a time of high infant mortality. Until well into the twentieth century, the graves of the very poor were
often marked with flimsy or unmarked stones or wooden crosses, and
most are no longer visible, while the graves of those then considered unfit
for heaven, like unbaptised infants and people who had died by suicide,
were generally unmarked, and often not even within formally recognised
graveyards. Graham's uncle, who died at just four months of age, is in a
'pauper's grave' in Dún Laoghaire, together with other members of the
community who died without funds. Countless others, young and old,
lie unmarked in their final resting places. Marty's mother gave birth to
a still-born child in 1947. The tiny body was placed in a wooden box
donated by a local greengrocer and buried in the middle of the night,
just inside the wall surrounding Old Rathmichael Church: 'they went
up after midnight with carbide lamps and my father got an old orange
box… and made a coffin'. Locally, everyone knew this was where to

bury unbaptised infants, but 'they probably didn't want too many people to know at the time'. Another Shankill resident, William, remembered hearing about unbaptised infants being buried in other people's graves at Old Rathmichael, while others recalled still-born, premature infants hastily baptised at home and buried in private gardens, their tiny lives unrecorded anywhere other than their now-elderly siblings' memories.

In death, as in life, the comfortably off and wealthy are much more visible, the graves of the very poor often completely unmarked, as if they had never existed at all.

* * *

As Dún Laoghaire-Rathdown is rich in history, unsurprisingly it is also rich in accounts of encounters with ghosts and spirits. Most of these narratives recount personal experiences and beliefs rather than conforming to known legend types. Janet lives in her former family home in Dún Laoghaire, in an area once home to hobblers and fishermen. All her childhood, her father told the children to open the door for the house ghost, a hobbler who had lived there before them and who perished in the infamous hobbler disaster discussed in 'A Roof Over Their Heads'. He was experienced as a rather benign ethereal presence. Pádraic, from the Kilternan area, described several anomalous experiences: he once saw a man who had died shortly before walking along the road, and another who later turned out to have been buried in the wrong grave. Tom and Molly live in a beautiful old farmhouse, said to have been built on the site of an old castle, in the Kilternan area, which is rich in both prehistoric and historic sites. Many people, they say, have had strange experiences there, seeing the various ghosts associated with the property, each of which appears to evoke a different time. They include one census collector, who left the house in a hurry: 'Effed if I'd live here,' he said. But for Tom and Molly, strange experiences and sights are not frightening, but rather a reminder of their home's extraordinary past.

Do accounts of ghosts belong in a book about memory and the past? Of course. It is not necessary to believe in ghosts to recognise that these stories provide insight into the relationship of the narrators with the past and speak loudly of just how much the past – even when quite remote – continues to resonate and how those who have gone before us continue to matter and to make their presence felt, as symbols or metaphors for times gone by if not as provable supernatural phenomena.

LOOKING BACK,
LOOKING FORWARD

The past is, by definition, over. But it is also with us all the time. We see and interact with the past in innumerable ways, often even without realising it: as we pass through the built and natural environment, doing our shopping or admiring the view; when we remember our families' distant or recent past; and when we use what we know from our personal and collective experiences to make decisions about the future.

Children with a toy boat, c.1912. Kind permission of Rosaleen Miller and Jennifer Nuttall.

Among the built elements of history in Dún Laoghaire-Rathdown are numerous archaeological sites, including megalithic structures from the remote past. Some are in prominent locations while others, like the large portal tomb near the Brennanstown Road, have been relatively hidden for years. For some, these places feel like points of connection between current residents and those who lived here in the distant past. Some report a deeply emotional sense of connection to them, manifesting as crying, or as a sense of joy or a profound feeling of togetherness with those who built these monuments. Ritual or semi-ritual behaviours, including hugging the stones, speaking to and around them in Irish, and diverse rites and ceremonies drawing on a range of spiritual and religious traditions, are also reported. Jackie described her feelings relating to the tomb mentioned here regarding 'a sense of connection with your ancestors… with our identity and who we are… life goes on and life continues'.

Life does go on. While there can be concern and anger about the construction of housing estates, sometimes in environmentally sensitive areas,

P. Farrell butchers, Cabinteely. Urban Folklore Project, Dublin City, July 1980. Patricia Boyle. Kind permission of National Folklore Collection.

it is also true that the new residents, just like those who created the ancient tombs, have chosen this place to put down roots and that, as soon as they do, they also become heirs to that ancient legacy, to those imagined ancestors. But in exploring the more recent past, and even today, the wealthiest residents from fashionable suburbs like Dalkey and Monkstown are much more present in the media and in historical writing than others, giving their experiences and voices disproportionate weight, while the complexities and nuances of most of the substantial local population are often overlooked. We already know that future historians, like historians now, will find it easier to piece together the lives and times of the wealthy and influential than of ordinary working families.

One of the striking qualities of this area is its stately homes and the estates once associated with them. While some have been destroyed, others have been reclaimed as public property, with their lands reimagined as parks and leisure spaces. Usually, the wealthy people associated with these impressive houses are well-recorded in history and the many servants and labourers whose lives were also played out here are more difficult to see, although without them the grand houses and their estates would have been unable to function. Lingering anger about the excesses of the colonial period – now relegated to an increasingly distant past – can be at least partly assuaged by the happy sight of young families and retirees enjoying demesnes once off limits to ordinary people. Other stately homes now serve as nursing homes, schools, hospitals, hotels or elements of apartment complexes, often surrounded by housing estates built from the mid-twentieth century onwards. Some are still the homes of elite members of society, although the social and cultural composition of the elite has shifted with the years. All those that survive are important elements of the built landscape, and testify not just to the skill of the architects who designed them but also to the multiple lives – the builders who constructed them, the wealthy owners and their families, the armies of indoor and outdoor staff who cared for and maintained them – influenced by them over the years. They are important aspects of our collective heritage and should be cherished – but their persistence in the landscape, while other elements of our built heritage slowly vanish, can also give a partial, even misleading, impression of the past, and impinge on how we see the present.

As a society, we are selective in terms of which elements of the material culture we choose to keep. It makes sense to designate beautiful stately homes as protected structures: they were expensive to build, used the best of materials and are often significant works of art. But when stately homes and other large buildings from the past that are deemed 'important' are all that remain, we get a skewed impression of bygone days. Vernacular architecture tends to vanish, for various reasons. The simpler vernacular homes disappear and are swallowed up by the landscape very quickly once they are uninhabited: there were people living in mud-walled homes in parts of Dublin as recently as the early twentieth century. Once empty, the roofs caved in, and those houses quickly melted into the ground, along with any record in the landscape of the lives of their inhabitants. Mid-twentieth century, some farmers and labourers in the Dublin uplands still lived in thatched houses. By the 1960s, most of them were slated. Vernacular furniture is now often found in a state of decay in outhouses and sheds. Brightly painted Travellers' wagons constructed by skilled artisans were quickly replaced by modern mobile homes and caravans in the 1970s and 1980s. Tents and other temporary dwellings once commonly used by Travellers were not built to last in the first place. Ireland is often thought of as a culture tightly bonded to tradition, but we were collectively quick to discard traditional architecture and design as incomes rose, and in the rush towards prosperity, few people stopped to think about the social and psychological consequences of removing from the landscape evidence of the way most people used to live. None of us want to return to living in draughty homes with six children in every bed, but is there a way to maintain a connection with those elements of the built landscape that were associated with the majority of the population? To make the material record of those countless lives more visible and to honour it? To keep the best of our vernacular traditions and marry them with our needs as twenty-first-century people?

Industrial features of the landscape, with the passage of time, can also become beloved landmarks and symbols of local pride, like the lead mines of Ballycorus, where a tall chimney is visible from many parts of Dún Laoghaire-Rathdown. Almost-vanished industries can sometimes be discerned under ivy, behind walls or reworked as new enterprises. Again, there are questions to be asked about the extent to which we could and should preserve aspects of this part of our history. For future generations, developments – whether industrial or residential – that were greeted with dismay when they were built can also become the focus of nostalgia for the past, while new developments are often experienced as threatening and as destroying all that is good about a community. Dramatic changes to the built landscape are often experienced as particularly challenging by residents who live in areas that, until very recently, were farmland. Elinor, who grew up in the Kilgobbin area when it was still rural, understands, she says, the need to develop the area for housing, but feels that planning 'leaves a lot to be desired', with rural families often prohibited from building on family land, while developers seem to have a much easier time getting planning permission. Failures of planning can be seen retrospectively in the form of housing developments of the 1960s, 1970s and 1980s, when many of the new estates were almost entirely settled by young couples in their twenties and thirties with small children. Now elderly, those couples have happy memories of when they were all young together in pleasant environments, with comfortable homes and plenty of green space. But today the downside of a housing estate where everyone is the same age is apparent, as the residents of entire housing enclaves get old and approach death together, with the 'last survivors' often surrounded by new neighbours so far removed from them in age that they feel they have nothing in common. With the benefit of hindsight, many now feel they would prefer a development catering for residents of diverse ages, reducing the sense of being a 'last survivor' of a vanishing cohort.

The Traveller community, formally recognised by the Irish government as a distinct ethnic group since 2017, has a long and complex past

Travellers' chalets on Ballyogan Road, 1993. Photo by Maura Laffan. Our Own Place Photography Project, National Library of Ireland.

here, and still has a significant presence. In recent decades, many more Travellers have been completing advanced levels of higher education, and excelling in occupations not traditionally associated with their community. There are more official halting sites than there were in the dreadful days of the 1970s and 1980s, when conflict and tension between Travellers and settled people was endemic in some areas, and on average the standard of housing has improved. In countless ways, though, it has become more difficult for Travellers to continue to observe traditional ways of life because our society remains essentially hostile to the very idea of nomadism, with few accommodations made. New rulings regarding burial, for example, can prevent Traveller families from using graveyards traditional to their families, as they often do not have a local address – and Travellers who have settled may now want their loved ones to be buried nearby so they can attend their graves more easily. Many Travellers remain marginalised and on the fringes of Irish society, and provision for housing remains inadequate. In 2015, a Travellers' halting site in Carrickmines was devasted by a fire that killed ten members of an extended family and left innumerable people with trauma they will carry with them all their lives. A monument to this family on the Glenamuck Road, an area where the suburbs continue their march up and over the hills of Dublin, stands in their memory.

All of Ireland has become much more ethnically diverse in recent decades. While inner-city areas have greater diversity, Dún Laoghaire-Rathdown is now also home to people with roots all over the world. Massimo, who is Italian-Irish, spoke of the experience of his family, who immigrated to Ireland in the mid-twentieth century, anticipating by several decades the mass inward migration that would change Ireland dramatically from the late twentieth century onwards. In the experience of his family, he sees parallels with, and useful lessons for, the waves of immigration that have followed, saying that the Italian-Irish are 'probably one of the most successful integrations of [an] ethnic minority anywhere in the world, if you think about it… we're fully integrated now'. As Ireland, newly multicultural, is on a steep learning curve in terms of balancing competing rights and claims, the Italian-Irish and other long-established minority ethnic groups may have useful lessons for us to learn from. For those who have come from elsewhere, their experience of putting down roots and perhaps raising a family, or of staying for a while and then moving on, will in time all become part of history.

For Brenda, an Irish-speaker, hearing the linguistic diversity that is increasingly marked in urban and suburban areas makes her feel even more strongly about the Irish language. Some people come to Ireland with almost nothing, she said, but at least they have their own language to speak: '*Suíonn tú ar an mbus. Cloiseann tú na Polannaigh ag labhairt Polainnis. Agus mar a dúirt mé leis mo pháistí féin, "Tagann siad anseo agus níl rud ar bith acu… ach tá a teanga féin acu.*"' ['You sit on the bus. You hear the Poles speaking Polish. And as I said to my own children, "They come here and they have nothing… but they have their own language."']

She pointed out that there are few places where Irish-speakers can go and know that there will be someone there for them to talk to in Irish. For some, hearing different languages all around them is an impetus to explore and treasure Ireland's own first national language. Yet while fluent Irish-speakers are a minority here, as in most parts of Ireland, the Irish language is faring better than many have predicted. Far from de Valera's vision of Irish once more being the first language of the Irish people, today it is a second language for a large and growing number of former students of the Gaelscoil system – an important player in education in Dún Laoghaire-Rathdown, as well as a major contributor to the preservation of the Irish language – and small but active local groups get together to converse in Irish, such as one founded by Seámus: '*tá ciorcal comhrá ar siúl anseo anois. Roinnt de na daoine, iad go léir, is dócha, ba mhaith leo feabhas a chur ar a gcuid Gaeilge*' ['there's a chat circle going on here now. Some of the people, probably all of them, want to improve their Irish'].

Dorothy and Marie Fox on Verney Farm, early 1990s. Sisters Dorothy and Marie ran a large and successful dairy business in Kilternan for many years. Kind permission of Eddie Fox.

Many professions and occupations are significantly different today than they were in the past. The agricultural sector in the area, for example, has declined dramatically. There are still a few working in agriculture, but much of what was once farmland is now occupied by housing estates. In recent decades, farming has been increasingly restricted to upland areas, and even there it is moving towards becoming a thing of the past in this area. It has been in precipitous decline since the mid-twentieth century, with the vast growth in the suburbs, while the widespread use of refrigeration made it easier for farmers from distant places to provide dairy produce and other perishables to the Dublin market. For the last generations of farmers in areas that are now essentially urban, it has been difficult seeing a way of life disappear. Roy recalled his father, the final dairy farmer of Glasthule, the end of a line going back generations, struggling with the changes in the latter years of his life: 'I think towards the end of his life… he had no one to talk to that had anything in common with him, because, you know, there were no farmers left.' Stephen, who farms in Kilmashogue, asserted that the farmers of Dublin have been effectively abandoned by their respective county councils and are having to learn how to live with their lands being seen by many Dubliners as a playground for city people. But Gene, whose family have been farming in the Kilternan area for generations, takes a philosophical approach: 'if someone suddenly offered you a few bob for a field that you'd been killing yourself for fifty years working and got nothing out of it, and someone offered you a million for it. Hallelujah baby.'

The industrial sector has also changed dramatically. Whereas there were once many small to middle-sized enterprises in manufacturing, today most manufacturing takes place overseas in countries that are similar, in many ways, to Ireland in the earlier years of its industrialisation: places where people will work for less than in rich countries. Instead, many Irish people and recent immigrants work in sectors including finance and information technology.

Domestic service remains an important form of employment, although the numbers engaged in this sort of work are vastly reduced compared to the nineteenth century and first half of the twentieth century. Domestic staff today are still likely to come from working-class areas, and/or are also likely to be from ethnic minority groups and to be predominately women. While those employed in domestic service have more legal protections and better pay than their precursors, this is still an area characterised by high levels of casual work, relatively low levels of legal protection and the potential for abuse of workers' vulnerable positions.

Sports remain an important leisure activity. Perhaps the biggest change in sports has been the large number of clubs and societies that now admit girls as well as boys. Jimmy, a sports coach, remarked that he was happy to see girls and boys both training and benefitting from involvement in team sports. He said that it is 'lovely' to see so many girls actively involved in sports, when 'twenty, or thirty years ago… that door was closed to them'. Odhrán is also a coach, and he works with two teams, 'Gaelic for Mothers' and 'Hurling for Fathers'. He is also delighted to see more women in sports: '[the] Ladies' Gaelic Football Association. It's phenomenal now. It's just taken off, which is great.' The

The Martello tower at Seapoint. The Wiltshire Photographic Collection, National Library of Ireland.

big increase in the numbers of girls and young women doing sports – albeit still in lower numbers than their male peers – is symbolic of the broader social changes that have led to vast differences in the ways in which women interact with the economy, with their families and with society as a whole. Sports have also become much less closely aligned with political and ethno-religious groupings than before, making it easier for them to focus instead on matters such as performance and community building. Where once the GAA hurled insults at 'foreign' influences, today it welcomes young players with roots all over the world.

On trend with the rest of Ireland and much of the developed world, there has been a dramatic, even precipitous, decline in formal religious observance here. Even the ecumenical movement of the 1970s and 1980s, which strove to bring people of different Christian faiths together, largely failed to stop the flood away from formal religion. It is increasingly challenging for an aging clerical population to cope with their work at a time when religious vocations have essentially collapsed. Even if many fewer are turning up for Mass, it still needs to be said. Lina commented: 'we only have one priest in [our local parish church] and there's another priest brought in to help him… between… four churches, we all get a loan of a priest. And that's it… they're having an awful time.' Pádraic attended the arrival of the Papal Nuncio in Dún Laoghaire on the occasion of the Eucharistic Congress of 1932. He remembered clearly how the crowds then were so big, all the hotels in Dublin were full. Liners in Dublin Bay served as accommodation, and the bay was full of little boats bringing them to and fro. By contrast, the congress of 2012 barely caused a stir. 'One flag over here,' said Pádraic, with dismay, 'one flag in Sandyford. That's all that's in it!' He concluded: 'We've gone down the drain a big way.'

But amid the decline in influence of the established churches, popular and folk expressions of faith have remained relatively resilient and, sometimes, even witnessed a modest resurgence. In 2001, the remains of St Thérèse de Lisieux toured Ireland and attracted huge crowds,[1] while religious observance at traditional sacred spaces like holy wells has witnessed a modest increase. Today most wells – holy or otherwise – are now built over or are otherwise inaccessible. However, while religious behaviour around holy wells declined rapidly in the twentieth century, popular knowledge of sites and traditions has persisted more than one might expect and by the late twentieth century was even growing a little. In Dalkey, following renovations in Dillon's Park, where the local holy well discussed previously is located, it is once again a site of ritual observance, and the gate erected by the Dalkey Tidy Towns committee is festooned with votive offerings including rags and Rosary beads. One woman who has held ceremonies there said of the well that 'it did kind of feel that the well was waking up, because I think certain things… do you know… are ready to be discovered at a certain time'. A retired Church of Ireland rector with a long history in the Dun Laoghaire-Rathdown spoke of the importance to him of Colmcille's well, in Oldcourt near Tallaght. Not only has he been involved with ecumenical prayers services at the well, he visits on a personal basis, for quiet reflection.

Popular and traditional expressions of faith, in the absence of a formally recognised liturgy, are both more flexible and less demanding of adherents, and many traditional sacred spaces can mean different things to different people. Some of the archaeological sites mentioned in this book are the focus of ritual behaviours drawing on a range of inspirations that can be viewed as loosely aligned with neo-pagan philosophies with links to ideas of nationhood, heritage and what has been referred to as 'romantic nationalism'. The idea of a sense of connection to a 'Celtic' past can be expressed (although the ritual sites in question are often actually pre-Celtic), along with sometimes the idea that one should speak Irish – an 'older language' – in rites associated with these sites.[2]

Folklore and tradition persist – thrive, even – in the area too. Derek, who grew up in the Dún Laoghaire/Sallynoggin area hearing stories of the banshee, noted that the tradition is still alive among children: 'In the woods where we walk, Granddad,' his granddaughter told him, 'there was a [banshee's] white comb found and the next day [someone] died.' There are still individuals in the area providing traditional folk medical services with links to antiquity. In fact, thanks to mobile technology and the incredible speed with which information can spread within a community, some are busier than they have ever been before. While science-based medicine is generally used for ailments of all sorts, an ancient practice – the use of human blood for treating shingles – persists in this area, as well as elsewhere in Ireland, partly because modern medicine remains ineffective at treating the condition. Those who continue to provide their blood for treatment remain in demand, with some reporting that their services even have been requested on behalf of patients being treated in formal healthcare settings, like hospitals.

Dún Laoghaire-Rathdown remains a culturally vibrant area. For example, Comhaltas Ceoltóirí Éireann, still based in Monkstown, was giving lessons to more than 1,000 students a week by the 2020s, and catering to more than 35,000 members in eighteen different countries. Bernard O'Sullivan, a leader in the organisation, stated that many were initially attracted to traditional Irish music and dance by commercial offerings like *Riverdance* and, wanting to know more about the source – 'back to the well' – have become involved in studying and teaching Irish music all over the world. He also noted that the growing multiculturalism has had an interesting impact on music, with young people with roots outside Ireland bringing new influences to bear on the music they play. The decoupling of Irish music from the more vehement forms of nationalism that were common in the early decades of the twentieth century has not hurt the tradition in any way. Quite the reverse, in fact. Today Irish music is thriving, and is more recognised around the world than ever before.

As a society that tends to prefer simplified narratives of the past, we seem to also prefer simplified narratives of the present. It is much easier to think in terms of particular people and things being 'bad' or 'good' than to see the nuances of the past. Nor have we really confronted the fact that even changes that are generally experienced as overwhelmingly positive can introduce new, unforeseen challenges. For instance, the massive social revolution that took place within living memory and saw women's education and participation in the paid workforce change dramatically had far-reaching consequences, some of which were not foreseen, and some of which are not that obvious. Very few people would like to undo the huge social progress that has been made, but the huge cultural shifts that accompanied it has changed society in ways that can be difficult, and that will need new solutions. In the recent past, many Irish families had so many children that they could not feed them all adequately. While poverty has certainly not vanished, it is rare today for children to suffer from conditions such as rickets, which were endemic among the poor less than three generations ago. Today, like elsewhere in the developed world, most Irish couples are choosing to have small families, or none at all. In fact, Ireland is now approaching the situation of much of the developed world, whereby women are having so few children that in another generation or two there will be a demographic crisis. At the same time, while large and growing numbers of women have achieved excellence in many fields that women were excluded from for so long, women devoted full-time to home and family can feel overlooked. Even the dramatic fall in absolute poverty that took place as Ireland became one of the wealthier countries in Europe has introduced challenges; like most developed nations, we are contributors to an environmental crisis that is unfolding and that we do not yet fully understand.

Does that mean that the dramatic social and technological changes that marked the final decades of the twentieth century were 'bad'? Certainly not: it just means that when society changes, everything shifts, and when everything shifts, we do not always know how to react. For new circumstances, we need new responses. We can learn a lot from the past, but not everything, and we can certainly never repeat it.

We often look at the past through one of two competing perspectives. Thinking about the past can attract nostalgia for a time that is seen as simpler and more rewarding ('Life was tougher then… but it was also simpler. We had less, but we were happier. Things are worse now'). Thinking about the past can also evoke feelings of horror and revulsion ('Life was brutal, difficult, short and cruel. People were less enlightened.

Today, thanks to progress, we do things differently and better'). While each of these perspectives has its attractions, neither actually helps us in any way to understand the past and its impact on the present. Neither, in fact, gives us any insight at all. The former also induces despair, the latter complacency, emotions that are anything but helpful when it comes to living well now and planning effectively for the future. If thinking about the past is to actually teach us something, to give us any insights at all, we need to think about it in a different way.

Yet thinking about the past really *is* important. The people of Dún Laoghaire-Rathdown, like everyone in a place with a long history of human habitation, live in an area where the physical traces of history can be seen wherever they look – from sites associated with the ancient past, to swathes of development tracking modern social and economic history throughout the twentieth century and right up to the present. The past is everywhere. The dead are gone, but in many ways they are also always with us. They matter – including the ones whose names are completely lost to history – and they always will.

How does exploring the past inform people's experiences of the present? Stewart, whose family has lived in the Glencullen area for hundreds of years, making their living from the stone and the land, stated that it is 'a really nice feeling' to be 'sort of a living part of history… the fact that so many generations are in the one area'. Obviously, Stewart's family, with its long and rich history in one spot, has a fascinating heritage and we are lucky to have been able to hear about some of it, as the stories of families long established in this area give us remarkable insight into its history.

But *everyone* in any given area, including those who settled in recent times, is a living part of its history, and they will remain so even if they move on. Those who just passed through, who maybe stepped straight off a train and onto a mailboat, or who spent a few weeks or months at a children's home during a difficult time for their family – they are all part of the story too. And, like all histories, it is an absolutely *amazing* story, and the more we know, and the more people whose stories we can tell, the more amazing it gets.

The great thing about the past is that it is a spool that never runs out of thread.

NOTES

'Dún Laoghaire-Rathdown'

1   Ó Maitiú, 2003, 127.
2   Pearson, 2007, 47–50.
3   Oldham, 1848, 252.
4   'Ballybetagh Bog, Archaeological Excavations, Remains of Irish Elk', *Irish Times*, 25 October 1934.
5   They would publish their work 'The Bogs at Ballybetagh, near Dublin, with Remarks on Late-Glacial Conditions in Ireland' in the *Proceedings of the Royal Irish Academy* in 1937–8.
6   Corlett, 2013, 9; 11–15.
7   MacAonghusa, 2007, 54.
8   Goodbody, 1993, 113.
9   Pearson, 2022, 14.
10 Pearson, 2007, 338.
11 Turner, 1979, 82–93.
12 Clare, 2005, 17.
13 *Ibid*, 19.
14 Mac Aonghusa, 2007, 76.
15 Pearson, 2021, 5–7.
16 Ball, 1899, 239.
17 Bolton et al., 2021, 7; 21.
18 Pearson, 1981, 14–18.
19 *Ibid.*, 24; 41.
20 Galavan, 2017, 89.
21 Clare, 2004, 31; 35.
22 Dún Laoghaire Harbour Company, n.d.
23 Pearson, 1981, 31; 99.
24 G.R.D., n.d, 4–5. Killiney Bay has often been compared to the Bay of Naples, with the view of the Sugar Loaf standing in for Mount Vesuvius, inspiring the Italianate names that were given to many of the finer homes.
25 Goodbody, 1993, 90.
26 Duffy, 2000, 213.
27 Ball, 1895, 220.
28 Galavan, 2017, 82–4.
29 Edwards, 1938, 30.
30 Scannell, 2006, 84.
31 Crossman, 2017, 36.
32 Hearne, 1998, 61.
33 Galavan, 2017, 117; 126–7.
34 Pim, 1891, 5.
35 Galavan, 2017, 98.
36 *Ibid.*, 97.
37 Pim, 1890, 25; 9.
38 Pim, 1892, 30; 15.
39 Talbot Coall and Son, 1889, no number given.
40 Daly, 1998, 9.
41 Pim, 1890, 28.
42 Galavan, 2017, 4.
43 MacAonghusa, 2014, 7.

44 Reid, 2014, 7.
45 Galavan, 2017, 152.
46 Brady et al., 2002, 42–4.
47 Galavan, 2017, 116.
48 Kelly, 1992–3, 6–7.
49 https://www.cie.ie/en-ie/Who-we-are/History-of-CIE, accessed 28 April 2023.
50 Dún Laoghaire Borough Civil Week, 1948, 20–1; 67.
51 Curtis, 2011, 56.
52 Brady et al., 2002, 254.
53 Daly, 2016, 131.
54 Brown, 2004, 200.
55 Norris, 2016, 151.
56 Brown, 2004, 245.
57 Brady, 2015, 328.
58 Kennedy, 1987, 1.
59 Fitzpatrick, 2001, 186.
60 Ó Catháin, 1998, 17–30; Ní Fhloinn, 2001, 217.
61 Briody, 2007, 261; 449.
62 See MacPhilip, 2006, 103–22.
63 Johnson, 2003, 5.

'Who's Who'

1   Milne, 1989, 4.
2   MacAonghusa, 2014, 20–1.
3   Lyng, 2016, 41.
4   Leonard, 1979, 81.
5   Hearn, 1999, 13.
6   NFC UFP, vol. 1954, 314.
7   Connolly, 1985, 4.
8   O'Morchoe, 1934, 22.
9   Robbins, 2021, 239–56.
10 Talbot Coall and Son, 1889, no page number.
11 Donnelly b, 1907, 153.
12 Connolly, 1985, 43.
13 Carter, 2015, 69–70.
14 Brady, 2002, 65.
15 MacAonghusa, 2014, 10.

16 Edwards, 1938, 32.
17 Conlon, 2016, 16.
18 NFC UFP, vol. 1994, 50.
19 Pašeta, 1999, 491.
20 NFC UFP, vol. 1994, 54.
21 National Folklore Collection, Schools' Collection (henceforth NFC SC), vol. 797, 191.
22 Taylor, 2015, 212–13.
23 Protestant children's organisations similar to the Scouts, with a scriptural element.
24 Costello, 2003, 326.
25 Reid, 2009, 24–6.
26 Brown, 2004, 39.
27 Grimes, *Architectural History*, Vol. 52, 2009, pp. 147-168.
28 Reynolds, 1993, 47–9.
29 D'Auria, 2012, 308–9; Reynolds, 1993, 51.
30 D'Auria, 2012, 313.
31 Marcantonio, 1998, 131.
32 Reynolds, 1993, 3.
33 'Garden Robbers', *Saunders Newsletter*, 24 August 1774.
34 Magee, 2017, 265.
35 Traynor, 2021, 79.
36 NFC UFP, vol. 1994, 69.
37 *Ibid.*, vol. 1994, 93.
38 *Ibid.*, vol. 1984, 229–30.
39 See Nuttall, 2020, pp. 158–65 for a discussion of the role of the 'socials' in Irish Protestant courtship, marriage and endogamy.
40 Peter, 1907, 124; 127.
41 Whelan, 2018, 218–19.

'A Roof Over Their Heads'

1   Clare, 2004, 23.
2   For example, in the parish of Booterstown, in the lanes of Booterstown, Williamstown

and Merrion Avenue. Smyth, 1994, 4–5.

3 Ó Cathaoir, 1995, 111.
4 Galavan, 2017, 8.
5 Clare, 2004, 14–15.
6 Kelly, 1952, 5.
7 Scudds, 2014, 42.
8 Weafer, 2010, 26.
9 Leonard, 1979, 34.
10 Conlon, 2016, 95.
11 Pearson, 1981, 132.
12 Prunty, 2007, 190–3.
13 Ibid., 2007, 340.
14 Earner-Byrne, 2016, 40–1.
15 Clear, 2021, 256.
16 Muldowney, 2017, 47.
17 Rowley, 2019, 165–6.
18 Boyd et al., 2020, 6–7.
19 Ward, 2020, 138–40.
20 Pearson, 2021, 5–6.
21 Taylor, 2015, 133.
22 Aalen, 1988, 308.
23 Taylor, 2015, 171–2; 240.
24 Aalen, 1988, 311.
25 Magee, 2017, 246.
26 Aalen, 1988, 321.
27 Skehill, 2004, 188.
28 Crossman, 2017, 1.
29 Scannell, 2006, 154–5.
30 Skehill, 2004, 188.
31 Ó Cathaoir, 1995, 114.
32 Skehill, 2004, 189.
33 Clare, 1986, 1.
34 Pearson, 2007, 89.
35 Crossman, 2017, 2–3.
36 Ibid., 22; 171.
37 Hardy, 1913, 58.
38 Ó Cathaoir, 1995, 117.
39 Crossman, 2017, 159.
40 Ó Gráda, 2002, 143.
41 NFC UFP, vol. 1994, s 29.
42 Ó Cathaoir, 1995, 123–4.

43 Scannell, 2006, 157–8; 162.
44 Wills, 2001, 45–6.
45 Pearson, 1981, 132.
46 Earner-Byrne, 2007, 173.
47 Earner-Byrne, 2007, 176–7; Ferriter, 2009, 16; Luddy, 2001, 804.
48 Skehill, 2004, 207.
49 Talbot Coall and Son, 1891, no given.
50 Daly, 2016, 128.
51 Pearson, 1981, 132.
52 Redmond, 2018, 23.
53 Hogan 2019, 12; 14; 17.
54 http://www.childrenshomes.org.uk/DublinBirdsNest/ Retrieved on 2 May 2023.
55 Pearson, 1981, 131–2.
56 Goodbody, 2002, 56.
57 Talbot Coall and Son, 1889, no page given.
58 Goodbody, 2002, 59.
59 Skehill, 2004, 229.
60 Gilligan, 2014, 150.
61 Redmond, 2018, 14.
62 http://www.childrenshomes.org.uk/BooterstownStAnneIS/ Retrieved 2 May 2023.
63 Report of the Commission to Inquire into Child Abuse, 2009.
64 Daly, 2016, 171–2.
65 Skehill, 2004, 190.
66 Ó Cathaoir, 1995, 121.
67 Breathnach, 2017, 787.
68 'Starving Nurse-child; Scandalous State of Affairs', Irish Times, 5 March 1924.
69 Shiel, 2003, 15.
70 Pearson, 2022, 225–6.
71 Boyd et al., 2019, 3–4.
72 Boland, 1995, 156–7.
73 Ibid.
74 NFC SC, vol. 799, 51–2.
75 Ibid., vol. 799, 55.

76 Bhreatnach, 2006, 58; 61.
77 Halleiner, 2000, 61.
78 Bhreatnach, 2006, 44.
79 Daley, 2016, 168.
80 McDonagh, 1994, 95.
81 Bhreatnach, 2006, 58; 65; 89.
82 Murdoch, 2002, 68.
83 Hayes, 2006, 134.
84 Named after Saint Labre, the patron saint of beggars. McWeeny, 2007, 6.
85 Ó Riain, 2000, 2–4.
86 O'Callaghan and Hourigan, 1999, 29.
87 Crowley, 2009, 19.
88 O'Callaghan and Hourigan, 1999, 11; 32.

'Mouths to Feed'
1 Bell and Watson, 2008, 15.
2 'B', 1834, 1.
3 Curran and Ryan, 2020, 88–90.
4 O'Connell et al., 2016, xv.
5 Byrne, 2018, 93.
6 *Ibid.*, 2018, 95.
7 Pim, 1892, 6.
8 MacAonghusa, 2014, 17.
9 Breathnach, 2017, 784.
10 Kelly, 2013, 150.
11 Keegan, 2006, number not given.
12 Guinnanne, 1997, 66.
13 Edgeworth, 2007, 7; 9; 17.
14 Goodbody, 1993, 68.
15 Irish Countrywomen's Association, n.d., 5.
16 MacAonghusa, 2007, 101–2.
17 Cowman, 2001, 62.
18 Normoyle, 2006, 11.
19 Barnett, 2006, 17.
20 Curran and Ryan, 2020, 95–6.
21 Ryan, 1991, 112–13.
22 Curran and Ryan, 2020, 101.
23 Galavan, 2017, 135.
24 'The Glass Bottle Manufacture of Ireland', *Irish Times,* 10 September 1880: 6.
25 'New Product by Irish Factory: Clear Glass Bottles', *Irish Times*, 18 August 1933.
26 'Irish Glass Bottle Co.'s new £1m. Factory', *Irish Times*, 12 July 1967: 12.
27 Kiely and Keane, 2012, 31; 41.
28 For example, 'Girls, 17–20, Jobs Offered', advertisement, *Irish Times*, 10 May 1957.
29 Leon, 2005, 1–21.
30 McQuade and O'Donnell, 2007, 569.
31 Tully, 2012, 400.
32 Cannon, 2014, 35.
33 Tully, 2012, 401.
34 https://www.irishlights.ie/who-we-are/our-history.aspx. Retrieved 7 April 2022.
35 Long, 1993, 36.
36 Wilson, 1968, vii.
37 Long, 1993, 195.
38 *Ibid.*, 38.
39 Wilson, 1968, 84.
40 Long, 1993, 42.
41 Pearson, 1981, 151.
42 'Concrete Islands May Take the Place of Lightships', *Belfast Telegraph*, 24 August 1965.
43 See *Cold Iron, Aspects of the Occupational Lore of Irish Fishermen* by Bairbre ní Fhloinn for a discussion of aspects of fishing lore.
44 NFC UFP, vol. 1994, 140.
45 Hart, 'With Her Majesty's Mails to Ireland', *Strand Magazine*, 1895. https://www.swilson.info/wp/?_id=260. Retrieved 22 May 2023.
46 Cannon, 2014, 36.
47 Pearson, 2022, 43.
48 Conlon, 2016, 47.

49 Lowth, 1995, 94.
50 NFC UFP, vol. 1994, s 27–38.
51 Archer and Pearson, 1987, 25.
52 Pearson, 2021, 10.
53 Grayson, 2018, 15.
54 Hearne, 1999, 1; 34–5.
55 Crowe, 2006, 42.
56 Brown, 2004, 80.
57 Kennedy, 2001, 57.
58 NFC UFP, vol. 1994, ages 48–9.
59 Hearn, 1999, 89.
60 NFC UFP, vol. 1994, 58.
61 Hearn, 1999, 96-9-8; Farrell, 2013, 39.
62 NFC UFP, vol. 1994, 93–4.
63 McCabe, 2020.
64 Wills, 2001, 40–1.
65 Clear, 2000, 65.
66 Brady et al, 2002, 35.
67 Clear, 2000, 27; 46; 21.
68 Pearson, 1981, 123.
69 Drew, 2008, 6.
70 Kiely and Keane, 2012, 55.
71 Farmar, 2004, 112
72 Findlater's, 2000, 217.
73 Urban District Council of Dún Laoghaire, n.d., 19–20.
74 Leonard, 1989, 16–17.
75 Pearson, 1981, 148.
76 McManus, 2018, 44; 25.
77 NFC UFP, vol. 2004, 367–8.
78 *Ibid.*, vol. 1954, 158.
79 Bhreatnach, 2006, 44.
80 NFC SC, vol. 799, 56.
81 Bhreatnach, 2006, 115.
82 Gibney, 2014.
83 Ferriter, 2013, 542.
84 Brady et al., 2002, 29.
85 Jacobson, 1994, 64.
86 Skehill, 2004, 222.
87 Johnston and Muldoon, 1908, 7.
88 Budd and Guinnane, 1991, 498.
89 Ó Gráda, 2002, 126.
90 Johnston and Muldoon, 1908, 14.
91 *Ibid.*, 1908, 18.
92 Ó Gráda, 2002, 129; 134; 143.
93 Cousins 1993–4, 368.
94 Earner-Byrne, 2007, 111.
95 Daley, 2016, 169.
96 Cousins, 1993–4, 379.
97 Scudds, 2006, 16–17.
98 McKillop et al., 2006, 38–40; 59; 322.
99 Wallace, 2006, no given.
100 Gmelch, 1977, 45.
101 Pat O'Neill in Clare and Laffan, 2006, 27.
102 Dún Laoghaire Borough Heritage Society, 1991, 12.
103 Findlater, 200, 321–2.
104 Leonard, 1989, 18.
105 NFC UFP, vol. 1984, 251,
106 Ferriter, 2013, 575; 581.

'Earth and Heaven'

1   Donnelly, 1907, 142.
2   Goodbody, 2004, 173.
3   Raftery, 2021, 111–12.
4   Whelan, 2018, 213.
5   O'Dwyer, 2009, 11.
6   Brown, 2004, 25.
7   O'Dwyer, 2009, 55.
8   Boyd, 2007, 321.
9   Sobolewski, 2013, 8.
10 O'Dwyer, 2009, 47.
11 Lyng, 2016, 35.
12 Sobolewski, 2013, 7.
13 O'Dwyer, 2009, 23.
14 Smith, 2003, 11.
15 Shannon, cited in Holmes, 2012, 60.
16 Titley, 1983, 127.
17 O'Dwyer, 2009, 71.
18 D'Alton, 2017, 199–200.
19 Biagini, 2017, 213.
20 de Cléir, 2019, 4.
21 Girvin, 1986, 63.

22 Cooney, 1999, 204–5.

23 Lennon, 2012, 15.

24 Begadon, 2012, 35.

25 Lennon, 2012, 17.

26 Leonard, 1989, 14.

27 Maguire, 2012, 100.

28 NFC UFP, vol. 1994, 363–4.

29 Cullen Owens, 2005, 59.

30 Whelan, 2018, 203.

31 Cullen Owens, 2005, 305.

32 Kiely and Keane, 2012, 65.

33 Girvin, 2008, 75–6.

34 Carville, 2021, 545.

35 Fuller, 2005, 48.

36 Wills, 2001, 37.

37 https://www.irishtimes.com/
life-and-style/people/a-generation-
of-john-pauls-growing-up-the-pope-
s-namesake-1.3598375. Retrieved on
28 February 2024.

38 Girvin, 2008, 86.

39 Falconer, 1997, 83; 86.

40 https://www.umc.org/en/content/
easter-sunrise-services-a-celebrat
ion-of-resurrection. Retrieved on 23
May 2023.

41 Girvin, 2008, 68; 81–2.

42 Girvin, 1986, 61.

43 Brown, 2004, 366–9.

44 Turpin, 2006, 58.

45 See Taylor, 1995, 35–76 for
a discussion of a sacred geography
in the sort of area more usually
studied from this viewpoint, in
this case rural Donegal.

46 Crawford O'Brien, 2008, 331.

47 Ó Danachair, 1958, 68.

48 Ibid.

49 O'Reilly, 1902, 178.

50 Donnelly, n.d. 95.

51 O'Reilly, 1902, 178; Donnelly, n.d. 97.

52 MacAonghusa, 2014, 25; Mac
Aonghusa, 2007, 177.

53 W.F. Wakeman, Old Dublin 1887, 34,
cited in Ó Danachair, 1958, 79.

54 Branigan, 2012, 107.

55 Curran and Ryan, 2020, 146–7;
Magee, 2017, 264.

56 NFC SC, vol. 797, 249. The same
holy well was the site of a store
of arms used by the IRA during
the War of Independence. Brady,
2020, 87.

57 Edwards, 1938, 4.

58 NFC SC, vol. 798, 76

59 Branigan, 2012, 105.

60 Pat O'Neil, in Clare and Laffan, 2006,
28. See also Ó Danachair, 1958, 84.

61 Ó Danachair, 1958, 84–5.

62 NFC SC, vol. 797, 100.

63 Brady, 2020, 89.

64 NFC SC, vol. 795, 49.

65 Ibid., vol. 798, 25.

66 Ibid. vol. 798, 132. See also vol. 798,
110; vol. 798, 138; vol. 798, 148; vol.
783, 12–14; vol. 798, 39; vol. 798, 138;
vol. 798, 151 for other examples of fairy
lore in the Dalkey and Killiney areas in
the 1930s.

67 Ibid. vol. 796, 42.

68 Ibid. vol. 798, 263–4.

69 NFC UFP, vol. 1979, 110.

70 Ibid., vol. 1992, 222–3.

71 Aarne, 1961.

72 Thompson, 1966.

73 Uther, 2004.

74 Lysaght, 1996, 39; 154.

75 NFC UFP, vol. 1994, 145.

76 Ibid., vol. 1999, 67.

77 Ibid., vol. 1991, 217–19.

78 Ibid., 237.

'Fighting and Fighting Back'

1 Pearson, 1981, 79.
2 Ferriter, 2015 (*Nation and not a Rabble*), 137.
3 Yeates, 2013, 2.
4 Mannion, 2013, 17.
5 Devlin, 2013, 37; 29.
6 Taylor, 2015, 7.
7 Fitzpatrick, 1995, 1018.
8 Ferriter, 2015 *A Nation and not a Rabble*, 144.
9 Johnson, 2003, 54.
10 Fitzpatrick, 1995, 1,029.
11 Johnson, 2003, 50.
12 Taylor, 2015, 1.
13 Grayson, 2018, 32; Johnson, 2003, 44.
14 Grayson, 2018, 34.
15 O'Callaghan, 2016, 96–7; 99.
16 Grayson, 2018, 75; 101; 207.
17 *Ibid.*, 2018, 123–4; 43.
18 Findlater, 2000, 367.
19 Grayson, 2018, 82.
20 'For Our Soldiers and Sailors, Sale of Work at Monkstown', *Irish Times*, 11 February 1915.
21 Reid, 2014, 18.
22 Gunning, 2021, 92–4.
23 https://www.militaryarchives.ie/collections/online-collections/bureau-of-military-history-1913-1921/reels/bmh/BMH.WS0355.pdf# =51
24 Brady, 2020, 14; 28.
25 Dún Laoghaire Borough Heritage Society, 1991, 22.
26 Grayson, 2018, 147, quoting Monica Roberts, a Stillorgan woman who was a prominent campaigner supporting Irish soldiers in the First World War, and a diarist of the time.
27 Moran, 'Easter 1916: A British soldier's family reunion and death in Dublin', *Irish Times*, 6 April 2015.
28 Dún Laoghaire Borough Heritage Society, 1991, 22–3.
29 Grayson, 2018, 153; 157.
30 Fitz-Simon, 2007, 51.
31 Grayson, 2018, 166.
32 *Ibid.*, 232.
33 Johnson, 2003, 24.
34 Leonard, 1997, 61.
35 Taylor, 2015, 13.
36 Grayson, 2018, 224–5; 191; 204; 228–9.
37 Robinson, 2020, 71; 46.
38 Farrell, 2021, 148–9.
39 Cronin, 1986, 16.
40 Lehane, 2019, 41.
41 Cronin, 1986, 17.
42 Reid, 2014, 18.
43 Brady, 2020, 45.
44 Pearson, 1981, 147.
45 Grayson, 2018, 261.
46 Ó Caolaí, 2018, 6.
47 O'Brien, 2018, 7.
48 Grayson, 2018, 262.
49 Cronin, 1986, 26.
50 Leonard, 1997, 60.
51 Scannell, 2019, 237.
52 Johnson, 2003, 95.
53 With thanks to historian and Cabinteely resident Felix Larkin for drawing this to our attention.
54 Fitzpatrick, 2001, 191.
55 Kinsella, 2014, 25.
56 Milne, 2018, 126.
57 Scannell, 2019, 229–30.
58 NFC UFP, vol. 1992, 51.
59 *Ibid.*, 235.
60 Robinson, 2020, 79.
61 NFC UFP, vol. 1979, p 90.
62 *Ibid.*, vol. 1992, 51.
63 Gunning, 2021, 92; 96.
64 Grayson, 2018, 275.
65 Magee, 2017, 241.

66 https://www.dlrcoco.
    ie/news/general-news/
    what%E2%80%99s-name-dun-leary-
    %E2%80%93-kingstown-%E2%80%93-
    d%C3%BAn-laoghaire#:~:text=In%20
    1821%20the%20name%20
    Dunleary,original%20Irish%20
    name%20for%20Dunleary. Retrieved
    18 July 2023.
67 https://heritage.wick-
    lowheritage.org/topics/
    wicklow-the-war-of-independence/bray-
    henry-cairns-brian-white-james-scannell/
    bray-and-the-war-of-independence-
    1917-to-the-truce-by-henry-cairns.
    Retrieved 18 July 2023.
68 Reid, 2014, 20.
69 Marie Brennan, quoted in Clare and
    Laffan, 2006, 15.
70 Sobolewski, 2015, 70.
71 Grayson, 2018, 312.
72 Robinson, 2017, 319.
73 NFC UFP, vol. 1992, 52.
74 Robinson, 2017, 327.
75 Robinson, 2020, 111–13.
76 Kinsella, 2014,186.
77 Lehane, 2019, 41.
78 'Kevin O'Higgins', *Dublin Leader*, 27
    July 1927.
79 NFC UFP, vol. 1954, 130.
80 Taylor, 2015, 95.
81 *Ibid.*, 328.
82 *Ibid.*, 2.
83 Robinson, 2017, 317–18.
84 Farrell, 2021, 146.
85 Taylor, 2015, 93; 126.
86 Ferriter, 2015, 'Always in Danger', 194
87 Coleman, 2013, 203; 207.
88 Ferriter, 2015, 194–5.
89 Ferriter, 2015, 'Always in Danger', 195.
90 Coleman, 2013, 203.
91 Coleman, 2015, 216.

92 Ferriter, 2015, 'Always in Danger', 191.
93 Coleman, 2013, 202; 209.
94 Maume, 2019 Memoirs of a revo-
    lutionary secretary published, The
    Irish Times, 24 March 2014. https://
    www.irishtimes.com/culture/books/
    memoirs-of-a-revolutionary-secre-
    tary-published-1.1733972. Retrieved 2
    October 2022.
95 Taylor, 2015, 235.
96 Burke, 2003, 350.
97 Hanley, 2002, 53–6.
98 Brown, 2004, 164.
99 Leonard, 1979, 146.
100 Earner-Byrne, 2007, 96.
101 Bill Riordan in Clare and Laffan,
    2006, 29.
102 NFC UFP, vol. 1979, 74–5.
103 *Ibid.*, vol. 1954, 284.
104 Brown, 2004, 165.
105 Lyng, 2016, 50.
106 O'Brien, 2003, 51–2.
107 'Bombs Fall, People Injured, Craters in
    Roadway and Garden', *Irish Times*, 21
    December 1941.
108 NFC UFP, vol. 1994, 345.
109 Fanning, 2016, 362–3.
110 'German Government's Fine Gift',
    Irish Times, 14 February 1938.
111 'Court and Personal', *Irish Times*, 28
    February 1938.
112 O'Donoghue, 2007, 170.
113 'Herr Hitler's Death, Callers at
    German Legation', *Irish Times*, 3 May
    1945.
114 Hull, 2002, 697; 702; 704.
115 Molohan, 1997, 7–9.
116 Hull, 2002, 704.
117 Taylor, 2015, 247.
118 Also reported in the *Irish Times* on 18
    April 1949, 'Guns Salute the Republic
    in Midnight Ceremony'.

119 Hanley, 2018, 51.

120 *Ibid.*, 17; 26; 30.

121 'British Embassy Bombed as 8000 Protest', *Irish Press*, 2 February 1972.

122 Hanley, 2018, 32.

123 *Ibid.*, 36.

124 Hanley, 2018, 43; 46; 55.

125 Weinraub, 1976.

126 Kate Ewart-Biggs: 'We Were Greeted by a Line of Staff Crying… I Knew in that Moment my Father had Died', *Belfast Telegraph*, 8 February 2020.

127 Mrs Christopher Ewart-Biggs, *Irish Times*, 30 July 1976

128 Hanley, 2018, 56.

129 *Ibid.*, 2018, 140.

130 *Ibid.*, 2018, 140; 146.

131 Personal communication with Aoife O'Connor of the Irish Film Classification Office.

132 Ferriter, 2009, 24–5.

133 Prunty, 2007, 264.

134 Brady, 2020, 97.

135 Ryan, 2018, 11–12.

136 Ryan, 2015, 24.

137 Brady, 2020, 57.

138 *Ibid.*, 96–7.

139 Beaumont, 2018, 232.

140 Girvin, 2018, 1.

141 Beaumont, 2018, 235.

142 'Women and Jury Service; Opposed to Voluntary Panel Amendment', *Irish Times*, 4 March 1927.

143 Beaumont, 2018, 235–7.

144 Ferriter, 2009, 116–17.

145 Ripley, 1981, 14.

146 Ferriter, 2009, 150.

147 O'Flynn, 1981, 31.

148 Skehill, 2004, 278.

149 Ferriter, 2009, 146.

150 Connolly, 2002, 73.

151 Ferriter, 2008, 181.

152 Connolly, 2002, 74; 77.

153 Sobolewski, 2015, 90.

154 Kennedy, 2001, 107.

155 Sobolewski, 2015, 91.

156 Ferriter, 2008, 179.

157 Daly, 2016, 128–9.

158 Connolly, 2002, 99–100.

159 Kelly, 2019, 269–70.

160 Daly, 2016, 181.

161 'Dealing with Wife Beating', Letter to the Editor, *Irish Independent*, 8 May 1974.

162 Contraception Action Programme, 1977.

163 Quoted in Magee, 2019, 379.

164 Kelly, 2019, 270.

165 *Ibid.*, 280.

166 NFC UFP, vol. 1994, 65.

167 Daly, 2016, 182.

168 Cullen Owens, 2005, 177.

169 Marsh, 2022, 74.

170 Marsh, 2019, 149.

171 Ferriter, 2013, 661.

172 Kennedy, 2001, 109.

173 'Girls in Bikinis Invade Male Swimming Resort', *Irish Times*, 22 July 1974.

174 Ferriter, 2013, 678.

175 'Girls in Bikinis Invade Male Swimming Resort', *Irish Times*, 22 July 1974.

176 'Cyril McDermott, a Male View', *Irish Times*, 7 August 1974.

177 Ferriter, 2013, 668.

178 Ferriter, 2008, 190.

179 Girvin, 2008, 89.

180 '14-year-old Strike Continues', *Irish Times*, 5 June 1953.

181 See *Solidarity with Travellers* (Roadside Books, 2000) by Seán Ó Riain for a discussion of pro-Traveller activism involving collaborations between members of the Traveller and of the settled communities.

182 McDonagh, 1994, 99.

183 Keane, 1985, 3; Cumann Duiseachta na h-Inse, cited in Keane, 1985, 8.

184 'Bishops Plan Week to Aid Itinerants, Dr McQuaid Calls for Special Prayers', *Irish Times*, 1 December 1969.

185 Crowley, 2009, 18.

186 'An Irishwoman's Diary', *Irish Times*, 9 April 1973.

187 Crowley, 2009, 20.

188 'Itinerant Plan Opposed', *Irish Times*, 1 December 1981.

189 'Nowhere to Go', Letter to the Editor, *Irish Independent*, 28 July 1986.

190 Liam Clare in Clare and Laffan, 2006, 129.

191 Bhreatnach, 2006, 147.

192 Casey, 2018, 2020.

193 Ferriter, 2009, 223.

194 Carville, 2021, 545.

195 Casey, 2018, 219

196 Nolan, 2018, 109.

197 Ferriter, 2013, 583.

198 Ferriter, 2009, 488.

199 Casey, 2018, 219–20.

200 'Facing the Demons', *Sunday Independent*, 22 May 1988.

201 Nolan, 2018, 108–10.

202 Ferriter, 2009, 504.

203 *Ibid.*, 513–15

204 *Ibid.*, 2009, 503.

205 Brown, 2004, 372.

206 *Ibid.*, 316–18.

207 Medico-Social Research Board, 1984, 14; 4; 17–18.

'Getting Ahead'

1 The Carmelite convent in Blackrock would close in 1997 after 174 years. Connolly, Paul, 'Falling Numbers Force Nuns to Close Monastery', *Irish Times*, 19 February 1997.

2 De Cléir, 2019, 2.

3 Gilligan, 2014, 147.

4 Titley, 1983, 129.

5 Daley, 2014, 66.

6 Titley, 1983, 131; 143.

7 Pearson, 1981, 114.

8 Daley, 2014, 67–8.

9 Scudds, 2001, 18.

10 Titley, *Rejecting the Modern World*, 1983, 139.

11 Maguire and Ó Cinnéide, 2005, 635–6.

12 Daley, 2014, 70.

13 Jeffers, 2016, 133–4.

14 NFC UFP, vol. 1994, 359.

15 Maguire and Ó Cinnéide, 2005, 648.

16 Kiely and Keane, 2012, 16.

17 Daly, 2016, 126.

18 Ferriter, 2013, 542.

19 Daly, 2015, 223.

20 Magee, 2017, 318.

21 Ferriter, 2013, 610.

22 Turner, 1987, 39; Nuttall, 2020, 191.

23 Walsh, 2018, 92–3.

24 *Ibid.*, 110.

25 *Ibid.*, 106–7.

26 Daly, 2016, 215,

27 Coolahan, 2017, 150.

28 Walsh, 2018, 120–1.

29 Dwyer, 1988, 1.

30 *Ibid.*

31 Keane, 1985, 18–19.

32 Bhreatnach, 2006, 112

33 Dwyer, 1988, 1.

34 Wills, 2001, 51–2.

35 Castelyn, 1984, 186.

36 Larkin, 2019, 8.

37 Grimes, 1998, 3.

38 *Ibid.*, 26–8.

39 Geraghy, 2007, 4.
40 Grimes, 1993, 61; 154.
41 Castelyn, 1984, 211; 215.
42 Grimes, 1998, 35.
43 *Ibid.*, 43; 141.

'Fun and Games'
1 Talbot Coall and Son, 1889, no given.
2 Brück, 2013, 198.
3 Pearson, 1981, 112.
4 Dún Laoghaire Borough Heritage Society, 1991, 6.
5 Pearson, 2007, 51.
6 Brück, 2013, 196; 199.
7 Nuttall, 2020, 258.
8 Brück, 2013, 214; Shannon, 2001, 21.
9 Brück, 2013, 203; 207–8.
10 Pearson, 2021, 4.
11 Curtis, 2019, 72.
12 Shannon, 2001, 15.
13 Curtis, 2011, 51.
14 NFC UFP, vol. 1992, 165.
15 *Ibid.*, vol. 1980, 35.
16 Ferriter, 2009, 125.
17 Cullen Owens, 2005, 257.
18 Fleming, 2004, 232.
19 Sheridan, 2008, 24.
20 Riach, 1973, 231; 236.
21 Lewis, 1992, 38–9.
22 For example, in January 1954, the Borough Minstrels performed for patients at St Colmcille's Hospital in Loughlinstown. 'Hospital Concert', *Irish Weekly and Ulster Examiner*, 9 January 1954.
23 O'Duffy, 2022, 126.
24 O'Reilly, 2014, 6.
25 O'Duffy, 2022, 127.
26 Kearney, 2013, 77.
27 Fleming, 2004, 228.
28 Kearney, 2013, 76.

29 Johnson, 2020, 239.
30 Grogan, 2018, 64.
31 NFC UFP, vol. 1984, 250.
32 Pearson, 1981, 139–40.
33 See Jackson, 2008, for a selection of writings about 'fit-ups'.
34 Rouse, 2015, 150–1.
35 Griffin and Strachan, 2019, 299.
36 Rouse, 2019, 310.
37 Rouse, 2015, 3; 92.
38 Reid, 2012, 148.
39 Cronin et al., 2009, 21.
40 Pearson, 2022, 217.
41 Reid, 2014, 36.
42 Rouse, 2015, 118–21.
43 Reid, 2014, 127.
44 Rouse, 2019, 312.
45 Reid, 2014, 220.
46 *Ibid.*, 49.
47 Cronin et al., 2009, 25.
48 Rouse, 2015, 178.
49 Cronin et al., 2009, 37; 40.
50 Rouse, 2015, 179–81.
51 Eaves and Hassan, 2019, 963.
52 Cronin et al., 2009, 213.
53 McElligott, 2016, 6–8.
54 Cronin et al., 2009, 123; 144; 148.
55 McElligott, 2016, 14.
56 Dooley, 2019, 116.
57 McElligott, 2019, 1–18.
58 Hassan and McGuire, 2016, 53.
59 Cronin et al., 2009, 154; 50.
60 Billings, 2017, 39.
61 Rouse, 2015, 201–2.
62 Ó hÓgarthaigh, 2011, 169.
63 Cronin et al., 2009, 258; 317.
64 *Ibid.*, 31.
65 Reid, 2014, 217.
66 Ó Murchadha, Oifig an tSoláthair, 1932.
67 Ó Conchubhair, 2013, 7.
68 O'Callaghan, 2016, 105.

69   Moore, 2017, 505.

70   Curran, 2021, 800.

71   Daggs, 1944, 49; 53–4.

72   The Irish Ladies' Hockey Club, 1994, 8; 20.

73   Lucey, 2018, 44–7.

74   The Irish Ladies' Hockey Club, 1994, 12; 61.

75   Eaves and Lake, 2020, 610.

76   Henderson, 2011, 6–7.

77   Eaves and Lake, 2020, 615; 609.

78   Higgins, 2013, 16.

79   Mintel, 2001, 15.

80   Gibson, 1988, 169–70; 140; 235.

81   Pearson, 2022, 217.

82   Gibson, 1988, 163.

83   Higgins, 2013, 15; 21.

84   Dooley, 2019, 108.

85   Mulhall, 2006, 31–6.

86   Dooley, 2019, 105.

87   O'Duffy, 2021, 25; 34; 10–11; 72–5.

88   *Ibid.*, 5; 40.

89   Wall, 1962, 13; 16–17.

90   O'Duffy, 2021, 44; 46.

91   Pearson, 2022, 95.

92   D'Alton, 2019, 87; 94.

93   Pearson, 1981, 74.

94   O'Sullivan, 2020, 5.

95   D'Alton, 2019, 88.

96   Pearson, 2022, 106.

97   Tully, 2012, 403.

98   Slusar, 2015, 29; 82; 133–4; 195–6; 234.

99   Fulton, 2004, 16–17; 21.

100 Murphy, 2013, 114–17.

101 NFC UFP, vol. 1972, 282.

102 Pearson, 1981, 141.

103 Cullen Owens, 2005, 258–9.

104 Ó hÓgarthaigh, 2011, 170; 175.

105 Raftery and Delaney, 2019, 335.

106 Ó hÓgarthaigh, 2011, 176; 178.

107 Dún Laoghaire Christian Institute, 1992, 1–2.

108 Dún Laoghaire Borough Heritage Society, 1991, 10.

109 Scudds, 2003, 2.

110 Findlater, 2000, 377.

'(Before the) Cradle to (Beyond the) Grave'

1   Wilde, 1849, 12–15.

2   Conlon, 2016, 89.

3   McMahon, 2005, 158–9.

4   Bhreathnach, 2016, 34.

5   McMahon, 2005, 161.

6   Breathnach, 2016, 41.

7   McMahon, 2005, 167.

8   Earner-Byrne, 2007, 10.

9   Daley, 2016 (Hay) 20.

10   Earner-Byrne, 2007, 11.

11   Farmar, 2004, 152.

12   Ballard, 2021, 221–2.

13   Earner-Byrne, 2007, 163.

14   Clear, 2000, 100–2.

15   Farmar, 2004, 200.

16   'Society for the Prevention of Cruelty to Children', *Irish Times*, 7 June 1889.

17   'Society for the Prevention of Cruelty to Children', *Irish Times*, 25 July 1901.

18   Earner-Byrne, 2007, 187; 48.

19   Breathnach, 2017, 783.

20   Earner-Byrne, 2007, 197.

21   'Charge Against a Boarding-out Nurse', *Irish Times*, 14 October 1905.

22   Cullen Owens, 2005, 160–1.

23   Ferriter, 2009, 133.

24   Earner-Byrne and Urquhart, 2019, 9.

25   Garrett, 2000, 337.

26   Luddy, 2001, 808.

27   Ferriter, 2009, 129.

28   Earner-Byrne, 2015, 91.

29   Ferriter, 2009, 55.

30 Earner-Byrne, 2015, 76.

31 Luddy, 2001, 806.

32 Cullen Owens, 2005, 174.

33 Rattigan, 2008, 135.

34 Farrell, 2013, 247–8.

35 'The Recent Child Murder at Blackrock', *Irish Times*, 4 December 1884.

36 'Inquest at Kingstown', *Irish Times*, 18 June 1890.

37 Earner-Byrne and Urquhart, 2019, 12.

38 Breathnach, 2017, 785–6.

39 Breathnach and O'Halpin, 2014, 212.

40 Rattigan, 2008, 137.

41 Prior, 2010, 92.

42 Rattigan, 2008, 142.

43 NFC UFP, vol. 1991, 272–3.

44 Prior, 2010, 92.

45 Ferriter, 2008, 131.

46 NFC UFP, vol. 1991, 268.

47 Delay, 2019.

48 Ferriter, 2008, 198–9.

49 'Illegal Operation Charge', *Irish Times*, 8 July 1944.

50 Farmar, 2004, 154.

51 Hesketh, 1990, 364.

52 Earner-Byrne and Urquhart, 2019, 9; 103.

53 Wilde, 1849, 4–5.

54 Girvin, 2018, 5.

55 Daly, 2006, 574.

56 O'Brien, 2021, 20.

57 Girvin, 2018, 5–6.

58 McAvoy, 2012, 192.

59 Daly, 2016, 145–6.

60 Girvin, 2018, 7.

61 Daley, 2006, 580.

62 Foley, 2019, 148; 143–5.

63 Daly, 2016, 144–50.

64 Ferriter, 2009, 362.

65 Foley, 2019, 156–7.

66 Ferriter, 2009, 330.

67 Skehill 2004, 266–7.

68 Leonard, 1989, 137.

69 Gilligan, 2014, 149.

70 Earner-Byrne, 2015, 95. See also Ferriter, 2009, 56–7, for a discussion of this issue.

71 Redmond, 2018, 35.

72 Skehill, 2004, 212.

73 Earner-Byrne, 2007, 207.

74 Daly, 2016, 166–7.

75 Earner-Byrne, 2007, 101–2.

76 Clear, 2000, 58.

77 'Precautionary Measures Against Gastro-Intestinal Disease', *Irish Times*, 21 February 1951.

78 Clear, 2000, 130–1.

79 Ferriter, 2009, 301.

80 Clear, 2000, 133.

81 Brennan and Ryan, 2020, 154.

82 'I wouldn't have breastfed if I hadn't got support', *Irish Independent*, 2 May 2023.

83 'Breastfeeding Seminar', *Irish Times,* 25 April 1979.

84 Kelly, 2023, Chapter 2.

85 O'Morchoe, 1934, 33–4.

86 O'Rafferty, 1996, 8.

87 Cox, 2010, 60.

88 Geary, 2011, 190–1.

89 Cox, 2010, 58.

90 Hardy, 1913, 43.

91 Farmar, 2004, 102.

92 Hardy, 1913, 12.

93 Lehane, 2019, 133.

94 Lyng, 2011, 18.

95 Lehane, 2019, 152.

96 Kelly, 2013, 143; 150; 141.

97 Purcell, 1979, 25; 31; 53; 99.

98 'B', 1834, 1.

99 NFC SC, vol. 796, 15.

100 See Nuttall, 2019, 145–57, for a general discussion of the practice in contemporary tradition.

101 NFC UFP, vol. 1991, 275–6.

102 2016, 43.

103 Lyng, 2016, 43.

104 NFC UFP, vol. 1994, 157; 164.

105 *Ibid.*, vol. 1992, 265.

106 Drew, 2008, 18.

107 Whelan, 2018, 100.

108 NFC UFP, vol. 1992, 257.

109 *Ibid.*, vol. 1991, 251.

110 Whelan, 2018, 99.

111 Curl, 1975, 13.

112 Pearson, 2007, 191.

113 Brendan Reynolds, in Clare and Laffan, 2006, 18.

'Looking Back, Looking Forward'

1 Brown, 2004, 371.

2 Butler, 2015, 198–9; 209.

BIBLIOGRAPHY

Aalen, F.H.A., 'Homes for Irish Heroes: Housing Under the Irish Land Act 1919 and the Irish Sailors' and Soldiers' Land Trust', *Town Planning Review*, vol. 59, no. 3, pp.305–23.

Archer, Stella and Pearson, Peter, *Royal St. George Yacht Club* (Dublin: Iona Print, 1987).

Aarne, Antti and Thompson, Stith, *The Types of the Folktale: A Classification and Bibliography* (Helsinki: The Finnish Academy of Science and Letters, 1961).

'B.', 'Dalkey, County of Dublin', *The Dublin Penny Journal*, issue 85, 1834, vol. 2, pp.257–8.

Begadon, Cormac, 'Confraternities and the Renewal of Catholic Dublin *c.*1750–*c.*1830', in Colm Lennon (ed.) *Confraternities and Sodalities in Ireland: Charity, Church and Sociability* (Dublin: Columba Press, 2012), pp.35–57.

Ball, Francis Elrington, 'Residents of Monkstown in the Eighteenth Century', *Journal of the Royal Society of Antiquaries of Ireland*, vol. 9, issue 3, 1899, pp.233–44.

Ball, Francis Elrington and Hamilton, Everard, *The Parish of Taney: a History of Dundrum, Near Dublin, and its Neighbourhood* (Dundrum: Hodges, Figgis, & Company Ltd, 1895).

Ballard, Linda-May, 'The Handywoman', in Ryan, Salvador, *Birth and the Irish: a Miscellany* (Dublin: Wordwell Press, 2021), pp.221–4.

Banks, Mary, 'The Longest Strike', *A Trip Down Memory Lane – Memories of Growing up in the Borough of Dún Laoghaire* (Dublin: The Over 50s Activities Club, 2006).

Barger, Lilian Calles, *The World Come of Age: An Intellectual History of Liberation Theology* (Oxford: Oxford University Press, 2018).

Barnett, John, 'Quarries, Mines, and Railways of Dalkey', *Journal of the Mining Heritage Trust of Ireland*, vol. 6, 2006, pp.17–21.

Beaumont, Catriona, 'After the Vote: Women, Citizenship and the Campaign for Gender Equality in the Irish Free State (1922–1943),' in Ryan, Louise, *Winning the Vote for Women: the Irish Citizen Newspaper and the Suffrage Movement in Ireland* (Dublin: Four Courts Press, 2018), pp.231–50.

Beckett, T., 'The Mulberry Harbours – Undiminished After 60 Years', *Proceedings of the Institution of Civil Engineers – Maritime Engineering*, vol. 157, issue 4, December 2004, pp.171–4.

Bell, Jonathan and Watson, Mervyn, *A History of Irish Farming 1760–1950* (Dublin: Four Courts Press, 2008).

Bhreatnach, Aoife, *Becoming Conspicuous: Irish Travellers, Society and the State, 1922–70* (Dublin: University College Dublin Press, 2006).

Bhreathnach-Lynch, Sighle, *Sr Concepta Lynch O.P. (1974–1939): A Unique Contribution to Irish Art* (Dublin: Four Courts Press, 2010).

Biagini, Eugenio, '"Patrick, the First Churchman", in The Protestant Vision of Ernest Bateman of Booterstown (1886–1979)', in Hill, Jacqueline and Lyons, Mary Ann (eds), *Representing Irish Religious Histories* (Berlin: Springer International Publishing, 2017), pp.211–27.

Billings, Cathal, 'Speaking Irish with Hurley Sticks: Gaelic Sports, the Irish Language and National Identity in Revival Ireland', *Sport in History*, vol. 37, issue 1, 2017, pp.25–50.

Boland, Eavan, *Object Lessons; The Life of the Women and the Poet in our Time* (Manchester: Carcanet Press, 1995).

Bolton, Jason, Carey, Tim, Goodbody, Rob and Clabby, Gerry, *The Martello Towers of Dublin* (Dublin: Dún Laoghaire-Rathdown County Council and Fingal County Council, 2012).

Boyd, Gary A., 'Supernational Catholicity: Dublin and the 1932 Eucharistic Congress', *Early Popular Visual Culture*, vol. 5, issue 3, November 2007, pp.217–333.

Boyd, Gary A., Pike, Michael and Ward, Brian, *Irish Housing Design 1950–1980* (Abingdon-on-Thames: Routledge, 2020).

Brady, Joseph, *Dublin in the 1950s and 1960s: Cars, Shops and Suburbs* (Dublin: Four Courts Press, 2017).

Brady, James, *With the Sixth Battalion, South County Dublin and the War for Independence, 1916–1921* (Litter: Litter Press, 2020).

Branigan, Gary, *Ancient and Holy Wells of Dublin* (Dublin: The History Press Ireland, 2012).

Breathnach, Ciara, 'Handywomen and Birthing in Rural Ireland, 1851–1955', *Gender & History*, vol. 28, issue 1, 2016, pp.34–56.

Breathnach, Ciara, 'Infant life Protection and Medico-Legal Literacy in Early Twentieth-century Dublin', *Women's History Review*, vol. 26, issue 6, 2017, pp.781–98.

Breathnach, Ciara and O'Halpin, Eunan, 'Scripting Blame: Irish Coroners' Courts and Unnamed Infant Dead, 1916–32', *Social History*, vol. 39, issue 2, May 2014, pp.210–28.

Brown, Terence, *Ireland: A Social and Cultural History, 1922–2002* (London: Harper Perennial, 2004).

Brück, Joanna, 'Landscapes of Desire: Parks, Colonialism, and Identity in Victorian and Edwardian Ireland', *International Journal of Historical Archaeology*, vol. 17, issue 1, pp.196–223.

Budd, John W. and Guinnane, Timothy, 'Intentional Age-Misreporting, Age-Heaping, and the 1908 Old Age Pensions Act in Ireland,' *Population Studies*, vol. 45, issue 3, November 1991, pp.497–518.

Burke, Tom, '"Poppy Day" in the Irish Free State', *Irish Quarterly Review*, vol. 92, pp.349–58.

Butler, Jenny, 'Paganism in Ireland, Syncretic Processes, Identity, and a Sense of Place,' in Rountree, Kathryn (ed.), *Contemporary Pagan and Native Faith Movements in Europe; Colonial and Nationalist Impulses* (New York: Berghahn, 2015), pp.196–215.

Byrne, Sylvester, *I was Born on a Farm in Dublin 4* (Paris: Obelisk Press, 2018).

Cannon, Nuala, 'Mariners in the Blood: Pilot families of Bullock Harbour, Dalkey, Co. Dublin', *The Irish Genealogist*, vol. 14, issue 1, 2014, pp.34–45.

Carville, Gary, '"Scrupulous and Timid Conformism": Ireland and the Reception of the Liturgical Changes of Vatican II', *Religions*, vol. 12, issue 7, July 2021, pp.545.

Carter, Grayson, *Anglican Evangelicals: Protestant Secessions from the Via Media, c. 1800–1850* (Eugene: Wipf and Stock Publishers, 2015), pp.69–70.

Casey, Maurice J., 'Radical Politics and Gay Activism in the Republic of Ireland, 1974–1990', *Irish Studies Review*, vol. 26, 2018, pp.217–36.

Cassidy, Mark, Strobl, Eric and Thornton, Robert J., 'Gender Pay Differentials and Equality Legislation in the Republic of Ireland', *Canadian Public Policy*, vol. 28, pp.149–69.

Casteleyn, Mary, *A History of Literacy and Libraries in Ireland* (Aldershot: Ashgate Publishing, 1984).

Clare, Liam, *Loughlinstown Workhouse in the 1840s; a Talk to the Foxrock Local History Club* (Foxrock: Foxrock Local History Club, 1986).

Clare, Liam, *Enclosing the Commons: Dalkey, the Sugar Loaves and Bray, 1820–1870 (Maynooth Studies in Local History)* (Dublin: Four Courts Press, 2004).

Clare, Liam, 'The Kill and the Grange of Clonkeen: Two Early Settlements in South County Dublin', *Dublin Historical Record*, vol. 58, issue 1, 2005, pp.17–30.

Clare, L. and Laffan, P., *Foxrock and Cabinteely Memories* (Dublin: Nonsuch Publishing, 2006).

Clear, Caitriona, *Women of the House: Women's Household Work in Ireland 1922–1961* (Dublin: Irish Academic Press, 2000).

Clear, Caitrona, 'Birth in Ireland c.1900–1960', in Ryan, Salvador (ed.), *Birth and the Irish: a Miscellany* (Dublin: Wordwell Books, 2021), pp.255–8.

Coleman, Marie, 'Military Service Pensions for Veterans of the Irish Revolution, 1916–1923', *War in History*, vol. 20, no. 2, 2013, pp.201–21.

Coleman, Marie, 'Violence Against Women in the Irish War of Independence, 1919–21', in Ferriter, Diarmaid and Riordan, Susannah (eds), *Years of Turbulence; the Irish Revolution and its Aftermath*, (Dublin: University College Dublin Press, 2015), pp.131–56.

Commission to Enquire into Child Abuse, The, 'Carriglea Park Industrial School, Dún Laoghaire ('Carriglea'), 1894–1954', *Report of the Commission to Inquire into Child Abuse*, vol. 1, chapter 10, 2022.

Conlon, Tom, 'The Last Town They Saw, Friends of the Leinster', in Ó Caollí, Breasal; O'Hagan, Niall and Finlay, Ken (eds), *The Last Voyage of the Leinster: Remembering the Dún Laoghaire & Holyhead Mailboat* (Dún Laoghaire: Dún Laoghaire Holyhead Mail Boat Leinster Centenary Committee/Friends of the Leinster, 2018), pp.10–15.

Conlon, Tom, 'Amateur Entertainment in Kingstown and Blackrock from the 1890s Onwards', *Genealogical Society of Ireland*, vol. 20, issue 2, 2016, pp.201–221.

Conlon, Tom, *Victorian Dún Laoghaire: a Town Divided* (Dublin: The History Press Ireland, 2016).

Connolly, Linda, *The Irish Women's Movement; from Revolution to Devolution* (London: Palgrave Macmillan, 2002).

Connolly, S., *Religion and Society in Nineteenth Century Ireland, Studies in Irish Economic and Social History* (Dundalk: Dundalgan Press, 1985).

Contraception Action Programme, Ballinteer Family Planning Survey, 1977.

Coolahan, John, *Towards the Era of Lifelong Learning; a History of Irish Education 1800–2016* (Dublin: Institute of Public Administration, 2017).

Cooney, John, *John Charles McQuaid; Ruler of Catholic Ireland* (Dublin: The O'Brien Press, 1999).

Cooper, June Eleanor, 'The Protestant Orphan Society, Dublin 1828–1928', PhD thesis (Maynooth: Department of History, National University of Ireland, 2009).

Corlett, Christiaan, *Unearthing the Archaeology of Dún Laoghaire-Rathdown* (Dublin: Dún Laoghaire-Rathdown County Council, 2013).

Costello, Francis J., *The Irish Revolution and its Aftermath, 1916–1923: Years of Revolt* (Newbridge: Irish Academic Press, 2003).

Cousins, Mel, 'Social Welfare Adjudication In Ireland, 1847–1995: A Diachronic Analysis', *Irish Jurist*, vol. 28/30, pp.361–82.

Cowman, D., 'The Metal Mines of Dublin City and County, c.1740–1825', *The Journal of the Mining Heritage Trust of Ireland*, vol. 1, 2001, pp.61–6.

Cox, Catherine, 'Access and Engagement, the Medical Dispensary Service in Post-Famine Ireland', in Cox, Catherine and Luddy, Maria (eds), *Cultures of Care in Irish Medical History, 1750–1970* (London: Palgrave Macmillan, 2010), pp.57–91.

Crawford O'Brien, Suzanne J., 'Well, Water, Rock: Holy Wells, Mass Rocks and Reconciling Identity in the Republic of Ireland', in *Material Religion: The Journal of Objects, Art and Belief,* vol. 4, issue 3, pp.326–48.

Cronin, Mike, Duncan, Mark and Rouse, Paul, *The GAA; a People's History* (Cork: The Collins Press, 2009).

Cronin, Patrick, *South County Dublin and East Wicklow During the 1914–19 War, a Paper Read to the Foxrock Local History Club on 6th October, 1986* (Dublin: Foxrock Local History Club, 1986).

Crossman, Virginia, *Poverty and the Poor Law in Ireland, 1850–1914, Reappraisals in Irish History* (Liverpool: Liverpool University Press, 2013).

Crowe, Catriona, 'Stillorgan in the 1911 Census Records', *Obelisk: Journal of the Kilmacud Stillorgan Local History Society,* vol. 2, 2006, pp.41–6.

Crowley, Úna, 'Outside in Dublin: Travellers, Society and the State, 1963–1985', *The Canadian Journal of Irish Studies,* vol. 35, no. 1 (Spring/Printemps 2009), pp.17–24.

Cullen Owens, Rosemary, *A Social History of Women in Ireland, 1870–1970* (Dublin: Gill and Macmillan, 2005).

Curl, James Stevens, 'The Architecture and Planning of the Nineteenth-Century Cemetery', *Garden History,* vol. 3, no. 3, Summer 1975, pp.13–41.

Curran, Conor, 'Introduction: the Growth and Development of Soccer in Dublin', *Soccer & Society,* vol. 22, issue 8, December 2021, pp.799–804.

Curran, Peadar and Ryan, Nicholas, *Ticknock, A History of a Beautiful Valley in the Dublin Mountains* (Dublin: The Ballinteer Active Retirement Association, Local History Study Group, 2020).

Curtis, Joe, *Harold Country: Rathfarnham* (Dublin: First Return Press, 2011).

Curtis, Joe, *Mount Merrion, 1711–2011* (Dublin: First Return Press, 2011).

d'Alton, Ian, 'Religion as Identity: The Church of Ireland's 1932 Patrician Celebrations', in Hill, J. and Lyons, M. (eds), *Representing Irish Religious Histories* (London: Palgrave Macmillan, 2017), pp.197–210.

d'Alton, Ian, '"Aquatic Gentlemen…" the Sport and Status of Sailing in the Gentry's World from the 1830s to the 1920s', in Dooley, Terence and Ridgway,

Christopher (eds), *Sport and Leisure in the Irish and British Country House* (Dublin: Four Courts Press, 2019), pp.73–86.

de Cléir, Síle, *Popular Catholicism in 20th-Century Ireland: Locality, Identity and Culture* (London and New York: Bloomsbury Academic, 2019).

Dagg, T.S.C., *Hockey in Ireland* (Tralee: The Kerryman Ltd, 1944).

Daly, Mary E., 'The Growth of Victorian Dublin', in Daly, Mary E., Hearn, Mona and Pearson, Peter (eds), *Dublin's Victorian Houses* (Dublin: A.&A. Farmar, 1998).

Daly, Mary E., 'Marriage, Fertility and Women's Lives in Twentieth Century Ireland (*c.*1900–*c.*1970)', *Women's History Review*, vol. 15, issue 4, 2006, pp.571–83.

Daly, Mary E., '"The Primary and Natural Educator"? The Role of Parents in the Education of their Children in Independent Ireland', in Luddy, Maria and Smith, James (eds), *Children, Childhood and Irish Society 1500 to the Present* (Dublin: Four Courts Press, 2014), pp.65–81.

Daly, Mary E., 'The Social Context of Wartime Dublin', in Hay, Marnie and Keogh, Dáire (eds), *Rebellion & Revolution in Dublin: Voices from a Suburb, Rathfarnham, 1913–23* (Dublin: South Dublin Libraries, 2016), pp.11–28.

Daly, Mary E., *Sixties Ireland; Reshaping the Economy, State and Society, 1957–1973* (Cambridge: Cambridge University Press, 2016).

D'Auria, Déirdre, *The Impact of Italian Foodways on Irish Food Habits from the Late Nineteenth Century* (PhD thesis submitted to UCD in December 2012).

Delay, Cara, 'Holy Water and a Twig: Catholic Households and Women's Religious Authority in Modern Ireland', *Journal of Family History*, vol. 43, issue 3, April 2018, pp.302–19.

Delay, Cara, 'Pills, Potions, and Purgatives: Women and Abortion Methods in Ireland, 1900–1950', *Women's History Review*, vol. 28, issue 3, April 2019, pp.479–99.

Devlin, Martina, 'Hell on Earth, but at Least Heaven was Waiting for Them', in Mannion, Padraig (ed.), *Lockout Centenary: Dún Laoghaire 1913–2013* (Dún Laoghaire: Dún Laoghaire 1913 Commemoration Committee, 2013), pp.35–8.

De Vos, Gail, *Tales, Rumors, and Gossip: Exploring Contemporary Folk Literature in Grades 7–12* (Exeter: Libraries Unlimited, 1996).

Diskin, Mary, 'Dora Montefiore: An Unwitting Victim of Propaganda', in Mannion, Padraig (ed.), *Lockout Centenary: Dún Laoghaire 1913–2013* (Dún Laoghaire: Dún Laoghaire 1913 Commemorative Committee, 1913), pp.27–30.

Donnelly, Nicholas, *A Short History of Some Dublin Parishes: Part III, The Parishes of Booterstown, Blackrock, Stillorgan, Kilmacud, and Dundrum* (Dublin: Catholic Truth Society of Ireland, 1907).

Donnelly, Nicholas, *A Short History of Some Dublin Parishes: part IV, The Parishes of Monkstown, Kingstown, Glasthule, and Dalkey* (Dublin: Catholic Truth Society of Ireland, 1907).

Donnelly, Nicholas, *A Short History of Some Dublin Parishes: The Parishes of Sandyford and Glencullen, Killiney, Little Bray and Cabinteely* (Dublin: Catholic Truth Society of Ireland, 1907).

Dooley, Terence, 'The Big House, Aristocracy, and Golf in Ireland c.1890–1921', in Dooley, Terence and Ridgway, Christopher (eds), *Sport and Leisure in the Irish and British Country House* (Dublin: Four Courts Press, 2019), pp.102–20.

Drew, Ronnie, *Ronnie* (Dublin: Penguin Ireland, 2008).

Duffy, Patrick J., 'Trends in Nineteenth- and Twentieth-Century Settlement', in Barry, T. (ed.), *A History of Settlement in Ireland* (London: Routledge, 2000), pp.206–227.

Dún Laoghaire Christian Institute, *Centenary Kingstown Men's Christian Institute, 1894* (Dún Laoghaire: self-published, 1992).

Dún Laoghaire Borough Civil Week, 1948, souvenir handbook.

Dún Laoghaire Harbour Company, *The Construction of Dún Laoghaire Harbour* (Dún Laoghaire: Dún Laoghaire Harbour Company, n.d.).

Dún Laoghaire Borough Heritage Society, *In the Mind's Eye: Memories of Dún Laoghaire* (Dún Laoghaire: Dún Laoghaire Borough Heritage Society, 1991).

Dwyer, Sr Colette, '"Seven" Years of Progress? Third Report on the Educational Needs of Travelling People', submitted by the National Coordinator of the Education of Travelling People, Sister Colette Dwyer, *Irish Travelling People*, vol. 8, Education, part G, January 1981.

Dwyer, Sr Colette, 'The Education, Training and Employment of Travellers – 21 Years On', Report of the National Coordinator for the Education of Travellers, *Irish Travelling People*, vol. 8, Education, part G, 1988.

Earner-Byrne, Lindsey, *Mother and Child: Maternity and Child Welfare in Dublin, 1922–60* (Manchester: Manchester University Press, 2007).

Earner-Byrne, Lindsey, 'The Rape of Mary M.: A Microhistory of Sexual Violence and Moral Redemption in 1920s Ireland', *Journal of the History of Sexuality*, vol. 24, no. 1, January 2015, pp.75–98.

Earner-Byrne, Lindsey, *Letters of the Catholic Poor: Poverty in Independent Ireland, 1920–1940* (Cambridge: Cambridge University Press, 2017).

Earner-Byrne, Lindsey and Urquhart, Diane, *The Irish Abortion Journey, 1920–2018* (London: Palgrave MacMillan, 2019).

Eaves, Simon J. and Lake, Robert J., 'The Forgotten Powerhouse: Analyzing the Brief Rise to Prominence of Lawn Tennis in Ireland in the Late-Nineteenth Century', *The International Journal of the History of Sport*, vol. 36, issue 11, 2019, pp.959–81.

Eaves, Simon J. and Lake, Robert J., 'The Decline of Lawn Tennis in Ireland around the Turn of the Twentieth Century: Bad Management, Bad Luck, or Bad Homburg?', *International Journal of the History of Sport*, vol. 37, issue 8, June 2020, pp.607–32.

Edgeworth, Brendan, 'Rural Radicalism Restrained: The Irish Land Commission and the Courts (1933–39)', *Irish Jurist*, vol. 42, 2007, pp.1–28.

Edwards, B.L. and Stephens, Claire, *Dalkey: a Short Account of the Town Throughout its Changing History* (Dublin: J. Duffy and Co., 1938).

Falconer, A., 'Ecumenism in Ireland', *Kirchliche Zeitgeschichte*, vol. 10, no. 1, *Bürgerkrieg und Religion*, 1997, pp.74–88.

Fanning, Bryan, 'Jewish, Catholic and Collaborator Refugees in Ireland', *Studies: An Irish Quarterly Review*, vol. 105, no. 419, EUROPE IN CRISIS, Autumn 2016, pp.362–72.

Farmar, Tony, *Patients, Potions, and Physicians: A Social History of Medicine in Ireland* (Dún Laoghaire: A.&A. Farmar Book Publishing (with the Royal College of Physicians of Ireland), 2004).

Farrell, Elaine, *A Most 'Diabolical Deed': Infanticide and Irish Society, 1850–1900* (Manchester: Manchester University Press, 2013).

Farrell, Anthony, 'A Forgotten Generation: Medical Care for Disabled Veterans of the First World War in Independent Ireland', *Irish Studies Review*, vol. 29, issue 2, April 2021, pp.142–55.

Fealy, Gerard M., *Care to Remember; Nursing and Midwifery in Ireland* (Cork: Mercier Press, 2005).

Ferriter, Diarmaid, *Occasions of Sin* (London: Profile Books, 2009).

Ferriter, Diarmaid, *Ambiguous Republic: Ireland in the 1970s* (London: Profile Books, 2013).

Ferriter, Diarmaid, 'Always in Danger of Finding Myself with Nothing At All', in the *Military Service Pensions and the Battle for Material Survival, 1925–55*, in Ferriter, Diarmaid and Riordan, Susannah (eds), *Years of Turbulence; the Irish Revolution and its Aftermath* (Dublin: University College Dublin Press, 2015).

Ferriter, Diarmaid, 'Women and Political Change,' *Éire-Ireland*, vol. 43, no. 2, Summer 2008, pp.179–204.

Ferriter, Diarmaid, *A Nation and not a Rabble: the Irish Revolution 1913–1923* (London: Profile Books, 2015).

Findlater, Alex, *Findlaters – the Story of a Dublin Merchant Family 1774–2001* (Dublin: A.&A. Farmar, 2001).

Finn, Clodagh, 'Sr Clodagh Lynch, Businesswoman, Dominican Sister, and Painter of a Unique Celtic Shrine 1874–1939', in *Through Her Eyes: A New History of Ireland in 21 Women* (Dublin: Gill Books, 2019), pp.137–54.

Fitzpatrick, David, 'The Logic of Collective Sacrifice: Ireland and the British Army, 1914–1918', *The Historical Journal*, vol. 38, no. 4, December 1995, pp.1,017–30.

Fitzpatrick, David, 'Commemoration in the Irish Free State: A Chronicle of Embarrassment', in Ian McBride (ed.), *History and Memory in Modern Ireland* (Cambridge: Cambridge University Press, 2001), pp.184–203.

Fitz-Simon, Chris, *Eleven Houses: a Memoir of Childhood* (Dublin: Penguin Ireland, 2007).

Fleming, Rachel C., 'Resisting Cultural Standardization: Comhaltas Ceoltóirí Éireann and the Revitalisation of Traditional Music in Ireland', *Journal of Folklore Research* (Special Double Issue: Advocacy Issues in Folklore, May–December 2004), pp.227–57.

Foley, Deirdre, '"Too Many Children?" Family Planning and Humanae Vitae in Dublin, 1960–72', *Economic and Social History Society of Ireland*, vol. 46, issue 1, December 2019, pp.142–60.

Frazer, James, *The Golden Bough: A Study in Comparative Religion* (Oxford: Oxford University Press, 1994, orig. 1889).

Ó Caollí, Breasal, O'Hagan, Niall and Finlay, Ken (eds), *The Last Voyage of the Leinster: Remembering the Dún Laoghaire & Holyhead Mailboat* (Dublin: Dún Laoghaire Holyhead Mail Boat Leinster Centenary Committee/Friends of the Leinster, 2018).

Fuller, Louise, 'Religion, Politics and Socio-Cultural Change in Twentieth-Century Ireland', *The European Legacy, Toward New Paradigms*, vol. 10, issue 1, February 2005, pp.41–54.

Fulton, Tom, 'A Brief History of Hunting in Ireland', in Costecalde, Claude and Gallagher, Jack (eds), *Hunting in Ireland: a Noble Tradition* (Dublin: Booklink, 2004), pp.13–25.

Galavan, Susan, *Dublin's Bourgeois Homes: Building the Victorian suburbs 1850–1901* (Abingdon: Routledge, 2017).

Garrett, Paul Michael, 'The Abnormal Flight: The Migration and Repatriation of Irish Unmarried Mothers', *Social History*, vol. 25, no. 3, October 2000, pp.330–43.

Geary, Laurence M., 'The Medical Profession, Health Care, and the Poor Law in Nineteenth-Century Ireland', in Crossman, Virginia and Gray, Peter (eds), *Poverty and Welfare in Ireland, 1838–1948* (Newbridge: Irish Academic Press, 2011), pp.189–206.

Geraghty, Alan, 'Glencullen Library – 1907–2007', *Three Rock Panorama*, vol. 33, no. 6, 2007, p.4.

Gibney, John, 'Pioneers and Aviators: a Century of Irish Aviation', *History Ireland*, vol. 22, issue 3, May–June 2014, *Reviews*.

Gibson, William H., *Early Irish Golf: The First Courses, Clubs and Pioneers* (London: Oakleaf Publications, 1988).

Gilligan, Robbie, 'The "Public Child" and the Reluctant State?', in Luddy, Maria and Smith, James (eds), *Children, Childhood and Irish Society, 1500 to the Present* (Dublin: Four Courts Press, 2014), pp.145–63.

Girvin, Brian, 'Social Change and Moral Politics: The Irish Constitutional Referendum 1983', *Political Studies Association*, vol. 34, issue 1, 1986, pp.61–81.

Girvin, Brian, 'Church, State and Society in Ireland since 1960,' *Éire-Ireland*, vol. 43, no. 1–2, Spring–Summer 2008, pp.74–98.

Girvin, B, 'An Irish Solution to an Irish Problem: Catholicism, Contraception and Change, 1922–1979', *Contemporary European History*, vol. 27, no. 1, 2018, pp.1–22.

Gmelch, George, *The Irish Tinkers: The Urbanization of an Itinerant People* (Long Grove: Waveland Press, Inc., 1977).

Goodbody, Olive, 'The Cottage Home', *Dún Laoghaire Borough Historical Society*, no. 11, 2002, pp.55–63.

Goodbody, Rob, *On the Borders of the Pale: a History of the Kilgobbin, Stepaside and Sandyford area* (Belfast: Beyond the Pale Publishing, 1993).

Goodbody, Rob, *The Metals: from Dalkey to Dún Laoghaire* (Dublin: Dún Laoghaire-Rathdown County Council, 2010).

Goodbody, Rob, 'Blackrock Miscellany – Quakers in Monkstown', *Blackrock Society Proceedings*, vol. 12, 2004, pp.172–5.

'G.R.P.', *One, Two, or Three Days in the County of Wicklow: also a Day at Kingstown, Killiney and Bray National Folklore*, John Henry Powell (date not given, appears late nineteenth century).

Grayson, Richard S., *Dublin's Great Wars: the First World War, the Easter Rising and the Irish Revolution* (Cambridge: Cambridge University Press, 2018).

Griffin, Brian and Strachan, John, 'Introduction: Sport in Ireland from the 1880s to the 1920s', *Irish Studies Review*, vol. 27, issue 3, 2019, pp.299–308.

Grimes, Brendan, *Irish Carnegie Libraries; a Catalogue and Architectural History* (Newbridge: Irish Academic Press, 1998).

Grogan, Mary, 'Further Glimpses of the "Bug House"', *Dún Laoghaire Journal/Dún Laoghaire Borough Historical Society*, no. 27, 2018, pp.64–8.

Guinnane, Timothy W., *The Vanishing Irish: Households, Migration and the Rural Economy in Ireland, 1850–1914* (Princeton: Princeton University Press, 1997).

Gunning, David (ed.), *Shifting Foundations: the Big Houses of Dún Laoghaire-Rathdown* (Dublin: Dún Laoghaire-Rathdown County Council, 2021).

Gunning, David, 'The Big House in Dún Laoghaire-Rathdown during the Revolutionary Years', in Gunning, David (ed.), *Shifting Foundations: the Big*

Houses of Dún Laoghaire-Rathdown (Dublin: Dún Laoghaire County Council, 2021), pp.92–108.

Hanley, Brian, *The IRA – a Documentary History* (Dublin: Gill and MacMillan, 2015).

Hanley, Brian, *The Impact of the Troubles on the Republic of Ireland, 1968–79: Boiling Volcano?* (Manchester: Manchester University Press, 2018).

Hardy, H. Nelson, *The Medical Profession, the National Insurance Act, and the State of Poor Law Dispensaries in Ireland: Being the First Part of the Carmichael Prize Essay, 1913* (Dublin: University Press (Ponsonby and Gibbs) 1913).

Hart, W.A., 'Africans in Eighteenth-Century Ireland', *Irish Historical Studies*, vol. 33, no. 129, May 2002, pp.19–32.

Hassan, David and McGuire, Andrew, 'The GAA and Revolutionary Irish Politics in Late Nineteenth and Early Twentieth Century Ireland', in McElligott, Richard and Hassan, David (eds), *A Social and Cultural History of Sport in Ireland* (Abingdon: Routledge, 2016), pp.51–73.

Hay, Marnie and Keogh, Dáire, *Rebellion & Revolution in Dublin: Voices from a Suburb, Rathfarnham, 1913–23* (Dublin: South Dublin County Council, 2016).

Hayes, Michael, 'Indigenous Otherness: Some Aspects of Irish Traveller Social History', *Éire-Ireland*, vol. 41, issue 3–4, Fall–Winter 2006, pp.133–161.

Hearn, Mona, 'How Victorian Families Lived', in Daly, Mary E., Hearn, Mona and Pearson, Peter (eds), *Dublin's Victorian Houses* (Dublin: A.&A. Farmar, 1998).

Hearn, Mona, *Below Stairs: Domestic Service Remembered in Dublin and Beyond, 1880–1922* (Dublin: The Lilliput Press, 1999).

Helleiner, Jane Leslie, *Irish Travellers: Racism and the Politics of Culture* (Toronto: University of Toronto Press, 2000).

Henderson, Brendan, *Sandycove Lawn Tennis and Squash Club, 1886–2011* (Dublin: Sandycove Lawn Tennis and Squash Club, 2011).

Hesketh, Tom, *The Second Partitioning of Ireland?: The Abortion Referendum of 1983* (Dublin: Brandsma Books, 1990).

Higgins, Róisín, '"The Hallmark of Pluperfect Respectability": The Early Development of Golf in Irish Society', *Éire-Ireland: An Interdisciplinary Journal of Irish Studies*, vol. 48, issue 1 & 2, Spring–Summer 2013, pp.15–31.

Higgins, Tom, *The History of Irish Tennis* (Sligo: Sligo Tennis Club, 2006).

Hogan, Caelainn, *Republic of Shame: Stories from Ireland's Institutions for 'Fallen Women'* (Dublin: Penguin Ireland, 2019).

Holmes, David G., 'The Eucharistic Congress of 1932 and Irish Identity', *New Hibernia Review/Iris Éireannach Nua*, vol. 4, no. 1, Spring 2000, pp.55–78.

Lennon, Colm, 'Confraternities in Ireland: a Long View', in *Confraternities and Sodalities in Ireland: Charity, Devotion and Sociability* (Dublin: Columba Press, 2012), pp.15–34.

Horner, Arnold, 'Dún Laoghaire's Great Harbour', *History Ireland*, vol. 21, no. 5, September–October 2013. https://www.historyireland.com/dun-laoghaires-great-harbour/retrived 06/05/2022.

Hull, Mark M., 'The Irish Interlude: German Intelligence in Ireland, 1939–1943', *The Journal of Military History*, vol. 66, no. 3, July 2002, pp.695–717.

Hunt, Tom, 'The National Athletic Association of Ireland and Irish Athletics, 1922–1937: Steps on the Road to Athletic Isolation', in McElligott, Richard and Hassan, David (eds), *A Social and Cultural History of Sport in Ireland* (Abingdon-on-Thames: Routledge, 2016), pp.130–46.

Irish Countrywomen's Association, Rathfarnham Guild, *Rathfarnham: Gateway to the Hills: the Story of Rathfarnham Past and Present from the Dodder to Kilmashogue* (Dublin: Irish Countrywomen's Association, 1990).

Irish Ladies' Hockey Union, *The First Hundred Years 1894–1994, a Centenary History* (Dublin: Irish Ladies' Hockey Team, 1996).

Jacobsen, John Kurt, *Chasing Progress in the Irish Republic: Ideology, Democracy, and Dependent Development* (Cambridge: Cambridge University Press, 1994).

Jackson, Vikki and Ó hAodha, Mícheál (eds), *Gags and Greasepaint: a Tribute to the Irish 'Fit-Ups'* (Newcastle upon Tyne: Cambridge Scholars Publishing, 2008).

Jeffers, Gerry, 'Telling Tales: Cruelty and Abuse in Schooling in Ireland', *Education Research and Perspectives Special Issue – History of Education*, Crawley, vol. 43, issue 1, 2016, pp.101–36.

Jennings, Robert M., Swanson, Donald F. and Trout, Andrew P., 'Alexander Hamilton's Tontine Proposal', *The William and Mary Quarterly*, vol. 45, issue 1, 1988, pp.107–15.

Johnson, Nuala Christina, *Ireland, the Great War, and the Geography of Remembrance* (Cambridge: Cambridge University Press, 2003).

Johnson, Veronica, 'Dublin Cinemas in 1916: The Easter Rising, World War One Films and The Growth of the Middle-Class Audience', *Historical Journal of Film, Radio, and Television*, vol. 40, issue 2, 2022, pp.239–56.

Johnston, W.J. and Muldoon, M.P., *Old Age Pensions in Ireland; a Guide for the Use of Claimants, Pension Officers, Clerks, Postmasters, Local Pension Committees, and Sub-Committees, in Ireland* (Dublin: Eason and Son Ltd, 1908).

Keane, Hawley, *National Council for Travelling People, 1969–1985: A Short History* (Ennis: Ennis Committee for the Travelling People, 1985).

Kearney, Daithí, 'Regions, Regionality and Regionalization in Irish Traditional Music: the Role of Comhaltas Ceoltóirí Éireann', *Ethnomusicology Ireland*, 2/3, July 2013, pp.72–94.

Keegan, Anne, 'Our Gang, The Over 50s Activities Club', *A Trip Down Memory Lane: Memories of Growing up in the Borough of Dún Laoghaire* (Dún Laoghaire: Dún Laoghaire-Rathdown County Council, 2006).

Kelly, Aidan, 'Blackrock in the 1930s', *Blackrock Society Proceedings*, vol. 1, 1992–3, pp.2–10.

Kelly, James, *Sport in Ireland, 1600–1840* (Dublin: Four Courts Press, 2014).

Kelly, Laura, 'Rickets and Irish Children: Dr Ella Webb and the Early Work of the Children's Sunshine Home, 1925–1946', in Mac Lellan, Anne and Mauger, Alice (eds), *Growing Pains: Childhood Illness in Ireland, 1750–1950* (Dublin: Irish Academic Press, 2013), pp.141–58.

Kelly, Laura, 'Irishwomen United, the Contraception Action Programme and the Feminist Campaign for Free, Safe and Legal Contraception in Ireland, *c.*1975–81', *Irish Historical Studies*, vol. 43, issue 164, November 2019, pp.269–97.

Kelly, Michael Richard Lascelles, *Dalkey, Co. Dublin* (Ilfracombe: Arthur Stockwell Limited, 1952).

Kelly, Nicola, 'Airfield House', in Gunning, David (ed.), *Shifting Foundations; the Big Houses of Dún Laoghaire-Rathdown* (Dún Laoghaire: Dún Laoghaire-Rathdown County Council, 2021), pp.34–42.

Kelly, Ronan, *Every Branch of the Healing Art: A History of the Royal College of Surgeons in Ireland* (Dublin: Eastwood, 2023), Chapter 2.

Kennedy, Brian P., *South County Dubliners and the Building of Independent Ireland* (Foxrock: Foxrock Local History Club, 1987).

Kennedy, Finola, *Cottage to Creche; Family Change in Ireland* (Dublin: Institute of Public Administration, 2001).

Kerr, Peter J., Liu, June, Cattadori, Isabella et al., 'Myxoma Virus and the Leporipoxviruses: An Evolutionary Paradigm', *Viruses*, vol. 7, no. 3, pp.1,020–61.

Kiely, Elizabeth and Leane, Máire, *Irish Women at Work, 1930–1960, an Oral History* (Newbridge: Irish Academic Press, 2012).

Kinsella, Ken, *Out of the Dark, 1914–1918: South Dubliners Who Fell in the Great War* (Dublin: Merrion Press, 2014).

Larkin, Felix, 'Four Special Commemorative Stamps For The Carnegie Libraries In Ireland', *History Ireland*, vol. 27, issue 6, November–December 2019, pp.8–9.

Lee, Michael and Lee, Edward J.P., 'The "Model" Employer', in Mannion, Padraig (ed.) *Lockout Centenary: Dún Laoghaire 1913–2013* (Dublin: Dún Laoghaire 1913 Commemorative Committee, 2013), pp.19–22.

Lehane, Shane, *A History of the Irish Red Cross* (Dublin: Four Courts Press, 2019).

Lennon, Colm and Kavanagh, Robin, 'The Flowering of the Confraternities and Sodalities in Ireland *c.*1860–*c.*1960', in Lennon, Colm (ed.), *Confraternities and Sodalities in Ireland: Charity, Devotion and Sociability* (Dublin: Columba Press, 2012), pp.76–96.

Leon, Barbara C., 'Mesolithic and Neolithic Activity on Dalkey Island–A Reassessment', *The Journal of Irish Archaeology*, vol. 14, 2005, pp.1–21.

Leonard, Hugh, *Home Before Night* (London: Andre Deutsch Ltd, 1979).

Leonard, Hugh, *Out After Dark* (York: Methuen, 1989).

Leonard, Jane, 'Facing "The Finger of Scorn": Veterans' Memories of Ireland After the Great War', in Evans, Martin and Lunn, Kenneth (eds), *War and Memory in the Twentieth Century* (Oxford: Berg, 1997), pp.59–72.

Lewis, Peter and Blackmore, Gillie, 'Dún Laoghaire's Troubadour', *Dún Laoghaire Journal no. 2* (Dublin: Dún Laoghaire Borough Historical Society, 1992), pp.38–43.

Logan, Patrick, *The Old Gods: the Facts about Irish Fairies* (Belfast: Appletree Press, 1981).

Long, Bill, *Bright Light, White Water: the Story of Irish Lighthouses and Their People* (Dublin: New Island Books, 1993).

Lowth, Cormac, 'The Palme Shipwreck and the Lifeboat Disaster of 1895', *Blackrock Society Proceedings*, vol. 3, 1995, pp.94–105.

Lucey, John, 'Women's Hockey in Ireland – A Short History', *History Ireland*, vol. 26, issue 5, September–October 2018, pp.44–7.

Luddy, Maria, 'Moral Rescue and Unmarried Mothers in the 1920s', *Women's Studies*, vol. 30, issue 6, 2001, pp.797–816.

Lyng, Paul, *Booterstown: a Snapshot of the 1940s* (Peterborough: Choice Publishing Ltd, 2011).

Lyng, Paul, *Booterstown Parish: a Pastoral Journey Through Four Centuries, 1616–2013* (Peterborough: Choice Publishing Ltd, 2013).

Lyons, Muirne, 'Rathfarnham Castle, Rathfarnham, Co. Dublin', *History Ireland*, vol. 27, no. 5, p.39.

Lysaght, Patricia, *The Banshee; the Irish Supernatural Death Messenger* (Dublin: The O'Brien Press, 1996).

Mac Aongusa, Brian, 'From Foxrock to Blackrock 75 Years Ago; A Talk to the Foxrock Local History Club on 16 September 2014' (Foxrock: Foxrock Local History Society, 2014).

Mac Aongusa, Brian, *Hidden Streams: A New History of Dún Laoghaire-Rathdown* (Dublin: Currach Press, 2007).

MacWeeney, Alen, *Irish Travellers: Tinkers No More* (Henniker: New England College Press, 2007).

MacPhilib, Seamus, 'Dublin South County to North Inner City: An Urban Folklore Project 1979–90', *Béaloideas*, vol. 74, 2006, pp.103–22.

Magee, Sean (ed.), *A Local History of the Neighbourhood of Ballinteer Co. Dublin from Early Times: from a Rural to a Suburban Community* (Ballinteer Active Retirement Association (BARA) Local History Study Group, self-published, 2017).

Maguire, Martin, 'The Church of Ireland Parochial Associations: a Social and Cultural Analysis', in Lennon, Colm (ed.), *Confraternities and Sodalities in Ireland: Charity, Devotion and Sociability* (Dublin: Columba Press, 2012), pp.97–109.

Maguire, Moira and Ó Cinnéide, Séamus, 'A Good Beating Never Hurt Anyone: The Punishment and Abuse of Children in Twentieth Century Ireland', in *Journal of Social History*, vol. 38, no. 3, 2005, pp.635–52.

Mannion, Padraig, *Lockout Centenary: Dún Laoghaire 1913–2013* (Dublin: Dún Laoghaire 1913 Commemorative Committee, 2013).

Mannion, Padraig, 'James Byrne, Dún Laoghaire's 1913 Lockout Martyr', *Lockout Centenary: Dún Laoghaire 1913–2013* (Dublin: Dún Laoghaire 1913 Commemorative Committee, 2013), pp.16–18.

Marcantonio, Katia, 'L'Emigrazione Italiana in Irlanda', *Studi Emigrazione/ Migration Studies*, vol. 35, no. 129, 1998, pp.127–35.

Marsh, Courtney, *Irish Policing: Culture, Challenges, and Change in An Garda Síochána* (London: Palgrave MacMillan, 2022).

Marsh, Courtney, 'It's a Man's World, Try to Convince the Men Otherwise: The Role of Women in Irish Policing', *Women & Criminal Justice*, vol. 29, issue 3, 2019, pp.148–62.

Maume, Patrick, 'McKenna, Kathleen Napoli', in McGuire, James and Quinn, James (eds), *Dictionary of Irish Biography* (Cambridge: Cambridge University Press, 2009).

McAsey, Carmel, 'Booterstown', *Dublin Historical Record*, vol. 21, no. 3, June 1967, pp.81–94.

McAvoy, Sandra Ruth, '"A Perpetual Nightmare": Women, Fertility Control, the Irish State, and the 1935 Ban on Contraceptives', in Preston, Margaret H. and Ó hÓgartaigh, Margaret (eds), *Gender and Medicine in Ireland 1700–1950* (Syracuse: Syracuse University Press, 2012), pp.189–202.

McCabe, Ciarán, 'Charwomen and Dublin's Secondary Labour Force in the Late Nineteenth and Early Twentieth Centuries', *Social History*, vol. 45, issue 2, April 2020, pp.193–217.

McCarthy, Kevin, *Gold, Silver and Green: the Irish Olympic Journey 1896–1924* (Cork: Cork University Press, 2010).

McDonagh, Michael, 'Nomadism in Irish Travellers' Identity', in McCann, May, Ó Síocháin, Séamus and Ruane, Joseph (eds), *Irish Travellers: Culture and Ethnicity* (Belfast: Institute of Irish Studies, 1994), pp.95–109.

McElligott, Richard, 'Contesting the Fields of Play: the Gaelic Athletic Association and the Battle for Popular Sport in Ireland, 1890–1906', in McElligott, Richard and Hassan, David (eds), *A Social and Cultural History of Sport in Ireland* (*Sport in the Global Society – Contemporary Perspectives)* (Abingdon-on-Thames: Routledge, 2016), pp.3–23.

McElligott, Richard, '"Boys Indifferent to the Manly Sports of Their Race": Nationalism and Children's Sport in Ireland, 1880–1920', *Irish Studies Review*, vol. 27, issue 3, 2019, pp.1–18.

McGuire, Andrew and Hassan, David, 'Cultural Nationalism, Gaelic Sunday and the Gaelic Athletic Association in Early Twentieth Century Ireland', *The International Journal of the History of Sport*, vol. 29, issue 6, 2012, pp.912–23.

McKillop, Donal G., Goth, Peter and Hyndman, Noel, *Credit Unions in Ireland: Structure, Governance and Performance* (Dublin: The Institute of Chartered Accountants in Ireland, 2006).

McMahon, Anne, 'Regulating Midwives: the Role of the Royal College of Physicians in Ireland', in Fealy, Gerard M. (ed.), *Care to Remember: Nursing and Midwifery in Ireland* (Cork: Mercier Press, 2005), pp.158–71.

McManus, Ruth, *Dublin, 1910–1940: Shaping the City and Suburbs, The Making of Dublin City* (Dublin: Four Courts Press, 2002).

McManus, Ruth, 'Dublin's Lodger Phenomenon in the Early Twentieth Century', *Irish Economic and Social History*, vol. 45, 2018, pp.23–46.

McQuade, Melanie and O'Donnell, Lorna, 'Late Mesolithic Fish Traps from the Liffey Estuary', *Antiquity*, vol. 81, issue 313, 2015, pp.569–84.

Medico-Social Research Board, *Heroin Use in a Dún Laoghaire Borough Area, 1983–84* (Dublin: Medico-Social Research Board, 1984).

Milne, Ida, *Stacking the Coffins; Influenza, War, and Revolution in Ireland, 1918–19* (Manchester: Manchester University Press, 2018).

Milne, Kenneth, *Protestant Aid, a History of the Association for the Relief of Distressed Protestants* (Dublin: The Association for the Relief of Distressed Protestants, 1989).

Mintel, *Golf in Ireland*, Irish Series, May 2001.

Molohan, Cathy, 'Humanitarian Aid or Politics?', *History Ireland*, vol. 5, issue 3, 1997, pp.7–9.

Moore, Martin, 'The Origins of Association Football in Ireland, 1875–1880: a Reappraisal', *Sport in History*, vol. 37, issue 4, December 2017, pp.505–28.

Muldowney, Liam, *The Townland of Ballinteer: a History and Account of the Amazing People Who Once Lived there* (self-published, 2017).

Mulhall, Daniel, 'A Gift from Scotland: Golf's Early Days in Ireland', *History Ireland*, vol. 14, issue 5, September–October 2006, pp.31–6.

Murdoch, Fiona, *Victor Bewley's Memories* (Dublin: Veritas, 2002).

Murphy, William, 'Sport in a Time of Revolution: Sinn Féin and the Hunt in Ireland, 1919', *Éire-Ireland*, vol. 48, issue 1/2, March 2013, pp.112–47.

Nassau, Kurt (ed.), *Colour for Science, Art and Technology* (Amsterdam: Elsevier, 1997), p.197.

Ní Fhloinn, B., 'The Role of the Postal Questionnaire in the Collection of Irish Folklore', in S. Ó Catháin (ed.), *Northern Lights: Following Folklore in North-Western Europe: Essays in Honour of Bo Almqvist* (Dublin: University College Dublin Press, 2001).

Nolan, Ann, 'The Gay Community Response to the Emergence of AIDS in Ireland: Activism, Covert Policy, and the Significance of an "Invisible Minority"', in *Journal of Policy History*, vol. 30, issue 1, January 2018, pp.105–27.

Normoyle, Paul, 'The Ballycorus Leadworks', *Journal of the Mining Heritage Trust of Ireland*, vol. 6, 2006, pp.11–16.

Norris, M., *Property, Family and the Irish Welfare State* (Basingstoke: Palgrave Macmillan, 2016).

Nuttall, Deirdre, 'Cahill's Blood; Mr Cahill Makes the Cure', in Tuomi, Ilona, Carey, John, Hilliers, Barbara and Ó Gealbháin, Ciarán (eds), *Charms, Charmers and Charming in Ireland: From the Medieval to the Modern, New Approaches to Celtic Religion and Mythology* (Cardiff: University of Wales Press, 2019), p.145.

Nuttall, Deirdre, *Different and the Same: a Folk History of the Protestants of Independent Ireland* (Dublin: Eastwood Books, 2020).

O'Brien, Mark, 'Policing the Press: Censorship, Family Planning, and the Press in Ireland, 1929–67', *Irish Studies Review*, vol. 29, issue 1, 2021, pp.15–30.

O'Brien, Paul, 'Post Office Workers Flex Their Muscle', in Ó Caollaí, Breasal, O'Hagan, Niall and Finlay, Ken (eds), *Friends of the Leinster, The Last Voyage of the Leinster: Remembering the Dún Laoghaire & Holyhead Mailboat* (Dublin: Dún Laoghaire Holyhead Mail Boat Leinster Centenary Committee/Friends of the Leinster, 2018), pp.7–9.

O'Callaghan, Dominic and Hourigan, Kathleen, *Time for Action: a Report on Traveller Accommodation in Dún Laoghaire Rathdown* (Dublin: Southside Travellers Action Group, 1999).

O'Callaghan, Liam, 'Irish Rugby and the First World War', in McElligott, Richard and Hassan, David (eds), *A Social and Cultural History of Sport in Ireland* (Abingdon-on-Thames: Routledge, 2016), pp.95–109.

Ó Caolaí, Breasal, 'The Truth was Also a Casualty', *Friends of the Leinster, The Last Voyage of the Leinster: Remembering the Dún Laoghaire & Holyhead Mailboat* (Dublin: Dún Laoghaire Holyhead Mail Boat Leinster Centenary Committee/ Friends of the Leinster, 2018), pp.4–6.

Ó Catháin, Séamus, 'Institiúid Bhéaloideas Éireann 1930–1935' [Irish Folklore Institute 1930–1935], *Béaloideas*, vol. 73, 2005, pp.85–110.

Ó Catháin, Séamus, 'Súil Siar ar Scéim na Scol, 1937–8', *Sinsear*, vol. 5, 1988, pp.19–30.

Ó Cathaoir, Eva, 'The Rathdown Union Workhouse at Loughlinstown, 1838–1923', *Dublin Historical Record*, vol. 48, issue 2, 1995, pp.111–24.

Ó Conchubhair, Brain, 'Trying Irish in the Free State', *Éire-Ireland*, vol. 48, issue 1&2, Spring–Summer 2013, pp.7–10.

O'Connell, Michael, Kelly, Fergus and McAdam, James H. (eds), *Cattle in Ancient and Modern Ireland; Farming Practices, Environment, and Economy* (Newcastle upon Tyne: Cambridge Scholars Publishing, 2016).

O'Danachair, Caoimhin, 'The Holy Wells of County Dublin', *Reportorium Novum*, vol. 1, no. 2 (Dublin: Browne and Nolan, 1958), pp.68–87.

O'Donoghue, David, 'State within a State: The Nazis in Neutral Ireland', *Dublin Historical Record*, vol. 60, no. 2, Autumn 2007, pp.167–70.

O'Duffy, Eileen, *From Dirt and Dips to Dryrobes; Bathing in Dún Laoghaire Through the Ages* (self-published, 2021).

O'Duffy, Eileen, *Champagne, Cocktails, and Crêpes Suzette; Wining, Dining and Dancing in Dún Laoghaire Through the Ages* (self-published, 2022).

O'Dwyer, Rory, *The Eucharistic Congress, Dublin 1932* (Dublin: Nonsuch Ireland, 2009).

Ó Gráda, Cormac, '"The Greatest Blessing of All": The Old Age Pension in Ireland', *Past & Present*, no. 175, May 2002, pp.124–61.

O'Flynn, Thomas, *Frank Duff as I Knew Him* (Wrexham: Praedicanda Publications, 1981).

Ó hÓgáin, Daithí, *Myth, Legend and Romance: an Encyclopaedia of the Irish Folk Tradition* (Newcastle under Lyme: Ryan Publishing, 1990).

Ó hÓgarthaigh, Margaret, *Quiet Revolutionaries: Irish Women in Education, Medicine, and Sport, 1861–1964* (Dublin: The History Press Ireland, 2011).

Oldham, Thomas, *Journal of Geological Science*, Dublin, vol. 3, 1848.

Ó Leidhin, Seán, 'Coláiste Eoin', *Obelisk: Journal of the Kilmacud Stillorgan Local History Society*, no. 4, 2009, pp.65–9.

Ó Maitiú, Séamas, *Dublin's Suburban Towns, 1834–1930: Governing Clontarf, Drumcondra, Dalkey, Killiney, Kilmainham, Kingstown, Blackrock, Rathmines and Rathgar* (Dublin: Four Courts Press, 2003).

O'Morain, Padraig, *The Health of the Nation; the Irish Healthcare System, 1957–2007* (Dublin: Gill and MacMillan, 2007).

O'Morchoe, Thomas Arthur, *O'Morchoe's History of Kilternan and Kilgobbin* (Dublin: Church of Ireland Printing and Publishing, Dublin 1934).

Ó Murchadha, Tadhg, *An Cliathán Clé* (Dublin: Oifig an tSoláthair, 1932).

O'Rafferty, Tomás, *The Seapoint and Salthill Story, Monkstown: a View of Historical Monkstown, Co. Dublin* (self-published, 1996).

O'Reilly, Michael, *Dancehall Days: When Showbands Ruled the Stage* (Dublin: Gill and Macmillan, 2014).

O'Reilly, Patrick J., 'Tobernea Holy Well, Blackrock, Co. Dublin', *Journal of the Royal Society of Antiquaries of Ireland*, vol. 12, 1902, pp.178–86.

Organising Committee of the 51st International Eucharistic Congress, Dublin, *The Handbook of the Eucharistic Congress* (Dublin: Archbishop of Dublin, 1932).

Ó Riain, Seán, *Solidarity with Travellers: a Story of Settled People Making a Stand for Travellers* (Dublin: Roadside Books, 2000).

O'Sullivan, Donal, *The National: Chronicles of a Dún Laoghaire Yacht Club* (Dublin: The Liffey Press, 2020).

O'Toole, Shane, 'Stillorgan Shopping Centre – an Architect's Perspective', *Obelisk: Journal of the Kilmacud Stillorgan Local History Society*, issue 1, 2006, pp.15–17.

Over 50s Activities Club, The, *A Trip Down Memory Lane – Memories of Growing up in the Borough of Dún Laoghaire* (Dublin: The Over 50s Activities Club, 2006).

Pearson, Peter, *Dún Laoghaire-Kingstown* (Dublin: O'Brien Press, 1981).

Pearson, Peter, 'The Big House in Dún Laoghaire-Rathdown – an Overview', in Black, Deirdre, Pearson, Peter and Gunning, David (ed.), *Shifting Foundations* (Dublin: Dún Laoghaire Rathdown County Council, 2021), pp.3–21.

Pearson, Peter, *Between the Mountains and the Sea: Dún Laoghaire-Rathdown County* (Dublin: O'Brien Press, 2007).

Pearson, Peter, *The Granite Coast: Dún Laoghaire, Sandycove, Dalkey* (Dublin: The O'Brien Press, 2022).

Peseta, Senia, 'Nationalist Responses to Two Royal Visits to Ireland, 1900 and 1903', *Irish Historical Studies*, vol. 31, no. 124, 1999, pp.488–504.

Peter, Ada, *Sketches of Old Dublin* (Dublin: Sealy, Bryers and Walker, 1907).

Pilgrims' Souvenir Guide During Eucharistic Congress 1932, The.

Pim, Frederic W., *A Sketch of Sanitary Progress in Dublin: Being an Address Delivered at the Nineteenth Annual General Meeting of the Dublin Sanitary Association, 27th March, 1890* (Dublin: R.D. Webb and Son, 1890).

Pim, Frederic W., *A Sketch of Sanitary Progress in Dublin: Delivered at the Annual General Meeting of the Dublin Sanitary Association, 12th March, 1891* (Dublin: R.D. Webb and Son, 1891).

Pim, Frederic W., *Preventable Diseases, Why are they Not Prevented? An Address: Delivered at the Annual General Meeting of the Dublin Sanitary Association, 30th March, 1892* (Dublin: R.D. Webb and Son, 1892).

Prior, Pauline M., 'Psychiatry and the Fate of Women who Killed Infants and Young Children, 1850–1900', in Cox, Catherine and Luddy, Maria (eds), *Cultures of Care in Irish Medical History, 1750–1970* (London: Palgrave Macmillan, 2010), pp.92–112.

Prunty, Jacinta, *Dublin Slums, 1922–1973* (Dublin: University College Dublin Press, 2007).

Purcell, Mary, *A Time for Sowing; The St John of God Brothers in Ireland, a Centenary Record, 1879–1979* (Dublin: Hospitaller Brothers of St John of God, 1979).

Raftery, Deirdre and Delaney, Catriona, '"Un-Irish and un-Catholic": Sports, Physical Education and Girls' Schooling, *Irish Studies Review*, vol. 27, issue 3, pp.325–43.

Raftery, Deirdre, 'The Big House in Dún Laoghaire-Rathdown as Religious Institution', in Black, Deirdre, Pearson, Peter and Gunning, David (ed.), *Shifting Foundations* (Dublin: Dún Laoghaire Rathdown County Council, 2021), pp.109–28.

Rattigan, Clíona, '"I Thought From Her Appearance That She Was in the Family Way": Detecting Infanticide Cases in Ireland, 1900–1921', *Family & Community History*, vol. 11, issue 2, 2008, pp.134–51.

Rattigan, Clíona, '"Half Mad at the Time": Unmarried Mothers and Infanticide in Ireland, 1922–150', in Cox, Catherine and Luddy, Maria (eds), *Cultures of Care in Irish Medical History, 1750–1970* (London: Palgrave Macmillan, 2010), pp.168–90.

Redmond, Paul Jude, *The Adoption Machine: the Dark History of Ireland's Mother and Baby Homes and the Inside Story of how Tuam 800 Became a Global Scandal* (Dublin: Merrion Press, 2018).

Reed, Caroline M., 'Parrish's Chemical Food Never Contained Arsenic', *British Medical Journal*, vol. 317, issue 7,152, July 1998.

Reid, Myles, *Reverend Maxwell Henry Close: Local Historian and Irish Cultural Figure, a Talk by Myles Reid to the Foxrock Local History Club on Tuesday 20 October 2009* (Dublin: Foxrock Local History Club, publication no. 58, 2009).

Reid, Myles, *Two-Hundred Years of the History of Foxrock: Townland, Parish, Postal Area. Including a Miscellany of People and Social Activities; a Talk by Myles Reid to the Foxrock Local History Club on 26th August 2014* (Dublin: Foxrock Local History Club, publication no. 71, 2014).

Reid, Sean, 'Identity and Cricket in Ireland in the Mid-Nineteenth Century', *Sport in Society*, vol. 15, issue 2, 2012, pp.147–64.

Reid, Sean, *Cricket in Victorian Ireland 1848–1878: a Social History* (PhD thesis submitted to the University of Huddersfield, 2014).

Reynolds, Brian, *Casalattico and the Italian Community in Ireland* (Dublin: UCD Foundation for Italian Studies, 1993).

Riach, Douglas C., 'Blacks and Blackface on the Irish Stage, 1830–60', *Journal of American Studies*, vol. 7, no. 3, December 1973, pp.231–41.

Ripley, Francis J., *Frank Duff* (London: Incorporated Catholic Truth Society, 1981).

Robbins, Keith, 'The Disestablishment of the Church of Ireland', in Costello, Kevin and Howlin, Niamh (eds), *Law and Religion in Ireland, 1700–1970* (Basingstoke: Palgrave MacMillan, 2021), pp.239–56.

Robinson, Michael, '"Nobody's Children?": The Ministry of Pensions and the Treatment of Disabled Great War Veterans in the Irish Free State, 1921–1939', *Irish Studies Review*, vol. 25, no. 3, 2017, pp.316–35.

Robinson, Michael, *Shell-shocked British Army Veterans in Ireland, 1918–39, A Difficult Homecoming* (Manchester: Manchester University Press, 2020).

Rochford, Paddy, 'Some Memories of Old Stillorgan', *Obelisk: Journal of the Kilmacud Stillorgan Local History Society*, issue 1, 2006, pp.5–8.

Rouse, Paul, *Sport and Ireland: a History* (Oxford: Oxford University Press, 2015).

Rouse, Paul, 'The Sporting World and the Human Heart: Ireland, 1880–1930', *Irish Studies Review*, vol. 27, issue 3, July 2019, pp.309–24.

Rowley, Ellen, 'How We Might Live: The Architecture of "Ordinary" Housing from late 1940s to 1950s Dublin', in *Housing, Architecture and the Edge Condition* (Abingdon-on-Thames: Routledge, 2019).

Royal Irish Academy, *Proceedings of the Royal Irish Academy*, 'Section B: Biological, Geological, and Chemical Science', vol. 44, 1937, pp.205–60.

Ryan, Christopher and Hayes, Olivia, *Dundrum, Stillorgan and Rathfarnham: Gateway to the Mountains* (Donaghadee: Cottage Publications, 2002).

Ryan, Louise and Ward, Margaret, *Irish Women and the Vote: Becoming Citizens* (Newbridge: Irish Academic Press, 2018 (revised edition).

Ryan, Nicholas M., 'Minute Book of the County Dublin Stonecutters' Society of Stepaside and its Locality, 1889–1892', *Saothar*, vol. 16, 1991, pp.112–17.

Ryan, Salvador (ed.), *Birth and the Irish* (Dublin: Wordwell, 2021).

Sammon, Patrick J., *In the Land Commission: a Memoir, 1933–1978* (Dublin: Ashfield Press, 1997).

Samuels, Arthur, *Early Cricket In Ireland: A Paper Read Before the Kingstown Literary and Debating Society on the 2nd February, 1888* (Dublin: Kingstown Literary and Debating Society, 1888), p.6.

Scannell, James, 'St. Columcille's Hospital, Loughlinstown, Co. Dublin: From Workhouse Infirmary to General Hospital', *Dublin Historical Record*, vol. 59, no. 2, Autumn 2006, pp.153–65.

Scannell, James, 'From Kingstown to Dalkey By Air (The Atmospheric Railway 1844–1854)', *Dublin Historical Record*, vol. 62, no. 1, Spring 2009, pp.83–97.

Scannell, James, 'Christmas 1918 in Kingstown and Dalkey, Co. Dublin', *Dublin Historical Record*, vol. 72, no. 2, 2019, pp.228–38.

Scannell, James, 'Major Hermann Goertz and German World War 2 Intelligence Gathering in Ireland', *Journal of the Greystones Archaeological & Historical Society*, vol. 4, 2004.

Scudds, Colin, 'The Workmen's Club, Dún Laoghaire', *Dún Laoghaire Borough Historical Society*, no. 12, 2003, pp.2–9.

Scudds, Colin, 'McManus Jewellers, 92, Lower Georges Street', *Dún Laoghaire Borough Historical Society*, no. 5, 2006, pp.16–22.

Scudds, Colin, 'Conditions of the Poor in Kingstown 1850–70', *Dún Laoghaire Borough Historical Society*, no. 23, 2014, pp.42–50.

Scudds, Colin, 'St. Joseph's Orphanage, Tivoli Road', *Dún Laoghaire Borough Historical Society*, no. 23, 2014, pp.18–23.

Scudds, Colin, 'The Building of Dún Laoghaire Harbour', *Dublin Historical Record*, vol. 64, issue 1, Spring 2011, pp.69–75.

Shannon, Denis, *A History of the Parks of Dún Laoghaire Rathdown* (Dublin: Dún Laoghaire Rathdown County Council, 2001).

Sheridan, Pat, 'From Barn Dances to Rock and Roll', *Obelisk: Journal of the Stillorgan and Kilmacud Historical Society*, issue 3, 2008, pp.24–7.

Shiel, Michael, *The Quiet Revolution; the Electrification of Rural Ireland* (Dublin: The O'Brien Press, 2003).

Skehill, Caroline, *History of the Present of Child Protection and Welfare Social Work in Ireland* (Lampeter: Edwin Mellen Press, 2004).

Slusar, John, *Race Courses: Here Today and Gone Tomorrow* (self-published, 2016).

Smith, Brian, *The Streets of Glasthule* (self-published, 2003).

Smyth, Hazel P., *The Town of the Road: the Story of Booterstown* (Belfast: Beyond the Pale Publications, 1994).

Sobolewski, Peter, 'The International Eucharistic Congress 1932', *Obelisk: Journal of the Stillorgan and Kilmacud Historical Society*, issue 7, 2013, pp.70–2.

Sobolewski, Peter, 'Civil War Incidents in Stillorgan', *Obelisk: Journal of the Stillorgan and Kilmacud Historical Society*, issue 9, 2015, pp.6–14.

Sobolewski, Peter, 'Hilda Tweedy and the Irish Housewives' Association during the "Emergency"', *Obelisk: Journal of the Stillorgan and Kilmacud Historical Society*, issue 10, 2016, pp.87–99.

Stewart, Paul, McKearney, Tommy and Garvey, Brian, 'The Independent Workers Union: Class, Nation and Oppositional Labour Movements in Ireland from 1900 to the Celtic Tiger', *Labor History*, vol. 55, issue 4, 2014, pp.486–500.

Talbot Coall and Son, *Directory, Postal and General Guide for Kingstown, Monkstown, Killiney and Dalkey, Talbot Coall and Son, 1889* (estate agent's promotional material).

Talbot Coall and Son, *From Kingstown to Wicklow 1891, Talbot Coall and Son, 1889* (estate agent's promotional material).

Taub, Michael, *Jack Doyle, the Gorgeous Gael* (Dublin: The Lilliput Press, 2007).

Taylor, Lawrence J., *Occasions of Faith: An Anthropology of Irish Catholics* (Dublin: The Lilliput Press, 1995).

Taylor, Paul, *Heroes or Traitors? Experiences of Southern Irish Soldiers Returning from the Great War 1919–39* (Liverpool: Liverpool University Press, 2015).

Thompson, Stith, *The Folktale* (Berkeley: University of California Press, 1977).

Titley, E. Brian, *Church, State, and the Control of Schooling in Ireland, 1900–1944* (Montreal: McGill-Queen's University Press, 1983).

Titley E. Brian, 'Rejecting the Modern World: The Educational Ideas of Timothy Corcoran', *Oxford Review of Education*, vol. 9, no. 2, 1983, pp.137–45.

Traynor, Aiden, 'Memories of a Lost Village: Stillorgan in the 1940s', *Obelisk: Journal of the Stillorgan and Kilmacud Historical Society*, issue 15, 2021, pp.68–81.

Tully, Darina, 'Pilot Boats, Hobblers and Skiffs of Dublin Bay', in Mac Cárthaigh, Críostóir, *Traditional Boats of Ireland: History, Folklore and Construction* (Cork: The Collins Press, 2008).

Turner, Mrs. M.K., 'Rathmichael: A Parish in the Pale', *Dublin Historical Record*, vol. 32, no. 3, June 1979, pp.82–93.

Turpin, John C., 'Visual Culture and Catholicism in the Irish Free State, 1922–1949', *Journal of Ecclesiastical History*, vol. 57, no. 1, January 2006, pp.55–77.

Urban District Council of Dún Laoghaire, *Dún Laoghaire [Kingstown]: an Official Guide to the Attractions, etc. of Ireland's Premier Seaside Resort* (no date, apparently 1950s).

Uther, Hans-Jörg, *The Types of International Folktales: A Classification and Bibliography. Based on the System of Antti Aarne and Stith Thompson*, FF Communications no. 284–286 (Helsinki: Suomalainen Tiedeakatemia, 2011 [three volumes]).

Wall, Mervyn, *Forty Foot Gentlemen Only* (Dublin: Allen Figgis, 1962).

Wallace, Seanie, 'Dogs, Ferrets, Rabbits and Boxing the Fox', in *A Trip Down Memory Lane – Memories of Growing up in the Borough of Dún Laoghaire* (Dublin: The Over 50s Activities Club, 2006).

Walsh, John, *Higher Education in Ireland, 1922–2016, Politics, Policy and Power–a History of Higher Education in the Irish State* (Basingstoke: Palgrave MacMillan, 2018).

Ward, Brian, 'An Architecture of Connections: The Ballybrack Cooperative 1969–1972', in Ward, Brian; Pike, Michael and Boyd, Gary (eds), *Irish Housing Design 1950–1980* (Abingdon-on-Thames: Routledge, 2020), pp.134–58.

Weafer, John, 'The Bombing of Sandycove/Glasthule', *Dún Laoghaire Journal/Dún Laoghaire Borough Historical Society*, no. 15, 2006, pp.2–8.

Weafer, John, 'Glasthule Buildings', *Dún Laoghaire Journal/Dún Laoghaire Borough Historical Society*, no. 19, 2010, pp.26–32.

Weinraub, Bernard, 'Britain's Envoy in Dublin Killed by Mine', *New York Times*, 22 July 1976.

Whelan, Kevin, *Religion, Landscape, and Settlement in Ireland: From Patrick to Present* (Dublin: Four Courts Press, 2018).

Wilde, W.R., *Irish Popular and Medical Superstitions: Midwifery, a Short Account of the Superstitions and Practices Relating to Midwifery; and Some of the Diseases of Women and Children in Ireland*, 1849.

Wills, Clair, 'Women, Domesticity and the Family: Recent Feminist Work in Irish Cultural Studies', *Cultural Studies*, vol. 15, issue 1, 2001, pp.33–57.

Wilson, T.G., *The Irish Lighthouse Service* (Dublin: Allen Figgis, 1968).

Yeates, Padraig, 'The Lockout in Kingstown', in Mannion, Padraig (ed.), *Lockout Centenary: Dún Laoghaire 1913–2013* (Dublin: Dún Laoghaire 1913 Commemorative Committee, 2013), pp.2–5.

ARCHIVAL SOURCES

National Folklore Collection, Schools' Collection
National Folklore Collection, Urban Folklore Project